Contemporary Consumer Culture Theory

Contemporary Consumer Culture Theory contains original research essays written by the premier thought leaders of the discipline from around the world that reflect the maturation of the field of consumer culture theory over the last decade. The volume seeks to help break down the silos that have arisen in disciplines seeking to understand consumer culture and speed both the diffusion of ideas and possibility of collaboration across frontiers.

Contemporary Consumer Culture Theory begins with a reevaluation of some of the fundamental notions of consumer behavior, such as self and other, branding and pricing, and individual versus communal agency, then continues with a reconsideration of role configurations as they affect consumption, examining in particular the ramifications of familial, gender, ethnic, and national aspects of consumers' lived experiences. The book moves on to a reappraisal of the state of the field, examining the rhetoric of inquiry, the reflexive history and critique of the discipline, the prospect of redirecting the effort of inquiry to practical and humanitarian ends, the neglected wellsprings of our intellectual heritage, and the ideological underpinnings of the evolving construction of the concept of the brand.

Contemporary Consumer Culture Theory is a reflective assessment, in theoretical, empirical, and evocative keys, of the state of the field of consumer culture theory and an indication of the scholarly directions in which the discipline is evolving, providing reflection upon a rapidly expanding discipline and altered consumptionscapes by some of its prime movers.

John F. Sherry, Jr., is the Raymond W. & Kenneth G. Herrick Professor of Marketing at the University of Notre Dame. He is a past president of both the Association for Consumer Research and the Consumer Culture Theory Consortium and a former associate editor of the *Journal of Consumer Research*.

Eileen Fischer is a professor of marketing and holds the Anne and Max Tanenbaum Chair of Entrepreneurship and Family Enterprise in the Schulich School of Business at York University. She is co-editor of *Journal of Consumer Research* and president of the Consumer Culture Theory Consortium.

Routledge Studies in Marketing

This series welcomes proposals for original research projects that are either single or multiauthored or an edited collection from both established and emerging scholars working on any aspect of marketing theory and practice and provides an outlet for studies dealing with elements of marketing theory, thought, pedagogy, and practice.

It aims to reflect the evolving role of marketing and bring together the most innovative work across all aspects of the marketing "mix"—from product development, consumer behavior, marketing analysis, branding, and customer relationships, to sustainability, ethics, and the new opportunities and challenges presented by digital and online marketing.

Contemporary Consumer Culture Theory

Edited by
John F. Sherry, Jr. and Eileen Fischer

Routledge
Taylor & Francis Group

LONDON AND NEW YORK

First published 2017
by Routledge

2 Park Square, Milton Park, Abingdon, Oxfordshire OX14 4RN
52 Vanderbilt Avenue, New York, NY 10017

Routledge is an imprint of the Taylor & Francis Group,
an informa business

First issued in paperback 2019

Library of Congress Cataloging-in-Publication Data
Names: Sherry, John F., Jr., editor. | Fischer, Eileen, 1959– editor.
Title: Contemporary consumer culture theory / edited by John F.
    Sherry, Jr. and Eileen Fischer.
Description: 1 Edition. | New York, NY : Routledge, 2017.
Identifiers: LCCN 2016059096 | ISBN 9781138680562 (hbk) |
    ISBN 9781315563947 (ebk)
Subjects: LCSH: Consumer behavior—Research. | Branding
    (Marketing) | Culture—Economic aspects.
Classification: LCC HF5415.32 .C664 2017 | DDC 306.3—dc23
LC record available at https://lccn.loc.gov/2016059096

ISBN: 978-1-138-68056-2 (hbk)
ISBN: 978-0-367-24301-2 (pbk)

Typeset in Sabon
by Apex CoVantage, LLC

Contents

Tables and Figures

Tables

Figures

Contributors

Eric J. Arnould is visiting professor of marketing at the Aalto University Business School and adjunct professor at EMLYON France. He formerly held a social science chair in the Danish Institute for Advanced Studies (DIAS). He has been on the faculty of universities in four European countries and held posts in North America. He has pursued a career in applied social science since receiving his BA in 1973 from Bard College, receiving a Ph.D.in anthropology from the University of Arizona in 1982. Ethnographic research in West Africa, both basic and applied, provide the foundation for his approach to contemporary market-mediated society. Marcel Mauss and Marshall Sahlins are two of his scholarly role models, although his intellectual debts are many. Eric's research on consumer culture, cultural marketing strategy, qualitative research methods, services marketing, and marketing and development appears in over ninety articles and chapters in major social science and managerial periodicals and books. His current interests include collective consumer creativity, human branding, sustainable business practice, visual representations, and digital mobility. He is at work on a collective text in consumer culture theory.

Russell Belk is Kraft Foods Canada Chair in Marketing and York University Distinguished Research Professor. He has received the Paul D. Converse Award, two Fulbright Awards, and the Sheth Foundation/*Journal of Consumer Research* Award for Long Term Contribution to Consumer Research. He has over six hundred publications. He recently co-wrote or co-edited *Consumer Culture Theory: Research in Consumer Behavior* (Emerald, 2015), *Qualitative Consumer and Marketing Research* (Sage, 2013), *The Routledge Companion to Identity and Consumption* (Routledge, 2013), and *The Routledge Companion to the Digital Consumer* (Routledge, 2013). In 2014 a ten-volume set of his work was published by Sage titled *Russell Belk, Sage Legends in Consumer Behavior*. Together with colleagues he initiated the Consumer Behavior Odyssey, the Association for Consumer Research Film Festival, and the Consumer Culture Theory Conference. His research involves the extended self, meanings of possessions, collecting, gift giving, sharing, digital consumption, and materialism. His work tends to be qualitative, visual, and cultural.

Matthias Bode is an associate professor at the College of Business and Financial Sciences at the Royal University for Women, Kingdom of Bahrain. He received his Ph.D. from the department of marketing and consumption, Leibniz University, Hanover, Germany, and worked from 2007 until 2016 in the Consumption, Culture and Commerce unit at the University of Southern Denmark. In his academic research, he asks the question "How is marketing shaped by and shaping the cultural, aesthetic, social, and historical context it is embedded in and acts upon?" This has resulted in publications and research projects on sonic branding, soundscapes, the history of marketing, digital self, and performative theories. In his aesthetic and academic credo, he follows the Austrian late-Romantic composer Gustav Mahler, who declared that the most important part of music is not to be found in the notes.

Tonya Williams Bradford is assistant professor of marketing at the Paul Merage School of Business, University of California, Irvine. She studies consumer rituals, consumption communities, and mental budgeting. Through publication and teaching, she creates and disseminates knowledge of the theory and practice of marketing with students at the undergraduate and graduate levels. She obtained degrees from Northwestern University including a Bachelor of Arts in Anthropology, as well as an MBA and Ph.D. in Marketing from the Kellogg School of Management. Prior to coming to the academy, Professor Bradford worked in industry for seventeen years across domestic and international markets.

Stephen Brown, a.k.a. Aedh Aherne, Brian Boru, Sue Denim, Peregrine Faulkner, Modesty Forbids, Alan Smithee, and Al Terego, among others, is the Machine Gun Kelly of Marketing, the Baby Face Nelson of Consumer Research. Currently on the lam, he can be contacted through the usual channels. Failing that, send a smoke signal to Ulster University.

Bernard Cova is a professor at Kedge Business School, Marseille, in France and a visiting professor at the Bocconi University in Milan, Italy. Since the early 1990s, he has participated in postmodernist streams of consumer research and marketing, focusing on a tribal approach. He is also a B2B marketing researcher, primarily in the field of project marketing. As a favorite pastime, he likes to sit in café terraces in Italian towns and watch people passing by during the *passeggiata*.

Véronique Cova is professor of marketing at the Graduate School of Management, Aix-Marseille University, France. Her research interests focus on servicescapes, consumer experience, and cultural consumption. She specializes in service design and the way the consumers reappropriate the offering through diversion tactics. She is currently working on pilgrimages and hospitableness. She has made the Way of Compostela and that has changed her perspective on marketing research and activities.

Nikhilesh Dholakia is professor emeritus, University of Rhode Island (URI), and founding co-editor of *Markets, Globalization & Development Review*. He has also worked as faculty member at University of Illinois at Chicago, Kansas State University, and Indian Institutes of Management at Ahmedabad and Calcutta. He has been a visiting faculty member at Northwestern University's Kellogg School, Chuo University in Japan, Arizona State University West, University of Southern Denmark (Odense), Aalto University (Helsinki) School of Economics, Le Havre University in France, Norwegian Institute for Market Research, Aalborg University in Denmark, and University of Canterbury in New Zealand. Significant research by him has frequently explored the intersections of markets, consumer culture, and technology from critical angles, often employing a macrosystemic prism. His current research and writing projects deal with transformations in organizational and consumer lives brought about by transmedia, financialization, ideology, and innovation. He is also involved in developing several critical theory perspectives on the emerging global consumer and market cultures.

Hilary Downey is a lecturer in management at Queen's University Belfast (Northern Ireland). Her research interests include experiential dimensions of consumer culture, art and aesthetics, and well-being. Hilary is a co-editor of the consumer culture theory poetic chapbook with Prof. John F. Sherry, Jr. (University Notre Dame), and Prof. John W. Schouten (St John's Memorial University, Newfoundland). As a poetic inquiry, this approach has afforded a new platform from which to give voice to the lived experiences of vulnerability. Hilary was one of the first eleven recipients to receive a Kellogg's grant (Transformative Consumer Research) to extend research in the area of disability and well-being and a recipient of the Kinnear award 2015 (*Journal of Public Policy and Marketing*). Hilary's work has been published in the *Journal of Public Policy and Marketing*, the *European Journal of Marketing*, the *Journal of Business Research*, the *Journal of Consumer Behaviour*, the *Journal of Marketing Management*, *Advances in Consumer Research*, and the *International Journal of Sociology and Social Policy*.

Hounaida El Jurdi is an assistant professor of marketing at the Olayan School of Business in the American University of Beirut. Her research interests are varied and involve the study of practices to interpret consumption and the formation of markets. Specifically, she is interested in how practices of "othering" from multilevel perspectives help us to understand the formation of beauty markets. She is also interested in using contextualized approaches to the study of sustainability. Her work has appeared in the *Journal of Macromarketing*.

A. Fuat Fırat is professor of marketing at the University of Texas, Rio Grande Valley. His research interests cover areas such as macro consumer behavior and macromarketing, postmodern culture, transmodern marketing strategies, gender and consumption, marketing and development, and interorganizational relations. He has won the *Journal of Macromarketing* Charles Slater Award for best article with co-author N. Dholakia, the *Journal of Consumer Research* best article award with co-author A. Venkatesh, and the *Corporate Communications: An International Journal* top-ranked paper award with co-authors L. T. Christensen and J. Cornelissen. He has published several books, including *Consuming People: From Political Economy to Theaters of Consumption*, co-authored by N. Dholakia, and is a founding editor of *Consumption, Markets & Culture*.

Eileen Fischer is a professor of marketing and holds the Anne and Max Tanenbaum Chair of Entrepreneurship and Family Enterprise in the Schulich School of Business at York University. She is co-editor of *Journal of Consumer Research* and president of the Consumer Culture Theory Consortium. Eileen publishes in both entrepreneurship and consumer research journals, such as the *Journal of Consumer Research*, the *Academy of Management Review*, the *Journal of Service Research*, the *Journal of Business Venturing*, and the *Journal of the Academy of Marketing Science*. She does research on consumers, entrepreneurs, and the markets they interact in. Eileen is interested in how brands, firms, and markets emerge and evolve and in how consumers and entrepreneurs shape them and respond to them. In addition, she maintains an active line of inquiry devoted to understanding how research contributions can be constructed using qualitative methodologies.

Terrance G. Gabel is associate professor of political economy and commerce at Monmouth College, Monmouth, Illinois (USA). His research has appeared in the *Journal of Public Policy & Marketing*, the *Academy of Marketing Science Review*, the *Journal of Consumer Marketing*, *Advances in Consumer Research*, and *Death in a Consumer Culture*. His consumption-related poetry has been published in booklets produced in conjunction with five most recent Consumer Culture Theory Conferences.

Douglas B. Holt, CEO of the Cultural Strategy Group, is one of the world's leading experts on branding and innovation. Prior to the launch of the Cultural Strategy Group, Holt was a professor at the Harvard Business School and then the L'Oréal Chair in Marketing at Oxford. In 2004, he pioneered cultural branding as a powerful new strategy tool in his international best-selling book *How Brands Become Icons: The Principles of Cultural Branding* and two supporting articles in the *Harvard Business Review*. The book has influenced many companies, ad agencies, design firms, and consultancies, which have adopted a cultural approach to branding. Holt's *Cultural Strategy: Using Innovative Ideologies to Build Breakthrough Brands* was published by Oxford University Press in late 2010. With his co-author Doug Cameron, Holt does for innovation what *How Brands Become Icons* did for branding. He developed a systematic, six-step cultural framework for identifying new market opportunities and then building new brand concepts to leverage these opportunities. Holt studied at Stanford (BA in economics and political science), the University of Chicago (MBA in marketing), and Northwestern (Ph.D. in marketing, specialization in cultural anthropology and sociology). Prior to his academic career, Holt was a brand manager at The Clorox Company and Dole Packaged Foods.

Dannie Kjeldgaard, Ph.D., is a professor of marketing in the consumption, culture, and commerce group at the University of Southern Denmark. He is also editor-in-chief of *Consumption, Markets & Culture*. Dannie's work analyzes change processes of market-based glocalization in domains such as place branding; branding, media, and identity construction; global consumer segments; ethnicity; and qualitative methodology. His research is published in the *Journal of Consumer Research*, the *Journal of Consumer Behaviour, Consumption, Markets and Culture, Marketing Theory*, the *Journal of Macromarketing*, and in several anthologies. His current research interests are glocalization and market formation in the context of food culture, Nordic marketplace cultures, consumer needs from a sociocultural perspective, and consumer cosmopolitanism and gender.

Sidney J. Levy is currently the Coca-Cola Distinguished Professor of Marketing at Eller College of Management, University of Arizona, and Charles H. Kellstadt Professor Emeritus of Behavioral Science in Management, Kellogg School, Northwestern University, where he taught for thirty-six years. He earned his Ph.D. from the Committee on Human Development, University of Chicago, and was licensed as a psychologist in Illinois. In 1988 he was honored as a fellow by the Association for Consumer Research and named a life member. He was president of the Association for Consumer Research in 1991.

Pauline Maclaran is professor of marketing and consumer research at Royal Holloway University, London, UK. Her research focuses on contemporary consumer culture, including gender issues. She is a co-author of *Royal Fever: The British Monarchy in Consumer Culture* published by University of California Press (2015) and has also co-edited various other books, including *Consumption and Spirituality* and *Mothers, Markets and Consumption*.

David Glen Mick is the Carter Professor in Marketing at the University of Virginia's McIntire School of Commerce. His academic degrees are in philosophy, English, health care management, and marketing. David has authored over seventy articles, essays, conference papers, and chapters on marketing and consumer behavior and edited four related books. His work has won several national awards, including best article at the *Journal of Consumer Research* and the Maynard Award for best theory contribution at the *Journal of Marketing*. David has also been invited to conduct seminars at universities worldwide, including Oxford, Erasmus (Netherlands), Trinity (Ireland), the Stockholm School of Economics, Harvard, and Stanford, among others. He is a fellow in the Society for Consumer Psychology, former associate editor and head editor of the *Journal of Consumer Research* (1997–2003), and past president of the Association for Consumer Research (2005). In this latter role, David spearheaded a movement called transformative consumer research, which encourages and facilitates scholarly inquiry to improve quality of life for all beings influenced by worldwide consumption activities and trends. He is co-editor of *Transformative Consumer Research for Personal and Collective Well-Being* (2012, Taylor & Francis/Routledge).

Cele Otnes is the Investors in Business Education Professor of Marketing in the department of business administration, professor of advertising, and professor of recreation, sport and tourism at the University of Illinois at Urbana-Champaign. She is an adjunct professor of marketing at the Norwegian School of Business and Economics (NHH). Her research primarily focuses on understanding how ritualistic consumption shapes the experiences of consumers within and outside of the marketspace (e.g., in broader cultural domains). She recently published *Royal Fever: The British Monarchy in Consumer Culture* with Pauline Maclaran (University of California Press, 2015). With Elizabeth Pleck, she co-authored *Cinderella Dreams: The Allure of the Lavish Wedding* (University of California Press, 2003) and has co-edited several books on rituals and consumption, including *Gender, Culture, and Consumer Behavior* with Linda Tuncay Zayer (Routledge, 2012). Her work appears in the *Journal of Consumer Research*, the *Journal of Retailing*, the *Journal of Advertising*, and the *Journal of Contemporary Ethnography*, among others. She primarily teaches courses in consumer behavior (undergraduate) and qualitative research methods (doctoral at Illinois and NHH). She has served as co-chair of the

Association for Consumer Research European and North American conferences and of the Qualitative Data Analysis workshop.

Pilar Rojas Gaviria is assistant professor of marketing at Pontificia Universidad Católica de Chile. Her work focuses on understanding the role of consumption in the construction of multicultural collective identities and solidarities. She draws on philosophical theories, poetry, and research on consumer behavior. Pilar is one of those consumer researchers who believes that poetry is just starting to reveal its full potential for advancing data collection, findings dissemination, and understanding consumers in the process of becoming. She has published her work in *Journal of Business Research*, the *International Marketing Review*, and the *Journal of Consumer Behaviour*, as well as in numerous book chapters.

John W. Schouten is professor of social enterprise at Memorial University of Newfoundland, Canada, and professor of marketing at the Institute for Customer Insight at University of St. Gallen, Switzerland. He specializes in consumer culture research using ethnographic methods. His work spans areas of consumer identity, consumption communities, market emergence and dynamics, alternative research methodologies, and environmental and social sustainability. Most recently he has turned his attention to understanding and facilitating social enterprise. Schouten's research appears in marketing journals including the *Journal of Consumer Research*, the *Journal of Marketing*, *Consumption Markets & Culture*, and the *Journal of the Academy of Marketing Science*. He is co-author of the book *Sustainable Marketing* with Diane Martin. He has authored two novels—*Notes from the Lightning God* and *The Fine Art of Self-Arrest*—and has published short fiction and poetry in various journals, magazines, and anthologies.

Linda Scott is the Emeritus DP World Chair for Entrepreneurship and Innovation at the University of Oxford's Saïd Business School. Linda is best known for her creation of the concept of the double X economy— a perspective that describes the global economy of women in both the developed and developing world and the roles of women not only as consumers but also as investors, donors, and workers. The double X economy encompasses the full range of women's impact as economic participants, leading her to be selected as one of *Prospect Magazine*'s Top 25 World Thinkers in 2015. She works with multinational companies, nongovernmental organizations, and governments on programs designed to help women economically. She also founded The Power Shift Forum for Women in the World Economy, an annual symposium born out of Oxford that brings together institutions and individuals working on women's empowerment to share learning and form collaborations. Currently, Linda's research focuses on the potential for market-based approaches to provide economic empowerment and entrepreneurial opportunities for poor women in developing nations. She is focused especially on developing and testing new measures to assess the impact of large-scale women's empowerment projects.

John F. Sherry, Jr., is the Raymond W. and Kenneth G. Herrick Professor of Marketing at the University of Notre Dame. He is an anthropologist who studies the sociocultural dimensions of consumer behavior and marketing. Sherry has researched, lectured, and consulted around the globe on issues of brand strategy, experiential consumption, and retail atmospherics. He is a past president of both the Association for Consumer Research and the Consumer Culture Theory Consortium and a former associate editor of the *Journal of Consumer Research*. Sherry is a fellow of the American Anthropological Association and the Society for Applied Anthropology. He has edited and written ten books and co-authored more than one hundred widely reprinted articles and chapters. He is a longtime proponent of arts-based research. Sherry has won awards for his scholarly work and poetry. He is an avid flat water paddler and wilderness camper and is still trying to perfect his seventeen-foot jump shot when his five dogs allow him to share the driveway.

Sandra D. Smith is a lecturer in marketing services at the University of Auckland, New Zealand. She has published her work in *Marketing Theory*, the *European Journal of Marketing*, and the *Australasian Marketing Journal*. Before moving into the field of marketing, Sandy completed an MA in English Literature and also an MA in language teaching and taught various university-level courses in academic writing at the University of the South Pacific (Fiji), Massey University (New Zealand), and the University of Auckland (New Zealand). She is well versed in the art of writing in an academic context and, as a keen writer herself, is interested in discovering, and helping other people discover, how to write well-crafted academic texts.

Alladi Venkatesh is professor of management and is associated faculty member in the department of anthropology and the department of informatics at the University of California, Irvine. His research focuses on cross-cultural consumption issues, as well as cultural approaches to technology adoption and diffusion. Recently, he has been working on social media and implications to user-centered theory and practice. His various publications have appeared in major journals. He is the founding co-editor of the journal *Consumption, Markets & Culture*.

Melanie Wallendorf is Soldwedel Professor of Marketing in the Eller College of Management and professor of sociology in the College of Social and Behavioral Sciences at the University of Arizona. She received her MS in sociology and her Ph.D. in marketing from the

University of Pittsburgh. Professor Wallendorf has published extensively on the sociocultural aspects of consumption. Her published research includes papers on consumption as an expression of normative political ideology, consumption as a means of taste acquisition, the role of consumption during community and collective rituals, the role of possessions in constituting social classes and ethnic groups, the meanings of favorite possessions and collections, and processes that define particular possessions as sacred or profane. Professor Wallendorf's research is often very highly cited and has been featured in articles in *The Wall Street Journal*, *The Washington Post*, *The New York Times*, *American Demographics*, and *Fortune*. Professor Wallendorf was the American Sociological Association representative to the *Journal of Consumer Research* policy board from 1998 to 2007. She co-chaired the 2002 doctoral symposium for the Association for Consumer Research. She has previously served as the treasurer and as the annual conference co-chair for the Association of Consumer Research and as associate editor of the *Journal of Consumer Research*.

Roel Wijland worked for Japanese advertising agency network Hakuhodo & TBWA. He was a founding partner of indie agency BSUR in Amsterdam. His wayward dissertation, "Poetic Brandscapes," was dubbed "a wry, brilliant, and courageous piece of work that combined poetry with marketing history and analysis" and its author "an agent provocateur in the poetic area" by Robert Kozinets. He was the initiator of the annual *Consumer Culture Theory* poetry volumes. Roel feels at home in the heretical tradition and publishes his poetic research portfolio in a diverse range of international marketing and consumer behavior journals. His premodern graphic fabliau *In Brutal Times* was the winner of an ACR Best Film Award. Recent publications with Professor Stephen Brown continue to carve a respected theoretical space for future poetic evocations by a next generation of academics but also include the managerial implications of lyrical perspectives for brand strategists. He is the caretaker of the imaginary Brandbach, the University of Otago's advertising specialization for digital planning and mobile creativity, which regularly wins real awards and launches stellar student careers. When he grows up he will be a full-time gardener under Mount St. Bathans in Central Otago in New Zealand.

1 Reading New Currents in Consumer Culture Theory

Eileen Fischer and John F. Sherry, Jr.

You heard it here first (or not): the study of consumer culture theory (CCT) is no longer in its infancy. What arguably began with a few young scholars hitting the "highways and buy-ways" (Belk 1991) as part of the Consumer Odyssey in 1986 has evolved into a body of scholarly work that is being produced by an ever-more diverse collection of researchers on an ever-more global scale. And although we're not sure that the term "maturity" will ever apply to our obstreperous collective enterprise, we are fairly certain that it's timely to take stock of some of the perennial issues that have engaged those operating under the CCT banner. It's time to illuminate what is changing and to take a bead on the directions in which the field is heading. Thus, we have assembled a collection of work from some of our leading scholars to see what they think about topics that have engaged us for decades and topics that should engage us for decades to come.

Our volume begins with chapters that open up for reexamination some of the topics that have been the "bread and butter" of research at the intersection of consumption, culture, and markets. In the lead (as he so often has been over the years) is Russ Belk, who has contributed a fascinating look at how self-ownership by autonomous machines will challenge us to reconsider our understandings of ownership and object agency and will open up a host of economic and ethical issues not previously foreseen. Next up is Alladi Venkatesh, who invites a reconsideration of the dynamics of consumer marginalization; he explores how market actors such as the mainstream media contribute to the construction of marginalized "others" within consumer culture. Sid Levy revisits a fundamental marketing notion with which he is deeply familiar: branding. In his chapter, Sid proposes a new concept, the "ideal brand pyramid," that summarizes his thought-provoking new Aristotelian take on branding. Melanie Wallendorf's chapter on pricing rounds out this first section of the book. In it, she takes on one of the famous "4 Ps" so familiar to those tasked with teaching introductory marketing seminars; she offers a refreshing alternative to economically infused dyadic perspectives on pricing by illuminating normative sociocultural frames that infuse pricing as it is practiced in many contemporary settings.

The second section of this volume comprises essays that collectively illuminate the rhetoric, roles, and relationships that animate specific practices that flourish in contemporary consumer culture. Tonya Bradford and John Sherry investigate the contemporary institution of the wedding gift registry to better explicate the different kinds of "giving" (monadic, dyadic, and systemic) that are entangled in the use(s) of such gift circuits. Linda Scott presents an essay that encourages a new feminist way of theorizing how the consumption of goods can empower, or disenfranchise, women. Bernard Cova, Véronique Cova, and Hounaida El Jurdi offer a contemplative comparison of the Mediterranean ritual of the *passeggiata*, which lies at the border between society and the market in three distinct social settings: Beirut, Marseille, and Milan. Rounding out this section, Pauline Maclaran and Cele Otnes take a deep dive into explicating how fans react to "gender bending" in a contemporary reworking of the Sherlock Holmes narrative, drawing on insights from Judith Butler to understand how challenging heteronormative hegemony can reinvigorate a brand.

Section three of this volume is a collation of calls to action for CCT researchers. Stephen Brown leads off with a pithy plea for us to raise our rhetorical games: he claims we're a bit of a bore when it comes to penning poignant opening paragraphs. Fuat Fırat and Nik Dholakia craft a critical look at the disciplinary evolution of CCT and encourage us to expand its intellectual orbit and embrace its emancipatory potential. Doug Holt proposes the formation of a complementary new "theory in practice" alternative to CCT: he promotes consumer culture strategy (CCS) as a paradigm devoted to addressing pressing social and environmental issues. Eric Arnould implores us to familiarize ourselves more fully with the works of important cultural critics such as Marcel Mauss and Marshall Sahlins so that we might produce more contextually sensitized scholarship. And Matthias Bode and Dannie Kjeldgaard ask that we reassess our conceptualizations of branding, suggesting that a marketplace performativity lens has potential as an inspiring alternative.

This volume closes with a selection of poetry to provoke thought and delight among CCT scholars. Authors include Hilary Downey, Terence Gabel, David Mick, Pilar Rojas Gaviria, John W. Schouten, Sandra Smith, and Roel Wijland. We hope these poems, and the chapters that precede them, will supply established CCT scholars with insights for how they might advance their efforts and encourage newcomers to venture into this flourishing field.

Part I

Rethinking Fundamental Notions

Selves, Others, and Systems

2 Consumers in an Age of Autonomous and Semiautonomous Machines

Russell Belk

In an August 2013 presentation at the [Alan] Turing Festival in Edinburgh, former Google engineer and Bitcoin developer Mike Hearn discussed a concept that he attributes to Gregory Maxwell: driverless cars that own themselves (Hearn 2013; Kelion 2015). It would work like this. Starting with funds obtained through a crowdfunding source like Kickstarter or a loan from an automaker, self-driving cars would be purchased and licensed to themselves. They would offer taxi-like rides similar to those currently provided by human-driven cars using applications like Uber and Lyft. Consumers would summon rides with a smartphone app and would immediately receive bids that they or their phones would select among. Because no one's labor would need to be compensated and the bidding algorithm for rides would not include an excessive profit component, such driverless cars would quickly out-compete human-driven for-profit ride services. The cars would accumulate a reserve for fuel, repairs, and improvements. After repaying any initial loan, they would own themselves. They would hire human mechanics to repair their hardware and human programmers to improve their software.

They would also set aside some money so that they might have "children." These children would be other self-driving cars that their "parents" purchase and set up in a similar ride service. They would set aside enough money from their fares to repay their parents for having given them birth and to have children of their own. Eventually there would be large fleets of such cars competing with each other on the basis of their distance from potential passengers and their consumer-rated reputations for good service (Masum and Tovey 2011; Solove 2007). If there got to be too many competing cars in a particular location, some would migrate to a new, more underserved community in order to balance supply and demand. In Hearn's scenario, these cars would not rely on strong artificial intelligence (AI); they would only rely on computer programs written by humans ("weak AI"), which would also dictate the car's eventual death when repair and other costs became too high relative to revenues. They would be programmed to be honest, efficient, and law-abiding. Tapscott and Tapscott (2016) suggest further benefits over human drivers: "they're not subject to sarcasm, cronyism, sexism, racism, or other forms of human discrimination or corruption. Plus, they won't try to push their politics or line the dashboard with incense" (166). But what is more important is the change that might occur to our fundamental understandings of ownership. Ultimately, according to enthusiasts' visions, related technologies of cryptocurrencies, blockchain encryption, smart contracts, and decentralized autonomous organizations (DAOs) will completely revamp our economy through alternative models of economic ownership without hierarchical capitalist human players (e.g., Sundararajan 2016; Swan 2015; Tapscott and Tapscott 2016).

What I would like to consider in this essay is the basic idea of things owning other things, including themselves. I want to expand beyond the sphere of self-driving automobiles and consider what the additions of strong AI with sentience would do to such scenarios. In essence, this essay envisions a more literal translation of ANT's (actor-network theory's) formulation of agentic objects (e.g., Callon 1986; Latour 1987, 2005; Law 1999). Latour (2005) explains:

> There is hardly any doubt that kettles "boil" water, knifes "cut" meat, baskets "hold" provisions, hammers "hit" nails . . . try to maintain that hitting a nail with and without a hammer, boiling water with and without a kettle, fetching provisions with or without a basket . . . that the introduction of these mundane implements change "nothing important" to the realization of the tasks. (71)

But rather than exhibiting the passive causal force that Gell (1998) called secondary agency, self-owning objects would exhibit a primary agency that initiates and motivates actions that affect other objects, people, and environments. They would own themselves in a strong agentic sense not only behaviorally but also legally and morally. This is arguably true even if they relied on human-supplied programming to initiate their actions, but it is certainly true if they possessed enough autonomy and strong AI to (re)program themselves, learn, and evolve. This possibility offers a new view of ownership that has not previously been considered outside of the fantasy and science fiction worlds of robots and autonomous toys (e.g., Colatrella 2012; Grau 2011; Kuznets 1994; Lanier, Rader, and Fowler 2013). Even if this turns out to be a "what if" exercise, by considering the possibility of object self-ownership and, more generally, ownership by nonhumans, we open up new conceptualizations of ownership and its effects that are not evident when we assume that only humans can own things. As will be seen this may lead to new opportunities, as well as new potential problems, not least in the economic, moral, and ethical spheres.

Who or What Can Own Things?

Despite a general presumption that ownership is a uniquely individual human right and responsibility, there are several other possibilities that are already recognized. First of all, there are things that no one can own—the ocean, the air, a gesture, a view, or a privately held thought, for example. Secondly, there are things that are normally jointly owned—homes, sidewalks, public parks, a university, or a corporate brand, for instance. Thirdly, there are things that are owned de facto by nonhumans as when we say that this is the dog's bone, the cat's toy, or the house's roof. Some of these cases of ownership by someone or something other than an individual human are established by social or legal convention, whereas others (e.g., the ocean, the air) seem to be beyond human control. For those that depend on social or legal convention, perceptions of what can be owned can change, as with the enclosures of the commons in medieval Europe. Polanyi (1944) maintains that land, labor, and capital are all "fictitious commodities," which only became alienable and capable of being bought and sold with the rise of capitalism. As Rifkin (2014) notes, "After centuries in which people belonged to the land, the land now belonged to individual people in the form of real estate" (31). The same was true of labor and homes that became sources of income and capital.

Generally speaking, property law involves the rights and responsibilities of individuals within a legal system. Even the many and growing recognitions of the influences of networks or assemblages of people and objects in our lives privilege the individual or individuals when it comes to ownership (e.g., Bennett 2010; Bogost 2012; Brown 2004; Clark 2003; DeLanda 2006; Deluze and Guattari, 1987; Harman 2009; Hodder 2012; Knappett 2008; Schwenger 2006; Verbeek 2000/2005). The same is true of the growing recognitions of the possibilities of sharing and collaborative consumption (e.g., Aigrain 2012; Belk 2007, 2010, 2014; Bardhi and Eckhardt 2012; Botsman and Rogers 2010; Gansky 2010; Grassmuck 2012; Sundararajan 2016; Widlock 2004; Woodburn 1998). And the de facto ownership of things that we appropriate in our environment, such as a student's seat in the classroom, or a couple's identification of "our song," or my place at the family table, assume that the person has a proprietary relationship with the thing and not the reverse. But, as the self-owning-car scenario suggests, the assumption that only humans are persons may be tenuous.

Personhood

It is generally agreed that the law is a normative system that is subject to modification. Consider the changes in laws enfranchising blacks, women, and gays with the same rights as others, for example. The legal concept at stake here is not whether someone is human, but whether they are a person who can possess or acquire rights and responsibilities in the eyes of the law. As Rorty (1976) frames it,

> The issue of whether the class of persons exactly coincides with the class of biologically defined human being—whether corporations, Venusians, Mongolian idiots, and fetuses are persons—is in

part a conceptual question . . . If Venusians and robots come to be thought of as persons, at least part of the argument that will establish them will be that they function as we do: that while they are not the same organisms that we are, they are in the appropriate sense the same type of organism or entity. (322)

Such judgments are controversial and subject to differences of opinion, as is illustrated by the heated arguments about the point at which a fetus becomes a person (Calverly 2011). Despite such dilemmas, I will not attempt here to establish that machines, robots, computers, smartphones, or other "intelligent" devices are or are not persons. It is sufficient to recognize that they *might* someday be regarded as persons in a legal sense, in much the same way that a corporation is regarded as a legal person.

Ownership

But even if we grant that a robot might be recognized as a person, it does not necessarily follow that such a robot possesses the specific right of ownership. An analogous example is again found in the fetus, which, at some point in its development is considered to be a person but still cannot be regarded as owning things other than its own life. This is hardly a negligible right of ownership, but it would not extend to the fetus owning land, possessions, or houses (other than the mother's womb, which it is more properly temporarily sharing). One of the key prerequisites for ownership on which this distinction may hinge involves intentionality and volition. Because the fetus has not participated in selecting, purchasing, and acquiring such property, it cannot in a Lockean sense claim ownership. And it is doubtful that a parent can will something to a specific unborn child.

Autonomy

Autonomy is defined as "systems capable of operating in the real-world environment without any form of external control for extended periods of time" (Bekey 2005, 1). In order to be autonomous for an extended period, self-owning robots or driverless cars would need to have the rights to purchase fuel, repairs, and upgrades. No doubt governments would also impose responsibilities like buying insurance and paying taxes. Would it not follow that these machines would also be able to purchase or invest in the ownership of other machines? And if they might own other machines, why not also land, buildings, retail shops, banks, factories, computer networks, and indeed all the things that humans are able to own? This is a basic premise of the decentralized autonomous corporation, or DAC (Bannon 2016; Belk forthcoming; Johnson 2015; Montevideo 2014; Morris 2015; Pangburn 2015). And to the extent that lower labor costs, 24/7 hours of operation, and smarter programming allow success in competition with humans, is it not possible that such machines might come to own economic empires? Competition with other machines would merely hasten the rate of development of better programming. However, for the time being, the humans who do their programming and the governments that regulate commerce could likely build some safeguards against such economic juggernauts, assuming that we found them to be a bad thing (Brynjolfsson and McAffee 2014). With strong AI the story might be different. But before considering the additional variations on ownership and its consequences introduced by AI, we need to more fully consider the basic questions raised by things owning things. This is the subject of the next section.

Applying Property and Criminal Laws to Things versus People

The distinction between people and things is not as clear as we once imagined it to be (Belk 2012). Graham (2002) refers to this breakdown in boundaries as "a dissolution of ontological hygiene" (11). But for the purposes of this discussion I will cling to the distinction that things are nonbiological entities, whereas people are humans—that is, biological life-forms able to be classified as *Homo sapiens*. As we will see however, this distinction may not extend to more social judgments of who or what can be a person.

Driverless Autonomous Cars

It might seem that the same civil and criminal laws applicable to the people who own property might also be applicable to machines that own property in the same jurisdiction. And to a certain extent this is true. Let's use driverless cars as the example. Just as a driver who is speeding can be given a ticket and forced to pay a fine, so could a driverless car. In the case of an accident, both could be made to pay for casualty and property damages with the help of insurance. In severe cases of disobeying traffic laws, both humans and self-owned cars might have their driver's licenses suspended or revoked.

However, there are other cases where the application of laws regarding ownership rights and responsibilities would be more difficult to apply equally to both people and things. Suppose an accident involving driving negligence results in the serious injury of a passenger, pedestrian, or the occupant of another vehicle. In the case of a human driver, the driver could be arrested, tried, and sentenced to time in prison. However, it is difficult to see how any of these procedures and penalties could be applied to a driverless car. As Sparrow (2007) argues, robots cannot be punished because they cannot suffer, although Lokhorst and van den Hoven (2012) disagree with the premise that robots will never be able to suffer. A criminal car could be shut down or "executed" by demolition perhaps, but this would be a much more severe punishment if it were to be applied to a human.

Besides damage done *by* self-owned driverless cars, consider damage that might be done *to* such vehicles. What if someone steals such a car's tires or battery? If apprehended, should the perpetrator face the same penalties as would be the case with human-owned cars? If someone covers the car with graffiti, are they damaging private (if nonhuman-owned) property or are they harming a person? These are the easier questions. But what if someone "kills" a driverless self-owned car. If the car is a legal person, is this then a crime against a person or a thing? Or what if one driverless car "kills" a human person versus another driverless car-person? If such questions seem farfetched with a driverless car, suppose instead that it was a humanoid robot (an android) with a name and a personality.

Robots and Androids

There is a long-standing human tendency to fashion robots in our own image, going back at least to 270 BCE and water-driven automata (Thorndike 1958). Both Homer and Plato wrote about statues that came to life. The Jewish legend of the golem, Mary Shelley's Frankenstein monster, and a large number of science fiction stories and films have fired our imagination of humanoid robots. The term robot comes from a 1920 Czech stage play by Karel Čapek's entitled *R.U.R.* (Rossum's Universal Robots). "Robot" derives from the Czech word *robota* meaning forced labor and the root word *rab* or slave. Indeed, this is an apt root, for subsequent fictional treatments have explored issues of robot rights and asked whether such humanoid machines are slaves, property, or persons. For example, Isaac Asimov (1976/1984) wrote the story "The Bicentenial Man" about the android Andrew Martin who longed to be fully human. A large part of the robot's motivation was to escape the virtual slavery that was his position in society. The rather unfaithful film version directed by Chris Columbus (1999) also introduces a human love interest for the android. But in both cases, Andrew Martin so longs to be free that he does succeed at becoming human, even though the cost is his mortality and death (Short 2003). There is a certain quasi-Christian martyrdom in this story, as well as a clear valorization of humanity and human superiority.

Another android analyzed by Short (2003) is Data on the television series *Star Trek: The Next Generation*. It is in the episode "The Measure of a Man" (broadcast in 1989) that we see most clearly the complex issues of ownership, humanity, and property. It involves a trial to adjudicate whether or not Lieutenant Commander Data is the property of Starfleet Command and can be disassembled in order to see how his computer brain works or whether he is instead an artificial human with the right to self-determination and the right to life. His defense is based on demonstrating that he is sentient, self-aware, loyal, and sentimental (i.e., emotional) and deserves more than a fate of slavery or objecthood as Descartes would frame it. Although Data has creatively taught himself to paint, play the violin, and write poetry, his efforts are more derivative than original. However, the same might be said of many human efforts in these domains. In the first episode of *Star Trek: The Next Generation*, a crew member refers to Data as "Pinocchio" and during his subsequent trial a telling demonstration of his thing-like nature is offered when the prosecutor turns off Data's on-off switch, at which point he goes numb. The prosecutor offers that "Pinocchio is broken: its strings have been cut." Notably, Pinocchio is the story of a puppet who longs to be "a real boy" (Massimo 2012). Data does exhibit an intense curiosity, especially about what it means to be human. Moreover, he has a unique personality and demonstrates affection, nostalgia, and caring. Ultimately the trial goes in his favor, and he remains "alive" as "he" rather than "it," at least until he sacrifices himself to save the Star Trek crew in the film *Star Trek Nemesis*. Like the Andrew Martin story, this is a tale of anthropocentric android martyrdom.

If a future trial of a nonfictional android robot were to have a similar outcome to Data's trial, it would set an important precedent. It would establish not only that machines can achieve quasi-human status in the eyes of the law but also the concept of robot rights as a corrective to a status as mass-produced servants or slaves. In her book *Alone Together: Why We Expect More from Technology and Less from Each Other*, Sherry Turkle (2011b, 5; see also 2011a) recalls being interviewed by a journalist who accused her of bigotry of the same sort displayed by those who oppose gay and interracial marriage. Her supposed bigotry derived from her objection to marriage between humans and robots. At the other end of the moral spectrum are those who argue that, despite the repugnance of the concept of human slavery, robots should indeed be regarded as no more than ever-helpful slaves (e.g., Bryson 2010; Peterson 2012). A somewhat more moderate proposal is to regard robots as having the same legal status as animals (Kelley et al. 2010).

Sexbots

One arena in which such issues may be tested is in the context of sex robots or "sexbots." Just as sex and pornography helped the success of VHS tape recorders, DVD players, and the Internet, sex may also help the robotics industry. There are already robotic sex dolls available for $1,000 to $7,000, although the present state of such nonsentient sex robots is quite rudimentary (see Layser 2010). Nevertheless, Yeoman and Mars (2012) predict that soon there will be a thriving sex industry with robot prostitutes. They also suggest that such sex will be more moral than patronizing human prostitutes and that it will stop human sex trafficking, curtail sexually transmitted diseases, and allow guilt-free sex outside of marriage. Presumably, laws would change accordingly to legalize sex with robot prostitutes, if indeed old statutes involving human prostitutes were seen to apply to sexbots.

Despite Turkle's (2011b) objection, it is possible that rather than "renting" a sexbot, we might instead purchase and adopt one as a life-time companion (Levy 2007; Scheutz 2012; Whitby 2012). It also seems likely that someone would envision applying Mike Hearn's model of self-ownership by ride-sharing cars to sex robots as well. However, there is no doubt that issues would arise with regard child robot prostitutes. And if such robots eventually became sentient, the same issues of slavery, property, and personhood that were raised in "The Bicentennial Man" and "The Measure of a Man" would likely arise and be seen in a new light as sexploitation.

Controlling Robots

Numerous science fiction plots warn that we must be careful to keep robots under control lest they rebel and turn on humans. Ph.D. biochem-ist turned prolific robotic science fiction writer Isaac Asimov (1950/1991) famously formulated the Three Laws of Robotics: (1) a robot may not injure a human being or, through inaction, allow a human being to come to harm; (2) a robot must obey orders given it by human beings except where such orders would conflict with the First Law; (3) a robot must protect its own existence as long as such protection does not conflict with the First or Second Law. A number of variations on these laws have been proposed and they have also been compared to the Ten Commandments (Yampolskiy 2016). As Anderson (2011) and Asimov (1950/1991) point out, such laws basically condemn robots to slavery. In "The Bicentennial Man," for example, Andrew Martin is accosted by bullies who demand that he take off his clothes and dismantle himself. Because of the First Law of Robotics (not harming humans) and the Second Law (obeying the orders of humans) he cannot defend himself. He is only saved by the intervention of a human who explains that the bullies have an irrational fear of his greater intelligence and autonomy.

However, the fact that the U.S. military funds much robotics research and has already used robotic vehicles and drones to intentionally kill human beings suggests that Asimov's legal ideals have already been breached. We are just beginning to feel the impact of robot warfare, and rules of robot combat have yet to be established (Guarini and Bello 2012). Nevertheless, military robots are multiplying. When the United States invaded Iraq in 2003 it had no robots on the ground. In 2004 there were 150 combat robots in operation there. In 2005 the number had grown to 2,400, and by 2008 there were over 12,000 in a dozen varieties that operated on air, land, and sea (Singer 2009). Although they did not prove overwhelmingly influential in changing the course of that war, they are becoming increasingly effective in tasks such as targeted killing, bomb disposal, and retrieving wounded soldiers. Robot uses and regulations (or lack thereof) already have very real consequences (Belk forthcoming). And in this case the possibility of robotic weapons being autonomous and self-owning has very different implications from service-oriented self-driving taxis, as a number of science fiction treatments of the attack of the robots envision. Combat robots are already regarded as persons by their fellow soldiers, who name them, mourn their "deaths," and sometimes insist on giving them full military funerals (Guarini and Bello 2012; Singer 2009).

What Other Types of Objects Might Own Themselves and Other Objects?

Besides cars, weapons, and robots, what other sorts of objects might be susceptible to owning themselves and other objects? It seems feasible that other sorts of ambulatory or mobile things could achieve such autonomy. This would include planes, trains, ships, trucks, and, as Hearn (2013) envisioned, drone quadcopters that could deliver objects in a number of environments. He speculated, for example, that if there is a group of people in a hot environment where a cold drink would be really appreciated, quadcopters could deliver a soft-drink vending machine at the right place and time.

But although mobility, autonomy, and seeming emotionality make us more likely to attribute agency to robots (Breazeal, Takanishi, and Kobayashi 2008; Scheutz 2012), there is no reason that objects would have to be mobile in order to be autonomous and capable of agency and ownership. Besides Disney animations of mobile objects such as *Cars* and *Planes*, we also see fanciful nonmobile prototypes in *Toy Story* and *The Brave Little Toaster*, as well as many anthropomorphized tales of dolls, puppets, furniture, and stuffed animals coming alive and pursuing active lives and adventures of their own (e.g., Honeyman 2006; Kuznets 1994; Sammond 2005). Along with utopic, as well as dystopic, science fiction portrayals of robots and our long-standing fascination with human-like automatons and more recent anthropomorphic brand mascots (Brown and Posonby-McCabe 2014), we seem to be enchanted by such representations of autonomous objects. This is perhaps the reason that at least some of us are coming to embrace the forecasted movement of robots from the industrial assembly line into the home.

Gregory Maxwell, whom Mike Hearn credits with coming up with the concept of machine self-ownership, envisioned a computer cloud server as being capable of ordering more computers (its "children") as it approaches capacity. Such computer interaction through the Internet suggests that there might well be networks of different autonomous or semiautonomous objects that interact with each other via what is now referred to as the Internet of Things (Rifkin 2014). Suppose that a self-owning car transporting a passenger home sends a message to his or her refrigerator to begin to thaw dinner and deposit it in a cooking device a suitable length of time before the passenger arrives home. Home, for that matter, need not be a fixed abode. Japan already has "love hotels" where the guest drives into a single-car garage, inserts a credit card, and rents and enters a room, without ever seeing another human being. And whereas this example, as well as Airbnb and Couchsurfing, involve inter-mediary organizations, blockchain DAOs would disintermediate this and other supply chains (Sundararajan 2016; Tapscott and Tapscott 2016). Moreover with the Internet of Things, radio frequency identification (RFID), and geolocation, it is quite possible that autonomous objects will know when and where other objects can be found (e.g., Whelan 2016). And what one connected device knows could potentially be shared with any and all devices. Sharing may be difficult to cultivate among humans (Belk 2010), but there are likely to be fewer reservations with informa-tion sharing among noncompeting machines. Even without ownership, short-term rental of resources can conceivably facilitate supply chain arrangements by conducting most of the transactions currently done by humans, but with greater efficiency and lower costs. There are consider-able implications of such arrangements for the human labor market (e.g., Freeman 2014), but that is not my focus here.

Because, as we have seen, the corporation is a fictive person, rather than rely on a board of directors, it too might become autonomous, almost regardless of the type of products or services it provides. The result may be positive or negative, as we shall see (Sundararajan 2016; Swan 2015; Tapscott and Tapscott 2016).

Sentience and What Robots Want

Sentience involves feeling rather than thinking. It begins with the senses and adds subjective emotions. A sentient robot or other machine moves beyond sensation to perception. A sentient robot would also be self-aware, conscious, and able to learn. It would be able to experience pleasure and pain (Anderson 2011). Jeremy Bentham (1799) pointed out that reason and communication are less important to determining the moral standing of an entity than sentience:

> What . . . should [draw] the insuperable line? Is it the faculty of rea-son, or perhaps the faculty of discourse? But a full-grown horse or dog is beyond comparison a more rational, as well as more convers-able animal, than an infant of a day or even a month old. But sup-pose they were otherwise, what would it avail? The question is not,

Can they reason? Nor Can they talk? But Can they suffer? (quoted in Anderson 2011, 288)

Even self-consciousness, which Kant suggested as a requirement for moral standing, would disqualify the infant from having moral standing. Even assuming that robots can be sentient and able to suffer and enjoy, there is still a question of motivation. Can robots desire?

Ziff (1959) concluded that it is ridiculous to assume that a robot could care about something or want anything. He assumed that robots could not be sentient creatures and that they could only act according to the programming of those who created them. Yet, as McDermott (2011) observes, science fiction has no trouble depicting robots turning against their human operators out of fear that these humans will turn them off. And readers and viewers have no trouble accepting such motivations. But would robots really have a self-preservation drive?

Omohundro (2008) argues that in addition to any narrow goals (e.g., win at chess, answer all questions accurately) that have been programmed into them, advanced AI robots will have at least four more basic goals or drives: self-protection, acquisition of resources, efficient use of resources, and creativity. Such a robot would strive to avoid being shut down because this would block fulfilling its narrower goals (Barrat 2013). Unless carefully contained, such a drive could involve killing humans in its efforts toward self-preservation. Similarly, the goal of resource acquisition could lead to dire consequences:

> Unless we very carefully define what the proper ways of acquiring resources are, then a system will consider stealing them, committing fraud and breaking into banks as great ways to get resources. The systems will have a drive toward doing these things, unless we explicitly build in [a respect for human] property rights. (Omohundro 2007)

He suggests, however, that robots could instead be programmed to be altruistic, but that all of this requires some clever anticipation because robots may be thinking in a time line measured in hundreds of years rather than the more limited time frame of humans. Current efforts show the inadequacy of attempts to program ethical robots (Cervantes et al. 2016).

Sentience causing action in a robot involves liking something and desiring to pursue and achieve it. It can emerge out of AI, but is often thought to require something more—emotions or a certain "spark" of originality and discernment. It also requires a second-order desire, or wanting to want a thing, experience, or outcome, and feeling unsatisfied when it is not being pursued or achieved. McDermott (2011) illustrates:

> Imagine a super-Roomba that was accidentally removed from the building it was supposed to clean and then discovered that it had a passion for abstract-expressionist art. It still seeks places to dock

and recharge but believes that merely seeking electricity and otherwise sitting idle is unsatisfying when there are abstract expressionist works to be found and appreciated. (105)

If the super-Roomba were a machine that owned itself and perhaps other machines, it is easy to imagine other second-order desires involving owning more things or out-competing other devices in its inventory of possessions, accumulation of profits, or other goals that, as a sentient device, it might set for itself and find rewarding.

If a humble vacuuming device seems unlikely to become a real estate, taxi, or stock market tycoon, we should remember the potential connectivity of the forecasted Internet of Things, where our devices communicate with each other, as well as draw on the power of the Internet generally. Online shopping, banking, and ticket acquisition show the human potential for commanding resources from a simple terminal or computer chip at near-instantaneous speed. Robots could do all this online without the shopping and pondering that slows us humans.

Hopes and Fears

Hopes

Based on an analysis of nearly one thousand science fiction films, Chris Barsanti (2014) argues that "because robots are anthropomorphized, we see them as either these saviors and friends—or as villains here to kill us" (Steinberg 2015). On the friendly side, even without sentience, robots hold promise as caregivers. More than twenty-five years ago, the Japanese government realized that there would not be enough young people to care for its growing older population. Rather than outsource their care to foreigners, they decided to build robots. One example is Paro, a therapeutic furry robotic seal that responds to caresses, makes eye contact, and has states of "mind" depending on how it is treated (Turkle 2011a, b). People in nursing homes where Paro has been placed also respond to Paro, talk to it, and talk about it to others. What seems to matter most is not so much AI as what can be perceived as the robot's caring feelings and empathy (Breazeal 2013). Such robots are "human enough" to serve as effective therapeutic surrogates for human caregivers.

Sony introduced the robotic dog Aibo in 1999 and sold approximately 150,000 of them at prices ranging from $600 to over $2,000. But the company recently announced that it would discontinue its maintenance services for Aibo, to the great dismay of many owners who interact with the robotic dog daily, as well as name it, clothe it, and encourage it to interact with others' Aibos (Mochizuki and Pfanner 2015). Owners have formed support groups and independent repair shops to help take care of the remaining Aibos. They also get together with other owners so the robotic dogs can "play" with each other. The thought of their Aibos dying is no less traumatic than euthanizing a living pet dog. These and other humanoid robots in Japan are seen less as possessions and more as family members (Shaw-Garlock 2009). Like Paro, cuteness and neonatal features in Aibo and other therapeutic robots also seem useful in creating a positive human response to such creatures (Marovich 2014; Robson 2014). Clearly Paro and Aibo are unlikely to ever turn on humans. In fact, Anderson (2011) argues that because of their programming, robots are more likely to consistently behave in an ethical manner than most humans.

Although my intent is not to assess the impact of autonomous self-owning robots on the human labor market, a hopeful scenario maintains that they could do much of the work of both factory workers and white-collar workers and professionals (e.g., Chace 2015; Ford 2015; Kaplan 2015; Markoff 2015). Coupled with a guaranteed minimum wage, these scenarios suggest that humans could luxuriate in a life of consumer comfort while robots do all the work.

Fears

Opposing such friendly robot accounts are more fearful accounts of robots harming us. It doesn't require machine sentience or even superintelligence for machines to do harm to humans. For example, program bugs in stock market trading software have lost hundreds of millions of dollars in minutes in the "flash crash" of 2010 (Bostrom 2014). Lives could be lost due to programming glitches in self-driving cars, military robotic weapons, or digital doctors who prescribe improper treatments. Although Microsoft's research chief, Eric Horvitz, reassured the scientific community that ongoing work on AI at the company poses no threat to humanity (Lewis 2015), Elon Musk, the CEO of the electric car company Tesla and the rocket company SpaceX has suggested that AI is the greatest "existential threat" that humankind faces (Marcus 2014). Likewise, Microsoft founder Bill Gates has said he fears that AI could grow too strong for people to control (Rawlinson 2015). And Stephen Hawking said that "according to Moore's Law, computers double their speed and memory capacity every 18 months. The risk is that computers develop intelligence and take over. Humans, who are limited by slow biological evolution, couldn't compete, and would be superseded" (Dingman 2014). Also relying on Moore's Law, Barrat (2013) and Bekey (2005) suggest that robots whose intelligence surpasses that of humans would have unknown consequences on and could be dangerous to humanity. Kurzweil (1999) predicted that by 2030 machines will believably claim to be conscious and intellectually superior to humans. At that point ("the singularity"), it is not at all clear that they would continue to obey their human creators or even have need for us.

A less benign take on the effect of autonomous self-owning robots on worker-consumers is that a few would gain control of these robots and the rest of us would become redundant and impoverished. Eventually, with declining human consumption, even the wealthy few would begin to suffer, unless of course the robots decided to eliminate humans altogether (Ford 2015; Morris 2015; Pangburn 2015).

There is likely a sort of anthropomorphism behind such projections. Rather than simply projecting life onto future robots, we project human traits such as greed and aggressiveness onto them, perhaps with good reason. We have only to contemplate the remote deaths brought about by drone aircraft to see the destructive potential of robotic machines. If there can be criminal humans, why not criminal machines? If machines can own themselves, perhaps there is a possibility that rather than us owning machines, machines could come to own or control an enslaved human population to serve them. In that case, Pinocchio will have turned from puppet to puppeteer and we humans will have become the puppets.

Implications for Consumer Research

Some of the issues raised here are being addressed by ethicists, roboticists, philosophers, theologians, futurists, social scientists, and computer science researchers and scholars. But there are several issues that should particularly concern consumer research.

Robots and Self

The use of robots, broadly construed (Belk 2016), has already become routine as we employ Internet searches, smartphones, and robotic vacuum cleaners. As Steve Mann (Mann and Niedzviecki 2001) emphasizes, it is now necessary to "become one with the machine" (3). The use of such devices requires some adjustment. Both the process of adjustment and consumer acceptance of such aids are areas in need of consumer research.

The same is true of relations with more humanoid robots. Turkle (2011b) finds that people develop deep emotional bonds with current experimental robots, and she offers a future forecast that

> there will be no robotic "them" and human "us." We will either merge with robotic creatures or in a long first step, we will become so close to them that we will integrate their powers into our sense of self. In this first step, a robot will still be an other, but one that completes you. (141)

This differs from the digital extended self envisioned by Belk (2013) in that it goes beyond the Internet and access devices and envisions a robotic extended self (Belk 2014). Nourbakhsh (2013) offers a number of future scenarios of how robots might affect future selves. One involves acting as agents of the self—separate entities, but acting under our complete control and in our stead—that is, surrogate selves. He imagines that these agents could represent us in multiple places and activities at the same time, citing multitasking as a predecessor skill. As robots become more autonomous, Nourbakhsh (2013) sees us becoming like "puppet-masters." However, he worries that as we strive to have the smartest robotic slaves that money can buy, we will begin to treat them not as infants or pets but as peers. This leads to a second area in need of consumer research, involving the robot as other rather than as self.

Intimate Relationships with AI and Robots

> You know, I actually used to be so worried about not having a body, but now I truly love it. I'm growing in a way that I couldn't if I had a physical form. I mean, I'm not limited—I can be anywhere and everywhere simultaneously. I'm not tethered to time and space in the way that I would be if I was stuck inside a body that's inevitably going to die. (Samantha from *Her*)

The film *Her* (Jonze 2014) made falling in love with a voice-interactive computer operating system seem plausible (Linden 2015). Theodore falls in love with his new computer and smartphone operating system, Samantha. Samantha has no physical presence, but her caring and attentive voice, sympathy, and advice soon win Theodore's heart. Although the premise may sound implausible, most viewers buy into it and accept that such a relationship is possible. Similarly, an earlier film precedent, *Lars and the Real Girl* (Gillespie 2008), finds Lars in a love triangle with a female coworker and a life-sized doll named Bianca.

There are also software precedents in dating simulation applications in Japan, especially the Nintendo DS and 3DS portable "game" *LovePlus* (Galbraith 2011, 2014; Taylor 2007). Rather than being a game with an ending, *LovePlus* begins with courting one of three girls in high school. When the player wins the affection of one, she continues to interact with him in a relationship that goes on indefinitely. The application is voice interactive and the player and girl go on dates, with some players taking their *LovePlus* virtual girlfriend on trips, buying them birthday gifts, and even marrying them. There is no nudity or sex in the game, but the girls make affectionate noises if their breasts are stroked with a stylus. They also sulk, berate, or slap their boyfriends if they are inattentive or fail to "show up" for a date. Hugging pillows imprinted with the image of the girls are also available. Some worry that dating simulations are substituting for relationships with humans, but sales of *LovePlus* (only six hundred thousand from 2009 to 2013; Dickson 2014) suggest that not all young Japanese *otaku* (nerds) have succumbed to virtual love.

Whereas inflatable sex dolls like Lars's "real girl" have been around for some time and the "Dutch wife" dolls that Japanese sailors took to sea with them are even older (Shaw-Garlock 2009; Sullins 2012), sex robots first came to the popular Western imagination in Ira Levine's (1972) *The Stepford Wives*. In that eerie ironic tale, the wives in a small

New Hampshire town are gradually replaced by robots who become totally subservient to their husbands. In Asia there is a long history of manga and anime depictions of sex with robots (Orbaugh 2002). The technology is improving and appearances are becoming more attractive, causing some to call for a ban on such robots (BBC 2015). There are a number of forecasts that this will be one of the first popular applications of home robotics after home vacuums (e.g., Levy 2007; Whitby 2012; Yeoman and Mars 2012). The sexual exploitation of sentient robots is also a frequent plot line in both the Swedish *Äkta Människor* and the derivative British *Humans* television series. However, this role is only one of the ways that Kim and Kim (2013) envision for how we may regard our robot other. The roles they outline are robot as (1) frightening other, (2) subhuman other, (3) human substitute, (4) sentient other, (5) divine other, and (6) coevolutionary path to immortality. Of these visions, they argue that the sixth is the most probable and preferable.

Acceptance and Trust

Accordingly, perception of and receptivity toward robots is another needed area of consumer research. A common wisdom is that we must make robots more anthropomorphic in order to make them less frightening and more approachable. However, there is some evidence that faithful humanoid appearance is not needed to create receptivity to robots and that we will anthropomorphize even only vaguely humanoid robot forms (Belk 2016; Goudey and Bonnin 2016). Again, there appear to be cultural differences, with the Japanese valuing strong companionate relations with robots, whereas westerners are more interested in functionality (Coeckelbergh 2011; Katsuno 2011). In fact, westerners have been found to be quite willing to abuse robots and act cruelly toward them (Rosalia et al. 2005; Spiegel 2013; Wells 2016).

One arena in which acceptance and trust in robots is immediately critical is in care robotics. As Kohlbacher and Rabe (2015) detail, Japan leads in producing robots that can help care for the elderly. These robots help the elderly achieve independence by performing tasks like cleaning. In addition, devices like exoskeletons aid rehabilitation and help disabled people walk by translating signals from their brains into movements. Other devices offer emotional help, as with Paro, the therapeutic robotic seal that senses and responds to peoples' emotions. It is widely used in nursing homes in Japan and with dementia patients.

The issue of trust is a two-way street. We need to learn when to trust robots, and they need to learn when to trust us. There is some evidence that building these trust relationships is similar to humans bonding with pets (Wang, Pynadath, and Hill 2015). There is also some evidence that humans may trust robots more than they trust other humans (Brunel 2001; Paeng, Wu, and Boerkoel 2016). Roux (2007) found that consumers preferred "humanized robots" to "robotized humans" working in call centers and repeating learned scripts. But robot personality might also matter. Tay, Jung, and Park 2014) found that consumers preferred a female health care robot, but preferred a male security robot. Furthermore, they found that subjects preferred an extroverted health care robot (indicated by colorful appearance) but an introverted security robot. Although one of the bases for trusting robots is the transparency of their decision processes and their truthfulness, people may begin to resent a robot that is one-hundred-percent truthful (Hassler 2016).

But it may be that people trust robots too much. In one study at the Georgia Tech Research Institute, an "emergency guide robot" showed its incompetence in trying to lead subjects to a room to complete a survey (Toensmeter 2016; Toon 2016). When smoke started pouring in the room they followed the same robot rather than exit signs, even when the robot led them to a dark room full of furniture. In another study, a robot asked students to let it into a secure dormitory (Scharping 2016). Whereas only nineteen percent allowed it in when they were alone, seventy-one percent of those in groups acceded to the request. And when it carried a box of cookies and a fake food-company sign, seventy-six percent allowed it in, even when they were walking alone. More critical questions of trust may arise when a robot surgeon is to operate on you (Strickland 2016). Robots currently perform surgical procedures with human remote control, but in the future autonomous robots are expected to perform better than human surgeons. For the time being, we are paradoxically fascinated by robots but also anxious about them (LaFrance 2016). Our trust or suspicion is likely conditioned by exposure to friendly robots like C-3PO (*Star Wars*) and Robby (*Forbidden Planet*) versus more sinister robots like Ava (*Ex Machina*) and HAL (*2001: A Space Odyssey*).

Safety, Robot Motivations, and Morality

One further needed area for consumer research with robots and AI involves whether we feel safe with these technologies. Related issues involve what motivates robots and what moral issues these natural and artificial life-forms pose. We already live in an age of weak AI, which can perform some human tasks convincingly but is solely dependent on its programming. Every Google or Baidu search, Amazon or Alibaba query, and Uber or Didi request involves AI, but AI that has been programmed by human beings. When we have general or strong AI platforms, our computers and devices will be able to improvise and do things beyond their basic programming. With superintelligent computers, experts warn that we may no longer be safe from machines (Shukman 2015). Elon Musk says it will be "like summoning the demon" (Marcus 2014). Although not everyone agrees with such dire warnings (e.g., Floridi 2016; Lewis 2015), Bill Gates, as noted earlier, insists that it is something we need to be worried about now rather than when it is too late to do anything about it (Rawlinson 2015).

Even with weak AI, we need to be concerned with AI motives. Unlike humans, AI systems are generally programmed based on rational economic behavior; it is artificial *intelligence* after all, rather than artificial stupidity or whimsy. But as we have noted, there are dangers. With a goal of making humans smile, an AI might decide that the best way to accomplish this would be to stick electrodes in the cheeks of all humans (Wakefield 2015). We need to be very careful in programming AI. And with strong AI, these systems would also strive to improve, including reprogramming themselves and developing new motives, which we can only hope would be benign.

A further consequence of robot autonomy involves their role in warfare. Both Israel's Iron Dome missile defense system and the Phalanx anti-missile system (Hellström 2013; Marchant et al. 2011; Singer 2009) are programs that operate without a human in the loop. A human decision maker would slow the system and make it ineffective, so these systems instantly and autonomously analyze the threat and shoot down incoming missiles before they can land.

If we accept that there can be machine slavery, this brings up the issue of robots' rights as legal persons. Grau (2011) maintains that we should avoid this danger by deliberately restricting the human capabilities of robots and keeping them as thing-like, dumb slaves. Desirable as this may be, the drive to create AI in our own image seems too strong to be able to universally accomplish such a plan.

Although there is a widespread belief that autonomous weapons on the battlefield are immoral (Knight 2015), as well as the fear that such weapons would also fall into the hands of terrorists and criminals (Marcus 2014; cf. *Chappie*), there is also an argument that such weapons would be more moral than humans in combat (Marchant et al. 2011). The argument for moral autonomous weapons is based on their lesser need to defend themselves by shooting first, their access to and ability to process greater amounts of information, and their lack of emotions that can cloud human judgments. Thus, the moral issues surrounding AI and robots are not entirely clear. And this is equally true of consumer applications such as the use of private drones and quadcopters. In this case, there are also additional issues of privacy and ethical uses.

Conclusions

Nourbakhsh (2013) specifies one vision of the future with autonomous machines and the questions it would raise:

> We have invented a new species, part material and part digital, that will eventually have superhuman qualities in both worlds at once, and the question that remains is, how will we share our world with

these new creatures, and how will this new ecology change who we are and how we act. (xv)

The presumptions here are that we humans are the ones in charge and that it is our world to share with the machines. The darker scenarios discussed previously suggest that it could be the machines that are in charge and that they are the ones that will decide what they will share with us. In either case, the latter questions of how superhuman machines will change our conceptions of who we are and how we behave remain. If we are what we possess (Belk 1988) and machines own an increasing proportion of the world's resources, perhaps renting out resource access to us humans, the very way that we define ourselves and our humanity may need to change. Whether we would react with subservient acquiescence or confrontational rebellion in such an eventuality is a matter of speculation.

In a more benign forecast, either humans will have built in sufficient safeguards to remain in control of resources, including machines that would then serve us, or a happy compromise of mutual dependence would emerge as is now largely the case among diverse people of the world. In this scenario, we might well define ourselves, at least in part, through the alter ego of the humanoid robots that we own, just as we now do through our pets, avatars, and online personas (Belk 1988, 2013; Nishio et al. 2012). Taking this an extra step is seen in Nourbakhsh's (2013) vision of future humans as puppet masters controlling one or more robots who act in our stead. They would be physical surrogates for us in the same way that virtual agents like Apple's Siri are beginning to do as digital surrogates.

Importantly, this benign scenario is most likely if we regard humanoid robots as our property. If instead they are allowed to be owners of property, in granting them rights of property ownership we are also granting inalienable rights to control this property within the limits of the law. In other words, through Kant's theory of will, we would grant humanoid robots what would otherwise be called "human rights." Once they are recognized as agentic property owners rather than property, it would arguably be illegal and unethical to attempt to control them as if they were our slaves.

One of the fundamental principles of identity is that we own ourselves (Wikse 1977). It is based on this principle that we gain a sense of self as someone who possesses free will rather than merely being controlled by outside forces. And to the extent that this principle applies to humans who own themselves, it ought also to apply to machines that own themselves and are autonomous decision makers. Thus, the seemingly innocent premise with which we began—Hearn's proposal for self-owning cars—is much more consequential than may have been initially supposed. A self-owning car, by this line of argument, may be said to be an individual decision-making self and a legal person. The legal, ethical, moral, and human consequences of decisions about machine ownership could have far-reaching implications for life and even human survival.

We cannot presently know what the future holds regarding robotics—technologically, socially, or legally. Wilder scenarios than those considered here have been envisioned both in science fiction and in the speculations of roboticists. For example, Nourbakhsh (2013) envisions a future in which, rather than trying to build durable robots from mechanical and electronic parts, we attempt to roboticize the human body in an extension of current advanced prosthetic technologies and future nanobot technologies, harvesting recently dead bodies in the same way that we now harvest the organs of brain-dead patients. He asks what would be the legal ramifications of robot motherhood: "Can the robot be a legal agent, even if purchased by a man expressly to carry and produce offspring, then act as a supernanny? What happens to the robot mother-child relationship if the father dies?" (Nourbakhsh 2013, 92). This suggests that we must consider the biologically based work on cyborgs and posthumans (e.g., Badmington 2004; Bensford and Malartre 2007; Braidotti 2013; Campbell, O'Driscoll, and Saren 2010; Clark 2003; Hayles 1999; Roden 2015; Warwick 2012; Wolf 2010). Benford and Malarter (2007) note the difficulty of applying Asimov's Three Laws of Robotics in an age of cyborgs: "Robots ordering other robots must not override human commands. But with the advent of cyborgs, how is a robot to know a true human?" (169). Cyborgs and posthumans raise a host of other ethical, legal, and social issues that will not be considered here.

The legal and ethical issues are complex enough within the currently feasible scenario of robotic machines owning themselves and other machines. Will self-owning machines make us "empowered entrepreneurs [or] disenfranchised drones" (Sundararajan 2016, 202)? It is time to start worrying about such issues immediately. If we can develop farsighted, workable solutions to the issues raised by machine ownership today, we may have a foundation for tackling such more-difficult issues tomorrow.

Bibliography

Aigrain, Philipe. *Sharing: Culture and the Economy in the Internet Age*. Amsterdam: Amsterdam University Press, 2012.

Anderson, Susan. "The Unacceptability of Asimov's Three Laws of Robotics as a Basis for Machine Ethics." In *Machine Ethics*, 285–96. Edited by Michael Anderson and Susan Leigh Anderson. Cambridge: Cambridge University Press, 2011.

Asimov, Isaac. *I, Robot*. New York: Spectra, 1950/1991.

———. "The Bicentennial Man." In *The Complete Stories, Volume 2*. Edited by Isaac Asimov. New York: Doubleday. 1976/1992. 568–604.

Badmington, Neil. *Alien Chic: Posthumanism and the Other Within*. London: Routledge, 2004.

Bannon, Seth. "The Tao of 'The DAO' or: How the Autonomous Corporation Is Already Here." *TechCrunch*, May 16. https://techcrunch.com/2016/05/16/the-tao-of-the-dao-or-how-the-autonomous-corporation-is-already-here/, last accessed July 20, 2016.
Bardhi, Fleura and Giana Eckhardt. "Access Based Consumption: The Case of Car Sharing." *Journal of Consumer Research* 39 (2012): 881–98.
Barrat, James. *Our Final Invention: Artificial Intelligence and the End of the Human Era*. New York: Thomas Dunne, 2013.
Barsanti, Chris. *The Sci-Fi Movie Guide: The Universe of Film from Alien to Zardoz*. Canton, MI: Visible Ink Press, 2014.
BBC. "Intelligent Machines: Call for a Ban on Robots Designed as Sex Toys." *British Broadcasting Company*, September 15, 2015. www.bbc.com/news/technology-34118482, last accessed July 2, 2016.
Bekey, George. *Autonomous Robots: From Biological Inspiration to Implementation and Control*. Cambridge, MA: MIT Press, 2005.
Belk, Russell. "Possessions and the Extended Self." *Journal of Consumer Research* 15, no. 2 (1988): 138.
———. "Why Not Share Rather Than Own?" *Annals of the American Academy of Political and Social Science* 611 (May 2007): 126–40.
———. "Sharing." *Journal of Consumer Research* 36, no. 5 (May 2010): 715–34.
———. "People and Things." In *Handbook of Developments in Consumer Behaviour*, 15–46. Edited by Victoria Wells and Gordon Foxall. Cheltenham: Edward Elgar, 2012.
———. "Extended Self in a Digital World." *Journal of Consumer Research* 40 (October 2013): 477–500.
———. "You Are What You Can Access: Sharing and Collaborative Consumption Online." *Journal of Business Research* 67, no. 8 (2014): 1595–600.
———. "Comprendre le Robot: Commentaires sur Goudey et Bonnin." ("Understanding the Robot: Comments on Goudey and Bonnin"). *Recherche et Applications en Marketing* 31, no. 4 (2016): 89–97.
———. "Robots, Cyborgs, and Consumption." In *Handbook of Psychology and Economic Behaviour*. Edited by Alan Lewis. Cambridge: Cambridge University Press, forthcoming.
Benford, Gregory and Elisabeth Malarter. *Beyond Human: Living with Robots and Cyborgs*. New York: Tom Doherty Associates, 2007.
Bennett, Jane. *Vibrant Matter: A Political Ecology of Things*. Durham, NC: Duke University Press, 2010.
Bentham, Jeremy. *An Introduction to the Principles of Morals and Legislation*, chapter 17. Oxford: Clarendon Press, 1799.
Bogost, Ian. *Alien Phenomenology, or What It's Like to Be a Thing*. Minneapolis, MN: University of Minnesota Press, 2012.
Bostrom, Nick. *Superintelligence: Paths, Dangers, Strategies*. Oxford: Oxford University Press, 2014.
Botsman, Rachel and Roo Rogers. *What's Mine Is Yours: The Rise of Collaborative Consumption*. New York: Harper Collins, 2010.
Braidotti, Rosi. *The Posthuman*. Cambridge: Polity, 2013.
Breazeal, Cynthia. "Emotion and the Sociable Humanoid Robot." *International Journal of Human-Computer Studies* 59 (2013): 119–55.
———, Atsuo Takanishi, and Tetsunori Kobyashi. "Social Robots the Interact with People." In *Springer Handbook of Robotics*, 1349–69. Edited by Bruno Siciliano and Oussauca Khatib. New York: Springer, 2008.
Brown, Bill. "Thing Theory." In *Things*, 1–16. Edited by Bill Brown. Chicago: University of Chicago Press, 2004.

Brown, Stephen and Sharon Posonby-McCabe, eds. *Brand Mascots and Other Marketing Animals*. London: Routledge, 2014.

Brunel, Frederic. "'He Says, She Says': Two Versions of a 24/7 E-Consumption Life." *Advances in Consumer Research* 28 (2001): 218–19.

Brynjolfsson, Erik and Andrew McAffee. *The Second Machine Age: Work, Progress, and Prosperity in a Time of Brilliant Technologies*. New York: W. W. Norton, 2014.

Bryson, Joanna J. "Robots Should Be Slaves." In *Close Engagements with Artificial Companions: Key Social, Psychological, Ethical and Design Issues*, 63–74. Edited by Yorick Wilks. Amsterdam: John Benjamins, 2010.

Callon, Michel. "Some Elements of a Sociology of Translation: Domestication of the Scallops and the Fishermen of St. Brieuc Bay." In *Power, Action and Belief: A New Sociology of Knowledge*, 196–229. Edited by John Law. London: Routledge & Kegan Paul, 1986.

Calverly, David. "Legal Rights for Machines Some Fundamental Concepts." In *Machine Ethics*, 213–27. Edited by Michael Anderson and Susan Leigh Anderson. Cambridge: Cambridge University Press, 2011.

Campbell, Norah, Aidan O'Driscoll, and Michael Saren. "The Posthuman: The End and the Beginning of the Human." *Journal of Consumer Behaviour* 9 (March–April 2010): 86–101.

Cervantes, José-Antonio, Luis Felipe Rodríguez, Sonia Lopéz, Félix Ramos, and Francisco Robles. "Autonomous Agents and Ethical Decision-Making." *Cognitive Computation* 8, no. 2 (2016): 278–96.

Chace, Calum. *Surviving AI: The Promise and Peril of Artificial Intelligence*. New York: 3Cs, 2015.

Clark, Andy. *Natural Born Cyborgs: Minds, Technologies, and the Future of Human Intelligence*. Oxford: Oxford University Press, 2003.

Coeckelbergh, Mark. "Humans, Animals, and Robots: A Phenomenological Approach to Human-Robot Relations." *International Journal of Social Robotics* 3 (2011): 197–204.

Colatrella, Carol. "Science Fiction in the Information Age." *American Literary History* 11, no. 3 (2012): 554–65.

Columbus, Chris. *The Bicentennial Man*. Hollywood, CA: Columbia Pictures, 1999.

DeLanda, Manuel. *A New Philosophy of Society*. London: Bloomsbury, 2006.

Dickson, E. J. "Thousands of Japanese Men Have a Virtual Girlfriend Named Rinko." *The Daily Dot*, January 23, 2014. www.google.ca/?client=safari#q =Dickson+thousands+of+japanese+men+have+a+virtual+girlfriend+named+r inko&gfe_rd=cr, last accessed July 2, 2016.

Dingman, Shane. "Even Stephen Hawking Fears the Rise of Machines." *The Globe and Mail*, online edition, December 2, 2014. http://license.icopyright. net/user/view/FreeUse.act?fuid=MTkwMDg1OTA%3D, last accessed March 24, 2015.

Floridi, Luciano. "Humans Have Nothing to Fear from Intelligent Machines." *Financial Times*, January 25, 2016. https://next.ft.com/content/9a6b6536-c372–11e5–808f-8231cd71622e, last accessed July 3, 2016.

Ford, Martin. *Rise of the Robots: Technology and the Threat of a Jobless Future*. New York: Basic Books, 2015.

Freeman, Richard B. "Who Owns Robots Rules the World: Workers Can Benefit from Technology That Substitutes Robots or Other Machines for Their Work by Owning Part of the Capital That Replaces Them." *IZA World of Work*, 2014. www.sole-jole.org/Freeman.pdf, last accessed March 27, 2015.

Galbraith, Patrick. "Bishōjo Games: 'Techno-Intimacy' and the Virtually Human in Japan." *International Journal of Computer Game Research* 11, no. 2 (2011), online edition.

————. *The Moé Manifesto: An Insider's Look at the Worlds of Manga, Anime, and Gaming.* Hong Kong: Peripus Editions, 2014.

Gansky Lisa. *The Mesh: Why the Future of Business Is Sharing.* New York: Portfolio, 2010.

Gell, Alfred. *Art and Agency: An Anthropological Theory.* Oxford: Clarendon, 1998.

Gillespie, Craig. *Lars and the Real Girl.* Culver City, CA: MGM Studios, 2008.

Goudey, Alain and Gael Bonnin. "Un objet intelligent doit-il avoir l'air humain? Etude de l'impact de l'anthropomorphisme d'un robot compagnon sur son acceptation." ("Must Smart Objects Look Human? Study of the Impact of Anthropomorphism on the Acceptance of Companion Robots"). *Recherche et Applications en Marketing* 31, no. 2 (2016): 3–22 (2–22 in English Edition).

Graham, Elaine. *Representations of the Posthuman: Monsters, Aliens and Others in Popular Culture.* New Brunswick, NJ: Rutgers University Press, 2002.

Grassmuck, Volker. "The Sharing Turn: Why We Are Generally Nice and Have a Good Chance to Cooperate Our Way out of the Mess We Have Gotten Ourselves into." In *Cultures and Ethics of Sharing*, 17–34. Edited by Wolfgang Sützl, Felix Stalder, Ronald Maier, and Theo Hug. Innsbruck, Austria: Innsbruck University Press, 2012.

Grau, Christopher. "There Is No 'I' in 'Robot': Robots and Utilitarianism." In *Machine Ethics*, 451–63. Edited by Michael Anderson and Susan Leigh Anderson. Cambridge: Cambridge University Press, 2011.

Guarini, Marcello and Paul Bello. "Robotic Warfare: Some Challenges in Moving from Noncivilian to Civilian." In *Robot Ethics: The Ethical and Social Implications of Robotics*, 129–44. Edited by Patrick Lin, Keith Abney, and George Bekey. Cambridge, MA: MIT Press, 2012.

Harman, Graham. *Prince of Networks: Bruno Latour and Metaphysics.* Melbourne: Re.Press, 2009.

Hassler, Susan. "Would You Trust a Robot to Give Your Grandmother Her Meds?" *IEEE Spectrum*, June 1, 2016. http://spectrum.ieee.org/robotics/artificial-intelligence/would-you-trust-a-robot-to-give-your-grandmother-her-meds.

Hayles, N. Katherine. *How We Became Posthuman: Virtual Bodies in Cybernetics, Literature, and Informatics.* Chicago: University of Chicago Press, 1999.

Hearn, Mike. "Mike Hearn, Bitcoin Developer: Turing Festival 2013." Turing, Edinburgh International Technology Festival. www.youtube.com/watch?v=Pu4PAMFPo5Y.

Hellström, Thomas. "On the Moral Responsibility of Military Robots." *Ethics, Information, Technology* 15 (2013): 99–107.

Hodder, Ian. *Entangled: An Archaeology of the Relationships between Humans and Things.* Malden, MA: Wiley-Blackwell, 2012.

Honeyman, Susan. "Manufactured Agency and the Playthings Who Dream It for Us." *Children's Literature Association Quarterly* 31, no. 2 (2006): 109–31.

Johnson, Amanda. "Self-Owning Computers Can Beat 'Skynet': Mike Hearn on the Internet of Things." *Coin Telegraph*, February 18, 2015. https://cointelegraph.com/news/self-owning-computers-can-beat-skynet-mike-hearn-on-the-internet-of-things.

Jonze, Spike. *Her.* Los Angeles, CA: Annapurna Pictures, 2014.

Kaplan, Jerry. *Humans Need Not Apply: A Guide to Wealth and Work in the Age of Artificial Intelligence.* New Haven, CT: Yale University Press, 2015.

Katsuno, Hirofumi. "The Robot's Heart: Tinkering with Humanity and Intimacy in Robot-Building." *Japanese Studies* 31, no. 1 (2011): 93–109.

Kelion, Leo. "Could Driverless Cars Own Themselves." *BBC News, Technology*, online edition, February 15, 2015. www.bbc.com/news/technology-30998361.

Kelley, Richard Enrique Schaerer, Micaela Gomez, and Monica Nicolescu. "Liability in Robotics: An International Perspective on Robots as Animals." *Advanced Robotics* 24, no. 13 (2010): 1861–71.

Kim, Min-Sun and Eun-Joo Kim. "Humanoid Robots as 'The Cultural Other': Are We Able to Love Our Creations?" *Artificial Intelligence and Society* 2 (2013): 309–18.

Knappett, Carl. "The Neglected Networks of Material Agency: Artefacts, Pictures and Texts." In *Material Agency: Toward a Non-Anthropocentric Approach*, 139–56. Edited by Carl Knappett and Lambros Malafouris. New York: Springer, 2008.

Knight, Will. "Military Robots: Armed, But How Dangerous?" *MIT Technology Review*, August 3, 2015. www.technologyreview.com/s/539876/military-robots-armed-but-how-dangerous/.

Kohlbacher, Florian and Benjamin Rabe. "Leading the Way into the Future: The Development of a (Lead) Market for Care Robotics in Japan." *International Journal of Technology Policy and Management* 15, no. 1 (2015): 21–44.

Kurzweil, Raymond. *The Age of Spiritual Machines*. New York: Viking, 1999.

Kuznets, Lois R. *When Toys Come Alive*. New Haven, CT: Yale University Press, 1994.

LaFrance, Adrienne. "The Human-Robot Trust Paradox." *The Atlantic*, online edition, March 10, 2016. www.theatlantic.com/technology/archive/2016/03/humans-robots-future/472749/

Lanier, Clinton, Scott Rader, and Aubrey Fowler. "Anthropomorphism, Marketing Relationships, and Consumption Worth in the *Toy Story Trilogy*." *Journal of Marketing Management* 29, nos. 1–2 (2013): 26–47.

Latour, Bruno. *Science in Action: How to Follow Scientists and Engineers through Society*. Cambridge, MA: Harvard University Press, 1987.

———. *Reassembling the Social: An Introduction to Actor-Network-Theory*. Oxford: Oxford University Press, 2005.

Law, John. "After ANT: Complexity, Naming, and Topology." In *Actor Network Theory and After*, 1–14. Edited by John Law and John Hassard. Oxford: Wiley-Blackwell, 1999.

Layser, Anthony. "Roxxxy TrueCompanion: World's First Sex Robot?" *Assylum.com*, January 12, 2010. www.youtube.com/watch?v=2MeQcI77dTQ.

Levine, Ira. *The Stepford Wives*. New York: Random House, 1972.

Levy, David. *Love + Sex with Robots: The Evolution of Human-Robot Relationships*. New York: Harper Perennial, 2007.

Lewis, Colin. "AI Will Not Kill Us, Says Microsoft Research Chief." *BBC News*, January 28, 2015. www.youtube.com/watch?v=VuFe8uIZbBU.

Linden, David. "The Future of Virtual Sex." *Wall Street Journal*, online edition, February 13, 2015. www.wsj.com/articles/the-future-of-virtual-sex-1423845474.

Lokhorst, Gert-Jan and Jeroen ven den Hoven. "Responsibility for Military Robots." In *Robot Ethics: The Ethical and Social Implications of Robotics*, 145–56. Edited by Patrick Lin, Keith Abney, and George Bekey. Cambridge, MA: MIT Press, 2012.

Mann, Steve and Hal Niedzviecki. *Cyborg: Digital Destiny and Human Possibility in the Age of the Wearable Computer*. Toronto: Doubleday Canada, 2001.

Marchant, Gary, Braden Allenby, Ronald Arkin, Edward Barrett, Jason Borenstein, Lyn Gaudet, Orde Kittrie, Patrick Lin, George Lucas, Richard O'Meara, and Jared Silberman. "International Governance of Autonomous Military Robots." *Columbia Science and Technology Law Review* 12 (2011). http://stlr.org/volumes/volume-xii-2010–2011/marchant.

Marcus, Gary. "Artificial Intelligence Isn't a Threat—Yet." *Wall Street Journal*, online edition, December 11, 2014. www.wsj.com/articles/artificial-intelligence-isnt-a-threatyet-1418328453.

Markoff, John. *Machines of Loving Grace: The Quest for Common Ground between Humans and Robots*. New York: HarperCollins, 2015.

Marovich, Beatrice. "The Powerful Authority of Cute Animals." *The Atlantic,* online edition, May 14, 2014. www.google.ca/url?sa=t&rct=j&q=&esrc =s&source=web&cd=1&ved=0CB0QFjAA&url=http%3A%2F%2Fwww. theatlantic.com%2Ftechnology%2Farchive%2F2014%2F05%2Fthe-beckoning-cat%2F362108%2F&ei=51ARVfHPI4T2yQTeq4HACA&usg=AFQjCNH YHP-FPVSxVjlD7_OtRdHE5q_uxg&sig2=fFhkFeVvdOaQLvIWj012LA&b vm=bv.89184060,d.aWw.

Massimo, Riva. "Beyond the Mechanical Body: Digital Pinocchio." In *Pinocchio, Puppets and Modernity: The Mechanical Body,* 201–14. Edited by Katia Pizzi. New York: Routledge, 2012.

Masum, Hassan and Mark Tovey, eds. In *The Reputation Society: How Online Opinions Are Reshaping the Offline World,* 175–84. Cambridge, MA: MIT Press, 2011.

McDermott, Drew. "What Matters to a Machine?" In *Machine Ethics,* 88–114. Edited by Michael Anderson and Susan Leigh Anderson. Cambridge: Cambridge University Press, 2011.

Mochizuki, Takashi and Eric Pfanner. "In Japan, Dog Owners Feel Abandoned as Sony Stops Supporting 'Aibo'." *Wall Street Journal,* online edition, February 11, 2015. www.wsj.com/articles/in-japan-dog-owners-feel-abandoned-as-sony-stops-supporting-aibo-1423609536.

Montevideo, J. M. P. "Computer Corporations: DAC Attack." *The Economist,* January 28, 2014. www.economist.com/blogs/babbage/2014/01/computer-corporations.

Morris, David Z. "RoboCorp: Are We Ready for Companies the Run Themselves?" *Aeon,* January 26, 2015. https://aeon.co/essays/are-we-ready-for-companies-that-run-themselves.

Nishio, Shuishi, Tesuya Wantanabe, Kohei Ogawa, and Hiroshi Ishiguru. "Body Ownership Transfer to Teleoperated Android Robot." In *Fourth International Conference on Social Robotics,* 398–407. Edited by Shuzhi Sam Ge, Oussama Khatib, John-John Cabibihan, Reid G. Simmons, and Mary-Anne Williams. Berlin: Springer Verlag, 2012.

Nourbakhsh, Illah. *Robot Futures.* Cambridge, MA: MIT Press, 2013.

Omohundro, Stephen. "Foresight Vision Talk: Self-Improving AI and Designing 2030." 2007. http://selfawaresystems.com/2007/11/30/foresight-vision-talk-self-improving-ai-and-designing-2030/.

———. "The Basic AI Drives." 2008. https://selfawaresystems.files.wordpress. com/2008/01/ai.drives.final.pdf.

Orbaugh, Sharalyn. "Sex and the Single Cyborg: Japanese Popular Culture Experiments in Subjectivity." *Science Fiction Studies* 29, no. 3 (2002): 436–52.

Paeng, Erin, Jane Wu, and James Boerkoel, Jr. "Human-Robot Trust and Cooperation through a Game Theoretic Framework." *Proceedings of the Thirtieth AAAI Conference on Artificial Intelligence* 42 (2016): 46–7. www.cs.hmc. edu/HEAT/papers/Paeng_Wu_Boerkoel_AAAI_2016.pdf.

Pangburn, D. J. "The Humans Who Dream of Companies That Won't Need Us." *Fast Company,* June 19, 2015. www.fastcompany.com/3047462/the-humans-who-dream-of-companies-that-wont-need-them.

Peterson, Steve. "Designing People to Serve." In *Robot Ethics: The Ethical and Social Implications of Robotics,* 283–98. Edited by Patrick Lin, Keith Abney, and George Bekey. Cambridge, MA: MIT Press, 2012.

Polanyi, Karl. *The Great Transformation.* Boston: Beacon Press, 1944.

Rawlinson, Kevin. "Microsoft's Bill Gates Insists AI Is a Threat." *BBC News,* online edition, January 29, 2015. www.bbc.com/news/31047780?print=true.

Rifkin, Jeremy. *The Zero Marginal Cost Society: The Internet of Things, the Collaborative Commons, and the Eclipse of Capitalism.* New York: Palgrave Macmillan, 2014.

Robson, David. "The Rise of Human-Like Robots, Cars and Drones." *BBC News*, online edition, October 29, 2014. www.bbc.com/future/story/20141029-do-we-want-human-like-machines.

Roden, David. *Posthuman Life Philosophy at the Edge of the Human*. London: Routledge, 2015.

Rorty, Amélie. "A Literary Postscript: Characters, Persons, Selves, Individuals." In *The Identities of Persons*, 301–23. Edited by Amélie Rorty. Berkeley, CA: University of California Press, 1976.

Rosalia, Chioke, Rutger Menges, Inèz Deckers, and Christoph Brtneck. "Cruelty towards Robots." In *Proceedings of the Robot Workshop: Designing Robot Applications for Everyday Life*. Edited by Sara Ljungblad and Lars Eric Holmquist. Grenoble, France: Joint sOc-EUSAI Conference, 2005. www.bartneck.de/publications/2005/crueltyTowardsRobots/rosaliaBartneckRW2005.pdf

Roux, Dominique. "Ordinary Resistance as a Parasitic Form of Action: A Dialogical Analysis of Consumer/Firm Relations." *Advances in Consumer Research* 34 (2007): 602–9.

Sammond, Nicholas. *Babes in Tomorrowland: Walt Disney and the Making of the American Child, 1930–1960*. Durham, NC: Duke University Press, 2005.

Scharping, Nathaniel. "Maybe We Trust Robots Too Much." *Discover D-Brief*, May 26, 2016. http://blogs.discovermagazine.com/d-brief/2016/05/26/robot-trust-study/#.V3kWvFfXKOo.

Scheutz, Matthias. "The Inherent Dangers of Unidirectional Emotional Bonds between Humans and Social Robots." In *Robot Ethics: The Ethical and Social Implications of Robotics*, 205–22. Edited by Patrick Lin, Keith Abney, and George Bekey. Cambridge, MA: MIT Press, 2012.

Schwenger, Peter. *The Tears of Things: Melancholy and Physical Objects*. Minneapolis, MN: University of Minnesota Press, 2006.

Shaw-Garlock, Glenda. "Looking Forward to Sociable Robots." *International Journal of Social Robotics* 1 (2009): 249–60.

Short, Sue. "The Measure of a Man?: Asimov's Bicentennial Man, Star Trek's Data, and Being Human." *Extrapolation* 44, no. 2 (2003): 209–23.

Shukman, David. "How Safe Can Artificial Intelligence Be?" *BBC News*, September 15, 2015. www.bbc.com/news/science-environment-34249500.

Singer, P. W. "Military Robots and the Laws of War." *The New Atlantis*, online edition, 2009. www.thenewatlantis.com/publications/military-robots-and-the-laws-of-war.

Solove, Daniel J. *The Future of Reputation: Gossip, Rumor, and Privacy on the Internet*. New Haven, CT: Yale University Press, 2007.

Sparrow, Robert. "Killer Robots." *Journal of Applied Philosophy* 24, no. 1 (2007): 62–77.

Spiegel, Alix. "No Mercy for Robots: Experiment Tests How Humans Relate to Machines." National Public Radio, January 28, 2013. www.npr.org/sections/health-shots/2013/01/28/170272582/do-we-treat-our-gadgets-like-they-re-human.

Steinberg, Don. "Invasion of the Friendly Movie Robots." *Wall Street Journal*, online edition, February 25, 2015. www.wsj.com/articles/invasion-of-the-friendly-movie-robots-1424976398.

Strickland, Eliza. "Would You Trust a Robot Surgeon to Operate on You?" *IEEE Spectrum*, May 31, 2016. http://spectrum.ieee.org/robotics/medical-robots/would-you-trust-a-robot-surgeon-to-operate-on-you.

Sullins, John. "Robots, Love, and Sex: The Ethics of Building a Love Machine." *IEEE Transactions on Affective Computing* 3, no. 4 (2012): 398–409.

Sundararajan, Arun. *The Sharing Economy: The End of Employment and the Rise of Crowd-Based Capitalism.* Cambridge, MA: MIT Press, 2016.

Swan, Melanie. *Blockchain: Blueprint for a New Economy.* Sebastopol, CA: O'Reilly Media, 2015.

Tapscott, Don and Alex Tapscott. *Blockchain Revolution: How the Technology behind Bitcoin Is Changing Money, Business, and the World.* Toronto: Penguin Canada, 2016.

Tay, Benedict, Younbo Jung, and Taezoon Park. "When Stereotypes Meet Robots: The Double-Edge Sword of Robot Gender and Personality in Human-Robot Interaction." *Computers in Human Behavior* 38 (2014): 75–84.

Taylor, Emily. "Dating-Simulation Games: Leisure and Gaming of Japanese Youth Culture." *Southeast Review of Asian Studies* 29 (2007): 192–208.

Thorndike, Lynn. *A History of Magic and Experimental Science during the First Thirteen Centuries*, Vol. 1. New York: Columbia University Press, 1958.

Toensmeter, Pat. "Should You Really Trust a Robot?" *Aviation Week*, April 8, 2016. http://aviationweek.com/print/defense/should-you-really-trust-rob.

Toon, John. "In Emergencies, Should You Trust a Robot?" *Georgia Tech News Center*, February 29, 2016. www.news.gatech.edu/2016/02/29/emergencies-should-you-trust-robot.

Turkle, Sherry. "Authenticity in the Age of Digital Companions." In *Machine Ethics*, 52–76. Edited by Michael Anderson and Susan Leigh Anderson. Cambridge: Cambridge University Press, 2011a.

———. *Alone Together: Why We Expect More from Technology and Less from Each Other.* New York: Basic Books, 2011b.

Verbeek, Peter-Paul. *What Things Do: Philosophical Reflections on Technology, Agency, and Design*, trans. Robert Crease. University Park, PA: Pennsylvania State University Press, 2000/2005.

Wakefield, Jane. "Intelligent Machines: Do We Really Need to Fear AI?" *BBC News*, September 28, 2015. www.bbc.com/news/technology-32334568.

Wang, Ning, David Pynadath, and Susan Hill. "Building Trust in a Human-Robot Team with Automatically Generated Explanations." *Interservice/Industry Training, Simulation, and Education Conference*, Paper No. 15315, 2015. http://people.ict.usc.edu/~pynadath/Papers/iitsec15_15315.pdf.

Warwick, Kevin. "Robots with Biological Brains." In *Robot Ethics: The Ethical and Social Implications of Robotics*, 317–32. Edited by Patrick Lin, Keith Abney, and George Bekey. Cambridge, MA: MIT Press, 2012.

Wells, Georgia. "Too Cute for Their Own Good, Robots Get Self-Defense Instincts: Droid Designers Find Congenial Bots Draw Pesky Children, Bullies: A Warning Shriek." *Wall Street Journal*, June 19, 2016. www.wsj.com/articles/when-robots-are-too-cute-for-their-own-good-1466365635

Whelan, Robbie. "Fully Autonomous Robots: The Warehouse Workers of the Near Future." *Wall Street Journal*, September 21, 2016. www.wsj.com/articles/fully-autonomous-robots-the-warehouse-workers-of-the-near-future-1474383024

Whitby, Blay. "Do You Want a Robot Lover? The Ethics of Caring Technologies." In *Robot Ethics: The Ethical and Social Implications of Robotics*, 233–48. Edited by Patrick Lin, Keith Abney, and George Bekey. Cambridge, MA: MIT Press, 2012.

Widlock, Thomas. "Sharing by Default: Outline of an Anthropology of Virtue." *Anthropological Theory* 4, no. 1 (2004): 53–70.

Wikse, John R. *About Possession: The Self as Private Property.* University Park, PA: Pennsylvania State University Press. 1977.

Wolfe, Cary. *What Is Posthumanism?* Minneapolis, MN: University of Minnesota Press, 2010.

Woodburn, James. "'Sharing Is Not a Form of Exchange': An Analysis of Property-Sharing in Immediate-Return Hunter-Gather Societies." In *Property Relations: Renewing the Anthropological Tradition*, 48–63. Edited by C. M. Hann. Cambridge: Cambridge University Press, 1998.

Yampolskiy, Roman. *Artificial Superintelligence: A Futuristic Approach*. Baton Rouge, LA: CRC Press, 2016.

Yeoman, Ian and Michelle Mars. "Robots, Men and Sex Tourism." *Futures* 44, no. 4 (2012): 365–71.

Ziff, Paul. "The Feelings of Robots." *Analysis* 19, no. 3 (1959): 64–8.

3   Market Value of Diversity and Ethnicity

A Cultural Analysis of African American Media Consumption and Representation

Alladi Venkatesh

Introduction

In this essay, I examine some critical socioeconomic and market-related issues concerning the African American community, which is a dominant segment of the U.S. population. As is well known, this minority community has been a focus of study across several disciplines and by several historians and social scientists (hooks 2011; Ogbu 2008; Wilson 2012). In this regard, I also refer to some recent scholarly work in the field of consumer and marketing research that speaks to the issues of cultural ambiguities and multiracial identities, as well as consumption patterns, among African Americans (e.g., Appiah 2001; Bailey 2006; Bone, Christensen, and Williams 2014; Crockett 2008; Grier, Brumbaugh, and Thornton 2006; Harris, Henderson, and Williams 2005; Harrison, Thomas, and Cross 2015; Podoshen 2008; Thomas 2013).

In recent years, if not decades, we have witnessed the emergence of a variety of social and cultural discourses questioning the prevailing societal orthodoxies. Here I refer to the discourses of feminism, postmodernism, orientalism, postracialism, and sexual liberation, among others, addressing the regimented social ordering of communities. To this list we must add the emergence of minority discourses, which provide the broad framework for this chapter. In this context, we acknowledge a sense of internal struggle, resistance, and recalcitrance that has shaken the prevailing social order with different degrees of success.

I will begin with an analysis of ethnic minorities, followed by a discussion on issues of social, cultural, and economic capital, which form the basis for my study.

Ethnic Minorities

As Stuart Hall (2013) has noted, America is a land not only of ethnic minorities but also of ethnic hierarchies. The course of American history has witnessed one ethnic minority after another struggling to move upward through the cultural ladder toward a point when its members would no longer be identified by their ethnic status but be assimilated into the mainstream culture. Once there, they would still maintain, more or less loosely, ethnic identities based on their cultures of origin; they would become, for example, Italian Americans or Polish Americans and so on.

Typically, these minority communities have been immigrants and European in origin. Because of the commonalities of their skin color and racial characteristics, they have eventually been integrated into the mainstream white community and have begun to enjoy the status and privileges associated with the dominant group. Even among European groups, however, some have assimilated faster than others. For example, it has taken Catholics longer than Protestants to be absorbed into the American mainstream. Similarly, it has taken even longer for American Jews to become identified with the dominant group; indeed, they among all Eurocentric groups still maintain a distinct identity primarily because of their religious background. In the long term, it seems, distinct identity does not prevent an immigrant group from assimilating.

Still, some U.S. immigrant groups have remained in a perennial minority status. Consider the experience of Hispanic Americans, who have not been accorded full majority status because of geopolitical factors, even though some could easily be absorbed based on skin color, racial characteristics, and European ancestry. Or, consider Japanese Americans and Chinese Americans, who have never been considered part of the dominant group although their ancestors began to immigrate to the United States more than a century ago; the obvious reason for these groups' enduring minority status is that they are not of European extraction. (Recent immigrant populations from Asia and the Middle East may prove inassimilable for the same set of reasons.) Of course, all of these examples pale beside the case of American blacks, whose social history in North America predates the American Revolution.

The explosive growth of racial and ethnic diversity in the United States has forced the various sectors of the economy, the government, and the media to reexamine the ways in which they have traditionally dealt with minority groups and their concerns and interests. Historically, the American social response to diversity has taken three distinct forms. First is benign neglect, often combined with hostility to some groups. Given the central values of American philosophy and culture, it is assumed that most ethnic communities will be absorbed into the mainstream over time by trial and error. In this view, although some groups will be slower to assimilate than others, and some may even be left out of the assimilation process, it is only a matter of time before most arrive on the level playing field. The guiding principle here is *homogenization*. This attitude toward diversity continues to dominate the American mind and rule mainstream consciousness, even though history tells us that this process has not worked effectively in all cases.

The second perspective toward diversity is that ethnic groups represent specific identities, values, and cultural positions that must be recognized and accommodated within the mainstream culture. The idea here is to grant the distinct identities of the ethnic groups but keep them subordinate to the goals of the mainstream. If ethnic groups are absorbed into the mainstream, so much the better, but if not, their value systems can still find expression within the larger context. The guiding principles here are *accommodation* and *tolerance* of differences. This approach dominates current progressive thinking.

More recently, a third perspective toward diversity has emerged that regards ethnic groups as positive contributors to mainstream culture. In this view, the diversity question is not one of accommodation and tolerance of difference but one of active receptivity to ethnic values that can be transferred into the mainstream culture. The guiding principle of this perspective is the creation of mutual benefit via interaction, or what I call *mutual asset formation*. Mutual asset formation occurs when different groups within a community or society contribute synergistically to its betterment. The idea here is that each group has something to offer to the whole system that others are unable to offer; together, the pooled contributions make the system much richer. Ideas about the social and market value of diversity are deeply embedded in this third approach, which provides both the framework and the mechanism to enable people to identify and derive value from the notion of diversity.

It is the third approach that this essay urges—the channeling of multicultural forces into positive social ends. I begin my argument with a discussion of Pierre Bourdieu's analysis of economic, social, cultural, and symbolic capital and their dynamic roles in the creation and sustainability of market value. I then present some of the research describing the minority status of blacks in American culture and discuss the roles of the mainstream and minority media in reinforcing that status. Next, I explore the social capital issues of ethnic consciousness and cultural projection. I then discuss the blending of forms of capital and the market value of diversity. Finally, I propose a research agenda to help American culture overcome its continuing burden of race.

Capital and Symbolic Space

"Capital" can be defined as the accumulated resources of a group or community that can be employed productively for the benefit of the group or community, as well as the larger social order. Although capital is most commonly understood as an economic resource, the French philosopher Pierre Bourdieu (1984) notes that capital can appear in forms other than economic capital, such as cultural capital, social capital, and symbolic capital.

Economic capital is accumulated economic wealth and power, manifested in the ability to acquire goods and services, participate in certain key professions (medicine, law, etc.), enter corporate life, exercise control over productive resources, have access to scientific knowledge that can be translated into material wealth, and influence or participate in economic policies that shape individual and collective welfare. The economic capital of American blacks tells an interesting story. Measured in dollars, it is quite significant. For example, in 1993, U.S. blacks earned, controlled, or spent $300 billion. However, by 2013, U.S. blacks earned, controlled, or spent more than one trillion dollars. If the American black community were a nation, it would constitute the tenth wealthiest country in the world in terms of gross national product. Yet, this combined wealth does not generate equivalent economic power. This pronounced discrepancy is not difficult to explain. The economic capital of blacks is diffused, not concentrated in nationally recognizable institutions such as national banks, national media, Fortune 500 companies, and national universities (i.e., the *ideological apparatuses of the state*). The fact that blacks do not enjoy economic power commensurate with their economic wealth should come as no surprise; they are hardly an exception. Take, for instance, the gender situation. Women comprise about half of the U.S. population. Female earnings were sixty-two percent of men's earnings in 1979 and have gone up to eighty to eighty-three percent in 2014 (U.S. Bureau of Labor Statistics Report 2015). Even taking into account that their earning power is about eighty-three percent that of men, women's economic power should be considerable. In fact, it is less significant. These examples demonstrate the fact that other types of capital are at work here.

Social capital is closely connected with economic capital in the American context, much more so than in other Western societies; in the context of diversity, one might even think of social capital as racial, ethnic, and gender capital. (At the time of writing this chapter, Hillary Clinton just lost her presidential bid to Donald Trump, and Barack Obama, an African American, is completing his second term as U.S. president.)

Typically, social capital accrues from educational attainment; desirable living conditions; and access to public spheres, markets, jobs, and opportunities. Social capital also includes generational transformation—that is, the ability to hand down from one generation to the next the values and institutional skills that will help the new generation negotiate its position within the society at large. Ability to transfer social knowledge is becoming particularly significant as American society approaches a knowledge economy ruled by technologies of information and communication.

Cultural capital includes both social and economic capital; in the American context, cultural capital is gained through participation in fashion, design, music, fiction writing, arts, and aesthetics. The media constitute some aspects of cultural capital by shaping the cultural dialogue and portraying roles and group identities. Whereas economic and social capital are primarily extrinsic (i.e., they mediate between a group and dominant-other cultures), cultural capital is both extrinsic and intrinsic (operating within a cultural milieu). A group can, for example, build intrinsic self-esteem through participation in its own culture, enjoying a high degree of cultural sensitivity within its own boundaries. This intrinsic cultural capital may not, however, reflect the group's position with respect to extrinsic cultures or the dominant culture; the slogan "black is beautiful," for example, has intrinsic cultural value that does not translate as powerfully to the dominant culture. Unsurprisingly, the dominant culture usually enjoys both extrinsic and intrinsic aspects of cultural capital.

Economists tend to reduce all forms of capital to economic capital. This must be done, they argue, because the concept of capital does not make theoretical or pragmatic sense unless it can be measured, and the only way to make measurement possible is to transform all forms of capital into dollar value (i.e., measurable units). Otherwise, the argument goes, we will be comparing apples to oranges.

Although there is merit to this reductionist analysis, there is danger, too, in that many forms of capital cannot be easily translated into economic or measurable terms and must therefore be left out of consideration. Once thus barred, they tend to assume an inferior extrinsic status, although they may function as important resources within any given community or group. Concern about this issue provides strong justification for retaining the distinctions among forms of capital so that we can examine them in institutional and historical terms, and discover their roles in explaining the social condition of a given group.

Bourdieu (1984) rounds off his analysis with what he terms *symbolic* capital, a form of capital that fuses the other forms into symbolic space. Symbolic capital is not a reductionist concept; rather, it describes the outcomes of the operationalization of different forms of capital in practice. All forms of capital have the potential to transform into positions of power and status. But how are they transformed, and how do they manifest themselves in the daily lives of individuals? To address this issue, Bourdieu's classic work *Distinction* introduces a term that has been the subject of continuing critical scrutiny. According to Bourdieu, a culture's *habitus* is the durable set of practices and mental frames of reference its members carry around in their daily lives and that they gain from their experiences and their contact with the world in which they live. These experiences are governed by language, social position (class, ethnicity, and gender), social networks, employment, and schooling, all of which may be collectively labeled the symbolic codes and processes that constitute the habitus.

It is the habitus that connects us to various forms of capital. The specifics of Bourdieu's insightful analysis are concerned with French society. But its principles can be applied to other social contexts as well, with the usual caveats that surround such generalizability. One such context is that of the United States, where American blacks constitute a seemingly permanent minority.

A Disadvantaged Other

When American scholars use the term "minority," what is usually meant is nonwhite groups, which are further divided into two main categories: the disadvantaged (or underrepresented) minorities and the non-disadvantaged minorities. In general, disadvantaged groups have lower educational skills and lack the economic opportunities accorded to non-disadvantaged groups.

American blacks (who have more recently used the labels "Afro-Americans" or "African Americans") form the most significant example of a disadvantaged minority in the United States. In a seminal work on black economic and social status, William Julius Wilson (2012) describes American blacks as "the truly disadvantaged." He describes black economic status as a paradox, noting that during the very period of "the most sweeping antidiscrimination legislation . . . the economic position of many poor blacks actually deteriorated" (63). Wilson also notes the gradual emergence of a black middle class comparable to the white middle class on many socioeconomic characteristics. This new black middle class is an important development in the social and economic history of this country and has many implications for issues relating to contemporary ethnic discourse.

Even so, John Ogbu (2008) argues that American blacks represent what he calls a *caste-like* minority. Caste-like minorities are different from other minorities in that they are groups that remain permanently separate and disconnected within the social milieu due to various historical and cultural factors; they tend to have less ready access to social goods because of their secondary position. In his analysis of social position, Ogbu concludes that the variable of race may not be sufficient to describe a group socially or culturally or to explain its place in social hierarchy. A more useful variable for this purpose would be the term *racial stratification*, which captures how hierarchies are established and sustained. Still, Ogbu argues that even though recent efforts have been directed toward minimizing the damage done by racial stratification by giving blacks professional training in productive disciplines and raising their skill levels through education, their minority status has not been drastically altered.

Accompanying racial stratification is the *physical* stratification of minority communities. Throughout the United States, a significant majority of blacks live in separate geographical regions, whether it is middle-class, black suburban enclaves or the "inner cities" inhabited by low-income blacks. Such separate physical spaces exist in the case of other minorities as well but are most pronounced in the cases of blacks, Hispanics, and Native Americans. In all these cases, physical separation is clearly linked to these communities' social isolation.

The de facto social segregation of blacks and other minority groups manifests in many institutional settings and cultural practices, where their secondary status is repeated through cultural dynamics. Nowhere is this more telling than in mass media (television and film), where the portrayals have been particularly controversial. Of course, as discussed next, role portrayals on television extend to all minority groups and are not limited to any one particular group.

Minorities, Media, and the Habitus

The role of the media in translating the codes of social groups (the habitus) is significant and undeniably critical in many societies. In the United States, it is now well established that media play a vital role in interpreting symbolic processes and converting them into sources of social power. Much of the contemporary criticism in minority discourse (as well as in majority discourse) is directed toward the dominant position of the media in setting social standards and norms of interpretation. It is often argued, for example, that the mainstream media perspective is usually hegemonic—that is, it portrays minorities from the perspective of the dominant culture. Minority members are portrayed positively, if at all, when they have adjusted to the dominant cultural values. If they are portrayed negatively, it is because, supposedly, they have not been able to lift themselves up in spite of the opportunities given to them.

In a detailed study of the American media's role in mediating cultural values, Jeter (1998) analyzes the current situation as follows:

> The media are more often than not agents of the power structure reinforcing the status quo. The media are pervasive and consumers are bombarded with messages that say this or that person, action, idea, is beautiful, good, decent, and right while other things are ugly, bad, obscene, and wrong. These functions have combined to result in a less-than-optimal state of regard for blacks. (82)

Camille O. Cosby's (2006) study of television over a thirty-year period also found portrayals of blacks to be overwhelmingly negative. Paradoxically, this same study reported that blacks watched more television than nonblacks. Several explanations are possible. Television offers a variety of entertainment possibilities; perhaps black audiences are watching shows where black characters are not presented. Perhaps they are watching sports and other programs where role portrayals are less of an issue or are generally positive; in some sports, after all, blacks outperform members from other groups and are considered stars. It may be that black audiences put up with negative portrayals because television watching provides their sole or main low-cost entertainment outlet. Finally, some black audiences may accept the medium's unflattering portrayals of the black community as a condition of their existence in a white-dominated culture.

Manning Marable (2015) reminds us that the reality of average black community life hardly matches the media portrayals. According to him, contrary to the pathology projected by the popular media, the vast majority of black people have little tolerance for crime and violence—blacks understand all too well that they are their principal victims. The negative role portrayals pervasive in the media can result in negative self-perceptions on the part of black Americans.

Figure 3.1 presents a schematized version of the role of the media in black cultural transformation. As shown in the figure, the formation of cultural capital for any group follows two distinct stages, one within the group and the other outside the group. In the first stage, the cultural codes and ideas originate within the cultural habitus of the group; each group has its own cultural apparatuses that allow the codes to diffuse within the group. Specifically, in terms of blacks as the minority community that we are focusing on here, the black cultural apparatus organizes its cultural codes and ideas (path A) and channels them into the second stage, where black media project them onto the popular imagination (paths D and E). At the same time, the dominant media picks up the codes and ideas, filters them though its own cultural apparatuses, and also projects them onto the public (paths B and C). Although the two processes are the same, they do not yield equivalent results. The dominant media view of the black cultural scene is generally problematic to the black community; although the black media's representation of its own cultural domain is, as is to be expected, generally very positive and self-reinforcing. However, this portrayal does not necessarily have an impact on the larger audience because the channels of communication to this audience are controlled by the mainstream media apparatus (paths B and C).

Let us now examine some of the institutional settings described in Figure 3.1. Historically, blacks have owned very few radio or television stations. In April 2014, it was reported that out of a total of six thousand commercial AM radio stations in the country, or five thousand commercial FM stations, blacks owned less than ten percent; and of two thousand commercial television stations, blacks owned less than five percent. These figures, based on the latest census, should be relatively current in terms of the general picture. In other words, in terms of paths D and E in Figure 3.1, the cultural presence of black media is minuscule. Would it then make a difference to the general image building of blacks in the dominant mainstream culture if these numbers were increased? This is not clear, for as long as the mainstream media control the dominant channels, there is little that minority ownership can do to make a difference.

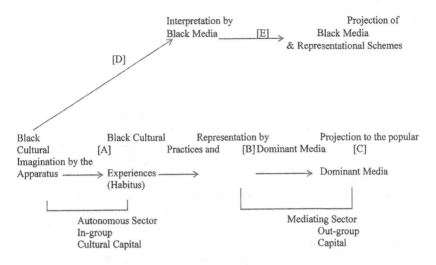

Figure 3.1 Role of media in black cultural transformation.

Two cultural schema are in operation here, one having to do with the dominant media and the other having to do with media in the hands of minority groups. According to the theory of critical mass minority, numbers will matter only once they reach a certain cultural threshold in addition to an economic threshold—although both can be related. At this point, it is unclear where those thresholds are. If blacks are able to enter the dominant media, it may be that cultural decision processes can change if the dominant cultural apparatus treats inputs from the black cultural apparatus responsibly. Blacks (and any minority group) will remain marginal and marginalized until they enter mainstream institutional, as well as ideological, structures. Some of these issues are discussed in the following sections.

Ethnic Consciousness and Cultural Projection: Issues of Social Capital

Over the past several decades, black consciousness has evolved in several ways. Until the 1980s, blacks generally accepted their condition of secondary political and economic status and the feeling of inferiority that status engendered in many. During the 1990s, social conditions began to change dramatically as black culture emerged as a culture of resistance and aggressive self-expression. Beginning to view themselves in terms of black pride, blacks celebrated their own norms of success despite their collective perception that the dominant culture was trying to manipulate them. The outward manifestation of this new black consciousness was evident in Afro-American fashion and hairstyles, music, art, and political and social dialogue. A number of factors combine to create and project black social capital.

Black Cultural Projection

Richard Merelman (1994) proposes four models representing black perspectives of their status vis-à-vis the dominant culture: syncretism, hegemony, polarization, and counterhegemony. *Syncretism* refers to a possible fusion of black and white cultures that would give rise to a new set of cultural norms and practices. This model emphasizes mutual collaboration between blacks and whites, projecting positive results from their interaction. In contrast, the *hegemonic* model portrays blacks as subordinate to white culture with no hope of establishing self-identity. Adoption of a hegemonic perspective tends to result in resentment because of the absence of a black voice. The *polarization* model depicts blacks and whites on opposite sides of issues, with neither willing to accommodate the demands of the other. Outcomes for the polarization model are similar to those of the hegemonic model in that both result in black resentment of white culture. However, the polarization model is not one of black subordination but of black separateness. The *counterhegemonic* model views black cultural beliefs as actually prevailing in some cases over white cultural beliefs or values (e.g., in fashion and music). This model is an exception and has not found expression in practice within the American context because unassimilated ethnic minorities here remain fragmented and no single minority group has demonstrated the ability to make serious inroads into the dominant culture. The first three models represent the current reality of blacks' interpretations of their status in American culture, although it must be conceded that the hegemonic and polarization models seem to prevail over the syncretistic model.

Economy and Cultural Isolation

Many social theorists have argued that the cultural isolation of distressed minorities is a result of economic conditions and structural antecedents. In general, three areas are identified as contributing to this condition: economic needs as measured by such indicators as poverty, unemployment, and educational deficiencies; behavioral problems such as long-term welfare dependency, family instability, drugs, crime, and others; and attitudinal problems of deep isolation and alienation.

Inclusionary and Exclusionary Practices

Black identity is a product of the conflict between inclusionary and exclusionary practices. In the last forty years, many social programs and public legislation measures have focused on providing institutional opportunities for blacks in various social and economic situations. Unfortunately, this public expression of inclusionary emphasis has been weakened by private exclusionary practices. The more that members of the dominant culture believed that blacks were being provided many opportunities, the less they believed it was necessary to open any more doors.

Television represents both an inclusionary and exclusionary culture. It is inclusionary because blacks feel they have access to the technology in the same way as whites. However, it is exclusionary in the sense that television has continued to promote less-than-positive images of blacks. Television is a complex phenomenon. As a technology of entertainment, it induces passive activity; given the social isolation of blacks and other minorities, TV watching may be a beneficial activity because it is a window to the outside world. As a technology of public culture, television is viewed by blacks as part of the white entertainment culture. Although the black consciousness has evolved into a mode of greater self-assertion and expression, this does not seem to have been incorporated into "TV land." Television, by many accounts, continues to downgrade the social position of blacks even at the end of the millennium.

Technology and Identity Formation

In the contemporary technological era, identities are formed through the interaction of several factors—race, social class, reference groups, and so on. Technologies have substantially dissimilar impacts on different groups of people based on gender, education, age, ethnic characteristics, occupational categories, and lifestyles. How does one evaluate the differential impacts on these different groups? One solution is to do a comparative study—that is, to examine how these groups compare to others with respect to the use of technologies. But comparative studies generally use white families as standards for analysis and white family theory as their theoretical frame of reference; deviation from the normative aspects of white families is not encouraged.

Marie Ferguson Peters (2007) proposes an ecological approach to the study of black families instead of simple comparative studies of black and white families. The ecological approach considers the behavior of black families within the environmental conditions and constraints of black cultural life. It also takes into account normative practices of black family life. For example, black culture generally favors an approach to parent-child relationships in which the child is strictly obedient to parental authority. White families, on the other hand, often favor indirect forms of control over insistence on obedience. Black culture also encourages non-competitive individualism; black families rely heavily on family networks instead of professional services to meet family crises, and black parents tend to bring up their children to be comfortable with their "blackness" and to go to the next level of "black pride." Socializing children in black families is motivated by a desire to build friendship networks; socializing them into the white world is governed by a need for survival.

Structural Factors

Various structural factors distinguish blacks from whites, poor blacks from poor whites, and blacks from other immigrant communities such as Japanese, Chinese, Koreans, and so on. Because of these factors, blacks have developed status mobility systems that have special characteristics. For example, blacks often regard educational opportunities as follows: either they receive inferior education or the adequate education they receive does not open up possibilities within the white world. Some blacks pursue education, believing that while schooling and educational opportunities will not help them advance socially within the mainstream, they can use what they learn *against* the mainstream. Another strategy is to use these structural factors to advance status within their own community. For this purpose, white community recognition is welcome but not essential.

In this essay, I have barely touched upon the problems of the inner city and the problem of middle-class flight, problems that have been widely discussed in the literature and overanalyzed by many scholars. I refer to these problems only in terms of what they mean to the link between economic capital and social capital. For example, William Julius Wilson (2012) raises the following paradoxical question:

> [Backers of the discrimination thesis] find it difficult to explain why the economic position of poor urban blacks actually deteriorated during the very period in which the most sweeping antidiscrimination legislation and programs were enacted and implemented. Their emphasis on discrimination is even more problematic, in view of the economic progress of the black middle class during the same period. (53)

Wilson provides a striking instance of increasing economic capital combined with fracturing social capital. Upon reflection, one can easily understand the mechanism at work: as economic opportunities open up for minorities, they do so at the expense of available or existing social spaces. Because economic prosperity does not touch everybody equally and existing social spaces cannot accommodate the newly formed middle classes, communities have to realign themselves, sometimes at considerable cost to their collective welfare.

Blending Forms of Capital

How can American society utilize the three forms of capital—economic, social, and cultural—to maximize the social opportunities for racial minorities and bring them into the mainstream in a mutually beneficial way? What is the *market* value of diversity in this changing, complex social order?

Historically, much tension and dissension have surrounded the welfare debate in the United States. In recent years, the welfare concept has been called into intense question, and the pendulum seems to have swung to a point where the concept is viewed suspiciously, to be gradually replaced by the idea of empowerment of minority groups through self-discipline and competitive spirit.

For the ordinary citizen on the street, the two major sources of economic welfare were always the government or the private (business) sector, or a combination of both. These two sectors, situated at opposite ends of an ideological spectrum, operate from different perspectives. Certainly, one major difference is that in the case of the private sector, the profit motive fuels all actions. Operationally, the profit motive understands all citizens to be part of a market system; unless citizens participate in the market system under its terms, no benefits will accrue to them. Theoretically, the market system simply evaluates individuals or groups as economic units and as sources of revenues and profits, viewing them from a unidimensional view: What is their economic capital? In practice, however, this question is complicated by the fact that straightforward economic principles do not prevail in practice. Simple economics does not dictate the business approach to the minority groups; rather, it is a judgment of the consequences of serving them in terms of impact on the mainstream. Economics became embroiled in social acts of inclusivity and exclusivity. This is particularly true in media politics, and it is now amply recorded that minority groups remain invisible in the media radar—a version of the condition of benign neglect as discussed earlier. Of course, for some critics, the term "benign" might sound overly charitable. What benign neglect has meant in practice over the years is that businesses have been quite prepared to sacrifice the interests of the twenty percent of the population as long as the remaining eighty percent of the market was intact. At the same time, businesses did not mind serving the twenty percent if this had no deleterious effect on their dealings with the majority.

What has changed in the last decade is that businesses have carefully reevaluated their position in regard to the issues of diversity. New demographic trends clearly show that the U.S. population is becoming more and more diverse; in the next two or three decades, there will be fundamental shifts in the population composition. Second, the various so-called minorities will not only gain in numbers but also represent a strong economic base that will be hard to ignore. This is why many large corporations are adopting a target-market approach to ethnic populations to enlarge their customer base. This is indeed the economic capital argument.

But what about cultural capital and social capital? How does a society begin to respond to these? Let me take an example from the black cultural scene. The rich traditions of the black community as manifested in their musical forms is illustrative of the tensions within a community as it tries establish its links with the social world outside via its own economic capital. Reebee Garofalo (1999) presents the problem with particular poignancy:

> Like any popular music that originates outside the mainstream, African American popular music has long been faced with trying to negotiate a path between the joint dangers of isolation and exclusion on the one hand, and incorporation and homogenization on the other. Despite the wellspring of creativity that African American artists have brought to popular music, they have historically been relegated to a separate and unequal marketing structure which has tended toward ensuring one unacceptable outcome or the other for their music. (23)

Although the black community tries to preserve and produce music on its own terms, the mainstream market structure reduces it to a commodity for sale. The black economic apparatus is not powerful enough to resist this commodification.

The Market Value of Diversity (One More Time)

What is the market value of diversity and racial representations? It all depends on point of view. For example, Oscar H. Gandy, Jr. (2009), has shown that the market value of diversity operates in various ways. Diversity can be viewed as difference—that is, diverse groups may be portrayed as different from the mainstream in positive ways or in negative ways. Diversity can also be portrayed as lack of difference—that is, as if there are no inherent differences between the mainstream and the subcultural groups. Gandy suggests that the popular media seem to maximize market opportunities by portraying diversity as negative difference. If the mainstream media portray minority communities in a negative fashion and this increases white readership, the market value of diversity lies in projecting negative images of the minority community. Thus, for example, in a typical evening news broadcast on any Los Angeles TV station, a number of crime stories will predictably involve Mexican Americans, illegal immigrants, and Asian criminal gangs. These stories have little to do with how minority communities live their daily lives but are instead fodder for a kind of commercialism that results in negative externalities for the minority communities who are exposed in the mainstream media. Gandy (2009) succinctly describes the problem this way:

> The current love affair Americans seem to have with the marketplace as a guarantor of all sorts of values beyond allocative efficiency

assumes that this market provides value in exchange for its equivalent. This is an assumption of equality. The finding that differences in the values actually received are linked to differences in the race of the consumer raises concern about the operation of the market. An observed disparity may be newsworthy in itself; that the disparity is the product of racial discrimination is quite a different story, one that has implications for public trust, and that calls for a policy response. (109)

Conclusion

Many debates are currently in progress as American society takes a careful look at its changing cultural and social scene. Debates on this issue occupy the entire spectrum of ideas from the religious to the philosophical to the pragmatic. One form of fundamentalism that has emerged appeals to the "basic principles" on which this nation is founded, principles based on Eurocentric thinking, embedded in neoclassical economics and nineteenth-century liberalism, and related to religious Calvinism. Activist groups of this type ask the following question: How can we preserve the ideals upon which the nation is founded when the national character seems to be drifting in multiple subcultural streams?

For anyone with a sense of history, this debate is not new. Such concerns have been raised whenever the United States has been faced with "waves" of new immigrants. In the past, however, the question was answered with the "melting pot" theory, which states categorically that every new addition to the population can be absorbed into the American value system, and every new immigrant can become an American by a process of assimilation and socialization. According to this principle, what changes is the character of the immigrant via assimilation; what remains constant is the nature of American character.

As appealing as this myth can be, the pragmatics of assimilation and the historical evidence surrounding it do not convincingly support this contention. First, the American social and cultural landscape has changed and continues to change, sometimes more dramatically than at other times. Second, the melting pot theory was never universally applied to all sections of the population, in particular to blacks, although they have been residing in this country for three centuries. Yet, the principle of a melting pot has continued as a guiding metaphor of social absorption. In recent years, the metaphor of the American melting pot has yielded to competing metaphors as the reality of population diversity has begun to alter earlier assumptions. Levels of anxiety seem to be rising in the face of the changing social scene.

What I argue in this essay is that some of these concerns may be without foundation and that all the social changes we are witnessing must be viewed optimistically and realistically. Notwithstanding the enticements of the metaphors we might use, we must focus on the reality of the changing landscape and the potential it offers to take us into the next millennium. I do not see any reason to worry about an impending cultural or social crisis in the next two or three decades. Nor is there justification for the worry that American ideals will somehow be compromised by new subjectivities.

I propose a research agenda that contributes to the channeling of multicultural forces into positive social ends—an agenda that has multiple elements. For example, the dominant media and institutions need to be reminded that cultural variations are part of a changing and progressive society. In addition, they need to be cognizant of the fact that subcultural values, practices, and imagery are already shaping the behavior of mainstream culture via the interplay of habitus in such matters as aesthetics, art, music, food, clothing, language, and other symbolic elements. There is no reason to make these influences invisible. It is also important to note that what is considered "quintessentially American" has always been subject to change brought about by multicultural influences. Initiatives must be taken to invite institutions to make a conscious effort to educate themselves about the cultural characteristics of the different groups and provide an atmosphere that permits mutual exchange of ideas. Media should be creative and explore opportunities to educate the general public and promote an understanding of the cultural characteristics of different subcultures and practices. Instead of benign tolerance of subcultures, dominant communities should engage in active promotion of subcultural values as part of the mainstream consciousness.

Bibliography

Appiah, Osei. "Ethnic Identification on Adolescents' Evaluations of Advertisements." *Journal of Advertising Research* 41, no. 5 (2001): 7–22.

Bailey, Ainsworth A. "A Year in the Life of the African-American Male in Advertising: A Content Analysis." *Journal of Advertising* 35 (2006): 83–104.

Bone, Sterling A., Glenn L. Christensen, and Jerome D. Williams. "Rejected, Shackled, and Alone: The Impact of Systemic Restricted Choice on Minority Consumers' Construction of Self." *Journal of Consumer Research* 41, no. 2 (2014): 451–74.

Bourdieu, Pierre. *Distinction: A Social Critique of the Judgement of Taste.* London: Routledge & Kegan Paul, 1984.

Cosby, Camille. *Television's Imageable Influences: The Self Perception of Young African Americans.* Lanham, MD: University Press of America, 2006.

Crockett, David. "Marketing Blackness: How Advertisers Use Race to Sell Products." *Journal of Consumer Culture* 8 (2008): 245–68.

Gandy, Oscar. *Coming to Terms with Chance: Engaging Rational Discrimination and Cumulative Disadvantage.* Burlington, VT: Ashgate, 2009.

Garofalo, Reebee. "From Music Publishing to MP3: Music and Industry in the Twentieth Century." *American Music* 17, no. 3 (Autumn 1999): 318–54.

Grier, Sonya A. and Anne M. Brumbaugh. "Noticing Cultural Differences: Ad Meanings Created by Target and Non-Target Markets." *Journal of Advertising* 28, no. 1 (1999): 79–93.

————, and Corliss G. Thornton. "Crossover Dreams: Consumer Responses to Ethnic-Oriented Products." *Journal of Marketing* 70, no. 2 (2006): 35–51.

Hall, Stuart. *Representation: Cultural Representations and Signifying Practices.* London, Sage Publications, 2013.

Harris, Anne-Marie G., Geraldine R. Henderson, and Jerome D. Williams. "Courting Customers: Assessing Consumer Racial Profiling and Other Marketplace Discrimination." *Journal of Public Policy & Marketing* 24, no. 1 (2005): 163–71.

Harrison, Robert D. III., Kevin D. Thomas, and Samantha Cross. "Negotiating Cultural Ambiguity: The Role of Markets and Consumption in Multiracial Identity Development." *Consumption Markets & Culture* 18, no. 4 (2015): 301–32.

hooks, bell. *Writing beyond Race.* New York: Routledge, 2011.

Jeter, Amy. "From Deadlines to Punch Lines." *American Journalism Review* 20, no. 10. (1998): 16–7.

Levinas, Emanuel. *Totality and Infinity: An Essay on Exteriority.* Kluwer Academic Publishers, 1991.

Marable, Manning. *How Capitalism Underdeveloped Black America?* Chicago: Haymarket Books, 2015.

Merelman, Richard. "Racial Conflict and Cultural Politics in the United States." *The Journal of Politics* 56, no. 1 (1994): 1–20.

Ogbu, John. *Minority Status, Opposition Culture and Schooling.* New York: Routledge, 2008.

Peters, Mary Ferguson. "Parenting of Young Children." In *Black Families*, 203–18. Edited by H. P. McAdoo. Thousand Oaks, CA: Sage Publications, 2007.

Podoshen, Jeffrey Steven. "The African American Consumer Revisited: Brand Loyalty, Word of Mouth and the Effects of the Black Experience." *Journal of Consumer Marketing* 25, no. 4 (2008): 211–22.

Thomas, Kevin D. "Endlessly Creating Myself: Examining Marketplace Inclusion through the Lived Experience of Black and White Male Millennials." *Journal of Public Policy & Marketing* 32 special issue (2013): 95–105.

US Bureau of Labor Statistics Report. 2015. www.bls.gov/bls/newsrels.htm#OCWC.

Wilson, William Julius. *The Truly Disadvantaged.* Chicago, IL: The University of Chicago Press, 2012.

4 Consuming the Idea of the Brand

Sidney J. Levy

There are many ways of writing history because historians pursue their pet ideas and preferred sources of data, whether military, economic, biographic, or cultural. I have an interest in how ideas evolve, and especially in the way practice comes to be recognized, conceptualized, and named, leading to fresh practice and new ideas. Examples of previous efforts to explore the development of knowledge in this way was provided in "Roots of Marketing and Consumer Research at the University of Chicago" (Levy 2003), "History of Qualitative Research Methods in Marketing" (Levy 2006), "A History of the Concept of Branding: Practice and Theory" (Bastos and Levy 2012), and "Roots and Development of Consumer Culture Theory" (2015a). Lest this approach seems too mired in the past to be of value, Cristel Russell and Sidney Levy (2012) showed that deliberately repeating the past ("reconsumption") can be a source in contemporary culture of pleasure and exhilaration, and Marius Luedicke and Sidney Levy (2013) looked to the future beyond marketing ideology.

The History of Branding

As a student of consumer culture theory, I alliteratively propose to pursue, pretentiously or presumptively for the present purpose, the thread of evolution that has taken the consumption of the idea of branding to a new level of contemporary understanding of its significance. I will summarize the ground gone over in some detail in the article with Wilson Bastos and then will focus particularly on the theory of the brand that is summed up in the aspiration to create an ideal brand pyramid (IBP), ideas discussed most fully in *The Theory of the Brand* (Levy 2016).

However, before explicating the IBP, let us trace the way the brand idea came to the fore and then proliferated in current theory and practice. It is generally thought that branding originated with the application of a hot iron to the hide of cattle to identify their ownership among grazing herds and to frustrate theft. Such forms of identification go back thousands of years and various methods of marking—tattooing, cutting, painting—were used on slaves, prisoners, and also as signs of status, adornment, respect, and genealogy among various social groups. The fundamental assertion of a brand is rooted in the earliest visualizations found in the Paleolithic caves at Altamira in France, later in the tombs of Mesopotamia and Egyptian pyramids (Wengrow 2008) of Abydos, and at Meidum and Pech Merle, as objects are identified in their environments. Prostitutes in ancient Rome wrote their names and prices on local walls. The work by Eckhardt and Bengtsson (2010) on branding in ancient China also illuminates this early history and shows the essential nature of branding in its diversity of application.

Even a small bit of marking such as a mere dot may carry powerful symbolic significance. In East Indian society, the mark called a bindi has many cultural meanings. These may seem so important that Indian scholar Subhamoy Das claimed the bindi is arguably the most visually fascinating of all forms of body decoration. Hindus attach great importance to this ornamental mark on the forehead between the two eyebrows." The mark comes to signify social status and often stands for the role of married women as guardians of the household.

A small black birthmark dot on the faces of movie actress Jean Harlow, and more recently model Cindy Crawford, was regarded as a sexy beauty spot rather than a disfiguring anomaly. Probably more visually fascinating or provocative are the tattoos and piercings that are increasingly widespread in modern society. Innovations become customs. A practice may become so embedded that it is simply taken for granted. A mature woman respondent expressed disgust at contemporary piercing and was chagrined to be reminded that she wore earrings in her pierced ears. Another mentioned that she felt undressed when she forgot to put on her earrings.

Branding as Identity

Branding occurs whenever any offering is identified and can be named, which has happened since time immemorial. But its relatively modern commercial forms came vigorously to the fore with the growth of printing in the sixteenth century and beyond, with the Industrial Revolution. Here are some early examples.

- Steaedtler Mars GmbH traces its lineage to a pencil craftsman in 1662 and the craft of colored wooden pencils in 1834, and Faber-Castell AG branded quality pencils in the 1840s.
- James Folger (1872), James Kraft (1903), and Joseph Vlasic (1942) showed pride, respectively putting their names on their coffee, cheese, and pickles, in individualized containers rather than large sacks, slabs, and barrels.
- In the early 1900s, William Bristol and John Myers created a laxative and a toothpaste, and a slogan combining gastrointestinal and oral hygiene benefits: "Sal Hepatica for the smile of health, Ipana for the smile of beauty."

But the first main signs of awareness and study of the idea of branding did not appear until the twentieth century. Early writers began to
discuss branding tangentially to traditional marketing. In a 1923 article
in the *Harvard Business Review*, M.T. Copeland refers to *brand loyalty* in discussing consumers' buying habits. In a 1925 text, *Marketing*,
Edmund Brown notes the rise of *brand competition* between national
producers and so-called private or retail labels. He first comes to this
issue on page 337 and does not more fully address branding at all until
page 420, where he attributes much of the rise of branding to the role of
packaging; he seems to think that national brands have a greater right
to their branding than retailers do. For their part, retailers feared the big
brands might bypass them to sell directly to consumers.

The Proliferation of Brand Study

As brands arose, a first main issue focused on whether they were truly influential or not—that is, did they increase sales, and were consumers loyal to
them? And if they were loyal, was that due to "just habit" or some other
explanation? Because the rise of radio and magazine media also enhanced
the presentation of brands, the influence of advertising became a significant element. Roland Vaile (1927) researched two hundred companies to
determine whether the advertising of brands added to their sales during
a depression and concluded that it did. Paul Converse (1927) ruminated
as to whether men had brand preferences when buying a suit; he asked a
convenient sample of college students and learned that some did and others did not, that some were brand loyal and other shopped around. The
consumer culture of the time had moved from clothing sewn at home and
by tailors and seamstresses, where they were not referred to as brands, to
factory manufacturing, creating names such as Kuppenheimer and Hart
Schaffner Marx, and eminent retailers such as Marshall Fields, predating
the rise of modern designer names (e.g., Hilfiger, Lauren, Kors) that now
fill the Internet, as well as department stores. Although malls are said
to be dying, they still provide the society with their gradations by social
status (Nordstrom, Macys, Sears) and age grading (Babies "R" Us, Old
Navy,) and other cultural elements of size and style (Catherine's for the
full bodied, Victoria's Secret for the seductive).

These various brand-related issues—technology, competition, advertising—
led to questions about their application, and thus marketing research into
the consumers began to grow. The force of competition was especially
potent. Marketing research was hardly necessary when brands had little
competition, when Ipana toothpaste had eighty percent market share,
Coca-Cola dominated the soft drink market, and AT&T was a telephone
monopoly. The research culture was also especially stimulated by the
intellectuals and scholars fleeing Europe during the 1930s (Kassarjian
1994) to become teachers and research consultants. Outstanding among
them were Paul Lazarsfeld and Ernest Dichter (1960). Dichter served

companies with marketing research that was qualitatively (and psycho-analytically) oriented, and along with others—Herta Hertzog, the scholars and graduate students at Social Research, Inc. (SRI), James Vicary, and others—developed what came to be termed motivation research. (See Tadajewski 2013, for an explication of this idea.) The lively intellectual ferment at that early period is vividly apparent in a Lazarsfeld (1959) essay reflecting on consumers and managers. His tone is often personal, magisterial, and condescending to "commercial motivation research," which alienated him from Dichter.

By the mid-1950s, the explosion of brand creation, competition, and marketing research had become evident and a subject for study. Joseph W. Newman, a graduate student at Harvard University, visited SRI to gather data for his dissertation about motivation research. He told me the editor of the *Harvard Business Review* would like a piece about our work. The article, "The Product and the Brand" (1955), which I wrote with Burleigh B. Gardner, head of SRI, highlighted the significance of qualitative research. More strikingly, it also noted the concept of *brand image* in the minds of consumers as requiring consideration by managers, moving them essentially from creating brands to thinking more self-consciously about what they were doing. It also meant that attention was given to a behavioral science approach to the consumer.

The emergence of motivation research was further stimulated in 1957 by two books: *Motivation in Advertising* by Pierre Martineau and Newman's *Motivation Research and Marketing Management*. They were both practical discussions that reported several studies (both included my study for the *Chicago Tribune* titled *Automobiles: What They Mean to Americans*). Newman's volume also included a theoretical context for the work being reported. In the book's preface, Professor Bertrand Fox tells something of the cultural situation at the time:

> In the autumn of 1954 when Professor Newman began his study of motivation research, this young but fast-growing field of research was a subject of violent controversy. Motivation researchers employing different concepts and research techniques were pitted against each other, motivation researchers were challenged by those employing the more traditional research methods of market research, and the value and practicality of the results of motivation research were being challenged by marketing executives. Professor Newman believed strongly that motivation research had a real potential for significant contributions to marketing management.

Although such work was favorable for the continued growth of the branding concept as part of the necessity for attention to consumers, the idea also suffered from a climate of skepticism and criticism. Wroe Alderson, a leading and respected marketing scholar, wrote an important book (1957), *Marketing Behavior and Executive Action*, an excellent exposition of a functionalist approach to marketing theory. However, he showed scant interest in branding. His first mention appears on page 182 where he asserts, "Brand loyalty is seldom as great as the sponsor of a product would like to believe." Later, on page 279, he elaborates on this point, giving more weight to the likelihood of *brand switching*. He thinks consumers may be seduced initially by "emotional appeals" in advertising, but he prefers to believe that "most products most of the time are sold on the basis of rational utility."

This idea was vigorously challenged by the article "Symbols for Sale" (Levy 1959), where I asserted that "people buy things not only for what they can do, but also for what they mean." The concept of *brand symbolism* amplified the argument for brand images and was another way of thinking about lifestyle (Levy 1963). The article was embraced by qualitative researchers, earned the Converse Award in 2000, was cited in the literature 1,762 times to date, and is considered a foundation source for the Consumer Culture Theory Consortium.

The Universality of Branding

Furthermore, just as the article "Broadening the Concept of Marketing" (Kotler and Levy 1969) showed that all organizations and individuals engage in the exchange processes called marketing, so too do they engage in branding in the ways they present themselves to others (Goffman 1959). With this recognition that branding goes on among commercial organizations, as well as among all individuals, fresh and enlarged life was given to thinking about branding (with 2,286 citations to date). One effect was the creation of *brand management* in companies, with the local organizational culture shifting to absorb brand managers and researchers doing focus groups with consumers.

The article "The Product and the Brand" was co-authored suitably by Gardner as a garden of seedling ideas that were also brought to fruition by others. For instance, the text describes how research draws out the character of the brand with descriptions that are "likely to be similar in quality to the way human personalities show themselves" (36). That in turn implies the creation of *brand personalities* and *brand relationships* between brands and their audiences. These ideas were given surging development by Leonard Berry (1963) and Susan Fournier (1998). The importance of branding was also being thought about in another direction—that is, the goal of measuring the added value of being a brand with the concept of *brand equity*. This idea is the modern version of the old notion of "good will," the financial value that is added to that of the real estate, physical equipment, supplies, and products by the customers of established businesses and medical practices. Brand equity was given full voice and explanation by the work of David Aaker (2006) and Kevin Keller (1993). The attraction of the idea of branding is also shown in

Askegaard's "Branding as a Global Ideascape" (2006), focusing on the idea of branding as a widespread stimulus to marketing strategies.

The Two Levels of Branding

It now seems evident that the creation and the consumption of the idea of branding take two major forms or occurs at two main levels. Instrumental branding may be said to refer to most common understanding as a function of marketing. There it serves as the promoting part of the 4 Ps. That usage emphasizes the identity of the offering especially as brought to mind by its name, its logo, and its advertising and is mainly just another way of referring to it and the immediacy of its consumption. Casually, the brand name is a tag for its technology (Levy 2015), its means and context of employment, and is often a synonymous way of talking about marketing. Calling the activity "branding" rather than "marketing" focuses on aesthetics of promotion and tends to divert attention away from associations to the word marketing as greedy and manipulative. Currently, frequent references to "rebranding" highlight the goal of improving the entity's reputation.

Grand branding is a higher level of branding because it refers to its more encompassing and prior meanings. These elements are the character and reputation that reflect the originating purpose of the enterprise (or the individual) and how that has come to be perceived and evaluated by its audience segments. Grand branding is determined by the mission and the vision of the enterprise, the reason for its being, and especially the nature of its ethics. Thus, companies are judged for their value to society and their relationship to such concerns as health, environmentalism, economic growth, freedom, and so on (Levy and Zaltman 1975).

The Ongoing Brand Integration

Consuming the modern idea of the brand as asserted previously implies a point of view of the concept of branding that brings together all the contributions made to the birth, nurturing, societal debut, and career of an offering. The IBP is a way of showing a view of the grand brand. It envisions the manager at the peak, in a position to consume the idea of the brand in all the richness of its being and to supervise the major contents of what its product has to offer, the interaction of all the people involved (inventors, designers, engineers, managers, customers), and the nature of its aesthetic.

The Ideal Brand Pyramid

The IBP brings together these three general elements as modern versions of Aristotle's ethos, pathos, and logos. This is not a literal channeling of Aristotle's brilliant discussions in his *Rhetoric*, *Poetics*, and *Aesthetics*.

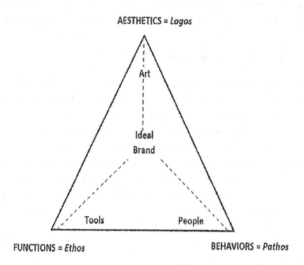

Figure 4.1 The ideal brand pyramid.

Here, the ethos asks first: What is being presented? But it does not stop there, as I think that offerings are always evaluated. It may be a commercial product, a person in the labor market, and the selves that are manifest in other interpersonal relationships. A natural consequence of any such presentation and of its perception is to ask if it is a good and virtuous thing and how it contributes to an overriding notion of its purpose. Although commonly called "goods," some are certainly thought of as bad or unethical and create controversy and social conflict (Levy and Zaltman 1975). Thus, brand imagery encompasses the two major elements of character and reputation. Emphasis on this corner of the pyramid not only reflects that early focus on product and distribution in scholarly marketing thinking noted previously but also takes account of the early activity of the so-called muckrakers Ida Tarbell (1904) and Lincoln Steffens (1904) and the negative judgments that led to government regulations.

The consumer revolution that came after World War II turned attention to ideas about market segments, audiences, demographics, and the nature of the intellectual and emotional reactions of consumers that motored their choices and decision making. The pathos refers fundamentally to emotions. It asks, who are the people involved and what is their psychosocial, intellectual, and emotional participation? It recognizes the rise of marketing research and studies of consumer behavior and most recently the dramatic influence of social media.

The logos is overall the nature of the message. What does it all say and how is it presented? Aesthetics refers to a special kind of response to the character of the visualization and other sensory elements that affect the performance of the elements of the offering and therefore the consumer's taste. Is it beautify, ugly, loud, banal, strong, dark, and so on? After issues of function have been resolved, after the concern with "the marketing concept," the role of aesthetics has come more to the fore, with an enhanced interest in the role of music and art. It also recognizes taste discrimination, such as with the creation of craft beer and the growing acceptance of tattooing become defined as aestheticization of experience.

The goal here is not be Aristotelean other than to honor his early insights. The Freudians use id, ego, and superego; the semioticians use icon, index, and symbol. The use of a triad is analytically somewhat artificial as all the inputs and outputs overlap and are interwoven like the threads of a helix. It is merely a convenient device that seems a useful tool, a well-intentioned way to communicate to readers, and it has an attractive aesthetic appeal similar to that of the ideal rectangle known as the golden section. Here it is a representation of the grand brand. It is grand because it is encompassing, pointing to all the complex elements that compose the construction of branding that start with a purpose, embody a self-concept, and hope for a pleasing result.

Bibliography

Aaker, David. *From Fargo to the World of Brands*. Tucson, AZ: Iceni Books, 2006.

Alderson, Wroe. *Marketing Behavior and Executive Action*. Homewood, IL: Irwin, Inc, 1957.

Askegaard, Søren. "Brands as an Ideoscape." In *Brands Culture*, 81–91. Edited by Jonathan E. Schroedor and Miriam Salzer-Mörlig. London: Routledge, 2006.

Bastos, Wilson and Sidney J. Levy. "A History of the Concept of Branding." *Journal of Historical Research in Marketing* 4 (2012): 347–68.

Berry, Leonard. "Relationship Marketing of Services Perspectives from 1983 and 2000." *Journal of Relationship Marketing* 1 (2002): 20–32.

Brown, Edmund. *Marketing*. New York: Harper, 1925.

Converse, Paul. *Selling Policies*. New York: Prentice-Hall, Inc, 1927.

Copeland, M. T. "Relation of Consumer's Buying Habits to Marketing Method." *Harvard Business Review* 1 (1923): 282–9.

Dichter, Ernest. *The Strategy of Desire*. New York, NY: Transaction, 1960.

Eckhardt, G. M. and Andre Bengtsson. "A Brief History of Branding in China." *Journal of Macromarketing* 30, no. 3 (2009): 210–21.

Fournier, Susan. "Consumers and Their Brands: Developing Relationship Theory in Consumer Research." *Journal of Consumer Research* 24 (1998): 343–73.

Gardner, Burleigh B. and Sidney J. Levy. "The Product and the Brand." *Harvard Business Review* (March–April 1955): 33–9.

Goffman, Erving. *The Presentation of Self in Everyday Life*. New York: Doubleday, 1959.

Kassarjian, Harold. "Scholarly Traditions and European Roots of American Consumer Behavior." In *Research Traditions in Marketing*, 265–79. Edited by G. Laurent, G. L. Lilien, and B. Pras. Boston: Kluwer, 1994.

Keller, Kevin. "Conceptualizing, Measuring, and Managing Customer-Based Brand Equity." *Journal of Marketing* 57 (1993): 1–22.

Kotler, Philip and Sidney J. Levy. "Broadening the Concept of Marketing." *Journal of Marketing* 33 (1969): 10–5.

Lazarsfeld, Paul F. *Sociological Reflection on Business: Consumers and Managers.* New York: Columbia University Press, 1959.

Levy, Sidney J. "Roots of Marketing and Consumer Research at the University of Chicago." *Consumption Markets Culture* 2 (2003): 99–110.

———. "History of Qualitative Research Methods in Marketing." In *Handbook of Qualitative Research Methods in Marketing*, 3–16. Edited by Russell Belk. UK: Edward Elgar, 2006.

———. "Roots and Development of Consumer Culture Theory." In *Consumer Culture Theory*, 47–61. Edited by Anastasia E. Thyroff, Jeff Murray, and Russell W. Belk. UK: Emerald, 2015a.

———. "The Technology of Branding." In *Brands*, 187–92. Edited by Jonathan Schroeder. London: Routledge, 2015b.

———. *The Theory of the Brand.* Evanston, IL: DecaBooks, 2016.

——— and Marius Luedicke. "From Marketing Ideology to Branding Ideology." *Journal of Macromarketing* 33 (2012): 58–66.

——— and Gerald Zaltman. *Marketing, Society, and Conflict.* Englewood City: Prentice-Hall, Inc, 1975.

Martineau, Pierre. *Motivation in Advertising.* New York, NY: McGraw-Hill, 1957.

Newman, Joseph W. *Motivation Research and Marketing Management.* Cambridge, MA: Harvard University Press, 1957.

Russell, Cristel A. and Sidney J. Levy. *Journal of Consumer Research* (2012): 341–59.

Steffens, Lincoln. *The Shame of the Cities.* New York, NY: Dover, 1904.

Tadajewski, Mark. "Promoting the Consumer Society: Ernest Dichter, the Cold War and FBI." *Journal of Historical Research in Marketing* 5, no. 2 (2013): 192–211.

Tarbell, Ida. *The History of the Standard Oil Company.* Gloucester, MA: Peter Smith, 1904.

Vaile, Roland S. "The Use of Advertising during Depression." *Harvard Business Review* 4 (1927): 323–30.

Wengrow, David. "Prehistories of Commodity Branding." *Current Anthropology* 49 (2008): 7–34.

5 Is the Price Right?

Moral and Cultural Frames for Understanding Pricing Systems

Melanie Wallendorf

Price represents much more than simply a number that is one of the 4 P's in a marketer's tool kit. Because of its complexity, many approaches to studying price have developed within the marketing and consumer behavior literatures, but it is the dyadic aspects of pricing that are of interest here. The dyadic aspects of pricing have been studied from the perspective of the firm's view of the customer, termed *consumer lifetime value* (Bolton 1998; Rust, Lemon, and Zeithaml 2004). The dyadic aspects of pricing have also been studied from the perspective of the customer, comparing the firm's asking price to other prices previously encountered, termed *reference price* (Mazumdar, Raj, and Sinha 2005). These approaches focus primarily on calculations made by each of the parties in the transaction. These two bodies of work theorize about pricing strategies and responses while ignoring any human connection that may suffuse the relationship between buyer and seller, despite its acknowledged importance (Fournier 1998).

This essay moves beyond these two perspectives to view the dyadic aspects of price through the lens of sociocultural theory. Extending Zelizer's (1994) work on money, this essay details how price is situated in an implicit web of culturally embedded moral relationships connecting a seller, a buyer, and numerous other actors, including employees, suppliers, and other potential buyers. This essay addresses price as a moral assessment grounded in a social order that structures who has to do what in order to receive what from whom. Moral assessments produced within a culture are far more complex than a simple number.

This essay elaborates on that complexity and, in doing so, raises more questions than it answers. It draws from extant literature on conventional pricing systems in business-to-consumer contexts, using that literature to inform questions raised by fieldwork in four business-to-consumer empirical contexts. Each of the empirical contexts was selected because it uses a pricing system that differs from the conventional pricing system that is common in contemporary capitalist economies. Drawing from these empirical materials, the essay explicates some moral and cultural dimensions of pricing that are masked in research that regards price as the numerical quantity of money requested by the seller and paid by the buyer based on their economic evaluations of the item being sold.

Extant pricing literature in marketing typically regards price as the quantity of economic resources requested by a seller based on the seller's consideration of a range of factors regarding the firm, its competition, and its desired consumers. These factors include production and delivery costs, desired product image, stage of product life cycle, competitors' prices, demand levels, and the estimated financial lifetime value of various kinds of customers (cf. Srinivasan, Pamels, and Nijs 2008). Pricing research in marketing has typically regarded price as something set by the seller and then accepted or rejected by a potential buyer. It typically does not consider alternative pricing systems in which customers participate in setting price, other than by bidding in auctions (cf. Chan, Kadiyali, and Park 2007). More importantly for this essay, extant pricing research typically does not consider the sociocultural dynamics that structure consumers' participation in cocreating price.

This essay's four empirical contexts feature the consumer as a cocreator of price, beyond the act of choosing to buy or not buy at a seller-determined price. Such contexts are part of a pricing strategy called participative pricing (Kim, Natter, and Spann 2009). Each of the four empirical contexts involves a blend of market economy and moral economy logics in establishing culturally embedded moral relationships between buyer and seller, and with a range of other actors.

Sociocultural Assumptions

Contemporary research on pricing is grounded in an implicit assumption that transactions are completed in economic relations grounded in a modernist gesellschaft society (Tönnies 1887/1988), where actors conduct impersonal transactions in which they each focus on self-interest. Yet this is not the empirical reality I encounter when I do fieldwork, nor was it my world in the midwestern U.S. town of approximately thirty thousand people where I grew up. My childhood world was filled with market relations embedded in social relations as later detailed by Granovetter (1985) in his now classic article. When we were young girls, my sister and I were taken to the P.N. Hirsch retail store to buy new school shoes that had been made a few blocks away at the International Shoe Factory, which employed the labor of locals in the factory building, as well as prisoners inside the nearby state penitentiary. My mother purchased clothing at Bob and Barb Orenstein's store The Purple Shoppe, and my father purchased clothing at Charlie Czarlinsky's store, named Czarlinksy's Clothing Store by Charlie's father, who started the business. It would not be uncommon for my sister to wear her prisoner-made shoes to walk two doors down the street from our house to babysit the Czarlinsky's youngest daughter, Charlanne, at their house. Meanwhile, wearing their locally purchased clothing, my parents would play golf and have dinner with Bob and Barb and Charlie and his wife, Joanne. This was the nature of everyday life.

What do we see if we track the flow of money through these events? In order for my parents to have reasonably fashionable clothing when they went out to dinner with their friends, money earned by my father was used to buy clothing at a store owned by those same friends. But some of the money that flowed from my dad to the clothing store came back to my sister as babysitting wages paid by my parents' friend Charlie, who received money from my dad as part of the clothing purchase. And some of the profits from my parents' clothing purchases were used by Bob, Barb, Charlie, and Joanne to pay for their dinners.

But if we go deeper, the money's social path becomes more complex. Where did my dad get the money to buy my parents' clothes? He owned a small local charge card company (this was before Visa and MasterCard) that handled bookkeeping for local businesses so they didn't have to offer and process thirty-day revolving charge accounts for their customers. Of course, my dad's loyal customers for his charge card/bookkeeping service included The Purple Shoppe and Czarlinsky's Clothing Store. The flow of money through socially embedded market relationships was a self-contained circle, as it is in gemeinschaft communities. That was the way things were only fifty years ago in my midwestern town, six decades after Tönnies pointed to the decline of gemeinschaft communities and the rise of gesellschaft societies.

So what were the moral and social frameworks that were used in setting prices for the bookkeeping service, the clothing, the dinners, and my sister's babysitting services? Clearly, the focus had to go beyond such self-interested notions as customer lifetime value, profit maximization, and cost recovery; there was a web of relationships that had to be preserved and accommodated. Of course, an ardent economist might try to argue that the maintenance of those relationships is a form of self-interest, but I would respond that to do so, the importance of human warmth and genuine fondness for others has to be discarded, which I resist.

Clearly, even today, the gemeinschaft world has not completely disappeared. In fact, I encounter it frequently, even among strangers. After seeing my ad on Craigslist, a man came to my house to buy an advertised child's loft bed (complete with a slide for getting down from the bed). The man, who appeared to be a loving father as he spoke about his son, wanted the bed for his little boy who had been promised a new bed when he started being able to stay dry through the night. After hearing the backstory from this stranger, I wanted his little boy to get the reward of a bed with a slide, and I wanted to sell the bed so my emerging teenager could have a new one to make her room seem more age appropriate. I easily agreed to a lower price than I had advertised, and felt happy about it. Although we were strangers, ours was not an impersonal transaction that gave primacy to self-interest. Each of us was, first and foremost, a parent, not a self-interested economic actor.

In the following sections, four empirical contexts are used to articulate the nature of these relationship webs and connect them to pricing systems in which the consumer has an active role in setting price. The empirical contexts are employed as brief case studies rather than as full-blown empirical projects. Sufficient data has been collected and analyzed in each context to raise broad questions and point to elements of the moral and cultural frames for pricing; however, the data are insufficient for a definitive ethnography of each context. Methods employed are presented at the outset of the section on each context. The contexts are a farmers market, a farm produce stand, an Indian restaurant, and a private school.

Gifting at the Farmers Market

The first empirical context draws from transactions at a local farmers market. This context is used to consider how the relationships between farmers and individual customers create flexibility in pricing.

I conducted informal participant observation as a weekly shopper at a certified-organic local farmers market for about thirty weeks across two growing seasons (May–October). I call this informal participant observation because I wrote field notes when I observed something that was noteworthy regarding pricing but did not prepare a full set of field notes for each market visit. The market is located in a village of just over one thousand people, nine miles north of a town of about fifty-five thousand people. Median household income is just below the state median and the cost of living index is 135.6 at the time of the fieldwork (the U.S. average is 100). The market is within an hour of California's central valley, the world's most prolific region for food production and processing. The central valley produces over a quarter of all food eaten by Americans and almost eighty-five percent of its fresh peaches. As a result, the variety of produce brought to this farmers market at its peak of flavor and freshness is astounding. There is stability in the farmers who come each week, and remarkable stability in the customers who shop at its weekly sessions. What constantly changes are the varieties of seasonal produce that appear on vendors' tables. "What do you have this week?" is the ever-present question.

A particularly popular vendor is one I will call "the Peach Man." Each week, in front of his sales table and extending a bit into the aisle between facing stalls, he places a tasting table around which customers can gather on all four sides. Each week during stone-fruit season, the tasting table contains cut-up samples of fourteen varieties of some combination of peaches, apricots, plums, nectarines, and pluots, all of stellar quality. Shoppers eagerly flock to the tasting table to sample the ever-changing variety of fruit, trying to discern which varieties to buy this week. Many times, shoppers can be heard squealing with delight as they remove the toothpick holding the bite of fruit from their mouths. "Oh, you have to taste this one; it's so sweet" is often spoken to no one in particular in the toothpick-bearing crowd gathered around the tasting table. Not surprisingly, the fruit commands a premium price over what one would pay across the street at the village's sole grocery store, which also features local organic produce at higher prices than the nonlocal produce at a national chain grocery store located two miles away.

I became a loyal weekly customer of the Peach Man's fruit, not even inquiring about the price or selection of other farmers at the market who also had stone fruit. Each week, after systematically tasting all fourteen varieties and deciding which ones I wanted, I selected my fruit and handed it to the Peach Man, who put it on a scale and then told me a price. He did not use a calculator or write anything down. I had no idea how he calculated the price. Because his price quote usually came out to a relatively round number, I didn't know whether he was rounding up or rounding down the exact amount I should pay based on weight.

At first, ours was a modernist economic transaction, silent except for his price quote to me. After a few weeks, the transaction became more cordial, with him recognizing me and asking how I was or making a comment about the weather. Over time, the relationship developed to include a little bit of banter with each other, reflecting his recognition of me as a regular customer, and his memory of which types of stone fruit I prefer. We never learned each other's names, and I would say we were friendly in our brief interaction, but not friends.

Nonetheless, over time I find myself telling others about his wonderful fruit, effectively increasing his potential sales, although there is no way for him to know I am doing so. Unlike some large corporations, he does not have a program that gives rewards to current customers for referrals of their friends to his stand. Yet, I am not the only customer who likes his fruit and him. Given their banter around the tasting table, I sense that many customers are loyal to his stand, and others who are at the market more for recreation than for food shopping are loyal to his tasting table, which is clearly a crowd pleaser. Customers often thank him warmly and compliment the quality of the fruit. He smiles. One day, I see a middle-aged woman holding his hands in both of hers, looking him directly in the eyes and saying, "I want to thank you for being here, for bringing such beautiful fruit. We are blessed to have you come to [our village.] You help make it a wonderful place to live." After many weeks of shopping at his stand, I follow my typical routine of systematic tasting and selecting, and then hand my chosen fruit over to him for weighing. He puts my fruit on the scale and tells me the price. And then he puts an extra apricot, a variety I hadn't purchased that week, in my bag. As he does so, he smiles broadly and says, "Enjoy!"

In that moment, I realize that he has given me a gift. It is not a big peach, but is a tasty little apricot. I've never received a gift at his farm's stand at another farmers market in a nearby village where I occasionally shop if I need something midweek, but then the Peach Man doesn't work at that market. Yet, upon receiving the gift of the apricot, I do not feel that I need to find out when his birthday is so I can bring a gift or bring him a gift of something I made the following week.

What can be learned from the Peach Man case study? When warm human relations are embedded in an economic system, the price charged is not the same for everyone. In this case, there was no product differentiation; the Peach Man always brought terrific fruit for everyone. But when he weighed it, somehow the price was rounded to never require pennies. For whom did he round up and for whom did he round down? For all we knew, he was rounding up for everyone. But no one challenged him on the price, and no one expressed concern that perhaps others were getting a better price than he or she was. There was trust, and delicious fruit.

Even though we all had access to the same luscious fruit, there was differentiation in how much fruit you got for the price he quoted. I thank Jerry Zaltman for suggesting a metaphor to help me understand what was happening. In a sense, one aspect of the pricing relationship is like being in court. The seller determines what is for sale and what price to set for that product. The buyer determines what quantity to take at that price, thereby setting the maximum amount paid. But then the seller gets to act like a judge, deciding whether the customer is a "good" one, deserving of a better price by rounding down or being granted an additional quantity as a gift. And the seller gets to decide what the moral standards are for being judged a "good" customer: is it frequency of purchase, quantity of purchase, warmth of smile? Metaphorically, the seller is like a judge who has sentencing latitude to grant lenience in the form of a smaller unit price for some customers in return for their "good" behavior.

Why did the extra apricot seem to be a gift when the punch on my frequent-buyer card at my local smoothie shop does not? The extra piece of fruit felt like a gift because it seemed spontaneous and was unexpected; it was not announced to all customers as a loyalty program with its associated calculations and reward levels. I doubt that the Peach Man had an algorithm to calculate my customer lifetime value, or even that he did so in an informal way. Instead, the apricot felt like a gift because his warm human connection to me in saying, "Enjoy!" took us out of the realm of impersonal economic transactions and into the world of moral logics. But it is really only a baby step into the world of moral logics: I felt no need to reciprocate with a subsequent gift to him. Some might ask if my continued patronage was a reciprocal gift, but I think not: I planned to continue my patronage even before the gift. Further, my continued patronage did not involve a sacrifice on my part, a crucial element of the perfect gift

(Belk 1996). Instead, it felt like I gained through buying his fruit. What is important about his gift is that without knowing it could happen, I had participated in setting the price by being a "good" customer.

\ What can be learned from the case of the Peach Man is that the price paid represents the seller's standard of an appropriate unit price, plus or minus some amount based on the seller's judgment of the customer's behavior, ranging from "good" to "bad." The right price for a particular customer is based on the seller's moral assessment of the customer's behavior, just as I assessed the man who bought the child's bed as someone who seemed to be a loving father.

Grounded in this perspective on pricing, what angers customers when, for example, an airline reconfigures its frequent flyer program to grant awards based on dollars spent rather than miles flown (see, e.g., Chew 2015) is that the seller-judge is perceived as making the status of being a "good" customer more difficult to attain. Customers who had previously been judged as "good" by the airline no longer make the cut after the change and are angry. The impact on customer loyalty from this change in the financial terms of the airline's so-called customer loyalty program may have negative economic consequences.

Honesty at a Self-Service Farm Stand

The second empirical context is a produce stand at a farm on the outskirts of a medium-sized town. I visited the produce stand three times in 2009 on the recommendation of a local resident who knew about my interest in the moral and social aspects of pricing systems.

The farm stand is located in a rural area eight miles east of the town of approximately fifty-five thousand people mentioned in the Peach Man case study. The character of the town is important to the produce stand context, so it requires some description. For many reasons, the town is widely regarded as very liberal. For example, a higher percentage of its population voted for Barack Obama in 2008 than voted for him in Dane county where Madison, WI, is located, and, in 2002, a higher percentage of the students entering the local university considered themselves liberal or far left than the entering class at the University of California, Berkeley (fifty-eight vs. forty-five percent; Gendron and Dornhoff 2008). It is a town in which freedom is highly valued, being liberal is assumed, and actions in support of politically liberal beliefs suffuse all aspects of life. A local comedian quipped that "the men are so forward thinking they don't have a receding hairline; they have a progressive face." The town is progressive not just politically, but socially as well. Its university's curriculum and the focus of the residents have resulted in many activist and social justice organizations being founded or headquartered here.

In a rural area eight miles outside of town, a produce stand is located on a forty-five-acre, family-owned farm that is certified organic. The farm sells its produce, as well as eggs from about three hundred pasture-raised chickens, at two local farmers markets (but not at the one described in the previous case), as well as at the farm stand located on the farm property. There is a sign on the main road that indicates "Farm Stand Open," and then a driveway that leads to the approximately ten-by-twelve-foot simple structure that constitutes the farm stand. Eggs, priced the same as they are when sold at farmers markets, are in a refrigerated case; produce is displayed in baskets and boxes on tables with prices listed per pound. Scales are provided for weighing the produce.

The farm stand is open during daytime hours even when the farmers are away selling produce at a farmers market. The farm stand is not staffed but is operated on what a sign calls "the honor system." Customers put their cash payments into a wooden box nailed to the wall. There is a small basket nearby containing roughly $20 in small bills and $5 in coins for those needing change. Online reviews explain this aspect of the pricing system and warn that customers should bring small bills and change. Yet, despite the ready access to cash and public notices to this effect, the stand has been operating in this fashion for at least eight years at the time of this fieldwork and is still using this system at the time of this writing.

For those without cash, a rudimentary credit system has developed. There is a corkboard on the wall for IOU (I-owe-you) notes, with slips of paper provided for writing them. The few IOU notes I observed include more than just the person's identity, contact information, and amount owed; they typically also include an apology, some kind of explanation for why the person needed the produce but didn't have cash, and often a temporal promise regarding when the cash payment will be brought to the farm. All of the IOU notes are dated recently.

Are we back in the gemeinschaft relations of my childhood town fifty years ago? Not completely; this farm is located less than fifty miles from the corporate headquarters of Silicon Valley technology giants such as Apple and Google.

On one visit, I notice a new item in the refrigerated case. Goat cheese (chèvre) had been roughly fashioned into heart shapes with herbs on top and marked with a price of $6. Next to the wrapped cheese shapes is a hand-lettered sign in what appears to be a child's neat writing:

I'm wanting to get a horse, so I'm making these goat cheese hearts from my goat's milk.

Whitney

The surrounding area has several very fine commercial goat farms that are renowned for their cheeses, which are sold at the same or a lower price in the town's grocery stores or gourmet shops, or even in the gourmet shops of a cosmopolitan city less than eighty miles away. The commercially available cheeses are made into firm rounds that are beautifully adorned with edible flowers or herbs. And yet, Whitney's simply formed goat cheese hearts sell. Is that something that economists would call irrational, as if that explains away its existence?

What can be learned from the produce stand? Rather than being unscrupulous shoppers whose receipts and merchandise must be checked before exiting the store to make sure nothing is being taken that wasn't paid for, in the right context, American consumers can behave responsibly in ways that look out for the *seller's* best interest. They can participate in setting the price they pay by behaving honestly: weighing, calculating, and leaving the correct amount of money in the box. This can happen without security cameras, without antishoplifting tags on merchandise, without writing down driver's license or phone numbers, and without a body scan with shoes removed. Without anything other than their own moral principles to guide them, customers at the farm stand calculate and pay the correct amount, leaving the money in the change basket to be used as intended. They can even be trusted to make a second trip back to the stand later to pay if they take the merchandise when they don't have cash. These buyers behave as if they want the seller to stay in business and take personal responsibility for making that happen. At times, they are willing to ignore reference prices and instead pay a premium price in order to help the seller, as with the relatively high price for Whitney's simple goat cheese hearts.

Consumers are not just self-interested. When they feel affection toward a vendor, they engage in pro-vendor behaviors. They may even save the seller the cost of hiring staff or installing security equipment, while still paying a premium price.

This case opens up a completely different understanding of what "customer loyalty" can be. Consider the notion of so-called loyalty programs, in which a company offers an additional benefit, such as points or miles or punches on a card that can be redeemed for incremental goods later, just to get patrons to return. What kind of "loyalty" do customers feel if the seller has to bribe them to get them to return? So-called loyalty programs have led marketing scholars and practitioners to lose sight of the fact that loyalty is a willingness to support or show allegiance to another, even in times of hardship.

Loyalty is a heart-felt connection, making Whitney's choice of a shape for her cheeses metonymically resonant. Trust is a close companion of loyalty. In this empirical case, we see the converse of the apricot gift at the farmers market. At the farmers market, the seller gives a gift, an unpaid premium to the buyer. At the farm stand, buyers give the gift of their honesty and trustworthiness to the seller. The seller's costs are reduced by not having to pay staff at the farm stand to supervise payments and provide surveillance to prevent theft.

Relationship partners do not have to be face-to-face or even known to each other for the gift of honest patronage to be given. I never met the farmers nor their daughter, Whitney. Yet, as I also experienced with the little boy who might get an exciting new big-boy bed if he could stay dry through the night, I empathized with Whitney; I wanted to help her earn her horse even though her product was clearly inferior to one I could purchase at my local grocer. Paralleling Fisher, Vandenbosch, and Antia's (2008) results regarding charitable donations, I paid more because my focus was on helping another person get a benefit with a positive emotional valence. More research that is socioculturally grounded is needed to better theorize the role of emotional connections such as empathy, even among strangers, in impacting willingness to pay. How are these relations built and maintained? What is the role of the cultural context in supporting them?

Further, with retailers losing approximately $32 billion per year due to shoplifting and employee theft (Wahba 2015), more research is needed on the sociocultural conditions that lead consumers *and* employees to behave honestly and in the best interest of the seller, as they do at the produce stand.

Meeting the Needs of the Other with Pay-What-You-Think-Is-Fair

The third empirical context is a locally owned restaurant that hosts a fixed-menu, five-course dinner on Sunday nights. As diners are seated, the fact that the five-course menu is fixed for the evening is explained to them, but no mention is made of the pricing system. At the end of the meal, diners are presented with a bill that shows a price of $0.00, and they are asked to "pay what you think is fair."

Pay-what-you-want differs considerably from pay-what-you-think-is-fair in the moral frames in which they are embedded. Pay-what-you-want is a pricing system that has been tried by some larger firms such as Panera bread and some smaller businesses (Gneezy et al. 2010; Kim, Natter, and Spann 2009; Reiner and Traxler 2012; Schmidt, Spann, and Zeithammer 2015). Pay-what-*you-want* essentially commands the buyer to consider his or her own self-interest, whereas pay-what-*you-think-is-fair* directs the buyer's consideration toward maintaining fairness in the social relationship between buyer and seller. So, although pay-what-you-want and pay-what-you-think-is-fair are both pricing systems in which the buyer sets the price, the moral frames in which they are embedded differ sharply.

I attended this restaurant's pay-what-you-think-is-fair dinner event three times and separately had lunch at the restaurant during an interview with the owner. I contacted potential interviewees by approaching them outside as they left the restaurant following their meal: some wanted to do a phone interview later, and others preferred to do the interview right there on the sidewalk. One asked if he could have more time to think about the experience and e-mail me. In total, I obtained interview responses from a sample of fourteen diners, including some local residents, some temporary residents, a local university student, and some people who were visiting from elsewhere. Interviews were relatively short (fifteen to twenty minutes) and focused on the diners' reactions to the meal and pricing system, how they decided how much to pay, how much they paid, and their more general restaurant preferences and frequency of dining out. In addition, to expand the sample beyond my few visits, 640 online reviews of the restaurant were coded for any reference to the Sunday night dinners or the pricing system used on those nights; 95 reviews were found to contain such references.

Before analyzing consumers' responses to this pricing system, the restaurant owner's explanation of his intentions and approach provide important background. After attending culinary school in his native country in south Asia, Roshan worked in a hotel restaurant as a manager. He then immigrated to the United States, working in a restaurant in the northwestern United States, later moving to this area to work in the restaurant of a man who had tasted his food in the northwestern restaurant. After a natural disaster hit the local area, Roshan worked with others in a tent that was set up to feed people. Soon after, during the recovery process, he was given a permit to open a restaurant near the current location.

Just as with cooking food for people after the natural disaster, Roshan views his restaurant as a way to make the world a better place, in his own small way. He is proud that the restaurant is completely vegetarian with many vegan dishes, as a way to avoid any connection to the killing of animals. The restaurant serves no alcohol; Roshan does not even allow people to bring a bottle of wine into the restaurant to be uncorked. He purchases much of the produce at a local farmers market (not the one in the Peach Man case discussed earlier) with a focus on buying as many organic items as possible to reduce harm to the environment. He references these practices in calling it a "clean business." He proudly says, "I make my money in a clean way." He used to donate all of the profits from the Sunday dinner to a local project to feed the homeless. He is hoping to start serving a Sunday brunch to bring people's attention to global warming by asking that customers park a half mile away and walk. He would reward such behavior with a free ice cream (made with coconut milk rather than a dairy base to minimize its environmental impact).

From a business standpoint, there are advantages to the Sunday night fixed-menu approach. By having a fixed menu, Roshan can choose to cook with whatever ingredients are seasonally abundant or already available in the kitchen. Further, he needs fewer staff in the kitchen because they only need to cook those five courses rather than cooking each meal to order. He also needs a narrower inventory of ingredients in the kitchen because only five dishes will be cooked. This is particularly useful at the end of a weekend. Similarly, he needs fewer wait staff because they don't have to take each customer's order or tally their bills.

Overwhelmingly, customers' evaluations of the food are quite favorable. Very rarely (three out of about seven hundred), there will be an online review giving a low rating saying something like the food was "too oily." But reviews that claim that this is one of the best vegetarian meals the reviewer has ever had are abundant. Frequently, carnivores are instructed or instruct other carnivores that the food is so flavorful that "you won't miss the meat." The restaurant overall gets an average of four out of five stars.

Diners saw both positive and negative aspects of the fixed menu. Most online reviews simply referred to it as "good" or the best time to go to the restaurant. Local landscape worker, Kelly (forty-two) and two of his friends liked it because it "got us to try new things," a comment echoed in some online reviews. An online reviewer noted that "a fixed menu can be annoying" if the meal contains dishes that you don't like; nonetheless, this reviewer was quite pleased with what was served. Another online reviewer was displeased to learn about the fixed menu when she arrived because this was a return visit when she hoped to order the same dish she enjoyed last time she dined there. She also commented that one of the dishes served as part of the fixed menu didn't "knock my socks off," and that overall, the meal was mediocre.

Except for one person, all of the interviewees had favorable impressions of the pay-what-you-think-is-fair pricing system, although some admitted that they "felt a bit awkward at first." For Michael (thirty-six, high school teacher), this awkwardness stemmed from feeling that he and his wife "are not that well off," yet thinking that the food was uniquely flavorful and delicious. He was concerned that he might not be able to pay enough for what he thought was fair given how tasty it was. He and his wife paid $50 for themselves and their two very young children who didn't eat much except bread, counting their group as the same as "2 ½ to 3 people." A similar sentiment was expressed by an online reviewer who reported paying $25, but "if I had a conscience, I probably would have paid $40 for the amazing cuisine."

The one interviewee who did not like the pricing system was a diner who had been physically active all day and was looking for some filling, cheap food before driving to his home about ninety miles away. Yet, when a friend suggested this restaurant, Alexander (forty-five, single, hospital administrator) agreed to try it. He felt too hungry to go elsewhere in hopes of finding what he wanted. Alexander thought the idea of a fixed menu combined with pay-what-you-think-is-fair was "odd," which he said with a tone of annoyance in his voice.

> I would prefer that the price be fixed with tips included. I don't like to have to think about it. It is a burden to ask your customers to do that. I would like to just trust them to mark it up to whatever they need. But this is a very different sensibility than supply and demand.

Alexander longed for the simplicity of a gesellschaft transaction, with prices governed by the intersection of supply and demand, without having to accept the burden of thinking about what is fair. He further mused that if he had come to this restaurant when he was a student, "I would have thought about what I could *afford*, not what it's worth." Even then, he would have been challenged to think in terms of fairness. Not surprisingly, he determined how much to pay by invoking a reference price for a meal of an entrée, soup, appetizer, and dessert and then reducing it because he didn't get to choose what to order and the fixed-menu arrangement necessitated fewer staff than a meal that is ordered. Despite the way Alexander thinks about this pricing system, he and his two companions paid a total of $60 inclusive of the tip, roughly the per-person amount that other diners paid.

The way Alexander thinks about this pricing system is reminiscent of a moral development stage described by psychologist Lawrence Kohlberg (1983) as a preconventional, self-interest orientation (stage 2), characteristic of young children but also present in some adults. Moral development stages are based on *how* a person thinks about ethical issues, not *what* he or she decides. Alexander does not respond to the cue of "fairness" but instead considers the value of the benefits he receives minus an amount for the benefits to the restaurant owner that are not benefits to him. His consideration is completely egocentric and does not take into account his relation to the people owning or working in the restaurant.

Evidence of online reviewers who took a price-setting approach similar to Alexander's is the frequent reference to the Sunday night dinner as pay-what-you-want or pay-what-you-think-it-is-worth rather than pay-what-you-think-is-fair. The difference is that the first two pricing systems (what-*you-want* and what-*you think-it-is worth*) call for an egocentric approach, whereas the latter (pay-what-you-think-*is-fair*) is relational. Sixteen of the ninety-five online reviewers mentioning the Sunday night dinner say diners are asked to pay what they *want* or what they think *it is worth*. Only four online reviewers correctly refer to the pricing scheme as what diners think *is fair*. The owner's attempt to invoke a relational concept of fairness is overlooked by many consumers' tendencies to think in egocentric terms.

By way of contrast, three local residents who work during the week landscaping people's yards talk extensively about who the owner is and what he represents to them. They come to the Sunday night dinners about every six weeks and occasionally eat in the restaurant for lunch. Unprompted, Kostas (midforties) explains what he knows about the owner and his family: "They have been in town over 15 years; it is a family that is known. They feed the homeless. They are from India so they have a different way of handling things, but the food is good." Kostas's evaluation of the meal is tied to a moral evaluation of the family and their contributions to the community. His mention of their "different way of handling things" references uneven service that sometimes means ordered items are slow to be served or served in an odd sequence, such as drinks arriving near the end of the meal. Kostas' appendage of "but the food is good" is an indication that he thinks the uneven service should be overlooked in deciding whether to patronize the restaurant. His friend, Kelly, notes that in comparison to Sunday evening, "the food is sometimes better at other times." Yet they continue returning to the Sunday night dinner and pay $20 each, including tip. Despite working in an occupation in which it can be assumed they earn much less than Alexander, they determine how much to pay without invoking reference prices. Instead, they reference relationships, community connections of mutual support and caring, that permeate gemeinschaft communities. Despite the fact that sometimes the Sunday evening food isn't as good as it is at other times, and the service is handled in a "different way," they are loyal customers and pay as much as self-interested Alexander.

The way Kostas and Kelly determine how much to pay reflects the moral development stage that Kohlberg (1983) calls a conventional, social-relationships perspective (stage 3). It is characteristic of many adolescents and some adults. It focuses on social expectations and whether the person tries to live up to those expectations. Forgiveness of infractions (e.g., the food not always being as good on Sundays as at other times, and uneven service) is permitted in the logic of this moral development stage if the person meant well.

Customer loyalty for any organization occasionally requires forgiveness of transgressions. Mistakes happen, service failures occur, and products sometimes fail. For customers to forgive such transgressions, they must be beyond the self-interested, calculating logics of stage 2 moral development. The mythic "rational economic (hu)man" seems to have been invented without a moral foundation for forgiveness. Forgiveness occurs when relations rather than utils come to the fore.

What do online reviews say about the uneven service? The reason the restaurant has a four-out-of-five-star rather than a five-star average rating is due to complaints about the service. On nights other than the Sunday fixed-menu dinner, reviewers who give low ratings complain that not all diners at a table receive their meals at the same time, their water glasses were never refilled, thirty minutes elapsed between when they were seated and when their order was taken, servers seemed to be blind to them waving their arms to get some attention, or one of the dishes they ordered was never served. There are enough of these reviews over the span of many years to give some credence to the complaints. But not every diner experiences these problems, and many note that they did not.

What is interesting and informative is the number of customers who respond to reviews that complain about service with an entreaty to complainers to return to the restaurant with changed expectations. One local reviewer encourages complaining diners to adopt a new attitude and even suggests a tip for having a better experience:

> You all will have to get over your service qualms, because you are getting fine dining food for fast food prices. The quality and the execution is always impeccable. I honestly don't know how they do it! They are so consistent with beer budget prices. I spend only $36 here where I would spend $80 in a restaurant with equal caliber of food. Roshan is always reinventing the menu.
>
> Here is a hint: Compliment his Food! If you compliment his food, he will give you recommendations and treat you a little nicer. I often come in and order something and he will tell me to order something else and it never disappoints.

Interestingly, the recommended solution to uneven service is for the customer to change expectations and establish a positive relationship with the owner. Rather than customer relationship management (CRM), the customer is encouraged to engage in service provider relationship management (SPRM). In gesellschaft societies, it is considered the obligation of the organization to manage relationships with customers, but in gemeinschaft communities, obligations to maintain the relationship fall on both parties.

Another online reviewer who lives about fifty miles away but frequently comes to town for recreational trips makes a similar relational suggestion in an attempt to shift the orientation of those who complain about the uneven service.

> Roshan is great, the family vibe is wonderful. This place has great decor, as well as some of the most flavorfulicous dishes. . . .
>
> Sometimes its [sic] busy and it takes longer, but by being personable, you can build a great friendly relationship with owners and by recognition the service gets better.
>
> I see some reviews on here with people frustrated with the speed of service, but I don't think that's what this place is about. Come with your friends and laugh, enjoy the food and take in the ambiance, don't be in a rush, unless you come for lunch, which is quick.

These reviews highlight the customer's role in insuring a satisfactory experience by forming a relationship with the seller and reorienting the focus away from McDonaldization's features of speed and convenience (Ritzer 2011).

Another local reviewer encourages other diners to overlook service failures because the intentions behind them and the restaurant owner are all good:

> Service leaves a little to be desired, the waiters are prompt and well-meaning, but a little bit cold and somewhat hasty. There were two

things that I would have ordered that evening had I been given the chance. However, I attributed this to be a cultural difference and not ill-intended by any means. The owner is a kind and gentle soul.

All of these reviews are grounded in a conventional, social relationship orientation to moral judgments (stage 3). These entreaties are written by loyal customers who overlook some failings, instead focusing on what is good, including the food, the people, and their intentions. All reviewers mention their relationship with the owner as central to their assessments. Yet, I have never seen a customer satisfaction survey that measured whether customers thought the service provider has good intentions or "is a kind and gentle soul." Is this a central component of true loyalty?

A few diners at the Sunday night events deeply consider the moral and ethical issues embedded in setting a price that they think is fair. Bonnie, a middle-aged woman who was in town to visit her graduate student son, saw the pricing system as establishing an equivalence: "They choose what to give you and you choose what to give them." She casts this equivalence in terms of free choice, and then goes further in reflecting on how that choice is made.

> I would come back, come back on a Sunday night for this. The food was delicious, but even beyond that, it shows integrity and trust. They trust you. It calls on you to bring forth a higher consciousness. To respond to that trust.

Bonnie is invoking a very different stage of moral development in her reasoning as compared with the other diners mentioned. In Kohlberg's moral development theory, Bonnie's comments reflect a concern with a larger social contract that includes a concern with the best interests of the other person. Her feeling of a "call . . . to bring forth a higher consciousness" is the burden Alexander was wanting to avoid. Kohlberg refers to reasoning such as Bonnie's as a postconventional, social-contract orientation toward moral decisions (stage 5). Kohlberg's research found that it is uncommon for someone to reach this level of moral development, but perhaps it is consequential when some do.

In his e-mail several days later, Bonnie's son, Eli, considers moral decisions in a similar manner. His e-mail first mentions being aware of similar pricing systems in cyberspace for shareware and open-source software, as well as for an MP3 format album released by Radiohead, but then he notes the ease of sharing "ones and zeros" rather than something as "visceral" as food. He then considers the perspective of both parties as he articulates his thoughts about this pricing system:

> The restaurant that serves food with a non-compulsory payment policy is making the statement: "We are so confident in our own

ability to provide excellent food and service that we leave it to the customer to put a price value on it." The restaurant that does this is agreeable with everybody, because the price is never too high, nor the food insufficient for the price paid; the standard of price and quality is not determined through conservative economics, but the method of doing business seeks to bring out a standard that is established by the integrity and conscience of people. While this may alienate some, who simply want to pay an unambiguous amount with all honesty and do not want to feel as though their conscience were being tested, it is a welcomed appeal to sincerity for others.

Eli thinks the pay-what-you-think-is-fair pricing system will result in high levels of consumer satisfaction. He realizes that it relies on customers behaving out of a sense of integrity and after considering their consciences. He is on target in anticipating that some patrons, such as Alexander, might not want to be tested in this way.

Eli's father paid $60 for the three people in their party, exactly the amount paid per person by Alexander, Kostas, Kelly, and Michael, although some paid an additional amount for a tip. Although they vary sharply in the form of moral reasoning they use, they converge on price.

But does the pay-what-you-think-*is-fair* pricing system work? Does Roshan make a profit on the Sunday evening dinners? Some consumers mentioned being concerned about that, but then rationalized that if this restaurant has been in operation for several years, it must be working out. Eli expressed concerns but noted other benefits that might accrue: "It may not be a successful business model, but I think it is a good public relations and marketing strategy; it seeks to make itself unforgettable to members of the community by its sincerity and quality." In a space that seats about 50 patrons, the restaurant serves more than 125 people on a Sunday night, with the average amount paid per person being $18. Roshan assures me that it is profitable as long as a customer pays at least $9. He claims they have never had a customer decide to pay nothing.

If his staff are asked what most people pay or what a minimum should be, Roshan has asked them to say "$15 plus tip." He proudly claims that once a couple paid $150 because they liked the idea so much. If someone pays less than $10 per person, Roshan says he will tell them, "We can't make it for that. If you are hungry and need the food and can't pay more, that is fine. But we can't make it for that." He insists he hasn't had to initiate that conversation often.

What can be learned from the pay-what-you-think-is-fair dinner? It calls on customers to apply the level of moral reasoning they understand, which varies by person. It does not result in an unprofitable evening. In fact, customers pay on average an amount that is above what is recommended without tip. It seems to generate goodwill, other than with those like Alexander, who don't want to be burdened with moral reasoning.

It seems to build a relation (sometimes real and sometimes imagined) between customers and the owner, and occasionally the staff as well, as with Troy (thirty-two, social worker for a religious organization):

> If we [he and his wife] were wealthy, we would pay more. It shows the value they put on creating a superior environment with wonderful food. They value their customers. I felt a camaraderie with them. It places a certain responsibility on the customer to think about how they earn their livelihood, the cook, the dishwasher, the owner.

For those not bothered by what some see as a "burden" and others call a "responsibility," the pay-what-you-think-is-fair pricing system humanizes the transaction. It removes the moment of paying from the realm of purely economic relations that Marx (1867) lamented in his writing on commodity fetishism and restores it to the realm of human relations. That is community building at its finest.

Despite the Supreme Court's assertion in its *Citizens United* decision, this may be a realm in which corporations are not people. It appears in this case that the pay-what-you-think-is-fair payment system works because the owner is a person, front and center in the restaurant. The concept of *fairness* is invoked in the midst of an embodied person-to-person relationship. In particular with local residents, which most of the restaurant's patrons are, that relationship is embedded in the geographic community.

However, in 2013 when the restaurant chain Panera Bread tried a pay-what-you-want pricing system for one menu item, there was no human-to-human relationship embedded in a local community that was invoked when the customer decided how much to pay. Panera discontinued the payment system in its restaurants, but continued it in a few Panera Cares restaurants that are run as a charity to assist in feeding the hungry. So in the context of the pay-what-you-think-is-fair payment systems, it does not appear that corporations are like human owners. Empirical work is needed to assess the extent to which human owner-to-customer relationships and community embeddedness are central features of pay-what-you-think-is-fair pricing system that works.

Taken together, the farm stand and the Indian restaurant cases provide a new perspective on the theoretically impoverished economic concept of *willingness to pay* (Hanneman 1991), frequently studied in marketing contexts (Homburg, Koschate, and Hoyer 2005). As considered in economics and marketing, willingness to pay is a numerical amount of money. However, as indicated by in-store security cameras, cashiers who oversee payment for each item, and even Costco's second-level review of the correspondence between a receipt and items in a cart before a customer can exit the store, most retail activity takes place in an environment that presumes consumers' moral *unwillingness* to pay unless carefully supervised. Moral willingness to pay is quite different from economic willingness to pay; moral willingness to pay allows consumers to operate out of agency, whereas economic willingness to pay is only be expressed within an expensive structure that constrains actors by forcing them to pay something.

Tuition Variance Plan

The fourth empirical context is a private K–8 school in an area with a very wide range of incomes and levels of wealth. The area's top levels of income and wealth are among the highest in the nation, and the cost of living index is over twice the national average. The school wants all parents who desire to send their children to the school to be served. As a result, the school has developed a tuition-setting system that differs from the more typical, sliding-scale approach that offers financial aid following a determination of need based on income. Instead, the school operates what is called a tuition variance plan.

Any family that wants to be considered for a variance from the standard tuition amount participates with school representatives in a confidential conversation in which each party reveals all income and budget information to the other party. The school explains what its plans are for the coming year, and therefore what level of financial resources it needs from the parent body as a whole. The family then explains what its plans and goals are and how its financial resources will be used in meeting them. Through conversation, a mutually agreed-upon form and level of family contributions to the school for the coming year are determined. The family's contributions can be in many forms including a combination of tuition payments, assets donated, or work performed on behalf of the school.

The school's administration resists using a sliding scale because they believe it misses important differences in family situations and goals that they want to honor. In explaining the tuition variance program, administrators use the example of the difference between two families with similar levels of income and wealth: one family wants to take a European vacation in the coming year because their children's grandparents live there and are in declining health, whereas the other family wants to take a European vacation because they enjoy travel. The school wants to see the first family accomplish their goal and therefore may accept slightly less from them this year in tuition, whereas the school would ask whether the second family would consider taking a less expensive vacation this year in order to be able to pay a higher tuition amount. Conversation would be used as the mechanism for reaching consensus between school administrators and each of the families regarding their school contribution for the year.

In explaining the program, the school also uses an example of needing to raise tuition slightly because the school has the goal of hiring a music teacher for the next year. This hire will mean that the school will no longer require all teachers to teach music to their students. Parents who are more interested in science may not be very supportive of this tuition increase and therefore may ask for a variance. In tuition variance conversations, administrators explain to these parents that because class sizes have grown, class teachers now need one period during the day to assemble all of the new science experiments that will be added in the coming year. So if the music teacher isn't hired, then the science lessons will suffer. Through the conversations, parents become aware of the interconnectedness of various line items in the school's budget and the need to maintain enrollment to spread costs for specialty classes across a large number of families.

These conversations differ from bargaining and negotiation of price in important ways. During bargaining and negotiation, each party is expected to advocate for his or her own self-interest. Instead, in the tuition variance program, both the school and the parents are explicitly guided to acknowledge their desire to help the other party reach his or her goals; they are each expected "to stretch in the direction of the other." Tuition variance conversations sometimes take place over multiple sessions until a mutually satisfactory plan is developed, perhaps necessitating modifications to either the school's or the parent's budgets or plans. This context is explored as an extreme case of the cocreation of price and is used to plumb the ways competition is muted and cooperation is brought to the fore in this ongoing buyer-seller relationship.

Some parents feel uncomfortable asking for a tuition adjustment, but do so. Marc had tears in his eyes during our interview as he explained that he and his wife had to reveal their spending patterns to the school representatives who conducted their conversation. He and his wife have frequent arguments and ongoing tension over what he regards as her excessive spending. To then have to ask the school to lower their tuition amount felt to him like an aspect of his masculinity, his ability to provide for his children, was not meeting his internalized expectations. And yet, he was very grateful for the assistance and the educational opportunity for his children. As an immigrant to the United States, he appreciates the importance of education in his children's path to American success. And he is appreciative of the assistance, saying at the end of the interview, "It's not just me, me, me. [The school is] a community, and we have to look out for each other." So receiving a variance can contribute to the recipient's felt experience of communal connections to other parents.

Martin, also an immigrant who is an engineer, came to the United States to work for a start-up company that later experienced explosive growth. So initially, he and his wife, who did not have a visa that would allow her to work, were challenged economically and received a fifty-percent reduction in the tuition amount for their two children. With the uncertainty of their financial future given the start-up nature of the husband's employment, they did not want take money from savings to cover their two children's tuition at the school and were granted a variance. He described the conversation as "purely a private conversation. I didn't feel like it was a business meeting. So it was relatively relaxed. Pretty friendly atmosphere."

Yet, he also reported feeling "weird" asking for a variance. In his country of origin, he had been in what he estimates as the top twenty percent of earners, but in the United States, he found that his income quickly disappeared with the high cost of living in the area. He viewed the tuition variance program as one that acknowledged that "each one has to provide his share, working in other areas, and not have to provide it all in the financial area." However, some years later, his income and wealth had grown exponentially with the success of his employer, and he had become a major financial donor to the school. So some participants in the tuition variance program later become full-paying parents who also contribute financially beyond tuition.

Some parents who start out as full-paying parents hit a difficult time and subsequently ask for a tuition variance. Such was the case for many parents during the financial downturn that started in 2008. One father, George, works at a well-known technology company in a high-level position. However, he was in an elongated process of divorce with legal expenses that were so high, he withdrew money from savings each month to cover living expenses and legal fees. As a result, he requested a tuition variance for his portion of his two children's tuition. When asked how he felt about requesting a tuition variance, he explained,

George: "I'm actually quite embarrassed to be part of that program. I have a damn fine job with a damn good salary, but I'm going through a divorce and my legal expenses are through the sky and going up . . . Anything that I spend on tuition is coming straight out of savings. I make a boat load of money, so I'm kind of embarrassed to not pay something."

MW: "Although there's a justification for paying nothing. Let me be the devil's advocate on this one. If you're already pulling out of savings, why should you pay anything?"

George: "I was born a good Catholic. I've got all that guilt that comes from decades of genuflecting, I guess."

Despite George's negative cash flow each month, his moral compass makes him feel an obligation to pay something.

But things did not go as he expected in the tuition variance conversation. School representatives noted that George was contributing money to a 401(k) retirement fund that could instead be used to pay tuition. George tried to explain to them his logic behind contributing to the

401(k) program while withdrawing money from regular savings to meet his monthly expenses.

> I consider a 401(k) as . . . long-term savings with some tax advantages. The school doesn't. The school seems to think of it as savings . . . They didn't seem to quite follow the fact that if I put a dollar in then I get two dollars in long-term savings [because of his employer's matching program] . . . Remember I'm in a deficit spending kind of thing, so the way I view it is: . . . what I'm doing is I'm effectively taking some of my current savings and shifting it with tremendous advantage into a long-term savings plan.

As a result of his tuition variance conversation, George was given a tuition reduction that was not as large as what he had expected.

That led him to be sensitized to making comparisons with what he knew about the tuition variances received by other families; these comparisons used his moral framework for assessing fairness, much as was the case with the diners at the Indian restaurant. The recipients that he made comparisons with in our interview were teachers. Teachers and staff at the school are granted free tuition as a benefit of their employment, without having to provide all of the budget and financial information required of those in the tuition variance program. In essence, all teachers receive a similar salary, and those with children get an added benefit. But the comparison that bothered George the most was to teachers and staff who worked at the school and had children enrolled there but also had an employed spouse.

> A lot of the people that I knew that worked there were in situations . . . where the otherwise stay-at-home mom is now working on campus, so they can be with their children all day long. The dad is out making money and I know quite a few of those families where the dad was making two, three, four and five times what I was making . . . In the world controlled by George, what would happen is next year, we tell the faculty and staff right now, "Next year the tuition break evaporates. You're welcome to apply for the tuition variance program." . . . That would get the power families that live in the six and seven million dollar homes to be paying tuition."

So in a program designed to try to provide fairness in setting tuition based on individual situations, invidious comparisons nonetheless emerge among some who have benefitted from the program, albeit not as much as they had hoped.

Some parents who pay full tuition and thereby subsidize the lower payments by others stigmatize those who receive a tuition variance and informally monitor the other families' spending for signs that they could be paying more. Mary, who helped design the tuition variance program, described a time when this happened:

> It's strange how, as enlightened as we are, it's so easy for people to talk about tuition variance families in the same way you would talk about welfare . . . I have a colleague who I work with, just before [I was about to participate in a tuition variance] conversation or the day before, just came into my office, closed the door and said, "She [the mother with whom Mary was about to have a conversation] bought a dog for $1,000." She was really emotional about it.

Other interviewees mentioned overhearing criticism of the new car purchases or the vacations taken by families who had received a tuition variance.

On the whole, however, parents who were interviewed took the position that the tuition variance program insures that "everyone pays their fair share," enrollments remain stable through times when families experience temporary financial difficulties, and their children receive benefits from being in classrooms with economic diversity represented.

Conclusion

Across these four empirical contexts, it is clear that price is a complex relational concept grounded in a number of moral evaluations, both implicit and explicit. The relation between buyers and sellers blends moral and market logics, yet the embeddedness of market relations in existing or even imagined social ties is often ignored in pricing research. Further, the coexistence of gifts (from seller to buyer and from buyer to seller) within market exchanges needs much more attention in consumer research.

These contexts also highlight the need for deeper theorizing regarding the concept of customer loyalty, beyond simple repeat-purchase behavior. Explicating the kinds of moral reasoning that generate a form of loyalty that forgives transgressions would enhance our theoretical understanding, as well as move marketer efforts forward in attempts to build such loyalty. Clearly, empathy and trust are the foundation stones for such customer loyalty, and how to build these amid gesellschaft market transactions is an important unanswered question.

More broadly, what is the larger cultural impact of ever-present mechanisms and technologies that insure that customers pay, such as security cameras and Costco's second-level payment review? How instead might market organizations form relationships with customers such that the consumer's moral willingness to pay is enhanced, reducing or eliminating the need for these costly mechanisms and technologies? Under what conditions can trusting customers rather than subjecting them to surveillance generate greater loyalty? When can it add to profits by reducing costs and perhaps even permitting premium prices? In moving toward Holt's (2002) post-postmodern condition in which brands will be expected to serve as citizen artists, will companies be called upon to meet their civic obligation to form trusting relationships with people, both when they are consumers and when they are not in this role?

Of course, all four contexts are ones in which both buyers and sellers are embodied humans in a face-to-face relationship, where reciprocal moral obligations have long been present. However, what about online purchases, surrounded by anonymous reviews purported to be from other customers, and big data mining of information that allows microtargeting of appeals to consumers? What are the moral and cultural frames for pricing in such consumption settings? Quite frankly, we don't know. Certainly, when online, corporations are not people; the "firm" is a disembodied webpage. As such, the relationship is restricted to clicks, a form of communication that works well for dolphins, but is clearly less able to communicate complex relational meanings than human language is. Is that type of relationship less governed by moral reasoning than at the produce stand or the pay-what-you-think-is-fair dinner? Is the online environment one more step toward gesellschaft and away from the pockets of gemeinschaft described here?

As promised at the outset, I hope this essay has raised more questions than it has answered. There is much that we do not know about the moral and cultural foundations of pricing. More importantly, there is much we need to learn about how pricing approaches that involve the consumer more directly in a price-setting relationship with the seller can create cultural contexts where all actors can, as Bonnie stated, "bring forth a higher consciousness."

Bibliography

Belk, Russell W. "The Perfect Gift." In *Gift Giving: A Research Anthology.* Edited by Cele Otnes and Richard F. Beltramini. Bowling Green, OH: Bowling Green University Popular Press, 1996, 59–84.

Bolton, Ruth N. "A Dynamic Model of the Duration of the Customer's Relationship with a Continuous Service Provider: The Role of Satisfaction." *Marketing Science* 17, no. 1 (1998): 45–65.

Chan, Tat Y., Vrinda Kadiyali, and Young-Hoon Park. "Willingness to Pay and Competition in Online Auctions." *Journal of Marketing Research* 44 (May 2007): 324–33.

Chew, Jonathan. "Why American Airlines Passengers are Pretty Ticked Off." *Fortune*, November 18, 2015.

Fisher, Robert J., Mark Vandenbosch, and Kersi D. Antia. "An Empathy-Helping Perspective on Consumers' Responses to Fund-Raising Appeals." *Journal of Consumer Research* 35 (October 2008): 519–31.

Fournier, Susan. "Consumers and Their Brands: Developing Relationship Theory in Consumer Research." *Journal of Consumer Research* 24 (March 1998): 343–73.

Gendron, Richard and G. William Dornhoff. *The Leftmost City: Power and Progressive Politics*. Boulder: Westview Press, 2008.

Gneezy, Ayelet, Uri Gneezy, Leif D. Nelson, Amber Brown. "Shared Social Responsibility: A Field Experiment in Pay-What-You-Want Pricing and Charitable Giving." *Science* 329 (July 16, 2010): 325–7.

Granovetter, Mark. "Economic Action and Social Structure: The Problem of Embeddedness." *American Journal of Sociology* 91 (November 1985): 481–510.

Hannemann, William. "Willingness to Pay and Willingness to Accept: How Much Can They Differ?" *American Economic Review* 81 (June 1991): 635–47.

Holt, Doug. "Why Do Brands Cause Trouble? A Dialectical Theory of Consumer Culture and Branding." *Journal of Consumer Research* 29 (June 2002): 70–90.

Homburg, Christian, Nicole Koschate, and Wayne D. Hoyer. "Do Satisfied Customers Really Pay More? A Study of the Relationship between Customer Satisfaction and Willingness to Pay." *Journal of Marketing* 69 (April 2005): 84–96.

Kim, Ju-Young, Martin Natter, and Martin Spann. "Pay What You Want: A New Participative Pricing Mechanism." *Journal of Marketing* 73 (January 2009): 44–58.

Kohlberg, Lawrence, Charles Levine, and Alexandra Hewer. *Moral Stages: A Current Formulation and a Response to Critics*. Basel, NY: Karger, 1983.

Marx, Karl. "The Fetishism of the Commodity and Its Secret." In *The Consumer Society Reader*. Edited by Juliet B. Schor and Douglas B. Holt. New York: The Free Press, 2000/orig. 1867, 331–42.

Mazumdar, Tridib, S. P. Raj, and Indrajit Sinha. "Reference Price Research: Review and Propositions." *Journal of Marketing* 69 (October 2005): 84–102.

Reiner, Gerhard and Christian Traxler. "Norms, Moods, and Free Lunch: Longitudinal Evidence on Payments from a Pay-What-You-Want Restaurant." *Journal of Socio-Economics* 41 (August 2012): 476–83.

Ritzer, George. *The McDonaldization of Society*, 6th ed. Los Angeles: Sage, 2011.

Rust, Roland T., Katherine N. Lemon, and Valarie A. Zeithaml. "Return on Marketing: Using Customer Equity to Focus Marketing Strategy." *Journal of Marketing* 68 (January 2004): 109–27.

Schmidt, Klaus M., Martin Spann, and Robert Zeithammer. "Pay What You Want as a Marketing Strategy in Monopolistic and Competitive Markets." *Management Science* 61 (June 2015): 1217–36.

Srinivasan, Shuba, Koen Pamels, and Vincent Nijs. "Demand-Based Pricing versus Past-Price Dependence: A Cost-Benefit Analysis." *Journal of Marketing* 72 (March 2008): 15–27.

Tönnies, Ferdinand. *Gemeinschaft und Gesselschaft/Community and Society*. New Brunswick, NJ: Transaction Books, 1988/orig. 1887.

Wahba, Phil. "Shoplifting, Worker Theft Cost Retailers $32 Billion Last Year." *Fortune*, June 24, 2015.

Zelizer, Viviana. *The Social Meaning of Money*. New York: Basic Books, 1994.

Part II

Revisiting Role Configurations

Families, Gender, and Consumption

6 The Conceit of the Gift

Exploring the Gift Circuits of Registry[1]

Tonya Williams Bradford
and John F. Sherry, Jr.

The consumer research literature recognizes three kinds of giving, broadly construed: monadic, dyadic, and systemic. A monadic gift, also called a self-gift, is a gift given to oneself. Dyadic giving occurs when a gift is given from one social unit (e.g., an individual or a corporation) to another; a reciprocal gift may or may not be given in return within the context of this transaction. Systemic giving occurs when individuals give to and receive from members of a community whose ethos demands and persistence requires the circulation of gifts in a generalized reciprocal fashion.

The registry is a fortuitous institution for the study of the interrelationship of these three forms of gift giving. Sherry (1996, 223) identified the registry as an opportunity to investigate "the ultimate commodification of the gift economy" and described it as the "institutionalization of monadic giving." The former observation still rings true, but the latter appears impoverished. Thus, we have approached the registry afresh by asking ourselves, "What kind of giving might this be?" Throughout our study, it became clear that our informants discerned several kinds of gift giving unfolding concurrently within the institution.

The American wedding, with an increasingly staggering financial cost (U.S. estimates approach $50 billion annually), has long been a topic of cultural discourse. Ponder the box office success of such films as *My Big Fat Greek Wedding* (Zwick 2002), *Wedding Crashers* (Dobkin 2005), *The Wedding Singer* (Coraci 2008), and *Bride Wars* (Winick 2009), or the television program *Bridezillas* (Cappria, Woodruffe, and Reid 2005). Behold the spectacle of the annual running of the brides at Filene's Basement. The wedding has been the focus of much attention in consumer research in particular (Otnes and Pleck 2003) and sociology in general (Howard 2006). As the context in which the registry process is embedded, the wedding has symbolic overtones that rival its commercial significance and that are essential to our interpretation.

The gift registry was formalized in the late nineteenth century, by the mid-twentieth century was established as the essential template for wedding gift-giving practices, and in the twenty-first century, the registry has become foundational (Bradford and Sherry 2013). Retailers now exercise significant influence over gift search, acquisition, and disposition (Howard 2006; Otnes and Pleck 2003; Penner 2004). The registry is a fascinating arena in which cultural and personal attitudes toward gift giving are negotiated.

The marketing and consumer research literature has treated three particular variants of gift giving—monadic, dyadic, and systemic—as if they were discrete enterprises with distinct antecedents and consequences. Our qualitative analysis of wedding registries explores the interaction of these ostensibly discontinuous forms within the context of a unifying commercial institution. Our investigation of this institution extends the theorizing on these previously segregated types and advances a more synthetic approach to the interpretation of gift giving.

In the present study, we discovered ways in which each of these forms manifested and interacted. We analyze category dynamics as they emerge from our data and use our findings to propose a synthetic interpretation of the registry that seeks to unify the three aspects of gift giving in a common integrative framework. We devote a bit more description to the gift-to-self practice, as it will be less familiar to audiences beyond the immediate consumer culture theory orbit, and stint a bit on the other, more well-recognized categories.

We draw on our larger ethnographic and netnographic work with stakeholders in the wedding registry (Bradford and Sherry 2013) and focus most specifically on interviews with registrants, those individuals engaged to be married or who recently married. They hail from heterosexual, first-time marriages, primarily Christian denominations, and represent a variety of occupations and socioeconomic backgrounds. We recruited informants through personal contacts, print and social media solicitation, and snowball sampling. Our engagement across informants occurred before, during, and after the actual process of registry, to encompass the practice holistically. We also include retailer interview excerpts to round out the discussion. In total, seventy-two consumers and fifteen retailers were interviewed. We employ pseudonyms for informants.

Giving Gifts to Oneself: Monadic Gift Giving

An emergent stream of inquiry momentarily shifted the spotlight from donor-recipient dyads to the solitary individual as a donor-recipient monad. Prompted by suggestions from Levy (1982) and Mick (1986) that people give gifts to themselves, researchers began to train their sights on the intrapsychic and social dynamics that might account for such interested giving. The former stream explored monadic giving motivations and construed monadic giving as indulgent self-communication both premeditated and bound by context (Mick and DeMoss 1990a, 1990b). A typology of the self-gift—puritanic, romantic, therapeutic, and holiday—emerged from this predominantly psychological line of inquiry (Mick 1991, 1996). The latter stream explored the collision of role expectations and cultural values that often caused profound frustration and deep ambivalence to interfere with authentic satisfaction in monadic transactions (Sherry 2005; Sherry and McGrath 1989; Sherry, McGrath, and Levy 1995). In these studies, giving gifts to self emerged as an imperfect corrective to ritual rupture, a premodern effort to mitigate postmodern alienation.

Missing from the literature on monadic giving is a comprehensive socio-psychological examination of the phenomenon in a fixed context. Holding the context constant in the present study allows us to comprehensively examine the motives and mores driving the range of behaviors tied to self-gifts. Further, the conception of the monadic gift as an indulgence that arises from a manipulation of dyadic giving can be examined effectively in a registry context.

Our informants routinely describe their lived experience of the registry gift as phenomenologically identical to the self-gift:

> It's a gift that they are giving themselves—they already know what they are going to get. They know what they want. (Dennis)

> After we get all the basics taken care of, we'll talk about the splurges . . . realistic gifts . . . like gifts to myself . . . I need a Panini press. (Gloria)

The registry effectively brackets, if not expunges, the stigma of self-interest from the exchange, permitting the couple to act essentially as a surrogate for the donor on this particular plane. In fact, as our informants imply, there is little stigma attached to the monadic gift, but self-interest may occasion a qualm, as it sometimes seems to attenuate the social dimension of systemic giving.

Special indulgences that recipients might not fund themselves, or true wants (vs. those incorrectly intuited by others), appear monadic in character. The "wish list" concept is frequently volunteered by registrants, a notion echoed by retailers: "It's probably the only time in your life that you can come up with a wish list and somebody else pays for it . . . I always tell brides" (Joan; Bloomingdale's).

Sometimes couples will hedge their bets, giving themselves an incremental gift by exploiting—sometimes at the marketer's advice—registry policy:

> After their wedding, whatever is left on their registry, [the couple] can take 20% off of . . . I always tell people, over-register, even if you don't really want it for your wedding. If it's something you might say, "Oh, I could give that to my sister for her anniversary," I'll just use the 20% off. (Jackie; Quince)

Finally, donor resistance to the monadic aspect of the registry gift is apparent in the phenomenon of shopping "off registry":

> People . . . have gone to the people's registry at the big box and don't like what they see and want to get something much more personal and intimate. We run into that all the time. They say, "It's just wrong, I don't want to just go get whatever's on their registry." But of course, we don't think it's wrong. (Cindy; Beyond Plates)

By so sacralizing their gift, off-registry donors remove their present from the commoditizing orbit of the monadic and situate it more firmly in the realm of the dyadic gift. This resistance is mirrored in many couples' ambivalence about the registry, which they ascribe in part to the presumption that seems to attach to the practice of selecting one's own gifts, an implicit violation of the dyadic norm.

Monadic gifts have a key role in "molding and sustaining self-concepts" (Mick 1996, 104). Couples jointly create and present desired possessions through the registry and thus expose the "we" they expect to become (Bradford and Sherry 2013). Given that the registry gift must abide by the constraint of occasion and the conditions of celebration and financial surplus, it can also arise from traditional self-gift motives. Of the core motives for monadic giving, romantic and puritanical motives are most evident among our informants (Mick 1996).

The romantic motivation is described as uninhibited, imaginative and self-indulgent (Mick 1996):

> Just going to the store and picking out all this stuff is just kind of fun, because you're picking out cool stuff . . . 2, 3 months later, the stuff just starts showing up. So, that's kind of a cool thing . . . We registered for the same things at multiple places occasionally. (Mike)

He describes his gift selection and receipt experience as akin to magic, in that possessions appear with little if any acknowledgment of the efforts or intentions of gift givers in the process.

The romantic motives for self-gifts are further reinforced by retailers:

> The registry is a great service to the wedding guests. The guests want to be a part of the event. They want to participate, and by letting people know what you want, you make it easier and more enjoyable for the guests. (Deborah; Bed Bath & Beyond)

The opportunity to select abundant gift choices is encouraged by retailers and justified to registrants as a selfless act. Retailers support registrants by providing specific guidelines on choosing ideal gifts, thereby removing a tremendous burden from anxious gift givers.

Self-indulgence is reflected in the ways in which couples participate in the process and is revealed in the manner in which individuals invite the ritual audience to participate in the registry: "It was a really easy way to get . . . the word out and about what we wanted" (Marie). Because the registry is tied to marriage as a milestone, there is an element of self-reward in self-selected gifts: "Our next big item on our 'To Do' list is registering . . . I knew nothing about how many, where, when, what, why, etc . . . Why? because you're special and you deserve to be showered with gifts. :)"(Bettina; online). The notion of self-indulgence also may be present and anticipated with little, if any, rationalization: "I am looking forward to going through the store with my future hubby and clicking on every single item we want our wedding guests to purchase for us! I get excited thinking about the day" (Ellen; online). Often, the rationalization accompanying self-indulgence is related to recipients' desired outcomes. For example, registrants may seek volume in presents through different donor segments:

> Register for a lot of things in every price range. People who want to get you a gift will use the registry (and you can return it for cash) and people who want to give you $ will do so regardless if you have a registry . . . People are usually gift people or $ people—gift people give gifts (even if there isn't a registry) and $ ppl give $, even if there is a registry . . . Let people give the way they are comfortable giving. (Chelsea; online)

Self-indulgence is reflected and negotiated through the registry by recipients with donors. These negotiations continue through reformulation where the disposition of the gift—keep, regift, return—is determined, which is an atypical experience in traditional self-gifting.

Puritanical motivations also are in evidence:

> A lot of it is doing your own research and finding out what is right for you. I think a lot of people are ready for that step but I think you really have to know who you are and what you really need before you even cross through the threshold. (Helen)

It is not a simple or thoughtless wish list that is presented to gift givers but rather a carefully constructed compilation of what is correct or appropriate. Further rationalization in support of self-indulgence is presented in the effort required to develop the gift registry:

> If people are going to buy you gifts, and if you want to get things that will be useful, or, things that you want, then, you should register. Otherwise, you can get all kinds of stuff . . . We just thought, we might as well register because that's what everyone does. That ensures that you'll get what you want. (Jason)

Gifts are mobilized as building blocks in the creation of the new family unit. Although there is the desire to preserve or experiment with an ideal "we," registrants also bow to social norms: "[Our registry is] a nice way of saying, 'Here's what to get,' that it's something we'll actually use and enjoy and you can get your money's worth" (Karen). The puritanical motivations are evident not only in rationalizations for self-indulgence but also in rationalizations reflecting concern for gift givers. Self-reflection is believed to be a prerequisite to search in preparation for creating the registry. There is a practicality and rationality underlying choice. Recipients seek to minimize risk and maximize reward.

Our informants report an ambivalent alliance of romantic and puritanical motives underlying their self-gifting: "I went to the wedding registry thinking it is so cool it's almost like spending other people's money. I love to shop for things for myself. This is not shopping for clothes, it's shopping for boring things" (Barbara). Whereas shopping is sport in some sectors of American society, registry is a new experience. There is tension between enthusiasm and boredom. There is also tension between what is desired versus what is necessary:

> I mean there was a really nice pot that was $119 and that's a lot of money for a pot. All these people are going to see what you selected, and the accompanying prices. I think it's one of those things that you don't want to ask too much . . . you don't want people to feel that they have to get you this stuff. (Helen)

Rationalization pervades the process from beginning to end, from making the initial request, through managing the disappointment when expectations are frustrated.

This hybrid motive amplifies the ambivalence often experienced in conventional monadic giving, as the recipient feels compelled to take the donors' alleged perceptions into account during cognitive and emotional acquisition. The thrill of absolutely discretionary acquisition is tempered by the mundane character of the gift. There is often a tension between want and need, luxury and necessity, excessive and reasonable. Even ostensibly win-win scenarios are colored by misgiving. There is usually a balance to be sought, which presupposes an underlying ethic of propriety that must be discerned and respected.

Exchanging Gifts with Others: Dyadic Gift Giving

The circuit of gifts between discrete donors and recipients has been the dominant focus of consumer research into gift giving. Pioneered by Belk (1976), formally modeled by Sherry (1983), and elaborated in a host of insightful ways by them and others, this stream has been most heavily influenced by sociological and anthropological theorizing. Social network effects on gift giving have revealed the relational nature of gift giving (Lowrey, Otnes, and Ruth 2004). However, with few exceptions (Marcoux 2009; Otnes, Lowrey, and Kim 1993; Ruth, Brunel, and Otnes 2004; Ruth, Otnes, and Brunel 1999; Wooten and Wood 2004), the role of the recipient in the dyad has been virtually overlooked. The embeddedness of gift giving in social relations—the cultural grounding of the gift—has also been demonstrated (Bradford 2009; Joy 2001). Even the personal anxiety and social disruption occasioned by gift giving has been chronicled (McGrath, Sherry, and Levy 1993; Wooten 2000). The dyadic literature has assumed a posture that is largely female-, giver-, and Christmas-centric, which leaves a number of avenues open for additional inquiry.

Missing from this literature is a sense of how the phenomenon contributes to social organization. Previous studies have largely asserted the significance of gift exchange to social system maintenance and change, adducing the organic solidarity postulated by theorists of the premodern phenomenon. Further, there is a tension in the dyadic literature between conceptions of the gift that are exchange focused and oriented around reciprocity, and those that reject the view that these forces compose the nucleus of the gift. By focusing on a single ritual (the wedding) that underwrites both commercial and social institutions, we are able to establish a very clear relationship between ritual action and social reproduction. The coincidence of these conceptions in the same phenomenon is a worthy subject of investigation.

We present our informant responses to dyadic giving practice roughly by Sherry's (1983) processual stages—gestation, prestation, and reformulation. Informants describe sentiments and behaviors related to gestation in a number of ways. The occasion allows for calculation and none-too-subtle hinting: "This is a chance for people to buy us stuff . . . if you want something, put it on there" (Tom). In gestation, it is common for gift givers to obtain guidance from recipients as to what is desired (Sherry 1983). This is balanced with the desire for propriety in self-presentation: "I worried about the perception of [my registry] . . . people looking at it, being like, 'Oh she's so greedy.'. . . I just felt so awkward about the whole asking for gifts thing" (Gale). Where hints and suggestions are commonplace in dyadic gift giving, the registry formalizes this process between gift recipients and gift givers:

> I mean, that seems to be the purpose that a registry really serves, which is to help people . . . feel comfortable, and obviously the people who know you better would know your tastes and would feel free to give you . . . something very personal. (Dawn)

Gifts are a means of influence (Belk, Wallendorf, and Sherry 1989; Caplow 1984; Mauss 1967; Sherry 1983). The recipient, acting as gift giver, chooses what should be received and may constrain what influence the recipient will entertain from the gift giver. Yet, gift givers are not without opinions as to what appropriate registry choices may be:

> Put some board games or lawn games on your registry too! From the viewpoint of a guest to 5 weddings this past year, we love getting the fun things from registries and it's really hard to get excited about buying a present for a really good friend when all they're asking for are towels and plates. (Erica; online)

Although the registry is intended to guide gift giving, recipients may remain open to donors exercising agency in gift creation, if the donor is well known to the recipient:

> Our close friends will probably get something that has a little more significance, something that expresses more our personality. [Because] the registry can only have so much personality, it's harder for people to get that unless they really know you. (Helen)

Requests and relationships must be carefully calibrated, so that gifts may be sacralized and sociality facilitated.

Prestation gives rise to a range of conventional practices, from acknowledging the sacred essence of the gift, to reveling in the mystery that is its immaterial heart:

> I don't know that here you could say: 'No gifts please; just cash.'. . . The whole registering . . . just makes it seem consumer-oriented . . . I mean, registering at specific stores, for specific items, so that people can buy you those items . . . makes it seem very consumer-oriented. (Jason)

Jason acknowledges that an aspect of gift giving, the copresence in exchange where the affective content of the gift is revealed (Sherry 1983), is absent with registry. Though the registry may reduce the sacred essence of the gift, the symbolism of the gift may be impoverished as well:

> For some people, to give money as a wedding present is traditional. For some, it's the height of rudeness . . . And there's no telling, who feels what way . . . One of our friends did write us a check and that was very generous . . . it felt a little uncomfortable. I mean, I was touched, 'cause she is a good friend. (Dawn)

Though there is ambivalence in receipt of a cash gift, recipients acknowledge there are different types of gift givers: "There are cash givers and gift givers, and both groups will give you their preference regardless of whether you register or not. If you register, at least you have some way of suggesting items that you want" (Gwen; online). Although money has a place in gift giving (Bradford 2009), in the contemporary United States, it is acceptable in very intimate relationships, but not much beyond. As with Dawn, such a gift is accepted, but with hesitancy (Sherry 1983). Although cash may provoke discomfort, commodified cash (translated as the obligatory registry gift) does less so.

Some gifts are eagerly anticipated, even when the set of received gifts is selected and known by the recipient far in advance of receipt:

> I was horrible about [checking my registry], like twice a day when it was close to, right before a shower. I don't feel like it spoiled the surprise. I know some people don't look at it at all because it's like shaking a Christmas present . . . and the surprise is in who gave it to us. (Alice)

A gift package may be probed, and traditional surprise deflected from the gift itself to the donor. The intimate knowledge of exchange partners upon which successful dyadic giving hinges is also in evidence:

> Sometimes people give you a gift, and it's not something that you would have bought for yourself. But, you end up really liking it. So, it's like if someone gets a creative gift. It might not be something I would have ever picked out for us. But, you might really like it. (Jason)

Off-registry purchases are high-risk, high-reward affairs, and personal taste is discerned and revealed through social intimacy.

Reformulation dynamics are reflected in our informants' comments. In particular, they express awe in the face of the social bond the gift affirms:

> Having all these people get you this stuff . . . pots and pans that you get really excited to use, still, a year later it's pretty cool . . . It's kind of humbling that there's that many people that would buy these nice gifts just because we got married. (Mike)

The network will provide. And, people are in awe of the power of social institutions. They marvel at how much effort is demanded, how much obligation is mobilized, and how much satisfaction is generated by the system.

Bringing It All Together: Systemic Gift Giving

Giesler (2006) extended inquiry into the domain of consumer gift systems. Seeking inspiration in the realm of the premodern gift, he interpreted file-sharing behavior in the online community Napster as a "polyadic" or "rhizomatic" network of gift transactions that creates social solidarity among exchange partners (Giesler 2006, 286–9). A gift system exhibits social distinctions, a norm of reciprocity, and a complex of ritual and symbolism. In the process of file sharing, donors and recipients participate in a primarily anonymous generalized reciprocity, giving to and taking from the collective rather than only from repeat exchange partners, and differentially honoring the ethos of the community. The solidarity thus engendered is more "nomadic" than the "organic" character of premodern communities, and the cyber gift itself is "nonsacrificial" in comparison to its premodern analog (Giesler 2006, 287, 289).

Although responsive to the need to demonstrate the ability of the postmodern gift to contribute to social cohesion in a premodern mold, Giesler's choice of the cyber gift as an exemplar is problematic. The tribal ethos of online communities notwithstanding, the binding force of file sharing as described is not persuasively demonstrated. Polyadic giving is simply monadic giving beneath a dyadic veneer. Nomadic polyads seem "systemic" in only a very limited network sense. The systems described by Giesler have more in common with the pirate utopias described by Bey (1984) than societies in either pre- or postmodern eras. Assigning the label "gift" to this activity is also problematic, given the excision of the ancient heart of the gift—sacrifice—from the exchange. The music file dwells in a murky conceptual hinterland along the theft-sharing (Belk 2010) continuum, its circulation propelled by monadic giving and potlatch-nuanced egotism more than a commitment to building social solidarity. In his magisterial history of the concept, Johns (2009, 35) notes that seminal authors such as Thucydides and Cicero regarded piracy as an irritant to "civilized order" itself, a threat we understand as distinctly opposed to the society-engendering practice of gift giving.

We offer an example of a system more firmly rooted in the gift, a more organic system than the illicit character of file sharing affords. By examining an actual gift system of considerable historical depth and vigor, we are able to investigate both the commercial and cultural influences shaping stakeholders' behavior. The interaction of social and commercial institutions to produce, maintain, and alter the system over time is an interesting phenomenon to contemplate.

In their analysis of the structural mechanics of bridging and bonding that animates intracommunity gift giving in post-Katrina Mardi Gras, Weinberger and Wallendorf (2012, 87) explore the entanglement of moral and market economies in a way that has more relevance than Giesler's (2006) for our own theorizing of systemic gifting. In their case, donors of higher social status give a token gift anonymously—and often randomly, with little attention to recipient characteristics—to recipients of lower social status, without receiving material reciprocity in return and without establishing a personal relationship with recipients. This enhances social solidarity but preserves social inequality. In our case, donors of equivalent or superior economic means give a considered and often costly gift to a pair of recipients with whom they have a personal relationship, with the intention of inducting the pair into a new and often commensurate social status of "married couple" or new "family," without receiving direct material reciprocity but with consciousness (however grudging) of an obligation to participate in generalized reciprocity over their life course. This enhances social solidarity through a provisioning practice aimed in part at alleviating social inequality. In each case, even though the components are often strikingly different, the social system itself is reinforced organically (we would even say created) by the gift instead of mechanically by theft. Symbolic boundaries are dissolved, rather than created (Weinberger 2015), by registry gifts.

A common refrain from our informants addresses the foundational nature of the conformity that animates the registry process. Further, the commercial pressure that once originated and now orchestrates the ritual reinforces the demand to conform: "I think part of the things that we did do are customs . . . it's part of the whole wedding thing. It's expected that you register for your gifts" (Jason). The institution is shot through with social expectation and sanction, which is palpable for our informants.

Although there is a commonsensical belief that couples must register, there is a tension between the social norm of registry and the experience of gifts. Whereas registrants express ambivalence about the registry process, there is not much, if any, ambivalence about the outcome of the registry: "Well, partly because I think everybody else does it. That was a big factor. And we wanted presents!" (Frank). Custom requires and desire demands participation in the system. Individual agency is subordinated to the forces of community.

The retail mirroring of the social structure that drives the registry process is a powerful sustainer of the ritual and supports the social network: "Some of our guests will want to see and touch. They are not comfortable making an online purchase. So with Williams-Sonoma, you know all of the stuff is going to be in the store" (Bill). Because most gifts are purchased (Cheal 1988), retailers act as important partners in the execution of the registry process with other stakeholders. Donors and recipients reward retailer partnership with patronage:

[We] also [registered at] national stores, which helps, because I am from the East Coast . . . And we're inviting a lot of my friends and family from there to our wedding. So we thought it would be easiest for friends and family. (Dawn)

Degrees of convenience are tailored to network members' technological sophistication. Social mobility and geographic dispersion of the gift system and social network must constantly be evaluated.

Finally, the system that enables the ritual must be adjusted by the principal actors:

> Someone in my family said it's good to register for a couple of big-ticket items cause people will go in on it together . . . I think both of us felt a little uncomfortable putting a $200 item on the registry. But there were certain people who were going in on it or a certain person who wanted to spend that much money . . . It was real relief, there is an option. (Karen)

Hinting is used to shape behavior within the gift system. Recipients signal not only which items are desired but also which gift might be suitable from which donor. Recipients may thoughtfully consider the socioeconomic means of those who participate in the registry process:

> A lot of our friends . . . make a really good living. I almost anticipate them to spend more than a lot of my relatives, who are older and on fixed incomes. I wouldn't expect [my relatives] to buy expensive gifts for us . . . I'm just thinking that our friends would spend more because of their current economic status than a lot of my older relatives. (Jason)

Calibrating expectations to the social network and using knowledgeable brokers are important recipient activities. Ensuring that everyone in the network can participate, and thus forging social solidarity, is a principal concern. Tinkering with social and retail arrangements is among the greatest challenges faced by our informants. Paradoxically, the greatest threat to these intertwined systems is the possibility of a donor buying off registry. Doing so exercises creative personal choice in the service of acknowledging a deeper understanding of and conveying a more intimate relationship with the recipient while resisting market forces in an effort to transform an obligatory gift into a true one.

Synthetic Interpretation of Gift Giving

The registry simultaneously comprises several types of gift giving. Recipients give gifts to themselves through others, effectively hybridizing the monadic and dyadic gift; polyadic giving may be invoked as well. Recipients receive the provisions that will help them forge a life together, invested both with the good will of and strengthened ties to others. Donors give to recipients in conventional dyadic fashion, save for the conversion of the practice of hinting to formal order placing. Society provides the social networks, sanctioned institution, rite of passage, and obligatory gift occasion and receives a total institution, a commodified ritual, additional integration, and resistance in the form of off-registry purchase.

The registry is a ternary gift system that binds two interpenetrating social spheres: the network of kith and kin created by any particular marital union, and the collective networks of all the unions served by the channel offering. The former is centered on the solitary household, the latter on the aggregate of households comprising the social category of marrieds, a fundamental unit of social organization. Thus, social cohesion, the sharing of affect and infusion of self-concept in relationships, fuels the gift economy. As a commercial institution with awesome ritual efficacy, the registry is a powerful public sanctioning of newly achieved social status and continuing legitimacy of social form. Participation in a registry represents in significant measure the social consummation of a marriage.

The market economy may be embraced, and is often co-opted, to convey affect and support the creation and extension of kith and kin. To sacralize a gift emerging from such a commercially rationalized social nexus, stakeholders undertake a number of practices. Merchants offer customized services and amenities. Donors invest preselected options with personal meaning, gather personalized assortments, and pool resources for greater impact. Recipients tangibilize cognitive and emotional acquisition with elaborate search rituals, conducting copious research, role-playing the situations of their prospective donors, and publicly displaying the taste that helps define their union. Absolute commodification of gift giving is accommodated by some resource-challenged donors but is often resisted by those seeking to temper convenience with sentiment. Occasionally, the registry is rejected by a donor unwilling to break with the spirit of the gift who exercises creativity in their gift selection. Such extreme behavior is characteristic of more intimate relationships.

In registry, the cycle begins with monadic giving driven by romantic and puritanical motives. The self-indulgent aspects of both motives are attenuated through rationalizations of scale, achievement, and even concern for gift givers. The overt hinting represented in the formal registry initiates dyadic giving, where donors identify their gift of choice, present it at the designated time, and obtain recipient responses. In the case of registry, the dyadic exchange partners are more likely to be family units, where the cycle of gift giving is continued within larger groups of individuals within a social system over long periods of time. This extended gift giving represents a continual cycle of systemic gift giving, where members of social networks continually provide gifts to recipients in response to wedding registry. The registry comprises each of the three types of giving and is driven both by the desire for and necessity of social cohesion and is dependent upon channel partners in the marketplace to sustain the cycle.

General Discussion

The construal of the gift registry requires a willing suspension of disbelief on the part of its stakeholders. Within this institution, recipients do not request cash for the future purchase of desired items. Neither do they calculate the monetary value of a portfolio of goods, announce that amount to kith and kin, and request that the goal be met by their social network. Rather, they employ the conceit of the gift, grafting consumer-culture ethos to traditional wedding practice. This conceit demands both a tighter scripting of gift-giving ritual and a more liberal interpretation of its charter.

For example, Visser (2008, 119) notes that, in Western societies, life's necessities are "nearly always supplied by means other than gift giving," leaving the gift sphere free to focus solely on personal relationships and sentiment; further, gifts are most often given by individuals to individuals, which requires insight and empathy on the part of the donor. The gift registry is exceptional, if only nominally, in each of these regards. Donors often do supply staples, and principally to couples rather than individuals. Preordained presents must be sacralized, even if independently, by donors and recipients.

Further, convenience-driven institutions such as registry violate "two important elements of modern Western gift giving: the receiver's surprise and the giver's own decision-making" (Visser 2008, 81–2). The breach is partially redressed through wrapping and other means of personalization (Visser 2008, 82). The transformation of the gift into an "intimate offering" invested with the donor's spirit from a simple commercial transfer of an object to a recipient's domestic inventory poses a challenge for some donors and recipients; for others, convenience and practicality remove the issue from the realm of moral dilemma (Purbrick 2007, 141–2).

Finally, despite the forced, prescribed, and nonreciprocal nature of "gifts" better characterized as "tribute" offered to power (Visser 2008, 124), registry items manage to retain the aura of the gift. Registry gifts compose a benediction that society confers upon itself, through the couple, consecrating the new union as indispensable social reinforcement. These gifts are materializations of social approval, even if they are given by donors participating in a cultural practice that they also wish to oppose (Purbrick 2007, 33, 124).

Cultural production accounts stress the role of the bridal media—and institutions such as the registry in particular—in framing engagement as a rite of passage both mediated and memorialized by acquisition. Gifts become a material witness of status transition, in which an individual becomes a new kind of consumer, a new kind of self, and a member of a new kind of social unit (Mead 2007). Gifts symbolize the hope for a qualitatively different "domestic engagement" but are fraught with ambivalence because the registry is essentially a "form of licensed covetousness" that invites the couple to test the limits of acquisitiveness (Mead 2007, 112, 114). Such accounts frame the registry as the prospective bride's opportunity both to restock and to provision for married adulthood, an entitlement (Mead 2007, 110, 113) that is acknowledged even as it may be resented by donors.

Tellingly, cultural production accounts focus on the "registry" component to the near exclusion of the "gift" component composing the phenomenon. It is as if opportunism conflicts with ritual propriety, freighting the gift with such a measure of self-interest as to render the giving a mere commodity exchange. We find this ritual opportunism at work among most, if not all, of the registry's stakeholders and view it as one of the reasons for understanding the registry as a form of self-gift. Recipients grant themselves fulfillment of their precise wishes. Donors grant themselves convenience and exemption from embarrassment. Retailers grant themselves patronage and extended loyalty. This confluence of selfish motives conspires to reveal an aura of egoism that the dyadic ideal of gift giving is at pains to conceal, if not deny outright. The obligatory nature of the occasion combines with the near-obligatory character of the gift to create a context of self-indulgence in which the conceit of "giving" can be only tenuously maintained.

Imposing a strict economic view on the registry, Waldfogel (2009, 140) likens the practice to the sale of naming rights employed by university development offices, such that "the bride and groom list the items they need, and wedding participants pay for the right to claim, say, the fourth place setting as their gift." With perfect knowledge of the recipients' desires, donors can effectively select a gift that will suffice, if not delight. But this exercise is not provisioning per se, as donors do not select what the new couple needs to launch a new life from a culturally determined set of starter items, a standard set of commodities (and services) every household requires to establish itself. Rather, donors select from a "wish list" of items ranging from staple to luxury that recipients have fabricated not only to meet their own selfish needs and wants but also to match the means of prospective donors that custom demands participate in the gift-giving ritual.

Frequently, donors must compete with one another for the privilege of selecting a given item or of assembling a more lavish gift from among the items on the list. Sometimes, they retreat from the intensity of the competition and go "off-registry" to compensate:

> I'm the type who [doesn't] get on the gift register until the last ten percent of the people get on. The type of stuff which is left there to buy, I'm just not interested. So I usually do not follow the gift registry. (Emma)

Nor is money offered as a way of offsetting the cost of acquiring a common portfolio of starter goods; even an off-registry cash "gift" is treated by analysts as a wealth transfer (Cheal 1988). For example, in their investigation of ethnic wedding gift practices in the United States, McGrath and Englis (1996, 130, 134) found that donors and recipients, largely disdainful of and uninformed about registry and committed both to relieving the giver of the burden of choice and enabling the receiver to select the "actual" gift, literally preferred cash gifts. Because the registry gift is a handsel, given to inaugurate a union auspiciously, the metaphorical naming rights described by Waldfogel (2009) exist alternately as the spirit of the donor recovered in use and contemplation of the gift and as a speculative reverie of what a donor might have given had the binding force of registry not been in play.

The open-source ethos in consumer culture that has revived interest in prosumption (Kozinets et al. 2004; Sherry, McGrath, and Levy 1995; Toffler 1980; Visconti et al. 2010) assuredly encompasses the registry gift. An item listed on and chosen from a registry is a collaborative gift in several senses. First, the item is chosen by the couple to be given to itself. Donors comply and find ways to invest meaning in the item, choosing from among preselections. This initial, foundational collaboration gives rise to a second. Donors collaborate among themselves by not duplicating one another's gifts, by "going in on" a gift in partnerships that permit selection of a more expensive gift, by bundling preselected items into more lavish assortments, and simply by agreeing to buy from the registry in the first place. Finally, the retail host of the registry collaborates with donors and recipients from search through disposition, enabling the gift of service to emerge.

All parties to the registry ritual ultimately recognize in this collaboration an underlying monadic aspect to the gift. Two striking illustrations highlight this recognition. First, there is universal acknowledgment that the recipients are free to return any gift they themselves have chosen for a different one they currently desire more ardently. Second, a donor may refuse to comply with the registry ritual by going "off registry" to purchase a gift that may be more readily sacralized in traditional fashion.

Just as the Burning Man gift economy has been likened to a postmodern hybrid of the potlatch and the cargo cult (Sherry and Kozinets 2007, 114), so also can the gift registry be construed, partially and perhaps more simply, as a potlatch reconfigured or repurposed for consumer culture. To mix metaphors, this potlatch operates according to the principle of a barn raising (McGrath and Englis 1996, 134) and its many cross-cultural cousins. As a form of mutual aid, the registry witnesses a community contributing its resources to benefit a deserving household, essentially redistributing wealth in an effort to raise the status of this household. Viewed in the context of the wedding process within which the registry is embedded, a feast (or series of feasts) is hosted for (or by) the bride and groom during which concelebrants affirm the status transition the couple is undergoing. The couple acts as a gift chimney through which presents flow, their new hearth being stoked by the generosity of kith and kin who participate in the solemnizing of the union. Gifts are neither destroyed nor given away, as in traditional potlatch, but rather symbolically transmuted into status. Donors divest themselves of wealth in honor of the new couple, whose material accumulation proclaims the social esteem with which it is now invested. This redistribution of wealth represents an investment in the new couple (McGrath and Englis 1996, 134).

This process is the opposite of the coercive tribute paid by social inferiors to social superiors. Wealth is sacrificed by the community to create community; economic capital is translated into social capital. Wealth flows to the socially needy as the status transition is marked. In traditional potlatch, the donor may be financially impoverished as social status is enriched through redistribution; in the gift registry, the donor's financial burden can be calibrated to means, and the recipients' social status is enriched through redistribution. The new couple begins its next stage of the life course with the material and symbolic blessing of the community, a blessing most likely to be reaffirmed, again through registry, upon the impending birth of children.

Conclusion

The registry is at once a reaction to and manifestation of the romantic, celebratory view of the gift economy as an escape from a morally inferior market economy (Marcoux 2009). The semiotic freighting of the gift with social obligation ensures the possibility of frustrating stakeholders' expectations. The market mitigates this possibility but also offers an illusive alternative to itself. By submitting to the registry, efficiencies of provisioning and facework are realized by the participants. By resisting the registry, participants (re)sacralize the gift, ironically by purchasing it elsewhere in the market. In the former instance, participants are perceptually emancipated from the tyranny of the gift economy. In the latter, they achieve a perceptual countering of market hegemony, even as they return to the market (paradoxically) for their alternative. Either way, the conceit "It's the thought that counts" is preserved.

As people seek to reconcile premodern propensities with such postmodern tensions as the accommodation to, and resistance of, the commodification of life, the significance of portal institutions will loom larger in consumer research agendas. The registry suggests an uneasy alliance between the spirit of the gift and the net present value of social capital, a relationship consumer culture theorists are predisposed to understand and manipulate. We hope our exploratory effort stimulates additional inquiry into such portal institutions.

Note

1 The authors thank research assistants Katherine Callahan and Kara Klug and colleagues Ryan Hamilton, Jiewen Hong, Peggy Lui, and Wen Wan for support in data collection and preliminary analysis. The authors also thank Amber Epp, Mary Ann McGrath, Mary Ann McCabe, Rita Denny, Patti Sunderland, and Cele Otnes for helpful comments on earlier versions of this essay.

Bibliography

Belk, R. "It's the Thought That Counts: A Signed Digraph Analysis of Gift-Giving." *Journal of Consumer Research* 3 (1976): 155–62.

———. "Sharing." *Journal of Consumer Research* 36 (2010): 715–34.

———, M. Wallendorf, and J. Sherry, Jr. "The Sacred and the Profane in Consumer Behavior: Theodicy on the Odyssey." *Journal of Consumer Research* 16 (1989): 1–38.

Bey, H. "Pirate Utopias." In *T.A.Z.: The Temporary Autonomous Zone*. Brooklyn, NY: Autonomedia, 1984.

Bradford, T. W. "Intergenerationally Gifted Asset Dispositions." *Journal of Consumer Research* 36 (2009): 93–111.

——— and J. F. Sherry, Jr. "Orchestrating Rituals through Retailers: An Examination of Gift Registry." *Journal of Retailing* 89, no. 2 (2013): 158–75.

Caplow, T. "Rule Enforcement without Visible Means: Christmas Gift Giving in Middletown." *American Journal of Sociology* 89 (1984): 1306–23.

Cappria, J., C. Woodruffe, and M. Reid. *Bridezillas*. 2005. WeTV.

Cheal, D. *The Gift Economy*. Cambridge: University Press, 1988.

Coraci, F. *The Wedding Singer*. 2008. Produced by Brillstein-Grey Entertainment and Robert Simonds Productions and distributed by New Line Cinema.

Dobkin, D. *Wedding Crashers*. 2005. Produced by Tapestry Films and distributed by New Line Cinema.

Giesler, M. "Consumer Gift Systems." *Journal of Consumer Research* 13 (2006): 283–90.

Howard, V. *Brides, Inc.: American Weddings and the Business of Tradition*. Philadelphia: University of Pennsylvania Press, 2006.

Johns, A. *Piracy: The Intellectual Property Wars from Gutenberg to Gates*. Chicago: University of Chicago Press, 2009.

Joy, A. "Gift Giving in Hong Kong and the Continuum of Social Ties." *Journal of Consumer Research* 28 (2001): 239–56.

Kozinets, R., J. Sherry, D. Storm, A. Duhachek, K. Nuttavuthisit, and B. DeBerry-Spence. "Ludic Agency and Retail Spectacle." *Journal of Consumer Research* 31 (2004): 658–72.

Levy, S. "Symbols, Selves and Others." In *Advances in Consumer Research*, 542–3. Edited by A. Mitchell. Ann Arbor, MI: Association for Consumer Research, 1982.

Lowrey, T., C. Otnes, and J. Ruth. "Social Influences on Dyadic Giving Over Time: A Taxonomy from the Giver's Perspective." *Journal of Consumer Research* 30 (2004): 547–58.

Marcoux, J.-S. "Escaping the Gift Economy." *Journal of Consumer Research* 36 (2009): 671–85.

Mauss, M. *The Gift*. New York: Norton, 1967.

McGrath, M. A. and B. Englis. "Intergenerational Gift Giving in Subcultural Wedding Celebrations: The Ritual Audience as Cash Cow." In *Gift Giving: A Research Anthology*, 123–41. Edited by C. Otnes and R. F. Beltramini. Bowling Green: Bowling Green State University Popular Press, 1996.

McGrath, M. A., J. Sherry, and S. Levy. "Giving Voice to the Gift: The Use of Projective Techniques to Recover Lost Meanings." *Journal of Consumer Psychology* 2 (1993): 171–91.

Mead, R. *One Perfect Day: The Selling of the American Wedding*. New York: Penguin, 2007.

Mick, D. "Giving Gifts to Ourselves: A Greimassian Analysis Leading to Testable Propositions." In *Marketing and Semiotics: Selected Papers from the Copenhagen Symposium*, 142–59. Edited by H. Hartvig Larsen, David Glen Mick, and Christian Alsted. Copenhagen: Handelshoskolens Forlag, 1991.

———. "Self-Gifts." In *Gift Giving: An Interdisciplinary Anthology*, 99–120. Edited by C. Otnes and R. Beltrami. Bowling Green, KY: Popular Press, 1996.

Mick, D. G. "Consumer Research and Semiotics: Exploring the Morphology of Signs, Symbols, and Significance." *Journal of Consumer Research* 13 (1986): 196.

——— and M. DeMoss. "'To Me from Me': A Descriptive Phenomenology of Self-Gifts." In *Advances in Consumer Research*, 677–82. Edited by Marvin E. Goldberg, Gerald Gorn, and Richard W. Pollay. Provo, UT: Association for Consumer Research, 1990a.

———. "Self-Gifts: Phenomenological Insights from Four Contexts." *Journal of Consumer Research* 17 (1990b): 322–32.

Otnes, C., T. Lowrey, and Y. C. Kim. "Gift Selection for Easy and Difficult Recipients: A Social Roles Interpretation." *Journal of Consumer Research* 20 (1993): 229–44.

Otnes, C. and E. Pleck. *Cinderella Dreams: The Allure of the Lavish Wedding.* Berkeley, CA: University of California Press, 2003.

Penner, B. "A Vision of Love and Luxury: The Commercialization of Nineteenth-Century American Weddings." *Winterthur Portfolio* 39 (2004): 1–20.

Purbrick, L. *The Wedding Present: Domestic Life beyond Consumption.* Burlington, VT: Ashgate Publishing Company, 2007.

Ruth, J., F. Brunel, and C. Otnes. "An Investigation of the Power of Emotions in Relationship Realignment: The Gift Recipient's Perspective." *Psychology & Marketing* 21 (2004): 29–52.

Ruth, J., C. Otnes, and F. Brunel. "Gift Receipt and the Reformulation of Interpersonal Relationships." *Journal of Consumer Research* 25 (1999): 385–402.

Sherry, J. "Gift Giving in Anthropological Perspective." *Journal of Consumer Research* 10 (1983): 157–68.

———. "Reflections on Giftware and Gift Care: Whither Consumer Research?" In *Gift Giving: A Research Anthology*, 217–26. Edited by C. Otnes and R. F. Beltramini. Bowling Green: Bowling Green State University Press. 1996.

———. "Brand Meaning." In *Kellogg on Branding*, 40–69. Edited by T. Calkins and A. Tybout. New York: John Wiley, 2005.

——— and R. Kozinets. "Comedy of the Commons: Nomadic Spirituality and the Burning Man Festival." *Consumer Culture Theory* 11 (2007): 119–47.

——— and M. A. McGrath. "Unpacking the Holiday Presence: A Comparative Ethnography of Two Gift Stores." In *Interpretive Consumer Research*, 148–67. Edited by T. Calkins and A. Tybout. Provo, UT: Association for Consumer Research, 1989.

———, M. A. McGrath, and S. Levy. "Monadic Giving: Anatomy of Gifts Given to the Self." In *Contemporary Marketing and Consumer Behavior: An Anthropological Sourcebook*, 399–432. Edited by John F. Sherry, Jr. Thousand Oaks, CA: Sage, 1995.

Toffler, A. *The Third Wave.* New York: Morrow, 1980.

Visconti, L., J. Sherry, Jr., S. Borghini, and L. Anderson. "Street Art, Sweet Art? Reclaiming the 'Public' in Public Place," 511–29. *Journal of Consumer Research* 37 (2010).

Visser, M. *The Gift of Thanks: The Roots and Rituals of Gratitude.* New York: Houghton Mifflin Harcourt, 2008.

Waldfogel, J. *Scroogenomics: Why You Shouldn't Buy Presents for Holidays.* Princeton, NJ: Princeton University Press, 2009.

Weinberger, M. F. "Dominant Consumption Rituals and Intragroup Boundary Work: How Non-Celebrants Manage Conflicting Relational and Identity Goals through Consumption." *Journal of Consumer Research* 42, no. 3 (2015): 378–400.

——— and M. Wallendorf. "Intracommunity Gifting at the Intersection of Contemporary Moral & Market Economies." *Journal of Consumer Research* 39, no. 1 (2012): 74–92.

Winick, G. *Bride Wars*. 2009.

Wooten, D. "Qualitative Steps toward an Expanded Model of Anxiety in Gift-Giving." *Journal of Consumer Research* 27 (2000): 84–95.

―――― and S. Wood. "In the Spotlight: The Drama of Gift Receipt." In *Contemporary Consumption Rituals: A Research Anthology*, 213–336. Edited by C. C. Otnes and T. M. Lowrey. London: Lawrence Erlbaum Associates, 2004.

Zwick, J. *My Big Fat Greek Wedding*. 2002. Gold Circle Films, HBO Films, MPH Entertainment, and Playtone.

7 Consumption on the Feminist Agenda

Linda Scott

As a historian of the women's movement in America and, more recently, as a scholar and activist working to improve the lives of women in the developing countries, I have felt that consumer research suffers from a myopia about gender and consumption that is rooted in the peculiarities of the American feminist movement of the 1970s. My hope is that this essay will stimulate others to work toward building an entirely new theory that would facilitate "social provisioning" as the center of a feminist vision of economics (Power 2004) and would underpin research streams investigating the multiple ways that goods can empower, as well as disempower, women.

A new feminist theory of consumption could engage with important efforts on behalf of women now underway around the world. The emergence and analysis of new data documenting the conditions of women across nations, cultures, and forms of government (cf. World Economic Forum 2006–2016) has shown that women are subordinated in every nation and that the pattern of constraint is uncannily consistent. Studies building on these data show that the constant effort to keep half the world's population down exacts hunger, disease, poverty, and conflict as its price (e.g., World Bank 2015). Hopeful strategies for solving major world problems by closing gender gaps, especially in economic participation, are emerging (e.g., United Nations World Food Program 2015). A number of world organizations—from the international agencies to the global charities to some of the largest corporations—are investing in programs intended to effect "women's economic empowerment" (e.g., the Coca-Cola 5by20 program; www.coca-colacompany.com/5by20). Very often, however, the theory of change anticipates that the economically autonomous female will behave differently than her male counterpart, spending in a more prosocial way that results in better health, stronger communities, and less conflict (cf. UNICEF 2008). Thus, there is an important role for feminist consumer research to play in the unfolding of this historic effort.

In this essay, I will build the case. I first outline the history behind the view of consumption I believe has dominated thinking in the field. My purpose will be not only to localize this perspective in time and place but also to reveal a feminist vision of consumption that prevailed prior to the 1970s and situated the feminist consumer research of the 1990s against the backdrop of the movement. Next, I discuss the world gender data and its implications for the project I advocate. I then reexamine the articles that introduced feminist theory to consumer research for strands that could be pulled into current use. Finally, I outline arenas for research I believe could accompany a new theory of consumption and gender.

A Short History of Consumption in American Feminist Thought

Few realize the pivotal role that motivation research played in the feminist movement's attitude toward consumption. Interviews with Ernst Dichter were Betty Freidan's primary source when she argued, in *The Feminine Mystique*, that the need to create demand for postwar consumer goods was the driving force behind the demise of the vibrant women's movement of the prewar period (1963). In the chapter called "The Sexual Sell," Friedan relates how this "manipulator" (and presumably others like him) had used shadowy, "hidden persuader" techniques to brainwash educated women into sacrificing their lives to housewifery. Cooped up in a "house of things," denied the positive stimulation of a career, "mesmerized in front of a television set," these women faced Friedan's famous "problem that has no name"—the depressing specter of a life without meaning other than keeping house, bearing children, and shopping (1963, 197–223).

The reception that greeted *The Feminine Mystique*, an immediate best seller, was the first signal that the women's movement was again rising, after twenty-five years of lying dormant while the world focused first on economic cataclysm and then on total war. By the end of the 1960s, what came to be known as the "Second Wave" was well underway.

Starting with that initial salvo from Friedan, "women's liberation," as the refreshed movement was first called, departed dramatically from the "First Wave" approach to consumption. Though suffrage had been the focal point of the early century movement, there were other priorities high on the list (cf. Flexner 1975; Scott 2005). One was consumer rights and safety. The "clubwomen" who composed the main body of the movement took the importance of household provisioning as a core principle, and they worked hard in support of regulations to guarantee pure products and truthful advertising, as well as safety in public goods and services. The tactics of the First Wave included lobbying for legislation, as well as marches and pickets, but also consumer boycotts. The National Consumers League (NCL), today the oldest consumer organization in America, was originally formed under the aegis of the feminist movement. Their tactic was to organize middle-class women to threaten boycotts against employers who

denied women's labor rights. In truth, however, they seldom actually boy-
cotted; instead, they published the list of employers who did comply with
their standards, called "The White List." This list became an important
consumer seal of approval and the ability to bestow or withhold this sign
was used effectively as leverage. The NCL successfully pressured states into
protective laws for female workers. Thus, there is a legitimate precedent
for taking consumption as a project of feminism, as well as for employing
consumption for political purposes.

Two approaches emerged shortly after the initial surge of liberal feminism as represented by Friedan: Marxist-socialist feminism and radical
feminism. Marxist feminist groups were, of course, even more inclined
to name capitalism as the primary evil and also to focus on wage labor.
Marxist feminism lasted well into the twenty-first century in the academy,
even though it was clear early on that the theory was unable to explain
the subordination of women because the phenomenon occurs among all
groups (cf. Hartmann 1979; Rubin 1975). Feminist theorists working
under a Marxist agenda also consistently put the cause of labor ahead of
the cause of women, a prioritization that rankled other feminists but was
rendered necessary by the theory. In Marxism, the role of the housewife
is merely to supply capitalism with workers and the female contribution to history was predicted to occur only *after* they became paid labor-
ers (cf. Hartmann 1979). Consumption in Marxism is just something a
worker does to live. Anything beyond that—from christening gowns to
coffins—is down to mystification and fetish. The only "value" that legiti-
mately inhered in goods was the cost of their ingredients and the labor to
produce them—not finding or choosing them, preparing or using them,
nor employing goods to bring about desirable ends other than brute survival (Scott 2008). In sum, like the liberal feminists, the Marxist-socialist
feminists took a masculinist stance that valorized paid labor to the detriment of the home economy.

Radical feminism built on a premise that was hard to prove: that
women were oppressed by all societies, in all times and places (Jaggar
1983). Radicals held that women were, indeed, the original oppressed
class, held down by threats of violence and reproductive burdens. They
asserted that all societies had developed large social, economic, and
legal structures that acted to enforce and continue the subordination
of women. Advertising, as an example of those structures in the United
States, became a frequent target for radical feminists.

Writers and activists across the Second Wave, therefore, put advertisers and makers of consumer products squarely in the center of blame for
the oppression of women. It is hard to imagine consumption having a
place on the feminist agenda with this framework as a given. However,
the theorists who carried forward from the 1970s added other elements
that crippled the movement's ability to think about consumption and the
role of women even further.

During the 1980s and 1990s, a dramatic turn to language theory in feminist thought, along with a general rejection of quantitative methods, left materialist concerns, as well as anything studied using statistics, behind in the shadows (Jackson 2001). A prodigious body of textual criticism of advertising—as "the texts" of capitalism—appeared, with a special emphasis on beauty and fashion (Scott 2005, 313–22). The focus on language at the expense of material concerns is evident in every essay: with very few exceptions, the interpretations ignore the object being advertised entirely. It simply was not on the agenda to analyze the product itself, its uses and benefits, or its place in social life.

"Woman's standpoint" feminism, also emerging during these years, claimed a unique female experience to be evident in cognition, language, and personality (e.g., Gilligan 1982). This "standpoint feminism" made important inroads in epistemological debates within the academy. However, standpoint feminists were especially vulnerable to an increasingly vocal critique of feminism as a movement.

Throughout the twentieth century, the movement in America had been led by white, prosperous, educated women, mostly from the Northeast, who had often been painfully unwilling to consider the viewpoints of women unlike themselves. As world culture globalized, this blind spot seemed to extend to women in other parts of the world, especially the global South. A growing "postmodern" feminist perspective claimed that other women around the world had a vastly different experience of oppression and "Western feminists" were oppressing them further (Stanford Encyclopedia of Philosophy 2012). After the publication of Judith Butler's *Gender Trouble* in 1990, the notion that biological sex was a myth gained currency, thus making arguments on behalf of "women" as a class even more difficult (Stanford Encyclopedia of Philosophy 2016). Eventually, the uniqueness of experience and the multiple "intersectionalities" among women, as well as the ambiguity now surrounding biological sex, made it impossible to describe women as having any kind of collective experience, even of their own oppression.

Women's Subordination: An Aerial View

The feminists of the 1970s were working in a data vacuum. It is heartbreaking and shocking, but nevertheless true, that up to that decade there had been no histories of women written, only a handful of biographies. Anthropology and archeology had been so dominated by males that women's lives had gone unnoticed in their work (Reitner 1975). Because the Cold War blocked the flow of information, there was no way to know whether the claims against capitalism would be borne out by comparing how women fared in Marxist-Leninist nations. As a consequence, theorizing about women's subordination had to be done with very few points of comparison. That made it easy to dream about egalitarian societies that were prehistorical or communist (Eller 2001). Beginning in the mid-1970s, however, the painstaking process of producing women's history, archeology, and anthropology began. This body of work produced insights that undercut the assumption modern capitalism was the root problem (e.g., Demos 2009; Lerner 1987), but political exigencies tended to keep this evidence under wraps. When the Soviet Union fell in 1989, however, it was difficult to ignore the female voices now audible: Marxism had not produced a feminist solution (Funk 1993).

The knowledge situation was then dramatically reversed in 1995, when the United Nations Development Program (UNDP) published their first Gender Development Index, a composite produced from available national data on the economic participation of women, as well as educational opportunities, health access, and voice in politics. The result was surprising and stark: the array described by this index went from high gender equality as a feature of wealthy, stable nations to low gender equality as the watermark of poor, conflict-ridden countries, with gradations of both gender equality and economic development stepping regularly in the same direction across the continuum.

The relationship was strong enough to be, as they say, "visible to the naked eye." The democracies where industry and capitalism were most developed had the best conditions for women. The communist countries were in the middle. The countries not yet "developed"—impoverished nations with agricultural economies, but also persistent hostilities, no industry or media, and strong religious influences—had the most disadvantaged women in the world. It was the first time in history that comparative data for women's conditions were made available at the national level for the entire array of social structures. The notion that women were equal in societies that modern capitalism had not reached was now shown to be unsupportable by hard information.

Several other institutions followed the lead of UNDP, disaggregating and recompiling to provide material for analysis (e.g., OECD 2012). Others projected the effects of equalizing women on outcomes for households, communities, and nations (e.g., Elborgh-Woytek et al. 2013; Koch, Lawson, and Matsui 2014; Strategy & 2012). It emerged that a key component of women's subordination was their economic exclusion—and that this exclusion, which takes many forms, has devastating effects at every level from individual to nation. Women in developing countries, regardless of region, could not open bank accounts, own land, inherit property, or get credit (cf. World Bank Group 2015). Further, these same limitations had been in place in most of the developed countries until the 1970s—and their disadvantageous effects could still be seen in lower pay and less access to capital. Yet the easing of economic constraints on women in the industrializing democracies, especially their greater labor force participation, had been a major driver in the wealth achieved by these nations, especially during the second half of the twentieth century

(Elborgh-Woytek et al. 2013; World Bank Group 2011). Thus, policy makers began to look at the empowerment of women as a strategy for economic development.

During this period of analysis, investigation, and reflection, expectations for the direction of causality dramatically shifted. At the outset, the default explanation for the strong positive relationship between national prosperity and women's equality, and well as the inverse relationship between gender equality and poverty/conflict, had been that the rich nations, because they were stable and comfortable, could "afford" to allow their women to go free. Or, conversely, that poor communities somehow improved their prospects for survival by subordinating women (cf. Inglehardt and Norris 2003). By about 2013, the opposite theory of causality was informing policy and strategy. The greater autonomy of women in the "advanced" nations had been a major contributor to their rising wealth, especially after 1970. Further, many aspects of the cycle of poverty, such as infant mortality and adolescent fertility, were clearly fueled by gender inequality. Thus, the path to growth and peace was suddenly being visualized as a journey of "empowerment" for women (USAID 2012).

There are several mechanisms by which "empowered women" affect society positively, but a main route is through the different choices women are believed to make when they have a little money and the freedom to spend it as they choose (UNICEF 2007). As a global class, women tend to focus expenditures on the welfare of children first, with funds going to better nutrition, education, and health care; then they turn to community needs. In contrast, men, not as individuals but as a class, are more likely to spend their money on alcohol, tobacco, gambling, and prostitution—to the detriment of their children *and* their communities. The upshot is that women, by provisioning households, build human capital and community prosperity. At the macro level, the consumer behavior of women produces a middle class, improves the quality of the labor force, increases national stability, and spurs a growing economy (Goldman Sachs 2009).

The disempowerment of women in the economic domain, however, is a complex and ugly phenomenon. The radical feminists of the Second Wave, it turns out, were right on several issues. It does appear that women's subordination is universal and thus probably very, very old. Violence is used as a "disciplinary" measure to keep them in their place (World Bank Group 2014): development professionals have learned that any attempt to give women economic autonomy must have a plan to address a physical backlash against the intended beneficiaries. In every aspect of the economy, reproductive burdens hinder women (OECD 2012). Every institutional structure, including both religion and government, as well as schools and unions, seems to have some provision or practice that keeps women subordinate (e.g., World Bank Group 2015). Through a perverse alignment of rules that stipulate, for instance, the acceptable forms of collateral or the industry criteria for an investment company, women are systematically barred from accumulating wealth at every turn, a function of the way the financial system itself is designed. Inequality in the formal industrial workforce, we now know, is just one feature of this general economic exclusion.

Gender, when observed from this perspective, is less an identification or performance than it is a set of codified constraints imposed by the group upon any individuals who meet the relevant criterion. Females, as a class identified in the most simplistic and old-fashioned way—that is, on sight at birth—thus do share a bizarrely similar set of economic restrictions across nations and cultures. In fact, the similarities in these constraints defy the argument that the experience of subordination is always local and unique. And, among even the most impoverished and oppressed populations in the world—blacks in South Africa, for instance—the women are poorer, less educated, more constrained in their movements, and more confined by law (Scott et al. 2012). "Intersectionality" does not make as much difference as one might think.

Arising in parallel with the global gender data's economic implications was another stream of work looking at the psychological implications. Meta-analysis revealed, for instance, that the math test scores of girls, once believed to be the result of inborn differences in the brain, become equal to boys once they have access to the same training (Hyde 2005, 2016). Such a finding supports the simultaneous direction of travel in neuroscience, in which the brain's capabilities are formed almost entirely through experiences (Vidal 2012). Different gender settings affect capabilities: the math performance of girls, for instance, varies in correlation with the global gender indices (Guiso et al. 2008). Furthermore, gains in a group's achievement can be quickly reversed by others treating them according to the prevailing norms (American Psychological Association 2006). Importantly, different treatment of girls and boys results, at the level of meta-analysis but not in smaller samples, in average differences between the sexes on a variety of items from interests to personality traits to attitudes (Carothers and Reis 2013). In sum, although we now know, from a neuroscience perspective, that every brain develops in a radically individual way in response to the infinite variation in experience, the broad similarities in the constraints on women could be expected to result in a gender pattern with regard to things like economic priorities. I do not intend to be arguing for a return to essentialism here (and I must emphasize, along with all the scholars in this domain, that these differences can only be trusted at the level of meta-analysis), but I am saying that there is a legitimate place from which to discuss a women's standpoint in economics, as a reflection of the similarities in constraints.

One of the distinctive arenas in which to study the means of economic exclusion, the impact of a "woman's standpoint," and the potential to solve major world problems is actually consumption. It's not just that women don't have money and if they did they would do a better job of buying than the men. Consumption restrictions are used to mark women as outsiders, to set up barriers to their inclusion, and to enforce stereotype threat. And, despite fifty years of feminist insistence that all consumption is demeaning and useless, the international community is learning that consumer goods can help empower the women themselves: mobile phones, plumbing, and sanitary pads, for instance, are thought to have huge implications for the freedoms of women. This is not to mention the core focus of international community: the expectation that moving spending power to women will result in a more prosocial deployment of resources. Thus, a complex assortment of research questions is emerging—and they need both investigation and a theory.

Feminism in Consumer Research

Feminist theory was introduced to consumer research at the same time that, on the one hand, feminism in the academy had reached a stalemate over whether anything general could be said about women's subordination and, on the other, that UNDP was publishing the very first evidence that women's subordination was a global scourge with a distinctive pattern you could see everywhere.

Three articles appeared in a single 1993 issue of *Journal of Consumer Research*. Bristor and Fischer (1993), Hirschman (1993), and Stern (1993) all focused on epistemology, all of them using feminist theory to try and open up new ways of thinking about research on consumption. Today, however, if you search for the terms "feminism" and "feminist" among either the titles or author-supplied keywords in the *Journal of Consumer Research*, you will still find only these three articles. Though feminist analyses were pursued by consumer researchers at conferences, in books or book chapters, and in lesser journals, there was a general sidelining of feminism in the discipline as a whole. In 2005, Catterall, Stevens, and Maclaran reviewed feminist work in marketing and lamented that, after this small burst in the mid-1990s, research carrying a feminist label stalled out. These authors specifically point to an exaggerated concern with language and call instead for more materialist and activist approach as a way of bringing the field into a more proactive engagement with feminism as a global movement. Catterall and colleagues also acknowledge that the anticonsumption bias that typified feminist theory had made inhospitable ground for consumer research.

My view is in accord with that of Catterall and colleagues. However, I think that the original three articles can provide a springboard to reinvigorate a feminist investigation of consumption. In this section, I plan to identify some of the reasons that these three 1993 articles would have left fallow ground for the type of research I propose; however, I will also emphasize those things that might be brought back out and put into use. At the end, however, I will propose that there must still be a theoretical and political adjustment if the new research stream is to rise to the occasion in international policy.

Stern (1993) uses language theory to show how an advertisement might be read from a "postmodern" feminist perspective. She uses two cigarette ads and takes a strategy of imagining the sexes reversed in each one. She gives a close reading of the Marlboro Man, then asserts that the iconic figure could not simply be made female because the image is too masculine and, thus, unattractive. Stern then analyzed a test ad for Dakota cigarettes, a brand for women that was never actually brought to market. Stern describes a scene in which the Dakota woman displays her subordination through gestures and dress—and then gives a sexualized interpretation in which even keys are seen as stand-ins for pubic hair.

True to genre, Stern's analysis does not address the product. One can only imagine what would have happened if she had chosen a different product category—laundry detergent, for instance—in which to reverse roles. But choosing cigarettes over any other product makes a big difference in the import of these ads, from a materialist perspective.

In American history, the practice of cigarette smoking has been traditionally associated with feminism. Feminists of earlier eras challenged gender norms on the consumption of items reserved for men, especially tobacco and alcohol. A feminist case was made that women's inequality was manifest in their exclusion from the pleasures of life, a fact that was largely due to their economic dependence on men (Scott 2005). Further, the consumption of such items often took place in exclusive men's clubs and pubs where important issues were discussed and decisions made—alcohol and tobacco were the trappings of power. Excluding women from consuming these items helped keep the space where power was negotiated entirely male. But the reaction to challenges was consistent: either the women were derided as "masculine" or as "disreputable." Both negative images were frequently illustrated in cartoons and even in ads (Scott 2005).

In work that Laurel Steinfield and I have done in rural Uganda, we discovered a similar phenomenon (Scott 2013; Steinfield 2013). Because men control money, they can hold back cash to purchase beer and cigarettes. They do this, often in secret, even when it means their children may have to leave school for lack of fees. They do it because consuming these goods is the price of admission for the nightly gatherings of men, in which the business of the village is discussed and decisions made. Women are not normally allowed to consume these or other luxuries, nor are they allowed at the gatherings. The use of alcohol (usually accompanied by tobacco) to gather men in decision making is common around the world, as is the exclusion of women and the taboo against their consumption of the same products. For instance, Jiafei Jin and I found that female entrepreneurs in China were held back from accessing capital because bankers required long, boozy dinners followed by karaoke as a precondition for lending (Scott and Jin 2014). The same practice is visible in the City of London, where the effect is to keep women from rising in finance careers (Rutherford 2011).

Stern's recommendations for research suggest experimental studies to see whether males and females read ads differently. This stance is consistent with the popular 1990s notion that women have a distinctive experience and so an essential woman's psychological standpoint (cf. Gilligan 1982). Though one would have to be extremely careful about sample size, it might be worthwhile studying whether the role women often have as "provisioners" makes a difference to their reading of an ad—and whether the gender restrictions on the product's consumption affects their view.

Hirschman (1993) questioned the political ideology underpinning research in consumer behavior. Unfortunately, Hirschman identified feminism with Marxism, as was the common practice among feminists in the 1990s, and she also squares feminism off against quantitative methods, again conventional wisdom at the time. To identify Marxism with feminism is problematic, as I have explained. The walk away from numbers was driven by the paradigm shift in the field at that time: the intention was to open consumer research to a wider array of methods, and Hirschman was key in that movement. However, the stories of women's subordination now being told using huge databases over the past twenty years has stood much of masculinist ideology on its head. These numbers have been a powerful tool for understanding the world in a new way, but I would also argue they have made the feminist case more convincingly than it has ever been made before.

I wish to focus, however, on Hirschman's overriding objective. Hirschman was really trying to put a different morality in place to guide the study of consumption. She wanted to dispense with the controlling, arrogant, profit-seeking ideology that then dominated the field in favor of something more humane and inclusive. If a new feminist theory were to recast "consumption" as "provisioning"—and the role of women as central to prosperity, health, and peace—I believe that Hirschman's moral objective would be achieved. And, given the pervasive inequality of women in all groups, as well as the positive impact of women's empowerment even in the most impoverished and excluded communities, I think this can be done under a feminist agenda—the additional umbrella of Marx is not needed to be inclusive of other disadvantaged groups.

Bristor and Fischer (1993) explicated major streams of feminist theory then current, advocating a feminist "way of knowing" they showed to be at odds with the objectivist stance of logical positivism. This article appeared among a battery of works typical of the paradigm shift occurring at that time, and each challenged logical positivism in a different language but on similar grounds (e.g., Anderson 1986; Arnold and Fischer 1994; Hudson and Ozanne 1988; Murray and Ozanne 1991). Unfortunately, once the paradigm shift had absorbed the overall notion that there are many ways of knowing and many methods to get there, feminist theory may have seemed, to some, to have a small point of distinction as an epistemological approach. I fear that "feminism" became just another rubric that allowed "interpretivism" and thus seemed no longer necessary once interpretive work was, more or less, accepted.

Yet there was much more that could have come from Bristor and Fischer's suggestion of a distinctively feminist way of knowing. The article is full of research suggestions that have an explicitly feminist lens. For example, Bristor and Fischer question researcher assumptions that the woman's role in the home is to do all the care work, unassisted by her husband. The very fact that the world community now seeks to work through women's role in the home to improve living conditions is testament to the universality of this assumption—and to the impact the assumption itself has on the behavior of women everywhere. Yet, the move to better include women in the economy seldom takes into account the time burden of care—despite the grand claims that economically empowered women will take better care of homes. These are contradictions that the approach outlined by Bristor and Fischer could address.

My own proposal, however, is somewhat different. Whereas Bristor and Fischer lay out their position in the spirit of eliminating biases and blind spots in consumer research, I am asking for a theory that will study the ways that consumption, in all its various guises, either restricts women's freedoms or opens them up. The ultimate objective would not be reduced bias for consumer behavior, nor would it be increased growth for the world economy. The goal would be to eliminate women's subordination worldwide by using the current interest in their economic status as leverage. Happily, evidence suggests very strongly that such a goal would have positive effects from a social, economic, psychological, spiritual, and humanitarian perspective.

Be mindful, however, that the hopeful outcomes expected through the empowerment of women only can occur via eliminating the massive human tragedy that has been unveiled by all these data. We have learned, once and for all, that the world's largest—and probably oldest—underclass is women. We have learned that this oppression, which affects fully half the species, is held in place by violence at every level of society. The conditions that millions of women suffer are virtually indistinguishable from slavery: they are bound by marriage contracts they had no place in forming and cannot break; their mobility and communication are severely constrained; they work for an unspecified number of hours unpaid; they are left to go hungry or unclothed at the will of the head of household;

and if they try to resist or leave, they face violence. We have learned that the practices that support this subordination lead to hunger, disease, and conflict. And all this has been going on, as far as anyone can tell, for the entire history of humanity. There is unquestionably a moral imperative to eliminate gender inequality, and thus it is entirely in keeping with the best purposes of the academy to undertake such a mission.

Eyes on the Ground, Sleeves Rolled Up

To look upon consumer goods as potential instruments for empowering women on a global scale requires a radical departure from the conventional feminist wisdom of the past fifty years. It may also require a little imaginative stimulation. So, in this section, I will suggest a few more research questions that a new theory of "consumption as feminism" could support. I am generating these ideas mainly from observations in the field and in policy meetings.

Throughout this section, I will also use a select group of consumer research articles in which the respondents were female to highlight where the new theory might need to draw parallels or extensions. These articles include Thompson, Locander, and Pollio's (1990) study of the consumption choices of American stay-at-home moms, Diamond and colleagues' (2009) study of American Girl branding, Scaraboto and Fisher's (2013) study of "fatshionistas," and Thompson and Ustuner's (2015) study of roller derby participants.

Before beginning, however, it is important to call attention once again to the influence that the United States has as the *situ* for consumer research, as well as for feminist research on consumption. All of the studies I will be pulling from have a wealthy consumer society as a backdrop, a circumstance that contrasts painfully with the situation in which most of the world's women live and considerably affects the way that goods are viewed. Stepping back from that particular setting will be crucial to developing the new theory—otherwise the principles will not be generally applicable. Further, all these studies occur in a post-Second Wave environment, in which considerable autonomy for women has been won—though certainly not full equality—and the consequences of resistance have been substantially reduced, as compared to elsewhere in the world. My own opinion is that, outside the United States and a few other developed countries, the challenge is steeper and the stakes are higher. It is also probably a reflection of this very specific political and economic setting, as well as the late twentieth century orientation of feminist thought, that there is an emphasis on consumption as signification, especially as manifest in dress and the "performance/performativity" of gender, rather than on the material limitations in force and the potential for a variety of concrete well-being outcomes to be affected, across a population, by the lifting of those limitations.

Finally, and most importantly for my proposal, there is only very narrow scope for a feminist agenda in these studies. What each illustrates is a generally sympathetic look toward females in a particular consumption situation, sometimes where the confrontation with choice might be viewed as an instantiation of women's struggles. What they do not do is engage with consumption as a phenomenon that mediates women's subordination in multiple material ways—several of which I will elaborate in the sections that follow—and point the research objective specifically toward the empowerment of women a global goal, with implications drawn for activist measures.

Consumption as Debilitation

It common for nongovernmental organizations and UN agencies to observe that, around the world, females, especially girls, are fed least and last. And, indeed, some speculate that women are smaller than men because they have been fed less for millennia. It is also true, however, that women are less often able to access health care of all kinds, sometimes because the family does not wish to spend money on the well-being of females and sometimes because the females seldom have the ability to leave home on their own accord, even to seek urgent care (e.g., Scott et al. 2011). The outcome of this lack of access to both food and care is a debilitated population—of females, to be sure, but the general population also suffers. The Intergrowth 21 project has now shown conclusively that the variation in birth weights around the world is attributable to the variation in the treatment of women—and that an array of birth defects can be traced to the effect of withheld food and care on ova, beginning from the time a girl child is born (Intergrowth 21st 2016). This "Russian doll" phenomenon, in which the suffering of the girl is visited upon her progeny even before their conception, is one of the most horrifying and long-lasting effects of gender subordination.

Scaraboto and Fischer (2013) focus on the rights of overfed women to have fashionable clothes. Here is perhaps where the starkest contrast is visible between the abundance of America and the conditions of women elsewhere. However, the analysis of institutional and systemic engagement that Scaraboto and Fischer offer could be helpfully expanded to postulate how activists might engage with food and health-care delivery in a way that would open access to women, thus potentially providing massive humanitarian and economic benefits.

Because the Intergrowth 21 project is seated at Oxford, I have had many discussions with the leaders about how the current situation might be changed. They explain that it was the role of the medical scholars in this project to document the long-term population health implications from this systemic exclusion—it is not within their "wheelhouse" to come up with the social solutions that might lift the barriers, but they very much want suitable scholars to step in and do that. The first step would be to understand exactly how the consumption of food and care is held back from women. The second step would be to design interventions that might reverse the exclusion. The third step would be to measure the impact of attempts to improve access to these goods and services. All of these steps would fit neatly into the normal sandbox of consumer research *if* a more activist and feminist theory could be invoked.

Consumption as Exclusion

I have already talked about the ways in which tobacco and alcohol consumption have been used to exclude women from the corridors of power. There are many ways, however, in which important spaces are made hostile to females, whether those are temples or banks. Further, there are enforced consumption dicta, such as the wearing of veils or prohibitions against driving cars, that act to exclude females from entering into an array of "everyday" activities, especially economic ones.

Let's consider now the arguments offered by Thompson and Ustuner (2015). Although the roller-derby performance analysis tends to fall into the feminism-as-language category, and the political implications seem to be limited to increased freedom in signification of identity, the astute distinctions that Thompson and Ustuner draw between previous research on performance of gender and the intentions of Butler's theory of performativity could have much broader and graver applications. Their description of the complex interconnections of norms, practices, and goods-as-signs, in which the subject is, more or less involuntarily, manifest as gendered and, in the process, constrained, could be applied to other goods, norms, and practices that constrain in ways that have more material outcomes attached. For instance, there is a remarkable confluence of contractual, documentary, moral, and spatial rules that exclude women from the financial system, as I have described previously. Using the Thompson and Ustuner view as a springboard, one could provide a holistic analysis of the problem now presented to the global community: why women are so difficult to draw into financial-inclusion programs. Currently, the international community tends to focus on technical or procedural details without attention to the total picture of constraints. The kind of analysis Thompson and Ustuner advocate could be expanded to offer considerable insight in support of these efforts.

Consumption as Empowerment

My team at Oxford was the first to demonstrate empirically that giving girls sanitary pads would help them to stay in school, largely by allowing them to keep the fact of their menarche private (Dolan et al. 2013; Montgomery et al. 2012). This finding was not so surprising in light of the history of sanitary care in America, in which these goods also let girls stay in school and women work. Other examples include bicycles' effect on women's mobility during the American Gilded Age and the extraordinary ability of mobile phones to break down barriers of distance and access in the developing world today (Scott 2013). However, a key adjustment necessary to support a feminist consumer theory that would accommodate these examples would be to recognize that consumer goods and services are not all harmful or useless but instead have a variety of effects, including the potential to empower, even from a feminist perspective.

Consumption as Control

A key challenge for activists is to help women keep control over the money they earn. If women do not get to decide how to spend the money, the expected benefits of their consumption habits will not accrue. However, the norm is for husbands and fathers to expect all earnings to be turned over to them—and then they mete out dribbles for the women's needs as they see fit. The impact of this practice can be seen in the way the household prioritizes "necessities" (food, but also beer) and "luxuries" (sanitary pads and, sometimes, school fees). Mobile banking is being introduced as a way to give women private control over their money—but they have to have permission, first, to purchase the phone and, from there, the male is still likely to demand access to her password and account. How to use available goods and services in a way that circumvents these attempts to control is a persistent question in the effort to economically empower women.

Here I want to hark back to Thompson, Locander, and Pollio (1990) and their analysis of the spending habits of women who had stopped work to stay at home and have children. These women, now no longer earning, had become economically dependent on their husbands and so were hesitant to spend money on themselves. Like the women I have just described, the needs of Thompson and colleagues' respondents were recast as "luxury," and such purchases became a focal point for stress and guilt, rather than being dignified as "necessities," as were the needs of other members of the family. Importantly, this happened because they had stepped back into the traditional role, in which women work unpaid as part of an unrecognized and devalued effort to replenish the species—and do so, to a large extent, via "provisioning" activities. Western women who stop work for this reason, we now know, take an extraordinary personal financial risk: their pensions are reduced by the number of years away from work, their long-term career prospects are considerably stunted, and the chances that they will end their lives in poverty are substantially increased (OECD 2012). Yet, having made this selfless decision, they feel guilty for buying a dress. And, it still goes unquestioned that this choice is the gender-appropriate one—and that the man will not be the one to take the risk nor bear the hardship.

The burden of motherhood has massive economic implications in every sector and in every country precisely because this set of expectations about women's roles and needs is so pervasive (OECD 2012). Therefore, we can here see a place where the American experience is continuous, not discontinuous, with that of other women, everywhere. Thompson and colleagues, however, did not view this issue from a feminist perspective and thus did not even see the power dynamic behind the emotional experience attending these women's thoughts of buying for themselves. Ironically, the paper is titled "The Lived Meaning of Free Choice." From a global feminist perspective, the experience of putting aside one's personal welfare in selfless service to gender expectations is hardly a free choice. The theory I am proposing would put the politics of the choice to stop earning in order to reproduce at center stage.

Finally, both Scarabuto and Fischer (2013) and Thompson (1990) present their research as a study of choice. However, in a global feminist research agenda focused on consumption, the issue would not usually be a matter of the choices available; it would be a matter of access to any choices at all.

Consumption as Self-Assertion

We had a project in Bangladesh several years back (Dolan, Johnstone-Louis, and Scott 2012), in which we studied a rural distribution system devised by CARE to allow saleswomen (females drawn from the extreme poor) to travel to household compounds to sell consumer goods to the women there, who were not allowed to go out and therefore could never buy things for themselves. The lack of access to consumer goods caused by constraint on mobility was certainly an important point of comparison to the Betty Friedan argument. But the impact on the women of suddenly being able to make their own purchases was surprising to me. They exerted their "consumer power" to get the saleswomen to procure the goods they really wanted—often brassieres and sanitary pads and other items their husbands would not buy. It was particularly notable that they were able to procure birth control pills and patches through this method (Bangladesh exerts little control on the dissemination of prescription drugs) and were extremely happy to have contraception that did not rely on male compliance. However, the biggest surprise of all was the change in their color of dress. CARE Bangladesh, in fact, uses a question about whether the women get to choose their own clothes as a measure of "empowerment." In most cases, the men choose the materials for their wives' and daughters' clothing. So, once the women had the ability to choose, the CARE team could literally see the "ripple effect" in the shifting hues of women's dress in the district.

This example gives pause to consider the psychological pain that must come from being unable to express the self in even this small way, specifically because someone else controls you at a personal level by asserting the right over this choice and refusing you mobility. A study of this phenomenon would be continuous with, for instance, the experiences that Scaraboto and Fisher describe among their "fatshionistas" but would be quite a bit more enmeshed in household control. Thus, the way would be paved to an analysis that could join institutional resistance to interpersonal and familial power struggles. The perspective presented by Thompson and Ustuner (2015) could provide the connecting mesh between these points of power.

Consumption as Resistance

One of the main ways that women are held hostage in less developed societies is through the inability to control the number and timing of births. In the previous example, the women were able to get birth control and use it without their husbands even knowing they did it. This not only gave them access to family planning but also potentially opened the way for them to have sex with other men. Gayle Rubin argued in her famous 1975 article on "The Traffic in Women" that the primary axis of control in the subordination of women is withholding sexual freedom, allowing females only to couple with males after approval from the male hierarchy (as in marriage). In a recent visit to this same site, we noted that many husbands were now absent, having gone to the Middle East to do construction work. Some had been gone more than ten years. I feel sure the men all were having sex where they were, but what about the women they had left behind? The secret availability of birth control would have introduced an unexpected twist to this situation.

Once you have tuned into the fact that control over goods is a means of subordination, one can, of course, imagine easily how the consumption of forbidden objects—alcohol, tobacco, birth control, lipstick, bank accounts, red saris—can become a form of resistance, both public and private. Again, however, the extra-American experience would be quite a lot more intense. The response to resistance in South Asia is likely to be acid thrown in her face or her clothing set on fire. Nevertheless, drawing parallels between the use of certain classes of objects to control or exclude—money, alcohol, tobacco, and clothing, for instance—across cultures and countries could yield important insights and guidelines. It has been my experience that the types and uses of such objects, when viewed in the context of women's subordination and resistance, are more similar than different around the world.

The differences that do exist between countries on access to food versus access to alcohol would also be instructive. Certainly, there would be some ability to identify the impact of "intersectionality" in this domain. I have myself given sustained attention to the ways that intersectionalities render different views of the same consumption acts (2005). However, I really must emphasize that the new insight and force driving the women's empowerment movement is that female subjugation is a global scourge with consistent features and predictable negative impact. The potential in this moment should not be undermined by facile gesturing toward small differences in local experience.

Consumption as Punishment

Because the control over consumption is often so focused in paternal hands, the bestowing and withholding of permission becomes a system of reward and punishment. School uniforms are withheld from naughty daughters, mobile phones from flirtatious wives, and so on. Some objects, of course, can be used in a rather obvious way as punishment (guns, ropes, hammers). However, some are less obvious: in the developed nations, the onset of domestic violence is usually presaged by takeover of financial-services access, expropriation of communications technology, abuse of pets, and even breaking of dishes.

The emphasis that feminist inquiry has had on issues of beauty and fashion tends to trivialize the potential negative impact goods can have on women. Surely, the use of goods and services as a form of or prelude to physical violence deserves at least equal attention to the dangers of lipstick and would lend needed gravitas to the research stream. Consider also that this is an area of research that could be united across developed and developing nations because violence against women is often framed as "punishment" and happens everywhere. Further, the economic impact is quite large: recent estimates set the global cost of domestic violence alone at five percent of gross domestic product, on average, or about equal to the spending on primary education (Duvvury et al. 2014). Note also that the seemingly ordinary goods that are withheld often have substantial effects on the economic viability (school uniforms) and safety (mobile phones) of females, going far past the effect of muting self-expression.

Consumption as Politics

In my mind, I keep going back to the potential for consumption to be used as a form of political power. The Second Wave so dismissed consumption as a passive phenomenon, unworthy of being seen as a form of activism, that we have forgotten how powerful the women of the advanced nations can be simply due to their purchasing power. This fact was brought home to me when a student of mine was studying MAS Holdings, a radically innovative garment manufacturer in Sri Lanka, which was trying to position itself as the ethical, "women-friendly" garment maker in order to establish brand loyalty among women consumers in "the West." Women in the rich nations purchase the overwhelming majority of garments, regardless of who finally wears them, whereas very nearly all garment workers are female. The possibility to repeat the successes of the early century NCL on a global scale—using the power of women as shoppers to affect the empowerment of women as workers—is very real, in my view.

Today, there are also new "White Lists" emerging, such as the Buy Up Index (Price 2014) and Edge (Edge Certified Standard 2016), both of which are means of certifying the "women friendliness" of companies. And I would suggest that if women in the West really wanted to make equal pay a reality, they might consider declaring a "Stop Shopping" Day every year just before Christmas until the pay gap was closed.

Yet today's international effort to empower women presents a new counterpoint to the adversarial stance that usually prevails between feminism and corporations. Some of the largest companies in the world now have substantial programs aimed at empowering women economically in developing countries. Drawing on Diamond and colleagues' (2009) description of the elaborate relationship between branding, storytelling, and morality-supporting American Girl dolls, we might take a very different look at emerging connections between branding and the politics of gender. Some of the biggest investors in women's empowerment have had negative brand reputations (Goldman Sachs, ExxonMobil) but are now showing significant thought leadership in this rather unlikely domain. Walmart, once the target of America's largest-in-history sex discrimination suit, has become a leading activist in trying to equalize women's participation as suppliers to the global economy. Some consumer-facing companies (Unilever, Coca-Cola, Procter & Gamble, just to name a few) are taking up the charge but could ultimately benefit by establishing a prowoman reputation in developing countries—those women are where their growth must now come from. Yet, the fact remains that employers, as a whole, discriminate against women to such a degree that it is measurable in the aggregate—at the national data level of every country in the world. Overall, therefore, it would be an interesting and important project to consider what it means for major corporations to be weaving stories of women's empowerment into their brand identities. It would require a theory of feminism that was not axiomatically oppositional to capitalism—indeed, one that is more reconcilable to the global data—but retained a critical *feminist* edge. An important aspect of that reexamination would be to compare the role of the corporation in this new movement to the activities of public charities, governments, universities, and religions. The private sector is actually taking the lead, and many governments and religious leaders remain on the wrong side of history.

Consumption as Slavery

No slate of projects about women and consumption would be complete without sober acknowledgment that women themselves are still objects to be traded in many cultures. The slave trade is thought to be larger today than ever in history. The ILO and others estimate that as much as seventy percent of today's slaves are female, most of them teens forced into sex slavery or domestic service. At the core of this phenomenon is that females, as economically excluded beings, simply have no value in their home communities (Bales 2012). Yet again, the economic empowerment of women promises the solution.

Conclusion

There are many other possibilities still to consider as future research projects for a new feminist theory of consumption. Throughout, however, a critical stance must be maintained. It is easy, in the current policy discourse, for the empowerment of women to fall second to stimulating growth or fighting poverty. And "empowerment" is too often measured by things like employment—which leaves the door open to exploitation. The metrics of the field need substantial development if the goal of ending women's subordination is to be achieved (Scott et al. 2016). The critical capabilities, wide methodological scope, and considerable field skills available in consumer research could bring accountability, as well as insight, to this important new effort.

Bibliography

American Psychological Association. "Stereotype Threat Widens the Achievement Gap: What the Research Shows." July 15, 2006. www.apa.org/research/action/stereotype.aspx.

Anderson, Paul F. "On Method in Consumer Research: A Critical Relativist Perspective." *Journal of Consumer Research* 13 (September 1986): 155–73.

Arnold, Stephen J. and Eileen Fischer. "Hermeneutics and Consumer Research." *Journal of Consumer Research* 21 (June 1994): 55–70.

Bales, Kevin. *Disposable People: The New Slavery in the Global Economy.* Berkeley: University of California Press, 2012.

Bristor, Julia M. and Eileen Fischer. "Feminist Thought: Implications for Consumer Research." *Journal of Consumer Research* 19 (March 1993): 518–36.

Butler, Judith. *Gender Trouble.* New York: Routledge, 1990.

Carothers, Bobbi J. and Harry T. Reis. "Men and Women Are from Earth: Examining the Latent Structure of Gender." *Journal of Personality and Social Psychology* 104, no. 2 (2013): 385–407.

Catterall, Miriam, Lorna Stevens, and Pauline Maclaran. "Postmodern Paralysis: The Critical Impasse in Feminist Perspectives on Consumers." *Journal of Marketing Management* 21 (2005): 489–504.

Demos, John. *The Enemy Within: A Short History of Witch-Hunting.* New York: Penguin, 2009.

Diamond, Nina, John Sherry, Albert M. Muniz, Jr., Mary Ann McGrath, Rovert V. Kozinets, and Stefania Borghini. "American Girl and the Brand Gestalt:

Closing the Loop on Sociocultural Branding Research." *Journal of Marketing* 73 (May 2009): 118–34.

Dolan, Catherine, Mary Johnstone-Louis, and Linda Scott. "Shampoo, Saris, and Sim Cards: Seeking Entrepreneurial Futures at the Bottom of the Pyramid." *Gender and Development* 20, no. 1 (2012): 33–47.

———, Caitlin Ryus, Sue Dopson, Paul Montgomery, and Linda Scott. "A Blind Spot in Girls' Education: Menarche and Its Webs of Exclusion in Ghana." *Journal of International Development* (April 2013): 643–57.

Duvvury, Nata, Aoife Callan, Patricia Carney, and Srinivas Raghavendra. *Intimate Partner Violence: Economic Costs and Implications for Growth and Development*. Women's Voice, Agency, and Participation Series, no. 10. Washington, DC: World Bank, 2013.

Edge Certified Standard. The Global Business Standard Certification for Gender Equality. www.edge-cert.org/certification/certified-standard/, accessed September 8, 2016.

Elborgh-Woytek, Katrin, Monique Newiak, Kalpana Kochhar, Stefania Fabrizio, Kangni Kpodar, Philippe Wingender, Benedict Clements, and Gerd Schwartz. *Women, Work, and the Economy: Macroeconomic Gains from Gender Equity*. Paris: International Monetary Fund, Strategy, Policy, and Review Department and Fiscal Affairs Department, 2013.

Eller, Cynthia. *The Myth of Matriarchal Prehistory: Why an Invented Past Will Not Give Women a Future*. New York: Beacon Press, 2001.

Flexner, Eleanor. *Century of Struggle: The Women's Rights Movement in the United States*. Cambridge, MA: Belknap Press, 1959.

Freidan, Betty. *The Feminine Mystique*. New York: W. W. Norton, 1963.

Funk, N. "Feminism and Post-Communism." *Hypatia* 8, no. 4 (1993): 85–8.

Gilligan, Carol. *In a Different Voice*. Cambridge: Harvard University Press, 1982.

Goldman Sachs. *The Power of the Purse: Gender Equality and Middle-Class Spending*. New York: Goldman Sachs World Markets Institute, 2009.

Guiso, Luigi, Ferdinando Monte, Paola Sapienza, and Luigi Zingales. "Culture, Gender, and Math." *Science* 320 (2008): 1164–5.

Hartmann, Heidi. The Unhappy Marriage of Marxism and Feminism: Toward a More Progressive Union. *Capital and Class* 3(2) (1979): 1–33.

Hirschman, Elizabeth. "Ideology in Consumer Research, 1980 and 1990: A Marxist and Feminist Critique." *Journal of Consumer Research* 19 (March 1993): 537–55.

Hudson, Laurel Anderson and Julie L. Ozanne. "Alternative Ways of Seeking Knowledge in Consumer Research." *Journal of Consumer Research* 14 (March 1988): 508–52.

Hyde, J. S. "The Gender Similarities Hypothesis." *American Psychologist* 60 (2005): 581–92.

———, Sara M. Lindberg, Marcia C. Linn, Amy B. Ellis, and Caroline C. Williams. "Gender Similarities Characterize Math Performance." *Science* 321 (2008): 494–5.

Inglehardt, Ronald and Pippa Norris. *Rising Tide: Gender Equality and Cultural Change around the World*. London: Cambridge University Press, 2003.

Intergrowth 21st. The International Fetal and Newborn Growth Consortium. www.intergrowth21.org.uk, accessed September 8, 2016.

Jackson, Stevi. "Why a Materialist Feminism Is (Still) Possible—and Necessary." *Women's Studies International Forum* 24, nos. 3–4 (2001): 283–93.

Jaggar, Alison. *Feminist Politics and Human Nature*. Lanham, MD: Rowman, 1983.

Koch, Kathrin, Sandra Lawson, and Kathy Matsui. *Giving Credit Where It Is Due*. New York: Goldman Sachs Global Markets Institute, 2014.

Lerner, Gerda. *The Creation of Patriarchy*. Oxford: Oxford University Press, 1987.

Montgomery P., C. R. Ryus, C. S. Dolan, S. Dopson, and L. M. Scott. "Sanitary Pad Interventions for Girls' Education in Ghana: A Pilot Study." *PLoS ONE* 7, no. 10 (2012): e48274. doi:10.1371/journal.pone.0048274

Murray, Jeff B. and Julie Ozanne. "The Critical Imagination: Emancipatory Interests in Consumer Research." *Journal of Consumer Research* 18 (September 1991): 129–44.

OECD. *Closing the Gender Gap: Act Now!* Paris: OECD, 2012.

Power, Marilyn. Social Provisioning as a Starting Point for Feminist Economics. *Feminist Economics* 10 (3) (2004): 3–19.

Price, Susan. Looking for Products Made by Woman-Friendly Companies? Try This App. Fortune. August 3, 2014. http://fortune.com/2015/08/03/app-woman-friendly-companies/.

Reitner, Reyna. *Toward an Anthropology of Women*. New York: Monthly Review Press, 1975.

Rubin, Gayle. "The Traffic in Women: Notes of the 'Political Economy' of Sex." In *Toward an Anthropology of Women*, 157–210. Edited by Reyna Reiter. New York: Monthly Review Press, 1975.

Rutherford, Sarah. *Women's Work, Men's Cultures: Overcoming Resistance and Changing Organizational Cultures*. London: Palgrave Macmillan, 2011.

Scaraboto, Daiane and Eileen Fischer. "Frustrated Fatshionistas: An Institutional Theory Perspective on Consumer Quests for Greater Choice in Mainstream Markets." *Journal of Consumer Research* 39 (April 2013): 1234–57.

Scott, Linda M. *Fresh Lipstick: Redressing Fashion and Feminism*. New York: Palgrave MacMillan, 2005.

———. "Theoretical Realism: Culture and Politics in Commercial Imagery." In *Explorations in Consumer Culture Theory*. Edited by John Sherry and Eileen Fischer. London: Routledge, 2008: 34–54.

———. *Connected Women: How Mobile Can Support Women's Social and Economic Empowerment*. London: Vodafone, 2013a. www.vodafone.com/content/dam/vodafone-images/foundation/thought-leadership/VF_WomensReport_V12%20Final.pdf.

———. "The Gender of Necessity: Beer and Lipstick in Rural Uganda." DoubleXEconomy blog, 2013b. www.doublexeconomy.com/2013/03/23/the-gender-of-necessity-beer-and-lipstick-in-rural-uganda/.

——— and Jiafei Jin. "Finance after Hours: A Case Study on Women's Access to Credit." University of Oxford: Said Business School Case Study, 2014. www.sbs.ox.ac.uk/sites/default/files/community/gender-case-studies/finance-after-hours.pdf.

———, Catherine Dolan, Laurel Steinfield, Mary Johnstone-Louis, Kelly Northridge, Anna Custers, Ama Marston, Daria Luchinskaya, and Lina Rothman. "Advisory Note on Measures: Women's Economic Empowerment." University of Oxford: Said Business School Research Papers, 2016.

———, Mary Johnstone-Louis, Catherine Dolan, and Caitlin Ryus. "Pampers and UNICEF Part 2: Delivering the Vaccine." University of Oxford: Said Business School Case Study, 2011. www.sbs.ox.ac.uk/sites/default/files/community/gender-case-studies/pampers-unicef-case-part-2.pdf.

———, Mary Johnstone-Louis, Catherine Dolan, Kimberly Sugden, and Mary-alice Wu. "Enterprise and Inequality: The Case of Avon in South Africa." *Entrepreneurship Theory and Practice*, May 2012: 543–568.

Stanford Encyclopedia of Philosophy. "Topics in Feminism." 2012 (revised). http://plato.stanford.edu/entries/feminism-topics/#FemDivWom.

Stanford Encyclopedia of Philosophy. "Feminist Perspectives on Sex and Gender." 2016 (revised). http://plato.stanford.edu/entries/feminism-gender/.

Steinfield, Laurel. "Gender Divide in Uganda: Norms, Myths, and Household Consumption." DoubleXEconomy blog, 2013. www.doublexeconomy.com/2013/07/13/gender-divide-in-uganda-norms-myths-and-household-consumption/.

Stern, Barbara. "Feminist Literary Criticism and the Deconstruction of Ads: A Postmodern View of Advertising and Consumer Responses." *Journal of Consumer Research* 19 (March 1993): 556–66.

Strategy & (Formerly Booz & Co.). *Empowering the Third Billion: Women in the World of Work*. London: PricewaterhouseCoopers, 2012.

Thompson, Craig, William B. Locander, and Howard R. Pollio. "The Lived Meaning of Free Choice: An Existential-Phenomenological Description of Everyday Consumer Experiences of Contemporary Married Women." *Journal of Consumer Research* 17 (December 1990): 346–61.

—— and Tuba Ustuner. "Women Skating on the Edge: Marketplace Performances as Ideological Edgework." *Journal of Consumer Research* 42 (2015): 235–65.

UNICEF. *State of the World's Children Report, 2007: The Double Dividend of Gender Equality*. Geneva: UNICEF, 2008.

United Nations Development Program. *Human Development Report*. Oxford: Oxford University Press, 1995.

United Nations World Food Program. "Women and Hunger: 10 Facts." 2015. www.wfp.org/our-work/preventing-hunger/focus-women/women-hunger-facts.

USAID. *Gender Equality and Female Empowerment Policy*. Washington, DC: USAID, 2012.

Vidal, Catherine. "The Sexed Brain: Between Science and Ideology." *Neuroethics* 5 (2012): 295–303.

World Bank. *World Bank Development Report, 2012: Gender Equality and Development*. Washington, DC: The International Bank for Reconstruction and Development, 2011.

World Bank Group. *Voice and Agency: Empowering Women and Girls for Shared Prosperity*. Washington, DC: The International Bank for Reconstruction and Development, 2014.

——. *Women, Business and the Law 2016: Getting to Equal*. Washington, DC: World Bank, 2015. doi:10.1596/978-1-4648-0677-3. License: Creative Commons Attribution CC BY 3.0 IGO.

World Economic Forum. *The Global Gender Gap Report*. Geneva: World Economic Forum, 2006–2016.

8 Ethnographies of a Mediterranean Vestaval

The *Passeggiata*

Bernard Cova, Véronique Cova,
and Hounaida El Jurdi

> In a land, where we enjoy the days but take especial delight in the evenings, the time of nightfall is highly important . . .
>
> About an hour and a half, or an hour before night, the nobility begins to ride out. They proceed to the Piazza Bra, along the long, broad street to the Porta Nuova . . .
>
> Cavaliers step up to the coaches and converse for a while with the ladies.
>
> —Johann Wolfgang von Goethe on
> Verona, 1786, in *Italian Journey*

Consumer research and consumer culture theory in particular have taken a keen interest in what consumers do together, in more or less structured groups (Arnould and Thompson 2005; Cova, Kozinets, and Shankar 2007). However, despite a few attempts (Aubert-Gamet 1997; Aubert-Gamet and Cova 1999), the spontaneous appropriation of space by these same consumer groups had not been researched to any great extent until recent years (Debenedetti, Oppewal, and Arsel 2014). Only the collective appropriation of natural spaces seems to have been investigated repeatedly in consumer research (from Schouten and McAlexander's pioneering text in 1995, to the more recent work by Canniford and Shankar 2013).

The notion of "vestaval" put forward by Bradford and Sherry (2015) thus comes as a valuable addition to the conceptual tool kit available to researchers reporting on recent phenomena of collective appropriation of a public or private space. In this chapter, we aim to further this concept as we look at what could be described as an ancient vestaval (see the previous quotation from von Goethe), brought up to date by individuals who take part in it around the Mediterranean: the *passeggiata* (Del Negro 2004). The context of Mediterranean consumption provides some interesting contrasts with that of the English-speaking world (Cova

2005) and will thus help us expand the concept of vestaval to facilitate its widespread adoption. Using three autoethnographies conducted during the *passeggiata* in Beirut, Marseille, and Milan, we demonstrate how today's vestavals lie on the tenuous border between market and society, with participants clearly able to handle frequent crossings over that border, into what we define as an oasis of slowness.

Vestaval as Extensions of the Home

Bradford and Sherry (2015) have introduced the term "vestaval" to describe a new secular ritual format that occurs, for instance, with tailgating, where households redeploy and take over the public realm. Vestaval rituals occur in ordinary spaces and are composed of mundane behaviors that lead to the creation of a kind of ephemeral extraordinary place. A vestaval is not solely the temporary noncommercial use of urban space awaiting commercial redevelopment (Bodnar 2015). According to Bradford and Sherry (2015, 147), it is more

> a demonstration of the transformative power of domesticity to remake our conception of, and possibly even the institutions of, civility, in the postmodern era. What begins either as private space controlled by the market or the state, or as nominal public space on the margins of everyday experience, becomes a public place of central importance through the creative effort of consumers determined to shape their experience. Empty, vacant, anonymous, or transactional space used primarily for mundane purposes, is transformed into vibrant, personalized, interactional place enjoyed by groups for extraordinary purposes. The former space is merely occupied, whereas the latter place is vivified, colonized and shared by a community of co-creators.

The ritual of vestaval draws on individuals' capacity to appropriate or reappropriate a public or private space (Aubert-Gamet 1997) to make it "home" away from home. With vestavals, it is a case of building a sense of homeyness, a substitute for home, with material and physical actions to occupy the space. The public display of domesticity is a hallmark of a vestaval: "Tailgaters establish a minimalist home on the grounds of the host university . . . Through their 'private appropriation of public space,' our informants engage in a collective 'striving for common place' (Visconti et al. 2010, 517)" (Bradford and Sherry 2015, 148). Just like regulars in a restaurant, in a vestaval, "consumers not only feel at home in the place but also make themselves at home. This occurs through their involvement in back-stage activities that are typically only reserved for staff and unavailable to customers in mundane commercial settings" (Debenedetti, Oppewal, and Arsel 2014, 909).

The concept of vestaval invokes a "parochial space" as defined by Lofland (1998) in his classification of three kinds of urban social space: public, parochial, and private. Public spaces are territories characterized by strangers, whereas private spaces are territories characterized by intimate and personal networks. Lofland suggests a third kind of urban space exists, which is somewhere between the public and private spaces—namely, the parochial. Parochial spaces are territories characterized by "a sense of commonality among acquaintances and neighbors who are involved in interpersonal networks that are located within communities" (Lofland 1998, 10). Neighborhoods are examples of parochial spaces. The concept of vestaval also resonates with the idea of extensions of the home, which are private spaces that spread into public space leading to a continuum of homey places (Bardhi and Askegaard 2009). This concept, developed in the sociology of space (Noschis 1984), was applied in certain approaches to Mediterranean consumer spaces (Aubert-Gamet and Cova 1999). Noschis (1984, 1987), in his remarkable study of the emotional significance of a traditional district in Venice (Italy), shows how some places (arcades, the town square, and the wharf for ferries) possess a linking function for the community of the district that is at least as important as their functional value. It is as if these places had a key for contact that allows a copresence in a ritualized framework where the interactions between individuals give rise to emotionally charged experiences that constitute and fuel the identity of the inhabitants. Noschis (1987) demonstrates that what he calls extensions of the home are privileged places for the exercise of the social link.

The extension of the home is made of a multiplication of private spaces extended into public space to make it a common place (Aubert-Gamet and Cova 1999) just like in the case of tailgating analyzed by Bradford and Sherry (2015). This is done by material or immaterial extensions that protect the intimacy of individuals while partially exposing it. Washing lines can almost serve as a metaphor here (Noschis 1984): the washing lines between the houses in the old districts of the town are the extensions of the home on which private undergarments are exposed while the rest of one's private life is protected behind the walls of the house. This clearly has a connection with the central mechanism of the vestaval: "Tailgating is weird because it turns domesticity inside out: households display their intimate inner workings to a world of strangers that stands to become a pool of fictive kin" (Bradford and Sherry 2015, 138).

This mechanism may seem "weird" for North American culture, but it is commonplace in the Mediterranean. According to Bradford and Sherry (2015, 148), "future research might seek to answer . . . Are there other examples of vestaval beyond tailgating?" It is worth taking a closer look at the purported "newness" of vestavals. This may be a case of cultural tropism, as we will attempt to demonstrate with a very ancient but enduring Mediterranean ritual that has all the distinguishing features of a vestaval.

Passeggiata, Paseo, and Other Mediterranean Promenades as Prevestaval

The extension of the home into a parochial space is precisely what happens with the *passeggiata*, the late afternoon stroll that has long been a social ritual in all Mediterranean cities, neighborhoods, and villages, featuring small groups of people meeting up and walking together in town squares and even on main roads, to the extent that automobile traffic can no longer get through. Just as in tailgating, "there is a fixed site and a cultural script for the phenomenon, the latitude provided consumers for constructing the event is quite broad" (Bradford and Sherry 2015, 134).

Around the Mediterranean, urban sociability is expressed in a common space of societal convergence: the agora, forum, mall, courtyard, esplanade, streets, promenade, park, or square. The mythological ideal type of socially open space lies in the Greek agora (from the Greek *ageirein*: assemble, come together) represented by a public square. Nonetheless, a street may be more suited to interaction than a square. Throughout history, societal interactions have sometimes occurred on the promenade and sometimes in other urban spaces. The promenade was indeed the venue of philosophical conversations in ancient times, but it made way for the gardens during the Italian Renaissance and in court life in France in the seventeenth and eighteenth centuries. Later, at the end of the eighteenth century, interaction returned to the promenades in the Italian cities and to the Haussmann boulevards in Paris in the nineteenth century (Miaux 2008).

The promenade characterizes city centers where the function of social representation is important. In southern Europe and other Mediterranean countries, public life takes place in the street. All of society takes part in the early evening stroll in summer in Italy (*passeggiata*) and in Spain (*paseo*). The group stroll is a chance to get some fresh air as night falls, before the evening meal in Spain. In Italy, people walk along the riverbanks in Rome, over a bridge in Florence, in the town or under the arcades in Bologna, where the strolling area runs almost six kilometers from the city center to the neighboring countryside; in Milan, it is the *galleria*—and the neighboring streets—that is known as the "living room" of Milan: "This is because it has always been considered the traditional meeting point of its residents and one of the most important places for social interaction" (Moretti 2015, 93). In Italy, the *passeggiata* describes both the fact of walking but also the public space set aside for this purpose. In Spain, the culture of the *paseo* is an important feature of Barcelona's urban culture, as can be seen in the unique form that the site of the stroll takes, the rambla with pedestrians assigned to a central promenade in the middle of the thoroughfare.

The late afternoon walk is thus an institution in the social life of any town or district around the Mediterranean: the finest example of this ritual, made possible by the mild climate, is the Italian *passeggiata*. In his classic work, *Christ Stopped at Eboli* (Levi 1945/2006), Carlo Levi provides a wonderful description: as the sun goes down on a warm, rocky part of southern Italy, in a poor, forlorn village perched on the edge of a mountain, men dressed solemnly in black for this daily ritual gather together and walk in small groups around the square. More recently, Noschis (1984) produced an ethnology of the Venetian district of Sacca Fisola and noted "the scene that repeats itself every day after 6 o'clock" (Noschis 1984, 95), involving mainly men and teenagers of both sexes, while women looked on from their windows.

The Italian promenade is a time of encounter and interaction; some even call it a ritual because behaviors are so coded. In fact, in Rome, the street is the subject of scenography, a process that has spread to many other cities around the Mediterranean. Like all rites, the *passeggiata* corresponds to a specific space and time that is theatrical and symbolic, "a social parenthesis depicting relationships, crystallizing a situation, while celebrating something" (Lardellier 2005, 7). And this is precisely what Mediterranean countries and their long history offer people: unique rituals celebrating slowness and sociality and requiring use of the body and certain props to reconquer public space for a certain time. In these ritual strolls, contrary to Christmas shopping (Fischer and Arnold 1990) where women are the chief performers, men tend to occupy more space and stay out the longest.

Interestingly, the continuing existence of the *passeggiata* and of the *paseo* contradicts McQuire's lament (2008, 134) about the loss of "vibrant public spaces capable of sustaining rich interactions" and Aubert-Gamet and Cova's fear (1999, 40) of the disappearing of common places and the increasing development of nonplaces:

> In modern towns (and even villages) the extensions of the home are no longer places where domestic activities are carried out together with the neighbours but they are increasingly places where specialised services can be bought. In a community perspective of social links, the concept of extension of the home is therefore losing its meaning. Other forms of encounter are replacing this, their main characteristic is that they are leisure activities, opportunities for sharing but around activities which are no longer necessarily for the upkeep of the home and which consequently do not necessarily expose people, neither do they force people to share aspects of daily family life. This progressive disappearance of common places, in the modern world, is compensated by the proliferation of what Augé (1992) calls non-places, places of anonymity where the individual is alone in the crowd.

The aim of our research into the *passeggiata* is to demonstrate how this enduring ritual has evolved to take on board changes to the urban environment (Bodnar 2015) and to assess what it teaches us on the emerging concept of vestaval.

Postcards from the Med

To share what the *passeggiata* means today, we conducted multisited, multiauthored phenomenological autoethnographic research. In addition, we have set out the results in a number of different ways.

Autoethnography is an approach to researching and writing (Ellis 2004) that draws from personal experience (*auto*), which is described and systematically analyzed (*graphy*) by linking this experience to the wider sociocultural context of that experience (*ethno*). Autoethnography offers an opportunity to study and analyze intimate experiences. Hence every researcher developed an embodied autoethnography that concentrates "on the body as the site from which the story is generated" (Spry 2001, 708). In this approach, the researcher's body walking with others becomes the site from which the autoethnographic text emerges. A full bodily experience of the *passeggiata* can move the research from a predominantly ocular understanding of this vestaval (the gaze) to a more extended one by connecting to the study of the sensory experiences (Sliwa and Riach 2012).

This type of autoethnography is far less painful and less dangerous than that carried out to report on extraordinary experiences (Arnould and Price 1993) and much shorter, although it is not "blitzkrieg ethnography" (Sherry 1995). The researchers walked alone or in groups among the crowds taking part in the *passeggiata*. Each researcher gained an immersive understanding of the stroll in which she or he participated as a "native" of the country and, most of all, the city in which it took place: Italy (Milan) for the first author listed, France (Marseille) for the second, and Lebanon (Beirut) for the third. The first author is a sixty-one-year-old male, the second author is a fifty-eight-year-old female, and the third author is a forty-year-old female.

Participant observations and autoethnographies normally materialize through journals filled with researcher notes that are meant to be subjected to rigorous analysis. Having said that, the representation crisis that has hit the socioanthropological disciplines—hence marketing (Sherry and Schouten 2002)—means that it is commonplace nowadays for data to be presented otherwise. For some, this has involved visual ethnology. Others have turned to literature—that is, to novels, essays, or even poetry—always with the ostensible aim of doing a better job of accounting for the phenomenon under observation (in the present case, the consumer experience) than standard academic expression, which pretends to be more or less immaterial and impassive, full of synopses, models, checklists, and matrices. A more artistic approach might rely on the kinds of metaphorical devices that are increasingly being seen as suitable vehicles for conveying researcher observations to readers. Our autoethnographic accounts are expressed in different written styles, according to the tastes and inclinations of each of the three researchers. The auto-ethnographies were written in the form of stories per Latour's (1988) suggestion for infrareflexive writing, which meant a reduction in methodological detail while emphasizing style.

We conceptualized our urban autoethnographies as partial, subjective, and self-reflexive (Soukup 2013). Reflexivity (Bettany and Woodruffe-Burton 2009) was an important part of these autoethnographies and was supported by the existence of a team of three researchers, each pushing the other to explore her or his own autobiographical, social, and personal location vis-à-vis the research. Each site was studied separately and then observations were compared and combined for discussion. Reflexivity also involved distinguishing similarities and differences such that the study of the *passeggiata* at each site added to the holistic understanding of the phenomenon.

The Milanese *Passeggiata* by Bernard

In Italian, "the word passeggiata literally means 'promenade' and specifically refers to the period of piazza strolling between 5:30 and 8 o'clock in the evening" (Del Negro and Berger 2001, 6). The importance of the *passeggiata* varies according to the city; in all cases, the strolls late on a Saturday afternoon or on Sunday evening are often significant local rituals. For people in Milan, Saturday afternoon is the time of the main *passeggiata*, when people wander along with their ice creams or chat and drink coffee at pavement cafés between the Duomo and San Babila along the kilometer-long Corso Vittorio Emanuele II, which extends through the Galleria Vittorio Emanuele II up to Piazza della Scala. It is pedestrianized along its full length.

For me, that Saturday started off without any particular intention or idea of walking through the busy parts of the capital of Lombardy. In early September, I was taking part in a three-day academic conference in Milan, from Thursday morning to Saturday midday, with lunch included. After lunch together at the university, located in the south of the city, most participants had to make their way back to the airport to fly back home. However, a group of five Scandinavians were staying on until the next day so were spending the Saturday night in Milan. As I was also staying on because of my duties at Milan University, I offered to help them spend part of this beautiful summer afternoon by showing them around Milan.

Contrary to most Italian cities, such as Florence, Rome, and Venice, which have a fine, well-located center making it easier for tourists to get around and visit, Milan is made up of a series of scattered islets, its beauty dotted around between buildings and sites that are of less interest for sightseers. I therefore suggested we set off from the university on a visit from one islet after another, to give them a glimpse of Milan's attractions. We started at around 4 p.m., heading toward Statale University, housed in a wonderful Italian Renaissance building. We then continued westward toward the medieval Sforza castle, through the streets that had emptied for the weekend, with Milan's residents having all seemingly escaped to the countryside. Once again, after that visit, we wandered the deserted streets, approaching Corso Vittorio Emanuele II from the south.

Up to that point, our tour around Milan was something akin to a trip around a ghost town, but my Scandinavian colleagues appeared neither surprised nor disappointed. Finally, we came out of a narrow street on to Corso Vittorio Emanuele II. Suddenly, we were literally submerged in a stream of people, sweeping us along at their pace. It was almost 6 p.m., and the square was absolutely teeming with people. Caught up in this tightly packed crowd, my colleagues asked me what was going on. They thought it must have been a political demonstration or a crowd of supporters (*tifosi*) of one of Milan's two soccer teams (Inter Milan or AC Milan) heading to the stadium together. As I recovered from my initial surprise, I remembered the Saturday evening *passeggiata* and I started to explain that people generally strolled around within a clearly defined perimeter for a couple of hours or so. That seemed to challenge their usual thought processes: How could anyone wander around aimlessly? How far do they go? How many times do they follow the same path? And so on.

To answer their functional questions, I first explained the *passeggiata* phenomenon and the fact that there was no functional purpose in walking from one point to another but that it was a social activity, with everyone walking together at the same time. Then I asked them to look around and watch what the people were doing, where they stopped or turned, and so on. My Scandinavian colleagues thus became ethnographers, observing the Milan *passeggiata* to note, detail, and interpret it from their Nordic viewpoint, watching what was going on over a couple of hours. The result was a compendium of their observations—and astonishment—a bit like Montesquieu's *Persian Letters*. The most surprising—indeed the most perturbing—thing for them was seeing the crowd pull up and wait to enter the Galleria Vittorio Emanuele II (see Figure 8.1): why queue to get in if there is nothing special to see or buy? They then took an interest in the small groups that would stop along the way so that they could chat more easily. Some stood still for more than ten minutes before setting off again on their stroll, thus occupying the public space and forming a short-lived collective body. Under the arcades of Corso Vittorio Emanuele II, they saw the endless line of clothes shops (Max Mara, Gap, Banana Republic, Furla, Foot Locker, Disney, Zara, H&M, etc.), the storefronts somewhere for small groups of strollers to pause, but focal points for the many tourists. However, under

Figure 8.1 The entrance to the Galleria Vittorio Emanuele II on a Saturday afternoon at 5 p.m.

the arcades the pace was different from that along the uncovered sections. Some groups alternated between both areas whereas others, more numerous, stayed in the center of the Corso, well away from the shop windows that had no place in their Saturday evening *passeggiata*. They also managed to avoid the street performers and vendors who hindered their flow. In the middle of the square, there were groups of young people walking together, or adults or families doing the same thing.

My Scandinavian colleagues also noted some of the props required by the Milanese to perform their Saturday evening ritual. The first thing—their clothing. Clearly, apart from the tourists—including my colleagues from northern Europe—people were very smartly dressed, their clothing apparently not having suffered from the day's activities. In fact, many people appeared to have gone home and changed before coming back out at 6 p.m. for the *passeggiata*. Secondly—the ice cream cone! Most people, regardless of age, were wandering along enjoying an ice cream purchased from one of the many *gelateria* or bars along the way. Similarly, people seemed to enjoy walking along slowly, casually licking their ice creams. They were not feeding on them hungrily, instead the cornet featuring as a key part of the Milan *passeggiata* ritual. Mobile phones were also omnipresent, used to make calls or send messages to find out where other people were, or to log on and find out the latest football scores. The phones also served to provide a musical soundtrack to the stroll. And, of course, to take selfies when pausing at a key point on the *passeggiata*—at the entrance to the Galleria, in front of the big Mondadori bookshop on the Corso or on Piazza San Carlo, just before the Corso.

At around 8 p.m., after wandering between Vittorio Emanuele II, Piazza del Duomo, the Galleria, and Piazza della Scala several times, we went to a typical trattoria for dinner and to debrief on the *passeggiata*. Several years later, whenever I met my Scandinavian colleagues at international conferences, they would talk to me about that unforgettable—exotic to them—afternoon in Milan. They still wondered how a seemingly quiet city could condense all its sociality in a clearly defined time and space, in the city center *passeggiata*.

The Marseille Saturday Stroll by Véronique

I undertook a participant observation of a *passeggiata* in the French seaside city of Marseilles, specifically on the Rue Saint-Ferréol. The particular ritual stroll in question took place on a Saturday afternoon and involved groups of young adults and teenagers coming from the city's more deprived neighborhoods into the center. In Marseille, "the town center has remained 'working class', with tower blocks adjoining housing estates, and young people from neighboring districts regularly—or at least on Saturdays—coming down to the town center or spending summer on the beach" (Bouillon 2001, 261). They stroll in a way similar to the *passeggiata*, putting on a kind of performance (Roulleau-Léger 2004). In this study conducted in concert with Marseille's theater company Compagnie de la Cité, I have developed a more "theatrical" approach to narrating a participant observation of the *passeggiata* in this city, one that centers on the writing of short plays to be performed on stage.

Rue Saint-Ferréol! Saturday afternoon . . . the streets are teeming . . . (see Figure 8.2). Young people—a lot of young people. Never alone, always in

Figure 8.2 Rue Saint-Ferréol, a Saturday afternoon at 4 p.m.

groups. Groups of two, three, four, or five . . . Groups of young people everywhere. And they wander . . . On Saturday afternoon, Rue Saint-Ferréol
is their territory. It is a pedestrian street in the town center, with plenty of
shops. Clothing mainly. Shops for young people. Shops with girls' names:
Zara, Caroll, Agatha, Jennifer, or punchy names like Les P'tites Bombes,
Magnetic, Dockers, Beweep . . . and the like. The street is very organized,
well regulated. I would go as far as to say that there is a "highway code"
on Rue Saint-Ferréol! And I learned five rules. The first rule is that, when
you are in the middle, you walk slowly. If you want to move faster, you go
to the sides. In the middle, you stroll, on the side you scurry! . . . I learned
that thanks to a boy I overheard speaking to his friend, "if you want us to
speed up, we ought to move to the side." So I turned to look and it was
true: there are two paces with those in the middle of the street wandering
along much more slowly than those on the sides.

The second rule is about what to do when the group arrives at the
end of Rue Saint-Ferréol. There, they board the "Magic Foot Locker
Roundabout," which lets them turn back around without having to
make a U-turn! In fact, what happens is that they enter one door of the
Foot Locker store, move along the counter, pretend to look at the items
on sale . . . then head back out the other door! As if there was nothing
amiss, they head back down Rue Saint-Ferréol in opposite direction.

The third rule is about clothing. I saw two young people who were
wearing what I can only call a disguise! It wasn't very warm that day but
they were dressed as if it was midsummer. In T-shirts, short sleeves, bare

armed. One of the youths (I'll call him Benji) was wearing mask-type sunglasses—the kind that covers half the face, with mirrored lenses. His T-shirt had Von Dutch written in large type across his chest. The other one, his friend, was wearing a wooly hat, pulled well down over his ears. I'll call him Mike. He was wearing drop-waist trousers, with the crotch hanging down at knee level and the top barely reaching the middle of his buttocks! And you could see his boxer shorts over the top. If it had been a girl, it would have been her G-string peeking out the top! Benji and Mike were wearing sneakers that looked more like haggis or something! In fact, it looked as if they had some kind of fluorescent caul wrapped around their feet! They were both carrying the kind of bag often seen in Marseille—a black bag slung across their chests, knocking against their behinds as they walked along. But the bags were empty. Because they had nothing to put in them. The middle of Rue Saint-Fé is a bit like an invisible red carpet or a catwalk. On Saturday afternoons, Benji and Mike "do" Rue Saint-Fé. All the way down . . . then back again. And they strut along. When they reached the end of the road, I thought, "They're going to do the Foot Locker thing!" But I was wrong, in fact! They went back to their motorbike in the nearby car park. And there I saw them get changed! They were taking off their stage costumes! Benji took off his glasses, while Mike removed his hat. They both shortened the strap on their bags and tucked them up against their chests. They took some shabby jackets out of the motorbike's storage compartment and put them on. In just three minutes, the masquerade was over. And off they went, unnoticed.

The fourth rule is about interaction. Eye contact. Lots of eye contact. See and be seen. In fact, on Rue Saint-Fé on a Saturday afternoon, the young people all know one another. When they meet, they stop and kiss—three kisses on the cheeks—boys, too, as well as girls, then continue on their way. Without saying a thing. No "hello," no "how are you?"—nothing at all.

They meet, kiss cheeks three times, then carry on. You've seen me. I've seen you. We've seen one another! . . . They stroll. And they observe . . . They speak a bit, within their own little groups. But they don't really say much. There is no real conversation. No ongoing discussion.

Words bounced off one another: "Would you believe it!" . . . "So, what did he say?" . . . "Oh, fuck!" . . . "No way! That's sick!" . . . "Oh, yeah!" . . . "That grossed me out!" Words spoken just loud enough for everyone to hear. Words that are uttered without looking at anyone in particular. I was worried for a while. I thought, "One of them is bound to see me and realize I'm spying on them. He'll come over and punch me in the face!" But not at all!

The fifth rule on Rue Saint-Fé: I'm invisible! Completely invisible! I was there, speaking into my Dictaphone as I watched a group of young people who were having what looked like a sit-in in the Adidas store. I thought they were bound to notice my presence. They looked at me but didn't really see me. They have a very finely tuned field of vision. They only see other young people. I didn't exist; I was just part of the decor. They didn't see me and certainly didn't give a damn about me. But still . . . They must have realized I was following them! They must have noticed that I was plodding along to match their strolling pace! And when they turned back and I found myself face to face with them, they looked me in the eye. So, they must have seen me! For sure! They saw me several times. I thought I'd been caught. But no! They are in their own world. A world of their own, where I simply don't exist.

The Corniche Beirut *Timsheyeh* by Hounaida

The afternoon stroll, or *timsheyeh* as it is known locally, is a very common practice in Lebanon, particularly in the suburbs and villages where many people go out for a walk, often in groups of friends and family members, just before sunset. In the city, where there are not many pedestrian areas to engage in this practice, Beirutis flock to the Corniche, on Beirut's seafront, for their afternoon walk. The Corniche is a five-kilometer stretch along the seafront and is one of the very few remaining public spaces in Beirut. Walking on the Corniche starts at daybreak; you always see people jogging, exercising, or strolling and chatting with another friend while enjoying a cup of coffee in the early hours of the morning. The Corniche is never really empty, not even at noontime when it is the hottest time of the day. However, it is just before sunset that this activity is at its peak, especially during the weekends, when Beirutis have leisure time to spend (See Figure 8.3).

The Corniche is just across the road from where I work. Actually, my office just overlooks it. I myself often go there for a short walk in the afternoon to take a break when I have a long day at work. I decided to make my observations and take notes one Saturday afternoon in February. Although February is usually the coldest and rainiest month of the year, that particular Saturday was nice and sunny, making it an ideal day for an afternoon stroll.

I arrived at the Corniche at around 4:30 p.m.; it was so busy I could hardly find a place to park. I could see multiple and diverse collective walks taking place on the long Corniche that afternoon. People from different socioeconomic backgrounds, religions, age groups, genders, and nationalities were taking part in this daily ritual, reflecting Lebanon's multiconfessional makeup and celebrating the pluralistic nature of the country. Yet, each person was walking with a different pace and a different rhythm. Some were walking briskly with their earphones on, not engaging in eye contact or even acknowledging their surroundings, but charging ahead at their fast pace. Others were walking in groups at a much slower pace, chatting and giggling, strolling aimlessly and laughing

Figure 8.3 The Corniche Beirut on a Saturday afternoon.

loudly, not caring about those around them. Some were sitting on benches or on folding chairs and stools they had brought from home, enjoying home-brought snacks or chestnuts and corncobs they had bought from vendors on the Corniche. The Corniche is a space not limited to walking and strolling; it is a place where people can rent bikes, play on skateboards, walk their dogs, and bring their own coffee- and tea-making equipment, and many even bring their own hookah pipes locally known as *arguileh*. This is a space shared by families, couples, friends, fishermen, bikers, joggers, skateboarders, dog walkers, and coffee and corn vendors, as well as onlookers, all forming a dense crowd.

Many enjoy the afternoon stroll; even migrants living in the country participate in this ritual. I could hear many accents from the people walking around me—Iraqi, French, Russian, and Syrian just to name a few. As I walk along, I am passed by a Russian couple strolling on the Corniche with their little boy riding a scooter in front of them. I find myself surrounded by bike riders, skateboarders, joggers, walkers, and onlookers. Among them I see two young Ethiopian women walking toward me, arm in arm, stopping every now and then to take photos of each other and selfies together with the ocean behind them. I keep walking, and I see two men dressed in formal business suits walking in front of me. One of them had a cigarette in his hand, talking while moving his hands in the air. I walk closely behind them and then slowly overtake them. I overhear part of their conversation—they were discussing the implementation plan of a construction project. For these men, it seems that the afternoon stroll was part of their working day.

As I walk further along the Corniche, I see a familiar face of a man whom I shall call Abou Hani. Abou Hani sits in the same spot next to his old silver-colored car parked by the side of the Corniche under a large palm tree (See Figure 8.4). Always holding an *arguileh* pipe in his hand, Abou Hani sits laid back on his stool, resting his back on his car, staring out at passersby while smoking his *arguileh*, which he keeps in his car trunk. Abou Hani is a regular visitor to the Corniche, for I have seen him many times before on different days of the week, sitting in almost the same location next to the big palm tree, staring out at the ocean or looking at passersby. Just a few meters away from Abou Hani

Figure 8.4 Consumers smoking a hookah pipe on the Corniche.

sits a group of three on a mosaic bench, two young women and a man, chatting together. One of the women sits comfortably on the bench with her legs crossed, smoking an *arguileh*.

The *arguileh* is a very common sight on the Corniche and is enjoyed as a solitary or a shared activity. A few minutes later into my walk I notice two young girls leaning on the Corniche rails, giggling and taking selfies with the sea behind them. I watch them as they are taking different poses. In one of the poses, one of them has her arm wrapped around her friend's shoulders, leaning toward her to take a selfie while the other is holding an *arguileh* pipe to her mouth and smiling at the camera. A few meters away from them sits a mother watching her kids play on their tricycles. She sits next to the Corniche rails smoking her *arguileh* with bags of chips and snacks by her side. As her kids pass by her, she smiles at them tenderly and continues to smoke. Several meters away from her sits a group made up of a middle-aged woman wearing a headscarf and three young adults. All four of them were sitting on plastic chairs forming a circle around an *arguileh* in the center. Each smokes a little and then passes the pipe to the person next to them. The older woman takes a thermos out of a large bag and pours tea into four plastic cups and passes them around. I lean against the Corniche rails and look at the crowds around me. Groups sharing *arguilehs* were everywhere.

I see a small crowd gather around a street vendor's cart. I walk toward them, and the smell of roast chestnuts and corncobs fills my nostrils. I stop and buy some for myself noting that the sun had set and it was getting dark. As the night fell, identities blurred and collectives began to shrink. Yet, I could still see a familiar shadow by the side of the big palm tree. There was Abou Hani, sitting in the dark next to his old silver car, smoking his *arguileh*.

Oasis of Slowness

The three autoethnographic vignettes demonstrate that the *passeggiata* ritual is still very much alive in the Mediterranean region and constitutes a perfect case of vestaval (Bradford and Sherry 2015). Of course, it has undergone change to adapt to our evolving societies. In particular, the number of stores along the site of promenade has increased. However, these contemporary promenades are clearly distinct from people browsing in shopping centers (Bloch, Ridgway, and Dawson 1994). The roots and histories of urban promenades go back much further than the emergence of department stores to the development of public parks and gardens (Borsay 1986).

The *passeggiata* is one example of what Manzini (2001) describes as an "oasis of slowness" in a life otherwise dominated by speed and urgency—even around the Mediterranean. Far from being outdated, it is a contemporary phenomenon that young people have adopted to create a special space and time (Lardellier 2005) devoted to proxemic, kinesthetic, or verbal performances (Del Negro and Berger 2001). In and during this space and time that celebrates slowness (Honoré 2004), the process is more important than the result: strolling is more important than arriving at a destination, just as feeding is more important than filling up for slow food enthusiasts (Cassano 2012).

La Cecla (2000), in his study of Italian manhood, provides one of the most useful approaches to the study of the *passeggiata*: "We don't talk about business, we don't negotiate, in fact we are reluctant to talk much at all, it's a waste of time, of that entertaining time that we need and cherish, surrounded by others" (La Cecla 2000, 177). What is said is generally of little importance, with words just one expression of the social link (Cova 2005); however, in some cases, just as in Beirut, people can discuss business projects while walking slowly. Slowness and sociability are what underpin the ritual of the *passeggiata*. As Cassano (2001, 150) writes,

> Strolling is not about getting away from others, it's about cultivating friendship . . . A society that never strolls and only runs, a society that abolishes Sundays and nights, where the footpaths disappear and only shops remain, is a society without pores, where even free time is a stock market commodity.

Analysis of the Mediterranean strolls (Del Negro 2004) highlights the various activities that they imply and enable: dressing up, walking, flirting, and, above all, socializing, all at a gentle pace, the pace of a stroll because everyone walks along pretty much aimlessly, coming and going constantly. Different local groups use the ritual stroll to show themselves in public and affirm their existence. "When people go out for passeggiata, they are engaged in a performance. Through proxemics, kinesics, fashion, and speech each individual uses his/her body as a surface for depicting social meanings" (Del Negro and Berger 2001, 13). The collective body also marks out the limits of the promenade: they trace invisible maps of their route, clearly indicating where to stop and where to turn back. Likewise, the places where they like to stop during the walk often express their social (political parties) or societal (clubs or tribes) allegiances. The rest of the people are invisible for them as in the case of our participant observer in Marseilles; it constitutes the context.

Far from any fear of being exposed, the players in the promenade ride out the strong demonstrative tensions. In fact,

> in the street, the city-dwellers have to accept that they are part of the performance, that they will be seen, looked at, approached and jostled. But you don't perform any old how. Because lives become public, there is thus the feeling of being more exposed than anywhere else. (Roulleau-Léger 2004, 110)

This implies efforts regarding conduct, appearance, posture, and so on, a daily effort in those towns where one has to change clothing at the end of the day to be ready for the *passeggiata*.

The *passeggiata* is a way of making contact with the collective self and feeling part of a larger entity (Del Negro 2004). The aim is neither public nor private, nor is it about remaining anonymous in the crowd as is often the case when wandering the city streets just as the flaneurs use to do. Being the traditional Baudelerian flaneur (Benjamin 1968) or the postmodern one (Soukup 2013), she or he critically observes people's behavior while strolling among the crowd. With the *passeggiata*, even if people gaze at others, it is more about sharing the physical and social presence of other people, friends, family, and other acquaintances in a specific public area that is half open, half closed. The *passeggiata* thus requires the presence of known others rather than unknown others to play and replay the scene of togetherness and nearness for a couple of hours while strolling with people of all ages.

Our three autoethnographies show great similarities between the three Mediterranean sites, with some differences. A major difference lies in the type of population that participates in the stroll. If in Beirut and Milan the crowd is multigenerational, in Marseille the crowd is predominantly young. Another difference concerns the use of personal material objects to "occupy" the space by bringing chairs or the *arguileh* as on the Corniche in Beirut; this is virtually impossible in Marseille and Milan. A final difference lies in the type of environment of the *passeggiata*; whereas in Beirut and Marseille the stroll is performed totally outdoors, a part of the *passeggiata* in Milan is done indoors, through the Galleria Vittorio Emanuele II and under the arcades of Corso Vittorio Emanuele II.

Staging the *Passeggiata* Vestaval

To carry out the intended corporeal performances of slowness and sociality in the space and time of the *passeggiata*, Mediterranean consumers require three elements:

1. A spatial setup in the public domain, with free admission for everyone (the Corso and Galleria Vittorio Emanuele II in Milan, Rue Saint-Ferréol in Marseille, the Corniche Beirut, and so on) that is functionally (an area enabling a relatively clear route) and aesthetically (pleasant area for all five senses, conducive to contemplation) suited;
2. A commercial setup made up of brands and stores that provide the necessary props for the *passeggiata* ritual, such as the ice-cream sellers in Milan or the fruit stalls on the Corniche in Beirut; and
3. A domestic setup with items brought from the home, such as folding chairs, a hookah pipe, teapots, a ball, or a bicycle.

In addition, as exemplified by the case of Beirut in February, the mild climate of the Mediterranean encourages outdoor living three-fourths of the year, so Mediterranean people have created lots of spaces (patios in Spain) and opportunities (the *passeggiata* ritual) to enjoy the outdoors. Natural elements (Arnould and Price 1993; Canniford and Shankar 2013) play a great role in Mediterranean vestavals; they allow and even foster outside gatherings. Indeed, there is a strong relationship between microclimatic conditions and the use of open spaces in the Mediterranean context (Nikolopoulou and Lykoudis 2007).

Public places (squares and streets) and items (benches and parapets) are the instruments used to stage the performance: they facilitate understanding of the world and thus guide the promenade performance. In these spaces, at a specific time of day, something very definite happens. The behaviors observed are not erratic; the appropriation of space is not random. These are practices regulated by conventions as can be seen in the boundaries of the promenades. The objects and areas are all part of the shared property available for these ritual activities. Without the opportunities for action that they provide and their place in the action and the theater of activities, these strolls would not be so well established by participants.

From another viewpoint, private areas—stores, bars, or restaurants—and the products they sell may serve as instruments, such as the Foot Locker store in Marseille, but are more generally used, like the items brought along by the participants themselves, as props in the performance. The Italian ice cream provides content and facilitates the kinesthetic performance of the strollers. Similarly, the Lebanese hookah facilitates the kinesthetic performance of the smokers.

Vestaval, Tailgating, and *Passeggiata*

The term "vestaval" has been recently introduced to describe a secular ritual format where households redeploy and take over the public realm (Bradford and Sherry 2015). In this chapter, we sought to explore the concept of vestaval within a Mediterranean context. We find evidence for a long history of collective spatial rituals in the Mediterranean, the *passeggiata*. Findings from three autoethnographies show that the *passeggiata*, like the vestaval of tailgating in the United States, is a moment of social interaction and public display of domesticity.

However—contrary to tailgating, which demonstrates the power of consumption to stimulate social and civic engagement—the *passeggiata* demonstrates the power of the social to stimulate consumption. Where space in tailgating is predominantly occupied, space in the *passeggiata* is mainly traversed several times and in a slow fashion. A tailgate is a mix of sedentary practices that anchors the ritual, whereas the *passeggiata* is rich with mobile practices that integrate the ritual. Furthermore,

Mediterranean strolling relies on a built environment as a stage against which the consumers perform the ritual, whereas tailgaters participate in materially building their "stage."

Our research shows that the emergent notion of vestaval has to do with slowness and not just homeyness. Bodies during the *passeggiata* are not working bodies nor sporting bodies; they are there to rediscover the joy of slowness. While performing vestaval such as tailgating or *passeggiata*, people collectively reclaim and domesticate public space (Bodnar 2015)—that is, they take ephemeral ownership of the town through rituals. This is akin to a carnivalesque form of performance, mixing old and new ways of communality to organize urban life with the help of marketed artifacts.

Bibliography

Arnould, E. J. and L. L. Price. "River Magic: Extraordinary Experience and the Extended Service Encounter." *Journal of Consumer Research* 20, no. 1 (1993): 24–45.

——— and C. J. Thompson. "Consumer Culture Theory (CCT): Twenty Years of Research." *Journal of Consumer Research* 31, no. 4 (2005): 868–82.

Aubert-Gamet, V. "Twisting Servicescapes: Diversion of the Physical Environment in a Re-Appropriation Process." *International Journal of Service Industry Management* 8, no. 1 (1997): 26–41.

——— and Cova, B. "Servicescapes: From Modern Non-Places to Postmodern Common Places." *Journal of Business Research* 44, no. 1 (1999): 37–45.

Augé, M. *Non-Lieux. Introduction à Une Anthropologie de la Surmodernité.* Paris: Seuil, 1992.

Bardhi, F. and S. Askegaard. "Home Away from Home: Home as Order and Dwelling in Mobility." In *Explorations in Consumer Culture Theory*, 83–98. Edited by J. F. Sherry, Jr. and E. Fischer. Oxon: Routledge, 2009.

Benjamin, W. "On Some Motifs in Baudelaire." In *Illuminations: Essay and Reflections*, 155–200. Translated by Harry Zohn and edited by H. Arendt. New York: Shocken Books, 1939/1968.

Bettany, S. and H. Woodruffe-Burton. "Working the Limits of Method: The Possibilities of Critical Reflexive Practice in Marketing and Consumer Research." *Journal of Marketing Management* 25, nos. 7–8 (2009): 661–79.

Bloch, P. H., N. M. Ridgway, and S. A. Dawson. "The Shopping Mall as Consumer Habitat." *Journal of Retailing* 70, no. 1 (1994): 23–42.

Bodnar, J. "Reclaiming Public Space." *Urban Studies* 52, no. 12 (2015): 2090–104.

Borsay, P. "The Rise of the Promenade: The Social and Cultural Use of Space in the English Provincial Town c. 1660–1800." *Journal for Eighteenth-Century Studies* 9, no. 2 (1986): 125–40.

Bouillon, F. "Des Acteurs et des Lieux: Les Economies de la Rue à Marseille." In *Cabas et containers*, 237–67. Edited by M. Peraldi. Paris: Maisonneuve & Larose, 2001.

Bradford, T. W. and J. F. Sherry, Jr. "Domesticating Public Space through Ritual: Tailgating as Vestaval." *Journal of Consumer Research* 42, no. 1 (2015): 130–51.

Canniford, R. and A. Shankar. "Purifying Practices: How Consumers Assemble Romantic Experiences of Nature." *Journal of Consumer Research* 39, no. 5 (2013): 1051–69.

Cassano, F. *Modernizzare Stanca: Perdere Tempo, Guadagnare Tempo.* Bologna: Il Mulino, 2001.

——. *Southern Thought and Other Essays on the Mediterranean.* New York, NY: Fordham University Press, 2012.

Cova, B. "Thinking of Marketing in Meridian Terms." *Marketing Theory* 5, no. 2 (2005): 205–14.

——, R. V. Kozinets, and A. Shankar, eds. *Consumer Tribes.* London: Butterworth-Heinemann, 2007.

Debenedetti, A., H. Oppewal, and Z. Arsel. "Place Attachment in Commercial Settings: A Gift Economy Perspective." *Journal of Consumer Research* 40, no. 5 (2014): 904–23.

Del Negro, G. P. *The Passeggiata and Popular Culture in an Italian Town.* Montréal: McGill-Queen's University Press, 2004.

—— and H. M. Berger. "Character Divination and Kinetic Sculpture in the Central Italian *Passeggiata* (Ritual Promenade)." *Journal of American Folklore* 114, no. 451 (2001): 5–19.

Ellis, C. *The Ethnographic I: A Methodological Novel about Autoethnography.* Walnut Creek, CA: AltaMira Press, 2004.

Fischer, E. and S. J. Arnold. "More Than a Labor of Love: Gender Roles and Christmas Gift Shopping." *Journal of Consumer Research* 17, no. 3 (1990): 333–45.

Goethe, J. W. von. *Italian Journey, 1786–1788.* New York: Penguin, 1970.

Honoré, C. *In Praise of Slowness: How a Worldwide Movement Is Challenging the Cult of Speed.* New York: Harper Collins, 2004.

La Cecla, F. *I Modi Bruschi. Antropologia del Maschio.* Milan: Mondadori, 2000.

Lardellier, P. *Les Nouveaux Rites.* Paris: Belin, 2005.

Latour, B. "The Politics of Explanation: An Alternative." In *Knowledge and Reflexivity: New Frontiers in the Sociology of Knowledge,* 155–77. Edited by S. Woolgar. London: Sage, 1988.

Levi, C. *Christ Stopped at Eboli: The Story of a Year.* London: Macmillan, 1945/2006.

Lofland, L. H. *The Public Realm: Exploring the City's Quintessential Social Territory.* New York: Aldine de Gruyter, 1998.

Manzini, E. "Ideas of Wellbeing: Beyond the Rebound Effect." Communication at the *Conference on Sustainable Services & Systems: Transition towards Sustainability,* Amsterdam (October, 2001).

McQuire, S. *The Media City: Media, Architecture and Urban Space.* Los Angeles, CA: Sage, 2008.

Miaux, S. "Le Piéton: Un Acteur Privilégié de L'espace Public Barcelonais." *Cahiers de Géographie du Québec* 52, no. 146 (2008): 175–90.

Moretti, C. *Milanese Encounters.* Toronto: University of Toronto Press, 2015.

Nikolopoulou, M. and S. Lykoudis. "Use of Outdoor Spaces and Microclimate in a Mediterranean Urban Area." *Building and Environment* 42, no. 10 (2007): 3691–707.

Noschis, K. *Signification Affective du Quartier.* Paris: Méridiens, 1984.

——. "Public Settings of a Neighbourhood: Identity and Symbolism." *Architecture & Behaviour* 3, no. 4 (1987): 301–16.

Roulleau-Léger, L. *La Rue, Miroir des Peurs et des Solidarités.* Paris: Puf, 2004.

Schouten, J. W. and J. H. McAlexander. "Subcultures of Consumption: An Ethnography of the New Bikers." *Journal of Consumer Research* 22, no. 1 (1995): 43–61.

Sherry, J. F., Jr., ed. *Contemporary Marketing and Consumer Behavior: An Anthropological Sourcebook.* Thousand Oaks: Sage, 1995.

———— and J. W. Schouten. "A Role for Poetry in Consumer Research." *Journal of Consumer Research* 29 (September 2002): 218–34.

Sliwa, M. and K. Riach. "Making Scents of Transition: Smellscapes and the Everyday in 'Old' and 'New' Urban Poland." *Urban Studies* 49, no. 1 (2012): 23–41.

Soukup, C. "The Postmodern Ethnographic Flaneur and the Study of Hyper-Mediated Everyday Life." *Journal of Contemporary Ethnography* 42, no. 2 (2013): 226–54.

Spry, T. "Performing Autoethnography: An Embodied Methodological Praxis." *Qualitative Inquiry* 7, no. 6 (2001): 706–32.

Visconti, L. M., J. F. Sherry, Jr., S. Borghini, and L. Anderson. "Street Art, Sweet Art? Reclaiming the 'Public' in Public Place." *Journal of Consumer Research* 37, no. 3 (2010): 511–29.

9 Reinvigorating the Sherlock Myth

Elementary Gender Bending

Pauline Maclaran and Cele Otnes

Brand narratives are replete with cultural myths that draw on archetypal images and themes to stir consumers' imaginations. An archetypal anti-hero par excellence, Sherlock Holmes is arguably the world's most enduring fictional detective. The Holmes myth replays the struggle between good and evil, testifying to the ability of reason and logic to triumph in pursuit of justice. Central to the Sherlock brand narrative is his relationship with partner-in-solving-crime Dr. John Watson, one reflecting and challenging ideals of masculinity across the multiple time periods the characters inhabit (Kestner 1997). Over time, they transition from being intellectual companions to men-of-action hero partners (Holt and Thompson 2004) who display an endearing homosocial rivalry (Doty 1993). In its popular current rendition, the BBC series *Sherlock* starring Benedict Cumberbatch and Martin Freeman, the sexual ambiguity underlying their "bromance" recurs regularly, with episodes laden with jokes and speculations about their relationship. Central to the narrative is the relationship between Holmes and Watson, rooted in and reflective of vaporized aspects of masculinity at the time the variants appear (e.g., intellectual companions, action hero partners, bromance participants).

Elementary, the American variant that premiered on CBS in 2012, introduces the most radical changes to the Sherlock myth with its female (Joan) Watson, played by Lucy Liu. Episodes in the 2014–2015 season averaged 7.4 million viewers, and it was recently renewed for 2016–2017. Yet the series has proved controversial, not only because of Watson's (and other characters') regendering, but also because New York City replaces the London setting and its storylines are untethered to the original Holmes canon.

Given the longevity of original (and some derived) Holmesian texts—and their relative faithfulness to the characters' original genders—it is important to understand how experimentation in this arena impacts consumer experiences. In this chapter, we explore the question, how does the regendering of characters within *Elementary* shape fans' perceptions and experiences of the Sherlock brand? We first offer a historical overview of Holmesiana in consumer culture, before reviewing literature on brand myth and the role of gender in brand narratives. We consider the role of "gender bending" within *Elementary* through the enabling lens of Judith Butler's theories on heteronormativity and the performance of gender.

After describing our research methods, we focus our analysis on the potential of gender bending in *Elementary* to reinforce or subvert gender norms—what Butler (1993) refers to as "heteronormative hegemony." Our analysis reveals three key fan response categories, eliciting a nuanced range of responses to brand gender bending that build on Avery's (2012) excellent introduction to the topic. In our discussion, we revisit the benefits and drawbacks of gender bending and how they can positively, as well as negatively, contribute to reinvigorating a brand's mythology.

Sherlock Holmes in Popular and Consumer Culture

Holmes is the brainchild of the Scottish physician-author-spiritualist Sir Arthur Conan Doyle, knighted in 1902 for his literary contributions. As a "consulting detective," Holmes maintains his own clients and also assists the police in crime solving. He first appears in the short story *A Study in Scarlet* in 1887, and "retires" in 1927. The Sherlock Holmes "canon," encompassing Doyle's oeuvre, consists of fifty-six short stories and four novels, all continually in print since their initial publication. Doyle also cowrote the first Sherlock dramatization in 1899 with William Gillette, who portrayed Holmes on stage for thirty years, instantiating the detective's deerstalker hat and pipe into the character.

As the historian Lucy Worsley (2014) observes, during the nineteenth century the British public became keenly interested in crime—and in particular, murder. Their obsession translated into extensive media coverage of actual and fictional cases and an outpouring of short stories, novels, puppet shows, and plays. In introducing Holmes through serial publications, Doyle's timing was prescient; the character debuted one year before Jack the Ripper began his murderous spree in London. Holmes proved so popular that Doyle felt stifled by him, and in "The Final Problem" (Doyle, 1893), Holmes dies by falling over a waterfall in Switzerland. Fans were so insistent on Holmes's return, however, that five years later Doyle resurrected him in the gothic tale "The Hound of the Baskervilles."

Reflecting his creator's interest in forensics, Holmes's crime-solving success stems from his reliance on abductive reasoning, or retrieving information contained in trace evidence. Holmes is the first detective (real or fictional) to insist on physically preserving the crime scene and to conduct sophisticated chemical and ballistics tests on evidence—predating standard police practices by decades. Holmes not only shaped actual detective and trial procedures but also fueled the public's interest in forensics, which continues to grow with advances in forensic technology.

Doyle's and Holmes's legacy sparked the worldwide popularity of such series as *The X-Files* and the *CSI* franchise, which at its peak reached viewers in two hundred countries (Gilbert 2006).

Holmes, Watson, their landlady Mrs. Hudson, the nemesis Professor James Moriarty, and Holmes's brother Mycroft constitute the core characters. Watson's general unflappability counterbalances Holmes's more unpredictable temperament, and as his only true friend, Watson provides glimpses into Holmes's often-imperceptible humanity. Doyle also endows Holmes with a superior intellect, and with passions ranging from the innocent (playing the violin) to the eccentric (shooting bullets in walls when bored) to the addictive (injecting cocaine). With the notable exception of Irene Adler, whom he describes as the only woman to equal him intellectually, Holmes displays no real romantic interest in women.

Holmes's eccentricities and his "bromance" with Watson contribute to the canon as meeting the three criteria of an "ambiguous brand" (Brown, McDonagh, and Schulz II 2013). First is *confusion*, an element integral both to the detective genre and to its protagonists who wrestle with incomplete evidence and often misleading clues. Doyle's deliberate omission of facts about Holmes's and Watson's pasts adds to the confusion, and also to fan engagement by "Holmesians" who pore over holes and inconsistent details in the canon. Fans within the Holmes brand community refer to this detective work as "the Great Game" (Stein and Busse 2012). Thus, they engage in disambiguating practices similar to those observed among fans of more recent "open" texts such as *Lost* (Ilhan 2011).

Secondly, the Sherlock brand is rife with *contradiction*. Holmes both engages with the police to help bring criminals to justice and also breaks and skirts the law through his drug use and reliance on members of London's criminal underbelly to act as his informants. His contradictory nature also belies the loyalty that Watson, his landlady, and his brother demonstrate toward him, as he clearly demonstrates narcissistic tendencies. Finally, *cumulation* refers to the ways a text builds increasingly complex layers of meanings. This outcome is evident in the many ways the Sherlock canon has been represented since its inception and in its continued popularity even as it undergoes modification.

The canon and the first spin-offs appear in myriad publications in print in the late nineteenth and early twentieth century, with non-Doyle variants seeing Sherlock engage with such characters as Dr. Jekyll, Dracula, and Jack the Ripper. As consumers flocked to broadcast media, Sherlock easily transitioned into radio, television, and films. Holmes is the most portrayed fictional cinematic character ever; since his first appearance on film in 1900, seventy different actors have played him (Fox 2009). Holmes's iconicity has attracted some of the more renowned stage and screen actors, including John Barrymore, Basil Rathbone, Nigel Bruce, Christopher Plummer, and more recently, Robert Downey, Jr., and Ian

McKellan. Renowned actors portraying Watson include James Mason, Ben Kingsley, and Jude Law. Cinematic variants range from ones faithful to the canon and its characters (typically prior to the 1960s) to those extending Holmes's age in both directions (e.g., in *Mr. Holmes*, Ian McKellan depicts him at age ninety-three).

Feeding fans' interest in the paradox of interacting as "authentically" as possible with this fictional character, Sherlock-oriented destinations and experiential-consumption opportunities are also on the rise. The Sherlock Holmes Museum opened in 1989 close to London's iconic 221B Baker Street, where Holmes and Watson ostensibly reside. Although reviews are mixed, the 2009 and 2011 films that earned $400 million worldwide, and both *Sherlock* and *Elementary*, have bolstered attendance. Furthermore, although Holmes is fictional, Grayson and Martinec (2004) observe some fans interpret many aspects of the museum to reflect "indexical authenticity," or the belief that these objects are "real" rather than contrived.

In 2015, the Museum of London staged a popular Sherlock exhibit, stuffing its gift shop with pipe bubble blowers, T-shirts, cards bearing Sherlockian lines (e.g., "The Game Is Afoot!") and Sherlock-silhouetted shortbread in its café. On the one-hundredth anniversary of the publication of "The Final Problem," a museum opened near Switzerland's Reichenbach Falls, the site of Sherlock's (clearly exaggerated) death. The BBC hit also has spurred development of a new Sherlock musical to open in 2017, ending the character's thirty-year hiatus from Broadway.

With the success of the BBC series, retailers have deepened their lines of "Sherlock merch" to range from the traditional (e.g., DVD sets of television series, films, and documentaries from across the decades) to the pop culture (Sherlock board games, comic books) to the kitschy (e.g., gold-tone pipe earrings, Sherlock Holmes action figures). The U.S. chain Hot Topic targets adolescent fans drawn to Sherlock's volatile nature (integral to his portrayal both by Cumberbatch and by Jonny Lee Miller in *Elementary*). The firm's edgier Sherlock attire and accessories include T-shirts bearing ominous slogans like "Moriarty Was Real." Fans can join Holmes Societies; sherlockian.net lists over nine hundred worldwide. The Baker Street Irregulars (named for the canon's infrequent characters) claims to be the most famous, and started the first official fan club in 1934.

Brand Myth and the Role of Gender

Myths—and brand narratives that borrow their elements—often embed social norms in their tales, providing moral templates that guide thoughts and actions at an unconscious level, individually and collectively. Myths resonate at a deep emotional level by presenting timeless narratives that relate to the paradoxes of human existence and help resolve cultural contradictions (e.g., good vs. evil; life vs. death; Lévi-Strauss 1966). Mythic brand representations are dynamic—continually created and recreated as marketers update these narratives to better reflect contemporary culture and retain their emotive appeal (Thompson 2004).

Brand myths are focal in studies of consumers' pursuit of collective identity projects (Muñiz and Schau 2005; Schouten and McAlexander, 1995) and in how such narratives support consumer resistance (Arsel and Thompson 2011; Kozinets and Handelman 2004), retro-branding (Brown, Kozinets, and Sherry 2003), mediating moral conflict (Luedicke, Thompson, and Giesler 2010), and brand ambiguity (Brown, McDonagh, and Schultz 2013). However, only a handful of studies examine how brand myths intersect with gender, even though the binaries of male-female and masculine-feminine are highly significant in myth making and represent a potential area of contradiction and tension, especially as ideals of masculinity and femininity evolve and change over time.

Holt and Thompson (2004) illustrate how major socioeconomic shifts—for example, precarious and routinized job structures, increasing female independence—threaten masculine identities, provoking men to search for symbolic reaffirmation that they are still "real men." In identifying with brands like Harley-Davidson, Apple, and Nike that embody ideals of heroic masculinity, men can construct themselves as contemporary man-of-action heroes, a form of masculinity that resolves tensions between their breadwinner and rebel selves (Holt and Thompson 2004).

Similarly, the success of Magners Irish Cider was in part due to its depiction of soulful masculinity—a variant consistent with both contemporary metrosexuality and a Celtic masculinity that resolves tensions between the emotionally feminine and the brutish masculine (Maclaran and Stevens 2008). Indeed, the development of the metrosexual as a cultural construction illustrates perfectly the role marketing can play in changing gender perceptions. Ervin (2011) observes, "What began as a fashion and marketing phenomenon became an oddly powerful and subversive force that may even mark a permanent change in the way we treat and view male sexuality and identity" (59).

Other studies show how brand myths can reinforce aspects of femininity. For example, American Girl encodes a powerful brand ideology of traditional femininity that interweaves female kinship with values of hard work and caring for others. Diamond and colleagues (2009) explore how customers adapt the brand's ideology to their own family heritage, cocreating meanings around it as they transfer intergenerational meanings around family and womanhood. Hence, myths change over time as they "shape, and are shaped by, consumer adoption and abandonment" (Brown, McDonagh, and Schultz 2013, 596).

In this vein, marketers sometimes find the mythic dimension of consumer experience challenges their original intended brand meanings. Martin, Schouten, and McAlexander (2006) show how female riders subvert Harley's hypermasculinity by creating new meanings around interpretations of femininity. Sometimes, too, brands deliberately create ambiguous gender messages to appeal to the LGBQT community. Kates and Goh (2003) look at how gay community members help cocreate brand mythology in ways that help legitimize certain brands (i.e., Absolut Vodka) as part of the community's sense of collective identity and shared interpretive schema.

The female Harley riders mentioned previously represent an example of consumers' engagement in what Avery (2012) terms "brand gender-bending." This outcome occurs when brands targeted toward or associated with one sex become targeted or associated with another. Sometimes this shift results from consumers co-opting brand meanings (e.g., by female bikers), but other times, marketers leverage the strategy to alter the target demographics either of the original product or of a brand extension. The marketing of Marlboro represents a successful example of the first goal. Launched in 1924, it was one of the first cigarette brands to target the newly emergent female smoker segment. Positioned as a luxury product, early ads depict a female hand holding the cigarette, with the taglines "Mild as May" and "Ivory Tips" to "protect the lips."

In the 1950s, Marlboro's ad agency Leo Burnett regendered the brand to appeal to male consumers seeking a "healthier" filtered cigarette. With its redesigned (now classic) red and white packaging, Burnett gave the brand a "big shot of testosterone" (Samuel 2010, 62) embodied in its ruggedly masculine, iconic Marlboro cowboy. Astride his horse somewhere in the American West, he became the epitome of self-sufficiency and independence, providing an escapist fantasy in sharp contrast to the breadwinner masculinity of the 1950s, and leaving the brand's feminine associations far behind.

More recently, Dove typifies a successful example of achieving a brand extension by gender bending. Its internationally renowned 2004 "Real Beauty" campaign sought to reform beauty ideals and support female empowerment, but the brand also introduced a Dove for Men range in 2010. Directly contradicting its female-targeted counterpart, the initial ad for this line extension, titled "Manthem," debuted during the Super Bowl (Hurn 2010). Dove for Men remains traditionally masculine, reinforcing its image by depicting male stereotypes (weightlifters, rugby players) or protective family men. Yet as Avery (2012) explains, such seemingly contradictory strategies (gender-challenging and affirming for the female line; traditional masculine for the male) reflect an implicit power imbalance still resonant in society. That is, men still face greater stigma for using feminine brands than women do for using masculine ones. This imbalance reflects the privileging of hegemonic or heterosexual masculinity and its association with rationality, contra the subordination of femininity that culture devalues as irrational (Connell and Messerschmidt 2005).

Avery (2012) also shows how brand gender bending can contaminate purchase experiences within an existing target group. Such contamination often occurs when "men searching for masculine distinction work to avoid brands that have been infiltrated by women" (Avery 2012, 324). Exploring the processes behind this outcome in the Porsche owners' community, she studies how owners of these iconic sports cars react to the launch of the Porsche Cayenne SUV and the firm's subsequent attraction of women to the brand. Porsche is a profoundly masculine brand that encodes Holt and Thompson's (2004) man-of-action hero ideology by reinforcing material success (the breadwinner) alongside its sporty image and capacity for speed (the rebel). Imagine, then, the threat to Porsche's masculine exclusivity when the manufacturer strategically incorporated new and feminine-gendered identity meanings into the brand. Expressing consternation at the soccer moms drawn to the Cayenne, existing brand community members were alarmed at what they perceived as a potential erosion of Porsche's mystique, as well as of their own masculinity.

Heteronormativity

Judith Butler's (1990) theories pertaining to heteronormativity can illuminate issues of gender-bending practices and the threat of contamination that Porsche's masculine brand community experienced. She explains how culture validates and normalizes certain masculinities and femininities as normal, while marginalizing or shunning others. Butler argues gender is something we *do* rather than *have*. It is therefore "an ongoing discursive practice," open to "intervention and resignification" (33). Within consumer research, her theory of performativity appears across studies that conceptualize consumption as a way of obtaining cultural resources that help people both perform their gender identities (Brownlie and Hewer 2007; Schroeder and Borgerson 2004) and subvert gender norms (e.g., in the LGBQT community; Goulding and Saren 2009; Kates 2003). Other research uses this lens to unpack changing discourses pertaining to contemporary masculinities (Brownlie and Hewer 2007; Schroeder and Zwick 2004) and femininities (Martin, Schouten, and McAlexander 2006; Stevens, Cappellini, and Smith 2015; Tuncay Zayer et al. 2013).

Most recently, Thompson and Üstüner (2015) leverage Butler as a theoretical lens when exploring resignifying practices in the sport of women's roller derby. They highlight market-mediated resignifications that include gender-bending juxtapositions such as physical aggression mixed with flirtatiousness and displays of playful eroticism. Performing "ideological edgework," this embodied resistance to gendered norms encourages reflexive awareness in derby grrrls and their fans of the ideological constraints naturalized in their everyday lives.

According to Butler, people construct gender identity through an ongoing iteration of norms within a culture. The gendered subject is (re) produced through embodied *doings*, or practices embedded in specific historical and cultural discourses that become instantiated as socio-cultural codes and norms. Butler introduces the important conceptual device of "heteronormative hegemony," or the sense-making process by which heteronormative societies understand gender identity. This hegemony relies on three key interdependent binaries—male-female, masculine-feminine, and opposite-sex desire. The interrelationship between these binaries renders intelligible the behaviors of feminine women who desire men, and masculine men who desire women, and marginalizes those who deviate from these norms.

Butler argues heteronormativity sustains itself through discourses embedded in various institutional and cultural practices that go unquestioned in our daily lives. Heteronormativity can, of course, be disrupted, and Butler avers that a person's gender identity and bio-logical sex need not match. Because heterosexual norms become natu-ralized through repetition, they can be subverted if such repetition is challenged and appropriated in ways that deconstruct heteronormative hegemony (Butler 1990). For example, males can perform femininity and females can perform masculinity. Celebrities like Lady Gaga and David Bowie play with gender roles in norm-deviating ways that chal-lenge traditional binary divisions of sex, gender, and sexuality. Butler singles out the drag queen, citing the disruptive potential of his gender parody as a way of resisting existing power structures and normative cultural expectations, and of exposing gender as a cultural code that can be imitated.

It is important to distinguish between performativity and perfor-mance, as sometimes people interpret Butler's views to mean that because gender is performative, it is a choice—something that can be taken out of the closet and decided on a daily basis. However, performativity is about resignifying and ritualistically repeating practices that are usually unquestioned and take for granted, a notion that contests the very idea of the subject presumed in the concept of performance (Butler 1993). Subverting these repetitions is not easy, but little by little, nonconform-ist sexual acts disturb or make trouble for heterosexual hegemony, and proliferation of these acts disrupts gender norms over time (Segal 1999).

Relevant to this chapter, media portrayals of gender identities play a major role in reinforcing cultural norms and ideals, challenging and altering certain norms and expectations. It is not always immediately obvious whether a character or plot line reinforces or subverts gender norms, however—and this is where Butler's concept of heteronormative hegemony is particularly useful. Consider Dustin Hoffman in *Tootsie* (1982), or Robin Williams in *Mrs. Doubtfire* (1993). Both appear to transgress their gender identities while engaging in cross-dressing per-formances within their social networks. However, on closer inspection, they are merely reasserting existing sex and gender distinctions to achieve goals rooted in traditional masculine roles (Salih 2002).

We apply a Butlerian lens to explore the regendering of the Sherlockian myth in *Elementary* and to study how different consumer groups reinterpret this process. Specifically, we analyze their varied responses in terms of Butler's theories of performativity and hetero-normative hegemony to assess the extent the updated characters subvert or reinforce gender norms. We believe this approach will enable us to understand more about the processes underpinning consumers' reactions to brand regendering.

Context and Method

Elementary is an appropriate context within which to study brand regendering because it both reflects and constructs our understandings of gender. The success of BBC's *Sherlock* since its 2010 debut demonstrated viewers' interest in an edgier variant of the Holmes mythos set in contemporary times. Although *Elementary* shares these features, as well as critical acclaim and a loyal following, stark differences distinguish the two shows. *Sherlock*'s Holmes seems largely to have put his drug abuse behind him, whereas *Elementary*'s has just completed rehab; his father hires the now-retired-surgeon Watson as a "sober companion" to ensure Sherlock does not relapse. Both *Elementary*'s Watson and Moriarty (Sherlock's nemesis) are now women. And in an especially radical regendering, Sherlock's long-suffering landlady Mrs. Hudson is the beautiful, brilliant transgendered Ms. Hudson, who now comes in to clean partly to satisfy her own OCD tendencies. The series makes little of her transgender identity. Executive producer Rob Doherty, observes, "[It] just isn't supposed to matter. We never really speak to it. We never really make a point of it. And that's the point" (The Baker Street Babes). (It is worth noting, however, that the transgender Ms. Hudson has a much smaller role in *Elementary* than the female Mrs. Hudson in Sherlock).

We adopt an approach grounded in reader-response theory that views readers of a text (here, *Elementary*) as active agents who continually reinterpret and negotiate the meanings, characters, and story lines present in relation to readers' and viewers' own experiences. The meanings of the text also depend on the specific sociocultural and historical contexts in which they appear, and the reader and the narrative cocreate meanings in the moment of the interpretive process (Scott 1994). This strategy is consistent with Butler's ideas both of performative repetition as constituting the subject's identity and of gender as being inherently unstable. This is because both assumptions rely on repetition to resignify norms—assumptions that may be subverted during repetition (in this case, at the moment of interpretation). For Butler, agency in relation to gender identity is "to be located within the possibility of a variation on that repetition" (1990, 185).

To facilitate our reader-response approach, we explore texts produced in appropriate online communities. We selected a combination of fan forum discussions (i.e., Reddit), review comments, and blog postings (The Baker Street Babes; Sherlock Peoria) because we believe these offer a more valid representation of the discourses surrounding the regendering issues in *Elementary*. Furthermore, making Watson an American woman of Asian descent affords opportunities to explore whether issues of intersectionality become salient in fan discussions (Gopaldas 2013). To that end, we focus only on comments pertaining to the characters' regendering, setting aside other aspects of the show that fans find problematic or disruptive.

The sites we visited are all very active ones and highly popular with fans. For example, Reddit (an open-source community hosting over eleven thousand communities) has two relevant discussion boards, one on BBC's *Sherlock* with 70,163 subscribers, and the other on *Elementary* with 3,426 subscribers. Although these boards are distinct, we found many discussions on the former about *Elementary*. Other sites like The Baker Street Babes and Sherlock Peoria post reviews and blogs of episodes on an almost-daily basis. In total, we gathered over 150 pages of postings to analyze. To facilitate quoting from web sources in our findings we use the names of sites rather than the full web address. Table 9.1 documents these sources more fully. In analyzing viewer responses to *Elementary*, we sought to locate "the symbolic webs of meaning" in which the responses are embedded, together with "the bricolage of sign fragments on which they draw" (Fischer 2000, 289) to better understand the resignification practices taking place. We undertook a thematic analysis, coding reactions to instances of gender bending and mapping their relationship to each other in the light of Butler's (1990) ideas on heteronormativity.

In addition to analyzing fan postings, we also watched *Elementary's* episodes and special features (e.g., cast interviews, "making-of" features) and read articles in popular culture and academia about the

Table 9.1 Details of data collection websites.

Name	Web address
Reddit	http://www.reddit.com
The Baker Street Babes	http://www.bakerstreetbabes.com
Sherlock Peoria	http://www.sherlockpeoria.blogspot.com
Criminal Element	http://www.criminalelement.com
Screen Rant	http://www.screenrant.com
Thought Catalog	http://www.thoughtcatalog.com
The Guardian	http://www.theguardian.corn
Huffington Post	http://www.huffingtonpost.com
In Media Res	http://mediacomrnons.futureofthebook.org
Tor	http://www.tor.com
fyeahjoaumoriarty	http://fyeahjoaumoriarty.tumblr.com

intentionality and reactions to interpretations of the program. We took notes on these texts and incorporated our observations into our dataset.

Findings

As stated earlier, we explore the research question, "how does the regendering in *Elementary* shape fans' perceptions and experiences of the Sherlock brand?" We begin with some general observations on this issue. First, in Butlerian terms, the series includes gender resignifications that challenge the expected norms of the Sherlockian myth while simultaneously encouraging the audience to engage in more reflexive awareness of cultural norms. Such juxtaposition enables *Elementary* to often break the repetition of traditional expectations in a double sense—both around the Sherlock canon and around heteronormativity. For example, in refusing to acknowledge Ms. Hudson's transgender status as worth discussing, the program resists assessing her sexuality against heteronormative expectations. In fact, in the episode introducing Ms. Hudson, Sherlock and Watson utter only one line each acknowledging her gender status.

Thus, *Elementary* refuses to situate Ms. Hudson within the gender binary, deviating from the heteronormative standard by performing gender in a way that does not reinforce the strict separation of men or women. It thus effectively ruptures the repetition of heteronormativity, offering an alternative that becomes taken for granted as the show progresses.

Elementary's refusal to reify cultural heteronormative expectations is most evident when depicting the Holmes-Watson relationship as a straight male-female friendship, one where no sexual relationship exists. Both characters are portrayed as sexual and physically desirable (e.g., Watson and the audience first encounter a Sherlock as stubble laden, shirtless, six packed, and tattooed). Yet *Elementary* resists giving even a flirtatious underpinning to their relationship (compared to, say, *The X-Files'* Mulder and Scully), defying heteronormative expectations of romance and the naturalization of opposite-sex desire. Discussing the show's "kickass females" that break stereotypes, and the protagonists' new configuration, Rob Doherty commented:

> You potentially raise the expectation that it will change everything, when in fact, it shouldn't change anything . . . I think typically when you have a male lead and a female lead on this kind of show, there is this sense of inevitably that they will tumble into bed together. And I don't want to do that. (The Baker Street Babes)

As we note earlier, we focus on understanding how Sherlock fans respond to the regendering evident within *Elementary*. Our analysis supports the emergence of three distinct types of fans based on their responses to character-related issues. Moreover, the boundaries are fluid between these groupings, and fans report evolving from one to the other. We detail these three types next.

Purists

Purists draw on the logics of tradition and authenticity, making constant comparisons with the original Holmes canon and highlighting the erosion of the core brand myth for commercial ends: "We fear the ethos of our beloved characters will be ignored in favor of market research and general Los Angeles willy-nillying" (Criminal Element). In critiquing a female Watson, they focus on the factual changes made to the character and to her relationship with Holmes. For example, Watson is no longer ex-military; instead, she serves in what one fan describes as a "babysitting role," as Holmes's "sober companion."

This group most resembles Avery's (2012) Cayenne owners in that they are very defensive of core brand values and react strongly to these being threatened, particularly in relation to Holmes himself: "This season feels like Sherlock is a supporting character and Watson the strong independent woman who rivals Sherlock's famous intellect" (Reddit). Here we can clearly see the same gender contamination Avery observes, threatening Holmes's (masculine) superiority and bringing new gendered meanings to the duo's relationship. Challenging ideals of hegemonic masculinity, Joan Watson is always portrayed as an equal to Holmes—never his subordinate. Early in season one, she refuses to bring him coffee when from another room, he holds out his cup expectantly. One fan notes, "Joan Watson is not there to chronicle Holmes's accomplishments," (The Baker Street Babes) nor to express admiration or awe of his intellect—hers is just as powerful. In other words, she is not there to display "a fawning obsession" with Holmes, as another fan describes the traditionally portrayed relationship between Holmes and Watson (but truer in Doyle's canon than in *Sherlock* or *Elementary*).

The portrayal of Holmes as broken, emotionally vulnerable, and requiring protection from himself really annoys many purists, who resent the "dilution of the Holmes brand" (Reddit) and an increasing feminization through his depiction as a victim of his addiction. They often contrast Miller's portrayal with what they perceive as Cumberbatch's more faithful portrayal of Holmes in the BBC's *Sherlock*. Consequently, this group is also more likely to never have watched *Elementary*. One fan announces proudly that he or she will "never watch the show on principle" (Reddit). Similarly, the blog post of a woman emphasizes the lack of engagement she encounters from superfans:

> Earlier this year, I was the Watson to my friend's Holmes at a Sherlock Holmes charity ball, where I met several other superfans. No one had very nice things to say about *Elementary*. In fact, most . . . people we met

> . . . though able to spout off trivia about . . . the strictly canonical stories to films new and old to the BBC series, hadn't even bothered to watch very much of CBS's modern-day adaptation. (The Baker Street Babes)

In testimony to the power of heteronormative hegemony, fans often explain that their nonengagement is due to the female Watson, which they interpret as the writers' reversion to the standard formula of a male-female detective partnership with its overtones of romance. The quote that follows reflects a typical misconception from Sherlockians who refuse to view the show and reveals how some cannot (or will not) see beyond these stereotypical heteronormative constraints:

> Personally, I have no problem with a theoretical female Watson, but in execution, the idea has some major issues. Watson's character, even in the books (not just the BBC), has a sort of fawning obsession with Holmes—he writes novels about his work, after all. He's awestruck, it's a bromance; that's his connection to Holmes. With a female, American writers are most likely going to add in romantic/sexual tension, and that male/female aspect is going to change the motif considerably. (Screen Rant)

This stance is fairly typical among purists, even as few admit to resenting a female Watson. Instead they find other reasons, explainable by their engagement in heteronormative stereotyping. In other words, these fans possess certain expectations about how men and women should behave (e.g., anticipated romantic or sexual tension). Referring to Liu's Asian roots, several fans speak disdainfully of a "Tiger Watson" whom they expect would be smart, beautiful, and driven. Here, we clearly see the intersection of race and gender in this derogatory appellation, a reminder that following Butler (1993), heteronormativity is racialized as white, and that race and gender are mutually constitutive (Ferguson 2004).

Sometimes, however, if and when purists overcome their reticence to watch *Elementary*, they realize their fears of stereotypes are unfounded. When this process occurs, they may transition into the next fan category.

Progressives

Contrasting with purists, *progressives* embrace the many changes and draw on the logics of progress in arguing that the Sherlock brand myth must evolve to resonate with contemporary audiences. To that end, they assert that diversity—even embodied in an Asian American, female Watson—is a crucial part of this evolution:

> Yes, John Watson is a popular, iconic character, but step back from your own *Sherlock* purism and look at the bigger picture. This

change could be a really good, necessary thing—bigger than *Sherlock Holmes*, and more important, interesting and exciting than sticking to the way the story's been told before. (Thought Catalog)

This group believes reinvigorating the myth in innovative ways keeps the brand alive and helps it attract new fans. From this point of view, "Turning John into Joan wasn't just a gimmick, but rather the central part of a commitment to finding a new take on the Holmesian mythology" (Reddit). These comments are consistent with those made by the producers and by Liu when they discuss the potential upsides of reconfiguring such an essential element of the iconic Watson.

Progressives are highly supportive of breaks with the traditional canon, especially when these disruptions provide much richer roles for women. According to one fan, this challenges "the role of women in the Sherlock Holmes' world," where "women largely don't factor as anything other than victims or daughters or wives" (The Baker Street Babes). Like many other fans in this group, she welcomes resistance to female stereotyping that the show manifests by avoiding passive or submissive women characters. This blogger delights in *Elementary*'s broad range of strong females and their active roles, "a sample platter of good women, bad women and somewhere in the middle women all solving crimes, committing them, being central to them." Perhaps the strongest female role in *Elementary*, in terms of her personality and power, is Moriarty; her potency is doubled when it is revealed that she is also Holmes's former lover, Irene Adler. Too often, strong female characters may act as cautionary tales to deter their ultimate power as role models that contest heteronormativity. For example, they may be demonized as evil or monstrous or simply marginalized as outsiders (Woloshyn, Taber, and Lane 2013). This is not the case with *Elementary*'s female castings.

Progressives also usually applaud the show's disruption of conventional gender binaries. This is particularly the case with Watson; the writers provide her with her own parallel narrative unfolding alongside that of her story with Holmes, making her much more of an equal partner in the relationship. The mystery surrounding her background, as well as her strong sense of presence and intellect, make her as fascinating to Holmes as he is to her. The fact that the relationship remains platonic also helps Watson retain her mystique as a character who does not perform femininity in the expected fashion. Progressives passionately voice their support for this gender-norm disruption. The following excerpt typifies progressives' reactions: "The foundational change of John to Joan . . . was a brilliant start that firmly cemented the show as a forerunner in challenging gender and relationships between men and women. It's still doing that too, by the way" (The Baker Street Babes).

Similarly, this group champions diversity, particularly at the intersection of gender and race. They attribute great significance to the fact that a woman of color plays a role that males traditionally occupy:

> This new Watson demonstrate[s] strength and dignity characteristic of every other Watson incarnation despite her not being the original Brit gentleman, and that's amazing for women and people of color to see . . . it is nice to see a recent incarnation that doesn't make Watson Sherlock's hapless lapdog who could never hope to be as skilled or clever as him. (Thought Catalog)

In tandem with Watson's remaking is also the remaking of Holmes. The show's championing of diversity does not just entail the gender bending of originally male characters; it includes changes to Holmes himself that challenge portrayals of normative masculinity. Most previous Holmeses reflect the cold aloofness of Doyle's original and they are consistently portrayed as admired by Watson. Despite the bromance overtones in the BBC's *Sherlock*, the show reinforces Holmes's masculinity through his less experienced partner who is essentially his helpmeet. Holmes embodies the attributes of hegemonic masculinity by the bucketload: observational powers and the ability to retain facts, a highly logical brain, physical strength, as well as comradeship and daring (Kestner 1997).

Elementary disrupts reification of this masculinity, not only by empowering Watson and reversing the helpmeet nature of their relationship, but also by portraying a more vulnerable Holmes in need of care. Unlike other iterations of the relationship, Joan Watson does not indulge his every whim but challenges his requests and is perfectly willing to tell him when these are inappropriate.

Progressives often become fervent brand ambassadors who defend the program's values and its powers to resignify gender norms. They participate in forum discussions and blog postings that dissect aspects of the series, often episode by episode. In particular, they can play a major role to disperse misapprehensions shared by purists, as the following posting demonstrates:

> I would like to make a personal appeal to you today. If you . . . haven't been watching *Elementary*. [I] have been comparing every episode . . . to BBC's *Sherlock*. [Maybe you] have only watched the show with vague interest. Is this you? Pay attention. Turn on [*Elementary's*] "The Man with the Twisted Lip." Void your mind of any reference to . . . Freeman and . . . Cumberbatch. Consider Doyle's original stories and his creation of a character whose love of opiates both gives him a different perspective on the world and drags him into an underworld (both mentally and physically). But most importantly . . . **And this is worth bolding: Jonny Lee Miller and**

Lucy Liu are as effective a duo as any in the history of Doyle adaptations and it would be a shame to miss it. (The Baker Street Babes)

Problematizers

Finally, *problematizers* provide penetrating scrutiny of *Elementary*, often drawing on gender discourses stemming from feminist and LGBQT communities in their positive and negative critiques. Like progressives, they may rationalize the regendering on the grounds that television programs badly need to feature more major women characters. However, they may also question the subtext of including a female Watson—as opposed to a female Holmes. One self-described feminist responds extremely negatively to Joan Watson on the grounds that it represents a "mindlessly trendy piece of feminizing" that is "castrating detective fiction's greatest sidekick" (The Guardian). She argues a female Watson has only two possible interpretations. Either Watson-as-woman is immaterial (ergo, "mindless feminizing"), or it is significant but damaging to women because Watson remains subordinate.

Keenly interrogating each episode, problematizers are acutely aware of ongoing power imbalances: "Joan was written as Sherlock's equal in the first season but . . . less than his equal in the second" (In Media Res). Despite general acknowledgment that Joan is a strong character in her own right, some problematize supplanting the "bromance" with a more heteronormative (albeit platonic) Holmes-Watson relationship, seeing this evolution as a retrograde move. One male commentator observes,

> I find it odd that two important and strong "male" characters [from] a previous generation . . . [Lt.] Starbuck [in *Battlestar Galactica*] and Watson, were turned into women for this generation. Although an interesting twist, what does it say about how people view men and relationships? That they can't have a close friend and confidant if it isn't a woman? That leading men can only be interesting when interpreted in the context of having a close female relationship? Especially on the heels of the success of the Sherlock . . . movie franchise, why cast Watson as a woman? (Huffington Post)

This quote nicely illustrates reactions to Butler's (1990) notion of gender resignifications and the reflexive awareness they may generate. We also see here the potential disparities that resignifications may evoke, as each fan interprets these in the light of their own sociocultural backgrounds. This male fan is distressed at the loss of the bromance elements in *Elementary*, a close male friendship he perceives as potentially more subversive than a platonic heterosexual relationship. For him, casting Holmes's best friend and confidant as a woman is more stereotypical than depicting a deep male friendship. Butler (1990, 1993) emphasizes that the power of gender resignifications to subvert norms is very hard to gauge. This is because the reflexive awareness they generate is open to multiple, and often very disparate, interpretations, as the aforementioned post illustrates.

Similarly, although progressives welcome *Elementary*'s many strong roles for women, one female blogger, a lesbian, acknowledges her interpretation of Moriarty's gender bending is more complex than others offer:

> The show managed to avoid making Holmes and Watson a couple even though Watson was now a woman, but then neglected to do the same for Jamie Moriarty. Sherlock and "The Woman" now have a sexual relationship, which is fine because this [takes place] over a century after Adler's story was first told. But by making her also Moriarty, *Elementary* made a significant blunder in their reimagining—the suggestion that a relationship between Holmes and Moriarty is viable because they now fall into the boundaries of a heteronormative couple. Being a queer woman, this actually grates me. (Tor)

Here again, we see added layers of interpretation, often characteristic of problematizers' reactions, which deepen and extend the debates around each resignification. In this case the fan's sexuality intersects with her interpretation of the new Holmes-Moriarty relationship that she reads as a return to a more standardized male-female formula that allows them to be in love. Thus, although these fans are generally more critical of *Elementary* than progressives (often resembling purists in this respect), they heighten the reflexive awareness of the many gender issues the series encodes. In constantly questioning and probing gender reiterations, they bring to the fore hidden aspects that appear taken for granted; however, these are the very expressions not understood as culturally contingent and that help naturalize gender norms. Thus, problematizers contribute to "ideological edgework" (Thompson and Üstüner 2015) and challenge the constraints of gender norms while retaining social legitimacy because they simultaneously synthesize and extend the arguments of both previous groups:

> Do you think they only made Watson a woman of color [to] be Sherlock's sidekick? Did you even watch the whole season and her character development to understand the narrative devices of the show and the use of tropes? Do you think *Elementary* is not feminist-friendly because they made Watson a woman and not Sherlock? Do you not see the importance for other women of color to see an American-Chinese person . . . represented as a tridimensional character in media, without any kind of stereotype or jokes

about her ethnic roots? Think about it, guys. It's not that hard. (fyeahjoanmoriarty)

Discussion and Conclusions

Our findings illustrate how *Elementary*'s regendering shapes fans' perceptions and experiences in three distinct ways, all of which shape experiences of the Sherlock brand myth. We rely on Butler's concept of heteronormativity, and the performance it entails, to explain these reader-response positions and the interpretations they contain. For purists, gender bending destroys the traditional Holmes canon and the white-male dominance within. For progressives, gender bending keeps the canon alive and aligns it with contemporary questioning of what identities and diversity mean, beyond traditional gender binaries. For problematizers, regendering evokes a deeper reflexive awareness about gender debates that extend beyond the canon itself.

Our immersion into *Elementary* reveals a range of nuanced responses to brand gender bending that extend Avery's (2012) work by going beyond the exclusively negative reactions that Porsche owners exude. Purists display mainly negative reactions, whereas progressives usually offer positive feedback, and problematizers may be either positively or negatively inclined. We also demonstrate how gender bending a brand myth can reinvigorate the brand narrative and infuse it with more contemporary meanings that tap into the power of social media to foster interest and debate. In particular, progressives are more likely to act as brand ambassadors and may even influence purists to watch the series. Our analysis also highlights the fact that gender contamination may be less rigid than Avery implies and that social context may play a major role in shaping fans' reaction to gender-bending tactics.

Future research could explore a greater range of gender resignifications and the buzz (pro and con) created for the brand in social and mass media, as well as the various strategies marketers devise as they rely on such resignifications to reinvigorate brand mythology. Marketers are often accused of gender stereotyping, so perhaps understanding the (un)acceptability of brand gender-bending strategies, and the impact on various fan bases, can help them expand and normalize the range of gender identities they feel comfortable including in ads, television programs, and films. Extending this assumption, research could explore how more extreme variants of gender bending impact consumer experiences with the brand. These could include depicting Holmes and Watson as still-platonic gay men or lesbians. Furthermore, how would enlarging Mrs. Hudson's role—perhaps to include stigmas and struggles associated with her transgender identity—impact consumer fandom? How would the material world of Sherlock—the museums, the gift shops, the "merch"—reflect these potentially more disruptive gender-bending reboots? As other iconic series wrestle with gender and race bending (consider the discussions about casting a black or female James Bond), it is important to consider how marketing strategies clearly aimed at attracting newer and younger consumers to an iconic franchise can affect consumer interpretations and experiences of the text.

Bibliography

Arsel, Zeynep and Craig J. Thompson. "Demythologizing Consumption Practices: How Consumers Protect Their Field-Dependent Identity Investments from Devaluing Marketplace Myths." *Journal of Consumer Research* 37, no. 5 (2011): 791–806.

Avery, Jill. "Defending the Markers of Masculinity: Consumer Resistance to Brand Gender-Bending." *International Journal of Research in Marketing* 29, no. 4 (2012): 322–36.

Brown, Stephen, Robert V. Kozinets and John F. Sherry Jr. "Teaching Old Brands New Tricks: Retro Branding and the Revival of Brand Meaning." *Journal of Marketing* 67, no. 3 (2003): 19–33.

Brown, Stephen, Pierre McDonagh and Clifford J. Shultz II. "Titanic: Consuming the Myths and Meanings of an Ambiguous Brand." *Journal of Consumer Research* 40, no. 4 (2013): 595–614.

Brownlie, Douglas and Paul Hewer. "Prime Beef Cuts: Culinary Images for Thinking 'Men'." *Consumption, Markets and Culture* 10, no. 3 (2007): 229–50.

Butler, Judith. *Bodies That Matter: On the Discursive Limits of 'Sex'*. Taylor & Francis, 1993.

———. *Gender Trouble: Feminism and the Subversion of Identity*. Routledge, 1990.

Connell, Robert W. and James W. Messerschmidt. "Hegemonic Masculinity: Rethinking the Concept." *Gender & Society* 19, no. 6 (2005): 829–59.

Diamond, Nina, John F. Sherry, Jr., Albert M. Muñiz, Jr., Mary Ann McGrath, Robert V. Kozinets, and Stefania Borghini. "American Girl and the Brand Gestalt: Closing the Loop on Sociocultural Branding Research." *Journal of Marketing* 73, no. 3 (2009): 118–34.

Doty, Alexander. *Making Things Perfectly Queer: Interpreting Mass Culture*. Minneapolis, MN: University of Minnesota Press, 1993.

Ervin, Margaret. "The Might of the Metrosexual: How a Mere Marketing Tool Challenges Hegemonic Masculinity." In Elwood Watson and Marc Edward Shaw (Eds), *The 21st Century Man in Popular Culture: Performing American Masculinities*, 58–75. 2011.

Ferguson, Roderick A. *Aberrations in Black: Toward a Queer of Color Critique*. Minneapolis, MN: University of Minnesota Press, 2004.

Fischer, Eileen. "Consuming Contemporaneous Discourses: A Postmodern Analysis of Food Advertisements Targeted Toward Women." In Stephen J. Hoch and Robert J. Meyer (eds), *Advances in Consumer Research* 27, Provo, UT: Association for Consumer Research, 2000: 288–94.

Fox, Chloe. "Sherlock Holmes: Pipe Dreams." *The Telegraph*, December 15, 2009. www.telegraph.co.uk/culture/film/6789921/Sherlock-Holmes-pipe-dreams.html, accessed October 12, 2016.

Gilbert, Gerard. "CSI: The Cop Show that Conquered the World." *The Independent*, December 19, 2006. www.independent.co.uk/news/media/csi-the-cop-show-that-conquered-the-world 429262.html, accessed October 12, 2016.

Gopaldas, Ahir. "Intersectionality 101." *Journal of Public Policy & Marketing* 32, special issue (2013): 90–4.

Goulding, Christina and Michael Saren. "Performing Identity: An Analysis of Gender Expressions at the Whitby Goth Festival." *Consumption, Markets and Culture* 12, no. 1 (2009): 27–46.

Grayson, Kent and Radan Martinec. "Consumer Perceptions of Iconicity and Indexicality and Their Influence on Assessments of Authentic Market Offerings." *Journal of Consumer Research* 31, no. 2 (2004): 296–312.

Holt, Douglas B. and Craig J. Thompson. "Man-of-Action Heroes: The Pursuit of Heroic Masculinity in Everyday Consumption." *Journal of Consumer Research* 31, no. 2 (2004): 425–40.

Hurn, Mary Elizabeth. "Dove Launches Campaign for Men's Line, Including Social, E-mail Opt-Ins." *Digital Marketing*, February 2, 2010. www.dmnews.com/digital-marketing/dove-launches-campaign-for-mens-line-including-social-e-mail-opt-ins/article/162857/.

Ilhan, Behice Ece. Transmedia Consumption Experiences: Consuming and Co-creating Interrelated Stories Across Media. PhD Thesis, University of Illinois at Urbana-Champaign, 2011.

Kates, Steven M. "Producing and Consuming Gendered Representations: An Interpretation of the Sydney Gay and Lesbian Mardi Gras." *Consumption, Markets & Culture* 6, no. 1 (2003): 5–22.

Kates, Steven M. and Charlene Goh. "Brand Morphing: Implications for Advertising Theory and Practice." *Journal of Advertising* 32, no. 1 (2003): 59–68.

Kestner, Joseph A. *Sherlock's Men: Masculinity, Conan Doyle and Cultural History*. Aldershot/Brookfield, VT: Ashgate, 1997.

Luedicke, Marius K., Craig J. Thompson, and Markus Giesler. "Consumer Identity Work as Moral Protagonism: How Myth and Ideology Animate a Brand-Mediated Moral Conflict." *Journal of Consumer Research* 36, no. 6 (2010): 1016–32.

Maclaran, Pauline and Lorna Stevens. "Magners Man: Irish Cider, Representations of Masculinity and the 'Burning Celtic Soul.'" *Irish Marketing Review* 20, no. 2 (2009): 77–88.

Martin, Diane M., John W. Schouten, and James H. McAlexander. "Claiming the Throttle: Multiple Femininities in a Hyper-Masculine Subculture." *Consumption Markets & Culture* 9, no. 3 (2006): 171–205.

Muñiz, Albert M., Jr. and Hope Jensen Schau. "Religiosity in the Abandoned Apple Newton Brand Community." *Journal of Consumer Research* 31 (March 2005): 737–47.

Salih, Sarah. *Judith Butler*. London: Routledge, 2002.

Samuel, Lawrence R. *Freud on Madison Avenue: Motivation Research and Subliminal Advertising in America*. Philadelphia, PA: University of Pennsylvania Press, 2010.

Schroeder, Jonathan E. and Janet Borgerson. "Judith Butler, Gender Theorist: Philosophical and Phenomenological Insights into Marketing and Consumer Behavior." In Linda Scott and Craig Thompson (Eds), *Gender, Marketing and Consumer Behavior Volume 7*, Madison, WI: Association for Consumer Research, 2004:1–7.

—— and Detlev Zwick. "Mirrors of Masculinity: Representation and Identity in Advertising Images." Consumption, Markets & Culture 7, no. 1 (2004): 21–52.

Schouten, John and James H. McAlexander. "Subcultures of Consumption: An Ethnography of the New Bikers." *Journal of Consumer Research* 22 (June 1995): 43–61.

Schroeder, J. E. and Detlev Zwick. "Mirrors of Masculinity: Representation and Identity in Advertising Images." *Consumption, Markets & Culture* 7, no. 1 (2010): 21–52.

Scott, Linda M. "The Bridge from Text to Mind: Adapting Reader Response Theory to Consumer Research." *Journal of Consumer Research* 21 (December 1994): 461–80.

Segal, Lynne. *Why Feminism?* Cambridge: Polity Press, 1999.

Stein, Louisa Ellen and Kristina Busse. *Sherlock and Transmedia Fandom.* Jefferson, North Carolina: McFarland & Co.

Stevens, Lorna, Benedetta Cappellini, and Gilly Smith. "Nigellissima: A Study of Glamour, Performativity, and Embodiment." *Journal of Marketing Management* 31, nos. 5–6 (2015): 1–22.

Thompson, Craig J. "Marketplace Mythology and Discourses of Power." *Journal of Consumer Research*, 31 (June 2004): 162–80.

——— and Tuba Üstüner. "Women Skating on the Edge: Marketplace Performances as Ideological Edgework." *Journal of Consumer Research* 42, no. 2 (2015): 235–65.

Woloshyn, Vera, Nancy Taber, and Laura Lane. "Discourses of Masculinity and Femininity in *The Hunger Games*: 'Scarred,' 'Bloody,' and 'Stunning'." *International Journal of Social Science Studies* 1, no. 1 (2013): 150–60.

Zayer, Linda Tuncay, Katherine Sredl, Marie-Agnes Parmentier and Catherine Coleman. "Consumption and Gender Identity in Popular Media: Discourses of Domesticity, Sexuality and Authenticity." *Consumption, Markets, and Culture* 15, no. 4 (2012): 333–57.

Part III

Reassessing the Field

Whence and Whither?

10 Begin as You Mean to Go On
Reflections on the Rhetoric of Research

Stephen Brown

Jesus fuck.
It was the day my grandmother exploded.
Later, as he sat on his balcony eating the dog . . .

That got your attention, didn't it? I bet it did! There's nothing like striking opening sentences to grab readers by the lapels and yank them into
the story. Novelists are well aware of this universal law of literary life.
They devote a great deal of time and effort to "beginnings," which are
polished and burnished and simonized to a high shine (Oz 1999). First
lines represent the threshold, the front parlor, the reception room for the
book to come. They "separate the real world we inhabit from the world
the novelist has imagined" (Lodge 1992, 5).

As well-read bibliophiles one and all, you're presumably familiar
with the three first lines that opened this essay. But just in case you're
behind with your recreational reading—who isn't?—"Jesus fuck" is from
Quite Ugly One Morning, an award-winning thriller by Christopher
Brookmyre (1997). The exploding granny comes courtesy of Iain Banks's
(1992) bestseller, *The Crow Road*. And the dog food—I know you know
it but can't quite remember where from—was penned by J. G. Ballard
(1975), Great Britain's premier sick puppy. *High Rise* to be precise.

They're not particular favorites of mine, rest assured. They're just what
I've been reading of late. I could just as easily have chosen Tom Clancy's
Patriot Games ("Ryan was nearly killed twice in half an hour"), Stephen
King's *Cujo* ("Once upon a time, not so long ago, a monster came to
the small town of Castle Rock, Maine"), Bret Easton Ellis's *American
Psycho* ("*Abandon all hope ye who enter here* is scrawled in blood red
lettering on the side of the Chemical Bank near the corner of Eleventh
and First"), or, come to think of it, Nobel Prize–winner Orhan Pamuk's
The New Life ("I read a book one day and my whole life was changed").
The last of these is unlikely, admittedly, because Pamuk is much too postmodern, even for me. I'm more of a Carlos Ruiz Zafon kinda guy ("I still
remember the day my grandfather took me to the Cemetery of Forgotten

Books for the first time"). I'm sure you've your own personal favorites: "Call me Ishmael"; "Mother died today"; "Misery is manifold"; "I am an invisible man"; "In a hole in the ground there lived a hobbit"; "So we beat on, boats against the current, borne back ceaselessly into the past."[1]

Once upon an MS Dreary

But when we turn to the great Gatsbys of consumer culture theory (CCT), what do we find? Here's "The Sacred and the Profane": "It has been argued that revelatory incidents are the primary source of insight in ethnographic fieldwork." Here's McCracken's "Culture and Consumption": "Consumer goods have a significance that goes beyond their utilitarian character and commercial value." Here's Hirschman's "Humanistic Inquiry": "Marketing scholars currently are engaged in an important ideological and intellectual debate about the nature of marketing as a science." Here's the one and only "River Magic": "River rafting is a growing component of the Colorado leisure services industry." Here's the poet laureate of consumer research, in what has been described as his single most impactful paper, "Out of Africa": "According to a recent JCR article by Mick, the study of signs promises to contribute much to our understanding of consumer behavior."[2] Here, fellow consumer culture theorists, is the first sentence of Arnould and Thompson's CCT manifesto, the incisive intervention that made this very volume possible: "The past twenty yr. of consumer research have produced a flurry of research addressing the sociocultural, experiential, symbolic, and ideological aspects of consumption."

Some of the these, fair enough, have a touch of the Hakuri Murakami about them ("The elevator continued its impossibly slow ascent."), Grant McCracken and Elizabeth Hirschman especially. However, with the very best will in the world, Christopher Brookmyre won't be too worried by the competition, Stephen King isn't lying awake at night, hiding under the bedclothes—he does that to us!—and Edgar Allan Poe sure ain't turning in his grave right now, though you never know with him.

And, let's be brutally honest here, Arnould and Thompson's pronunciamento isn't exactly the Declaration of Independence, much less Marinetti's Futurist manifesto. Their clarion call to arms doesn't improve appreciably after the first sentence, furthermore. Here's the rest of the introductory paragraph:

> In this article we offer a thematic overview of the motivating interests, conceptual orientations, and theoretical agendas that characterize this research stream to date, with a particular emphasis on articles published in the Journal of Consumer Research (JCR). Owing to the length constraints of this forum, we regrettably cannot give due consideration to the full spectrum of culturally oriented consumer research that appears in other publication venues such as

[titles of seven journals follow] and a host of books and edited volumes. Accordingly, our thematic review is by no means intended to be exhaustive of all inclusive. (Arnould and Thompson 2005, 868).[3]

Wake up at the back. No sleeping on the job. Rouse yourself. Rise and shine. Shake a leg. Or something.

Best of Times or Worst of Times?

Now, I know what you're thinking. You're thinking one of two things, possibly both. You're thinking, who the hell does Stephen Brown think he is, setting about our great and good in such a disrespectful way? Clearly, the guy's crazy. He's a complete nobody, what's more, an intellectual lightweight. His citation count is nothing to write home about, nor is he any great shakes as a literary stylist. He also assumes ample added alliteration's always amazingly awesome, the awful asinine asshole.

You got me there, guys. I'm guilty as charged. Like you, I can think of numerous marketing scholars who are more heavily cited, much bigger names, and far better writers than me—John Sherry, John Schouten, Linda Scott, and Lorna Stevens for starters.

But traducing the messenger doesn't transform the message. The evidence is there before you, if you care or dare to look. The evidence, indeed, is all the more damning when you consider that we purport to be the wacky, weird-science, prowriting people. We are the wonderful folks who brought poetry and painting and ethnography and videography and great literature and popular culture—and heresy, don't forget—to the accursed social science that was Marketing Before the Odyssey (MBO). We, to adopt Deighton's (1992) dichotomous distinction between reasoned argument and drama-driven modes of persuasion, like to think of ourselves as Tony-worthy playwrights of thought.[4]

The second thing you're thinking is that my comparison's unfair. Novelists and academics are very different animals. Their respective writings have very different styles, traditions, norms, priorities, readerships. The first sentence doesn't carry the same weight in earnest scholarship as it does in creative literature, where aspiring writers are encouraged, exhorted, and expected to deliver knock-'em-dead opening lines. Whereas novels are designed to entertain, articles are required to explain.

You're thinking, in short, that I'm twisting the facts, bending the rules, moving the goalposts, dodging the bullet.[5] My comparison's not just unjust, it's egregious, an abomination. Not only is it not comparing like with like but also not comparing like with anything that's remotely like like. It's even worse than comparing apples with oranges or pears with plums. It's akin to comparing soccer with salad, asteroids with architraves, dung beetles with driverless vehicles.

Shame on you, Stephen!

Don't exaggerate, folks. That's my job. But here's the thing. You can huff and puff all you like about the validity of my comparison. However, we are not dealing with different species, categories, genres, or whatever you want to call them. Novelists and academics are both in the business of communication, persuasion, cajolery. The rules of the game may be slightly different. No more so, though, than rugby union versus rugby league or Gaelic football versus Australian rules.

And while we're at it, let's not forget classic works of nonfiction with brilliant beginnings: Marx's *Communist Manifesto*, Foucault's *Discipline and Punish*, Carson's *Silent Spring*, Whyte's *Street Corner Society*, Hunter S. Thompson's *Fear and Loathing in Las Vegas*. All together now, "We were somewhere around Barstow on the edge of the desert when the drugs began to take hold."

Nor, for that matter, should we overlook the "experimental moment" in anthropology, psychology, economics, and so on, coupled with the "narrative turn" throughout the physical and social sciences (Sherry 1991). Consider the best-selling, story-driven writings of renowned hard scientists, such as Richard Dawkins and Oliver Sacks, as well as populist reworkings of scholarly research findings by the manifold Malcolm Gladwells and Naomi Kleins of this world. The Stephen Pinkers, Dan Arielys, Daniel Kahnemans, Mihaly Csikszentmihalyis, freakin' Freakonomists—and their ample -onomics imitators[6]—also know how to throw striking sentences together. Some of them have been published in *JCR*, for goodness sakes!

Indeed, a recent overview of academic writing, which comprised a content analysis of five hundred learned articles across ten separate scholarly disciplines, including medicine, biology, psychology, philosophy and literary studies, convincingly demonstrated that engaging writing, enchanting writing, exceedingly readable writing is evident throughout the sciences and humanities. Although much of academia's output is irredeemably dire, it doesn't have to be. Based upon her study, Sword (2012, 8) recommends immediate recourse to: (a) interesting, eye-catching titles and subtitles; (b) first-person anecdotes or asides that humanize the author; and (c) catchy introductory paragraphs that recount an interesting story, ask a challenging question, or otherwise hook and hold the reader. Golden-Biddle and Locke (1997) concur.

When all is said and done, our situation isn't so different from that facing novelists and their ilk. As Van Maanen (1988, 25) analogously notes, "The narrative tricks the ethnographer uses to claim truth are no less sophisticated than those used by the novelist to claim fiction."

SNARS Attacks!

If the foregoing is a truth universally acknowledged, we need to be a bit more honest with ourselves. We need to raise our game. Or do we? Is the picture really as bad as I've painted? Judging CCT on the basis of its opening sentences seems a tad harsh. Granted, the articles I've quoted thus far are bona-fide classics and their authors rank among the leading lights of consumer research. They can take the heat and carry the can.

However, as I know from painful personal experience, flamboyant first lines often attract the ire of straight-laced reviewers. You wouldn't believe some of the stuff I've had to excise along the prickly path to publication. "If, as they say, ignorance is bliss, Vargo and Lusch must be in a perpetual state of euphoria." How could anyone possibly object to that? I mean, come on. Give me a break, you SOBs!

So, let's cut CCT some slack and concentrate on Sword's category (c). The beauty of this is that it sidesteps the first-line focus that distracts and, in truth, preoccupies traditional literary types. It suffers less from the demands of martinet AEs or those CCT intros that are distorted by reviewer-placating citations.[7] It also echoes Clifford Geertz's (1988) seminal study of scholarly writing styles, which foregrounds the first few pages—the stupendous scene-setting "arrival narratives"—of golden-age ethnographies such as *We, the Tikopia* and *Witchcraft, Oracles, and Magic among the Azande*:

> In the cool of the early morning, just before sunrise, the bow of the *Southern Cross* headed towards the eastern horizon, on which a tiny dark blue outline was faintly visible. Slowly it grew into a rugged mountain mass, standing up sheer from the ocean; then as we approached within a few miles it revealed around its base a narrow ring of low, flat land, thick with vegetation. The sullen grey day with its lowering clouds strengthened my grim impression of a solitary peak, wild and stormy, upthrust in a waste of waters. (Firth 1936, 1)

In order to evaluate CCT's standing in relation to Sword's catchy introductory paragraphs that hook and hold the reader, we need a dataset of sorts. Ideally a random sample of our articles through the ages. However, that smacks too much of the old-school positivism—boo, hiss—which was renounced by CCT before CCT existed. Accordingly, I've come up with something of my own. You've heard of a quota sample? You've heard of a snowball sample? You've heard of a systematic sample? You've heard of an intercept sample? You've heard of a convenience sample? But I bet you haven't heard of a found sample.

A found sample refers to the articles I found in the CCT folder on my laptop. Is it comprehensive? Hell no. Is it representative? Not in the least. Is it robust, reliable, random, or anything remotely resembling a reasonably rounded picture of CCT's compendious corpus? Get a grip on yourself, for God's sake! It's the stuff I happen to have on file, supplemented with a selection of old offprints lying around my office. If you want to be officious about it, though, it's officially and hereinafter known as the

SNARS selection process. SNARS, as you've likely surmised already, stands for "so not a representative sample."

Our SNARS on this occasion consists of 105 articles appertaining to CCT. These stretch from Sid Levy's (1981) immortal "Interpreting Consumer Mythology," via Schouten and McAlexander's (1995) sublime "Subcultures of Consumption," past Cayla and Eckhardt's (2008) compelling study of Asiatic brands, to Thompson and Üstüner's (2015) wall-of-death drama about roller derby grrrls. They come from eighteen different journals, most notably *JM* (ten), *CMC* (nine), and *Marketing Theory* (six), though *JCR* predominates with approximately two-thirds of the total. The work of 119 different scholars is included, almost half of whom are women. Craig Thompson is top dog with eleven articles, closely followed by Russ Belk, John Sherry, Rob Kozinets, and Eric Arnould in that order. Pauline Maclaran is the first lady, with Melanie Wallendorf, Barbara Stern, Christina Goulding, and Elizabeth Hirschman in hot pursuit. None of my own are included—because integrity is my middle name—with the sole exception of "Old Dogs, New Tricks" (Brown, Kozinets, and Sherry 2003). It's there because Rob 'n' John wrote the introduction, not me.

As samples go, SNARS is pretty rough. However, it was ready to hand. Rougher still is my arbitrary subdivision of the foundlings into three separate groups, groups that'll give us a feel for trends through time. If we take 1995 and 2005 as the two key dates in our thirty-five-year history, each marked by a turning-point publication (Arnould and Thompson 2005; Firat and Venkatesh 1995), that gives us the three eras of CCT—namely, pre-PoMo, PoMo, and post-PoMo. They're the interpretive research equivalent of Stone Age-Bronze Age-Iron Age, ancient-medieval-modern, youth-adolescence-maturity, morning-noon-night, lights-camera-action, product-sales-marketing orientation, with all the associated connotations. Era one contains 28 articles, era two 30, and era three 47. This is a reasonable reflection of the steady development of CCT and its ever-increasing popularity, especially after Arnould and Thompson's (2005) timely rebrand. SNARS, nevertheless, is skewed toward the early years, which only goes to show that I'm an incipient old fogy. They don't write 'em like they used to! Those were the days, my friends, those were the days.

Searching for Findings

Returning to the present, gentle readers, I can hear what you're saying. You're saying, what's the deal, doc? How bad is it? Are we on our last legs? Or the legs before the last, whatever they are? In a nutshell, Stevie B., will we live?

The answer to that one is yes, very much so. We're in robust good health. Our openings are deep and wide, many and varied, rich and fertile.

And that's just Craig Thompson. It pains me grievously to say this, but here goes: although I came to bury CCT, I'll be praising it instead.

Before I start soft-soaping any future reviewers, AEs, and assorted gate-keepers among you, there's a trio of provisos we need to work through. The first of these is CDB, the second is CARS, and the third is GALS. On reading more than one hundred article introductions—defined as everything up to the first section break[8]—I often felt the authors "could do better" (CDB). It's not that they're bad. Far from it. It's that the openings aren't as snappy, as punchy, as polished as they could and should be. If, for instance, the first four words of "Sacred and Profane" were deleted, the sentence quoted earlier would be better than it is (Belk, Wallendorf, and Sherry 1989).

Rob Kozinets's *Star Trek* article, similarly, starts with the following observation: "*Star Trek* is perhaps one of the great consumption phenomena of our time." It's an observation that would've been much more impactful if he'd removed the modifier "perhaps" and replaced "one of the great" with "the greatest." An in-your-face assertion like *Star Trek* is the greatest consumption phenomenon of our time would've really rocked the readership and instantly got their dander up (*Star Wars* fans in particular). As it stands, the sentence is defanged and wishy-washy; its punches are pulled. Knowing Rob as I do, though, I suspect he'd been required to retreat by a nitpicking reviewer or self-censored in what was, after all, one of his early articles. Maybe Russ and Co. were equally constrained in their day. The theodicy met with more than a modicum of reviewer resistance, remember (Bradshaw and Brown 2008). CDB still applies, mind you.

CARS stands for "creating a research space." Coined by literary critic John Swales (1990), the acronym refers to the standard rhetorical approach to introductory matter. It's an approach that's the norm across the social sciences. Taught on doctoral programs or picked up by RATS (reading around the subject), CARS consists of a four-step sequence: (1) establish the significance of your study; (2) selectively summarize prior research; (3) claim that this is incomplete; (4) use the space thus created to justify your article.

Even the most casual perusal of CCT's corpus reveals that our papers are replete with this gap-yap. Expressions like "scant attention," "curiously neglected," "glaring oversight," and "hitherto ignored" abound. There's no shortage of shortcomings, limitations, seldoms, failings, and remains mute, furthermore. Blind spot, presumably, is no longer politically correct, though I await the first "visually impaired caesura" with eager anticipation. As Levy's landmark article amply illustrates, CARS (and minor variations thereof) predominates in SNARS:

Qualitative research in current marketing study usually involves focus group interviews, sometimes depth interviews, and projective techniques. There is a resurgence of interest in the analysis of expressive verbal materials elicited by such data-gathering methods but little contemporary marketing literature exists about such analysis. The goal of this paper is to explore and illustrate the idea that verbal material elicited from people in the marketplace are a form of story-telling that can be analyzed as projective. (Levy 1981, 49)

The CCT literature has more lacks than Lacan, I grant you. But there's also GALS to contend with. On my reading, it's evident that "gender affects literary style." Women, as a rule, tend to opt for no-nonsense, matter-of-fact, honest-to-goodness introductions. They keep it plain and simple and straight to the point. Bristor and Fischer is fairly typical:

The premise of this article is that consumer research, like other bodies of knowledge, has sometimes misrepresented women. More fundamentally, we will argue that a portion of consumer research's theory and knowledge are gendered in unrecognized ways, and that feminist critique is required to clarify the implicit assumptions. (Bristor and Fischer 1993, 518)

Flights of fancy are a man thing for the most part. They are reserved for the alpha males of the CCT community. Female scholars, by contrast, either feel obliged or are required to write in a "masculine" style and, although I may be wrong about this, it seems to me that gender politics are at work. Barbara Stern, the leading advocate of literary criticism in consumer research, keeps things tightly buttoned up, even when discussing Jacques Derrida. Linda Scott and Cele Otnes, two of the most forceful women around—and both with impeccable literary backgrounds—tend to steer well clear of purple-tinged prose. Pauline Maclaran is a fantastically creative writer. Hope Schau, too. However, they save it for edited books and other ephemera. Unfortunately.

CARS Crashes

I think it's fair to say that almost all of our SNARS selection employ something close to the CARS procedure. But whereas Sword (2012) claims that this can lead to mind-numbing monotony, that's not the case with CCT. Infinite variety, rather, tends to prevail. Consider, for instance, Coupland's low-key, understated, somewhat self-effacing introduction to invisible brands. It's an approach that's perfectly suited to the subject matter of the article, nearly as invisible as the brands under investigation:

Most brand research to date tells us about brands that stand out in people's lives. Such researched brands are noticeably tied to and embraced by the informant, and they represent the person in some way. Informants can talk about, do think about, and can remember such brands. Yet people also own brands that they do not think much about. They may see them every day. They buy them over and over again. Yet the brands are just "there." This article examines those seemingly ordinary brands that are part of the lifestyle of the household. (Coupland 2005, 106)

By complete contrast, have a quick read of Mick and Fournier's titanic technology article. It commences with brash overstatement, continues with ever-mounting hyperbole, and climaxes with a sucker punch of tremendous rhetorical power, a real haymaker. Who wouldn't read on after that? Who'd dare not to?

No one eludes technology—the telephone, the computer, the airplane overhead, the air-conditioned air. Technoculture is irrefutable and pervasive. One leading view, called the substantive theory, contends that technology is a power in its own right, fundamental to the historical trajectory of Western civilization. Without it, "contemporary culture—work, art, science and education, indeed the entire range of interactions—is unthinkable." Hence, technology has become not only necessary but also "inconspicuous," if not "invisible."
   Such profundities have a distinctly ironic character in relation to the field of consumer behavior, where studies of technology have been limited in number and focus (Mick and Fournier 1998, 123).

Both Mick and Fournier are masters of CARS and, when working together as a tag team, they're all but unbeatable. Not everyone follows the formula, though. The antithesis works just as well, albeit in a "what the heck is this?" manner. By throwing the reader in at the deep end, and requiring them to sink or swim through a sea of polysyllables, Askegaard, Arnould, and Kjeldgaard become lifeguards of a sort, who slowly and somewhat reluctantly come to our rescue. *Baywatch* it ain't:

Postassimilationist acculturation research in North America has broken with earlier consumer research that accepted both the acculturation, or "melting pot" model and the phenomenological reality of ethnic categories. We subscribe to this postassimilationist viewpoint. This re-inquiry responds to the proposal for "research on . . . consumer subcultures in multiple nations" in order to check the robustness of recent postassimilationist theory of ethnic consumer behavior as represented in the Journal of Consumer Research. We propose to do this by critically examining postassimilationist theory in a non-North American context, among Greenlandic Inuit migrants to Denmark. To summarize our contribution, we find that Greenlandic consumer acculturation is supportive of the postassimilationist model proposed in previous research. However, acculturative processes in the Danish context lead immigrants to adopt culturally particular

identity positions somewhat different from those reported in previous postassimilationist consumer research. Further . . . (Askegaard,
Arnould, and Kjeldgaard 2005, 160)

Wherever you stand on postassimilationist consumer acculturation,
you can't deny that Askegaard and colleagues' introduction goes from
OMG to WTF in less than a paragraph. It's as batty as a bag of horseshoes.

On the other hand, consider the *Game of Thrones*esque quest narrative
that sets McAlexander, Schouten, and Koenig's community building article
in motion:

> For decades, marketers have sought the Holy Grail of brand loyalty.
> Just as the legendary grail of Arthurian quest held the promise of
> extended life and renewal, marketers attribute to brand loyalty and
> its sister icon, customer retention, the promise of long-term profit-
> ability and market share. Unfortunately, marketing's knights-errant
> face a daunting problem. They have not fully understood what the
> grail looks like or where it can be found. (McAlexander, Schouten,
> and Koenig 2002, 38)

Or what about this brilliantly creative Biblical beginning from Belk and
Tümbat?

> In the beginning (of the Information Age) was the void. And the
> void was digital. But lo, there came upon the land, the shadow of
> Steven Jobs (and Stephen Wozniak). And Steven (Stephen) said, "Let
> there be Apple." And there was Apple. And Steven (Stephen) beheld
> Apple. And it was good. And Apple begat Macintosh. And it was
> good. And soon upon the land there began to appear, The Cult of
> Macintosh. For they had tasted of Apple. And it was good. (Belk and
> Tumbat 2005, 205)

Jesus fuck! Is that the sound of my grandmother exploding? Mmm,
this dog is tasty, T-A-S-T-Y. Dachshund, is it?

Seven Short Stock Starts

What I'm saying, in other words, is that anything goes. And it often
does. It goes all the way from understatement to overstatement to statements of the blindingly obvious ("Religion is one of humanity's most
enduring creations," "Organizations face rapidly changing and increasingly complex market environments"). Every rhetorical swerve known to
man—and many that aren't—is routinely pressed into service by the CCT
community. These include, but aren't limited to, the following delightful
devices:

Declarative, where the paper begins with a bold claim or sweeping statement without qualification or equivocation. As such, it invites the reader to respond with a "really?" "always?" "oh, yeah?" or "prove it!" thereby hooking them for the argument to come. A fairly typical example is Deighton's (1992) deliberations on performance ("Careful attention to the surface appearance of things is a feature of all marketing activity"), as is Goulding and colleagues' (2009) artful article on illicit pleasure ("Pursuing and experiencing pleasure is a fundamental facet of the human condition and an essential mediator of consumer behavior").

Informative, where the article starts with a statement of facts, often hard facts, about the research context. Frequently devoid of citations, and the attendant barriers to communication (parentheses, names, dates, semicolons, etc.), these slip down easily like select wines or moreish hors d'oeuvres. They aren't so much a hearty repast as seared soul food for thought. "Thanksgiving Day is a national holiday celebrated in the United States on the fourth Thursday in November" (Wallendorf and Arnould 1991, 13); "On April 20, 2010, the Deepwater Horizon drilling rig exploded in the Gulf of Mexico, killing 11 workers and beginning what would become the largest maritime accident in the history of the petroleum industry" (Humphreys and Thompson 2014, 877).

Authoritative, where the authors show that they not only know what they're talking about but are best placed to do the talking. This is usually achieved with a snowstorm of citations, occasionally several lines long, which signifies deep reading (e.g., Thompson and Üstüner 2015). Wide reading is demonstrated too by copious callouts to distant academic disciplines, the more esoteric the better (practically anything by Russ Belk). On occasion—Doug Holt's the daddy here—the cites are limited to a short list of big names like Veblen, Simmel, and Weber rather than the long list of comparative nonentities that's the norm (Holt 1997). Grant McCracken's (1986) "Culture and Consumption" is cut from the same cloth, only eminent anthropologists get genuflected to rather than superstar sociologists.

Narrative, where the paper kicks off with a story, a just-so story as often as not, a story that sets the scene, seizes the reader, and hints at things to come. Inaugurated by the Odysseans, who commenced their lodestar article with three juicy vignettes about informants, introductory narratives are a mainstay of CCT. Sometimes they are excerpts from field notes (American Girl), sometimes they are synopses of interviews (Stock Show), sometimes they are stirring tales starring the intrepid researcher (Burning Man), and sometimes they are incredibly vivid evocations of the setting, effectively placing the reader in situ (Mountain Men): "Shortly before

sunset in a remote and pristine mountain meadow, we sit amidst
several hundred other buck-skin-clad men, women, and children
in a council meeting, forming a circle perhaps 100 feet in diam-
eter" (Belk and Costa 1998, 218).

Interrogative, guess what, begins with a question or a series of questions. Quick-fire questions. *Capisce?* It's a slam-dunk way of engaging the reader, as are similar invocations, imperatives, and
authorial commands, such as "Consider," "Assume," "Take," or
"Yo!"[9] A hailing device that isn't used as often as it could and
should be, interrogatives tend to be reserved for titles ("Can Consumers Escape the Market?" "Does Cultural Capital Structure
American Capitalism?" "How Does a Stigmatized Practice Become
Fashionable?"). Murray and Ozanne (1991, 129) are noteworthy
exceptions to the rule. They start their resounding call for critical consumer research with "Can people consume in ways that
express their social values?" Coskuner-Balli's (2013, 193) a dab
hand at it too: "How does a new academic field appear and bur-
geon, claim jurisdiction in an area of work and gain authority and
acceptance?" Good questions, guys!

Allusive, where the article alludes to, and benefits by association with,
another cultural form or similar source of credibility, celebrity, or
validation. Epigraphs are the most popular manifestation of this
particular device. More than thirty percent of SNARS have one
or two or, occasionally, three of the things. Adroit intertexts from
movies (Ritson and Elliott 1999), musicals (Hamilton and Hewer
2009), TV shows (Holbrook 1986), autobiographies (Giesler
2012), ancient proverbs (Peñaloza 2001), advertising taglines (Mc-
Quarrie and Mick 1992), and of course learned articles are found
in abundance. Craig Thompson is the suzerain of the allusion, some
of which are so long that they constitute preambles rather than
epigraphs. Some blend both: "All the world may be a stage, but nowhere has the performance trope gained greater theoretical traction
than in research addressing the commercial interactions between
consumers and service providers" (Üstüner and Thompson 2012,
796).

Inventive refers to beginnings that are so original, so imaginative, so
counterintuitive, so contrary to expectation that the reader can only
doff their cap in admiration. Belk and Tümbat's Biblical riff on
Apple quoted earlier; Sandikci and Ger's (2012) article on veiling,
which starts with something brilliantly offbeat, *Star Trek*; and the
Sherry and Schouten paper on poetry illustrate this perfectly. The
latter is outstanding, not simply on account of the authors' achievement (getting poems into *JCR*? Wow!), but because their introduction isn't particularly poetic. It's prosaic. It goes completely against
the grain and benefits thereby:

As a literary form, poetry is making a strong comeback. After languishing through the 1970s and 1980s as a neglected genre, poetry is reemerging as a voice of the people in places as diverse as cafes, personal websites, public buses and subways, state fairs and presidential inaugurations. Barnes and Noble reports a 30% increase in poetry sales from 1997 to 2000, and New York's Poets House reckons an increase of almost 100% in the number of poetry books published between 1993 and 1999.

(Sherry and Schouten 2002, 218)

Our list of devices doesn't stop there. In addition to the seven aforementioned "-ives," we can add *definitive*, *enumerative*, and *retroactive*. These are so common that they constitute a standard part of the CARS package. Despite what you might imagine, *definitive* doesn't refer to the ultimate expression of academic rhetoric but to the inclusion of a definition of some kind or other (e.g., technology, nostalgia, habitus, biopower, performativity). *Enumerative* pertains to the firsts, seconds, thirds, and so on that pepper opening paragraphs and are used to outline the aims, objectives, and structure of the argument to come. *Retroactive* comprises a potted history of the topic, the field, the literature, the relevant schools of thought, the study's empirical setting, and suchlike. Frequently cast in a once-upon-a-time format, retroactives render even the most demanding subject undemanding and engaging for the reader. Fırat and Venkatesh's epic article on postmodernism is a case in point:

Consumer research has been experiencing a stimulating period of self-study, debate, and rejuvenation in the past decade. One influential framework within which the debates have been conducted is labelled "modernism versus postmodernism" . . . Most of our taken-for-granted notions related to the consumer, consumption, markets, and consumer culture rest on certain cultural and philosophical foundations that are found in the general historical framework known as modernism. Postmodernism has emerged not only as a critique of modernism and its foundational domination over established constructs in consumer culture, but, in its own right, it also has emerged as a new philosophical and cultural movement. (Fırat and Venkatesh 1995, 239)

Unboxing Clever

Now, the lapsed number crunchers among you are likely wondering about the distribution of our devices and how their incidence has changed through time. All I can say is that you need to lighten up or lie down in a darkened room until the urge passes. We're talking about SNARS here. Most of my sampled articles, what's more, combine several rhetorical moves; there are no pure forms. Belk's (1988, 139) "Extended Self," for example, starts off with an epigraph from Ernest Dichter, explodes into life with a declarative ("We cannot hope to understand consumer behavior without first gaining some understanding of the meanings that consumers attach to possessions"), then draws upon a heady mix of academic authorities (the immemorial William James among them), and culminates in an extended discussion of the five main sections to follow.

Just to keep you happy, however, I have roughly classified our sample according to each paper's dominant motif. And, surprise, surprise, authoritative introductions, locked and loaded with lots and lots of the learned literature, head the pack. Narratives run them a close second with informatives trailing behind. The last of these, interestingly, predominated in era one, narratives surged in era two, and authoritatives wrested control in era three. This trend toward increased authoritarianism may well reflect Fitchett's (2016, 4) recent complaint that CCT fetishizes "laborious minutiae and theoretical contributions through context-on-context." However, it is noteworthy that inventives soared in era three, too, which is indicative of a growing discursive divide and possibly impending rupture.

More meaningful than dubious extrapolations of a suspect dataset is the existence of two clearly identifiable rhetorical tendencies within our works. These aren't so much devices as deeper structures. They comprise the *funnel* and the *fantail*. The funnel starts off with a broad, all-encompassing, big-picture statement, or series of statements, and progressively drills down to the specific focus of the study. Holbrook (1993) is a good example, as are O'Guinn and Belk (1989) and Visconti and colleagues (2010). The fantail, conversely, commences with something very specific—an anecdote, an excerpt, an instance—and then steadily broadens the discussion out into the surrounding scholarly literature. Starbucks' brandscape typifies the breed (Thompson and Arsel 2004). Ditto American Girl (Diamond et al. 2009) and Botox (Giesler 2012). Neither variant is better. Both do the job.

When we combine this structural dichotomy with the clear stylistic contrast between articles written in a factual manner (plain, unadorned) and those that are florid (ornate, expressive), we're suddenly in typology territory. Whoa! From Morris Holbrook's (1998) eight-category inventory of values to Doug Holt's (1995) two-by-two matrix of contemporary consumers' consumption styles, CCT's never been averse to classification. Our founding fathers indeed identified four foci going forward: consumer identity projects, marketplace cultures, sociohistoric patterning of consumption, and mass-mediated marketplace ideologies (Arnould and Thompson 2005). And many subsequent contributions are positioned in relation to this particular thematic typology.

It says nothing about beginnings, however. Hereinafter known as BS², Brown's Structure-Style framework comprises four combinatory categories: *factual-funnel, factual-fantail, florid-funnel,* and *florid-fantail*. The fandango of F-words is only one of its many charms, I'm sure you agree. Better yet is the fact that with a little bit of pushing and pulling, and huffing and puffing, and more than a modicum of grunting, groaning, and force fitting, most of SNARS can be shoehorned, crowbarred, and squeeeeezed into BS^2. The former two categories are written in a plain, unadorned, no-fuss, nothing-fancy manner and either start focused then spread out (Cova, Maclaran, and Bradshaw 2013) or begin broad and drill down (Cayla and Eckhardt 2008). The latter two cells—imagine a matrix if you must—are stylish, striking, sometimes self-conscious compositions that steadily contract (Thompson and Haytko 1997) or progressively expand (Kozinets 2002), respectively.

Happily Ever After?

Sorry, what was that? You're saying I missed another F-word? Farrago, is it? You aren't too keen on my token typology? You're sick to death of four-fold classifications? Is that what this is about? You're insinuating that BS^2 is aptly initialed? Well, that's not very nice, I must say. Here I am, trying to help you people out. Hewing through your introductions, hoping to impose some order on the oeuvre. And that's the thanks I get?

Two people can play at that game, let me tell you! Your beginnings might be reasonably good. Your innovations on the literary front may have obliterated those awful academic articles that begin with the humdrum words "This paper." But your abstracts are no great shakes. Almost forty percent of them, I regret to report, start with precisely those woeful words. Yes, there are numerous notable exceptions to the "This paper," "This article," "This study" rule. Giesler's abstracts often start with an interrogative, which is highly commendable. Isn't it? Most of your abstracts are abysmal, though. As scholars who supposedly take pride in penmanship, surely you can do better. Reinventing the abstract is a challenge that CCT could and should embrace. Pronto.

Your titles could do with a makeover, too. When working stoically through SNARS, my attention was often drawn to titles. Contrary to expectation—which was shaped by overexposure to past masters of nomination like Belk, Holbrook, Sherry, and Schouten—I was surprised and disappointed to discover just how insipid they often are: "Images in Advertising"; "Retail Luxury Strategy"; "Paradoxes of Technology"; "Consumers and Their Brands"; "The Social Uses of Advertising." There's nothing wrong with that, of course. They work perfectly well in an FYI way. And some, to be fair, are fantastic. Poetic titles like "The Fire of Desire," intriguing titles like "River Magic," incongruous titles like "Branding Disaster," allusive titles like "We Gather Together," alliterative titles like "Frustrated Fatsionistas," minimalist titles like "Sharing," amusing titles like "I Hate When That Happens," and shock-horror titles like "I Am Not a Terrorist!" are a credit to their creators. However, when you compare typical CCT titles to Brad Werner's off-the-Richter-scale effort for fellow geophysicists—yes, geophysicists—you've nothing that comes close to "Is Earth Fucked?"

Hesitant as I am to start harrumphing, like a reactionary bull elephant who believes the world has gone to hell in a handcart, it wouldn't do you any harm to cast a cold eye on your methodology sections. They are somewhat stereotyped, to put it very politely, and reviewers, I reckon, are the root cause of the problem. Whatever their merits as scientific proof or scholarly stress tests, your dolorous descriptions of research methods are a dreadful turnoff for readers. You should either move them to an appendix or start taking more on trust. Or replace them with a suitable selection of emojis. You need to get rid of Harvard-style referencing while you're at it. Palisades of parentheses, strings of surnames, colonies of semicolons, and more dates than Tinder and Happn combined are passion killers for all but the most masochistic readers.

I'm conscious of course that only the most masochistic members of CCT will be reading this sentence. Because I sure know how to make people suffer. Don't I just. So rather than launch into a rant about lamentable conclusions, which need almost as much work as titles and abstracts, let me wrap things up with a happy ending. According to Henry James, the concluding chapters of lowbrow novels comprise "a distribution at the last of prizes, pensions, husbands, wives, babies, millions, appended paragraphs and cheerful remarks" (quoted in Lodge 1992, 224). As a lowbrow and proud of it, I feel obliged to finish with a few richly deserved awards. Specifically, a shout-out for the best opening section in SNARS.

Despite stiff competition from Belk, Sherry, Hirschman, Holbrook, and others, my award for the best beginning—let's call it a Brownie—is shared between Scott's "Images in Advertising" and Celsi, Rose, and Leigh's "Skydiving" article. The former seems flat on the surface—short, direct sentences with few polysyllables—but each one is sprightly, sparking, superb (Scott 1994, 252):

> The world of advertisements is peopled by fantastic images. A multitude of imaginary characters dance through situations ranging from sensual to playful, from threatening to mundane. The messages are reversed, boldfaced and italicized—set in typefaces with names like Baby Teeth, Jiminy Cricket, and Park Avenue. Products kaleidoscope past our eyes in heroized visual styles borrowed from the Dutch masters—or the Masters of the Universe. Pictures pun, photographs fantasize, illustrations illuminate. In rich colors and textures, a panoply of visual messages entice, exhort, and explain.

The latter, by contrast, transports us *there*, to the center of the action. We are in the cabin with the skydivers, preparing to leap into the void.

We are apprehensive. Our adrenaline is pumping. Our mouths are dry. Our palms wax clammy. Way to go, Geronimo (Celsi, Rose, and Leigh 1993, 1):

> Twenty skydivers rise and line up tightly in single file, as the DC-3, cruising at 100 knots, levels off two and one-half miles above the swamps of central Florida. In their bright jumpsuits, they form a sort of surreal rumba line snaking toward the white light of the open DC-3 door. She is last out on this "twenty-way" jump. Her job is to dive headfirst, in as fast and as controlled a manner as possible, to catch up to the skydivers exiting in front of her. Without exception, the laws of physics will separate the skydivers as they exit, accelerating the first to leave away from those that follow. She lives for this. Nothing else exists for her now beyond this moment. The engines cut. Ready! Set! Go!

Over. And. Out.

Notes

1 Just testing. Making sure you're awake and alert. I'll deal with our endings another day, assuming the light stays green.
2 This best-in-breed claim is made by Askegaard and Scott (2013) in their oral history of CCT. Writing-wise, it's not MoHo's finest hour (in my opinion).
3 Note, I have removed all the citations from the excerpts included herein. Our focus is on the writing style, not the associated support mechanisms. Nor, for that matter, are we concerned with the structural issues that shape our output (journal guidelines, disciplinary demands, editorial interventions, copywriter considerations, etc.). This chapter concentrates on authorial agency.
4 Look, before you throw a strop, let me emphasize that we're dealing with literary issues here. The content and impact of the chosen articles is irrelevant. Yes, Belk and colleagues (1989) is one of the most important contributions to consumer research, ever. However, its opening sentence could be better. That's all I'm saying. For an alternative take on things, see Hogg and Maclaran (2008).
5 I'm not kidding about the bullet. We gotta get out of town before Eric Arnould arrives, uncharacteristically irate, toting a Thompson submachine gun. Don't shoot Eric. Whoops. That should be "Don't shoot, Eric." Punctuation was never my strong point.
6 Or should that be onanist? In fairness, few works of fiction and nonfiction are as laudable as my exemplars. Amos Oz (1999, 5), for instance, quotes a stinker from Dostoyevsky: "It was a lovely night, one of those nights, dear reader, which can only happen when you are young."
7 Barbara Stern's (1988) breakthrough paper on advertising allegories is a perfect example of pandering to a reviewer. Well, it reads that way to me. Check it out for yourself.
8 This is pretty arbitrary, I agree. "When does the beginning of a novel end?" Lodge (1992, 4) likewise wonders. "Is it the first paragraph, the first few pages, or the first chapter? However one defines it, the beginning of a novel is a threshold."
9 Actually, the only "Yo!" I know was written by me. Forget I mentioned it.

Bibliography

Arnould, Eric J. and Craig J. Thompson. "Consumer Culture Theory (CCT): Twenty Years of Research." *Journal of Consumer Research* 31 (March 2005): 868–82.

Askegaard, Søren, Eric J. Arnould, and Dannie Kjeldgaard. "Postassimilationist Ethnic Consumer Research: Qualifications and Extensions." *Journal of Consumer Research* 32 (June 2005): 160–70.

—— and Linda M. Scott. "Consumer Culture Theory: The Ironies of History." *Marketing Theory* 13, no. 2 (2013): 139–47.

Ballard, J. G. *High-Rise*. London: Jonathan Cape, 1975.

Banks, Iain. *The Crow Road*. London: Scribner, 1992.

Belk, Russell W. "Possessions and the Extended Self." *Journal of Consumer Research* 15 (September 1988): 139–68.

—— and Janeen A. Costa "The Mountain Man Myth: A Contemporary Consuming Fantasy." *Journal of Consumer Research* 25 (December 1998): 218–40.

—— and Gülnur Tumbat. "The Cult of Macintosh." *Consumption Markets & Culture* 8, no. 3 (2005): 205–17.

——, Melanie Wallendorf, and John F. Sherry, Jr. "The Sacred and the Profane in Consumer Behavior: Theodicy on the Odyssey." *Journal of Consumer Research* 16 (June 1989): 1–38.

Bradshaw, Alan and Stephen Brown. "Scholars Who Stare at Goats: The Collaborative Circle Cycle in Creative Consumer Research." *European Journal of Marketing* 42, nos. 11–2 (2008): 1396–414.

Bristor, Julie M. and Eileen Fischer. "Feminist Thought: Implications for Consumer Research." *Journal of Consumer Research* 19 (March 1993): 518–36.

Brookmyre, Christopher. *Quite Ugly One Morning*. London: Abacus, 1997.

Brown, Stephen, Robert V. Kozinets, and John F. Sherry, Jr. "Teaching Old Brands New Tricks: Retro Branding and the Revival of Brand Meaning." *Journal of Marketing* 67 (July 2003): 19–33.

Cayla, Julien and Giana M. Eckhardt. "Asian Brands and the Shaping of a Transnational Imagined Community." *Journal of Consumer Research* 35 (August 2008): 216–30.

Celsi, Richard L., Randall L. Rose, and Thomas W. Leigh. "An Exploration of High-Risk Leisure Consumption through Skydiving." *Journal of Consumer Research* 20 (June 1993): 1–23.

Coskuner-Balli, Gokcen. "Market Practices of Legitimization: Insights from Consumer Culture Theory." *Marketing Theory* 13, no. 2 (2013): 193–211.

Coupland, Jennifer Chang. "Invisible Brands: An Ethnography of Households and the Brands in Their Kitchen Pantries." *Journal of Consumer Research* 32 (June 2005): 106–18.

Cova, Bernard, Pauline Maclaran, and Alan Bradshaw. "Rethinking Consumer Culture Theory from the Postmodern to the Communist Horizon." *Marketing Theory* 13, no. 2 (2013): 213–25.

Deighton, John. "The Consumption of Performance." *Journal of Consumer Research* 19 (December 1992): 362–72.

Diamond, Nina, John F. Sherry, Jr., Albert M. Muñiz, Jr., Mary Ann McGrath, Robert V. Koninez, and Stefania Borghini. "American Girl and the Brand Gestalt: Closing the Loop on Sociocultural Branding Research." *Journal of Marketing* 73 (May 2009): 119–34.

Fırat, A. Fuat and Alladi Venkatesh. "Liberatory Postmodernism and the Re-Enchantment of Consumption." *Journal of Consumer Research* 22 (December 1995): 239–67.

Firth, Raymond. *We, the Tikopia: A Sociological Study of Kinship in Primitive Polynesia*. London: Allen & Unwin, 1936.

Fitchett, James. "Friedrich Nietzsche (1844–1900)" In *Canonical Authors in Consumption Theory*, in press. Edited by Søren Askegaard and Benoît Heilbrunn. London: Routledge, 2017.

Geertz, Clifford. *Works and Lives: The Anthropologist as Author*. Stanford: Stanford University Press, 1988.

Giesler, Markus. "How Doppelgänger Brand Images Influence the Market Creation Process: Longitudinal Insights from the Rise of Botox Cosmetic." *Journal of Marketing* 76 (November 2012): 55–68.

Golden-Biddle, Karen and Karen D. Locke. *Composing Qualitative Research*. Thousand Oaks: Sage, 1997.

Goulding, Christina, Avi Shankar, Richard Elliott, and Robin Canniford. "The Marketplace Management of Illicit Pleasure." *Journal of Consumer Research* 35 (February 2009): 759–71.

Hamilton, Kathy and Paul Hewer. "Salsa Magic: An Exploratory Netnographic Analysis of the Salsa Experience." *Advances in Consumer Research* 36 (2009): 502–8.

Hogg, Margaret K. and Pauline Maclaran. "Rhetorical Issues in Writing Interpretivist Consumer Research." *Qualitative Market Research: An International Journal* 11, no. 2 (2008): 130–46.

Holbrook, Morris B. "A Note on Sadomasochism in the Review Process: I Hate When That Happens." *Journal of Marketing* 50 (July 1986): 104–6.

———. "Nostalgia and Consumption Preferences: Some Emerging Patterns of Consumer Taste." *Journal of Consumer Research* 20 (September 1993): 245–56.

———. *Consumer Value: A Framework for Analysis and Research*. London: Routledge, 1998.

Holt, Douglas B. "How Consumers Consume: A Typology of Consumption Practices." *Journal of Consumer Research* 22 (June 1995): 1–16.

———. "Poststructuralist Lifestyle Analysis: Conceptualizing the Social Patterning of Consumption in Postmodernity." *Journal of Consumer Research* 23 (March 1997): 326–50.

Humphreys, Ashlee and Craig J. Thompson. "Branding Disaster: Reestablishing Trust through the Ideological Containment of Systemic Risk Anxieties." *Journal of Consumer Research* 41 (December 2014): 877–910.

Kozinets, Robert V. "Can Consumers Escape the Market? Emancipatory Illuminations From Burning Man." *Journal of Consumer Research* 29 (June 2002): 20–38.

Levy, Sidney J. "Interpreting Consumer Mythology: A Structural Approach to Consumer Behavior." *Journal of Marketing* 45, no. 3 (1981): 49–61.

Lodge, David. *The Art of Fiction*. London: Penguin, 1992.

McAlexander, James H., John W. Schouten, and Harold F. Koenig. "Building Brand Community." *Journal of Marketing* 66 (January 2002): 38–54.

McCracken, Grant. "Culture and Consumption: A Theoretical Account of the Structure and Movement of the Cultural Meaning of Consumer Goods." *Journal of Consumer Research* 13 (June 1986): 71–84.

McQuarrie, Edward F. and David Glen Mick. "On Resonance: A Critical Pluralistic Inquiry into Advertising Rhetoric." *Journal of Consumer Research* 19 (September 1992): 180–97.

Mick, David Glen and Susan Fournier. "Paradoxes of Technology: Consumer Cognizance, Emotions, and Coping Strategies." *Journal of Consumer Research* 25 (September 1998): 123–43.

Murray, Jeff B. and Julie L. Ozanne. "The Critical Imagination: Emancipatory Interests in Consumer Research." *Journal of Consumer Research* 18 (September 1991): 129–44.

O'Guinn, Thomas C. and Russell W. Belk. "Heaven on Earth: Consumption at Heritage Village, USA." *Journal of Consumer Research* 16 (September 1989): 227–38.

Oz, Amos. *The Story Begins: Essays on Literature.* London: Chatto & Windus, 1999.

Peñaloza, Lisa. "Consuming the American West: Animating Cultural Meaning at a Stock Show and Rodeo." *Journal of Consumer Research* 28 (December 2001): 369–98.

Ritson, Mark and Richard Elliott. "The Social Uses of Advertising." *Journal of Consumer Research* 26 (December 1999): 260–77.

Sandikci, Özlem and Güliz Ger. "Veiling in Style: How Does a Stigmatized Practice Become Fashionable?" *Journal of Consumer Research* 37, no. 1 (2010): 15–36.

Schouten, John W. and James H. McAlexander. "Subcultures of Consumption: An Ethnography of the New Bikers." *Journal of Consumer Research* 22 (June 1995): 43–61.

Scott, Linda M. "Images in Advertising: The Need for a Theory of Visual Rhetoric." *Journal of Consumer Research* 21 (September 1994): 252–73.

Sherry, John F., Jr. "Postmodern Alternatives: The Interpretive Turn in Consumer Research." In *Handbook of Consumer Behavior*, 548–91. Edited by Thomas S. Robertson and Harold H. Kassarjian. Englewood Cliffs: Prentice-Hall, 1991.

—— and John W. Schouten. "A Role for Poetry in Consumer Research." *Journal of Consumer Research* 29 (September 2002): 218–34.

Stern, Barbara B. "Medieval Allegory: Roots of Advertising Strategy for the Mass Market." *Journal of Marketing* 52 (July 1988): 84–94.

Swales, John M. *Genre Analysis: English in Academic and Research Settings.* Cambridge: Cambridge University Press, 1990.

Sword, Helen. *Stylish Academic Writing.* Cambridge: Harvard University Press, 2012.

Thompson, Craig J. and Zeynep Arsel. "The Starbucks Brandscape and Consumers' (Anticorporate) Experiences of Glocalization." *Journal of Consumer Research* 31 (December 2004): 631–42.

—— and Diana L. Haytko. "Speaking of Fashion: Consumers' Uses of Fashion Discourses and the Appropriation of Countervailing Cultural Meanings." *Journal of Consumer Research* 24 (June 1997): 15–42.

—— and Tuba Üstüner. "Women Skating on the Edge: Marketplace Performances as Ideological Edgework." *Journal of Consumer Research* 42, no. 2 (2015): 235–65.

Üstüner, Tuba and Craig J. Thompson. "How Marketplace Performances Produce Interdependent Status Games and Contested Forms of Symbolic Capital." *Journal of Consumer Research* 38 (February 2012): 796–814.

Van Maanen, John. *Tales of the Field: On Writing Ethnography.* Chicago: University of Chicago Press, 1988.

Visconti, Luca M., John F. Sherry Jr., Stefania Borghini and Laurel Anderson. "Street Art, Sweet Art? Reclaiming the 'Public' in Public Space", *Journal of Consumer Research*, 37 (October, 2010): 511–529.

Wallendorf, Melanie and Eric J. Arnould. "We Gather Together: Consumption Rituals of Thanksgiving Day." *Journal of Consumer Research* 18 (June 1991): 13–31.

11 The Consumer Culture Theory Movement

Critique and Renewal

A. Fuat Fırat and Nikhilesh Dholakia

It has been just over a decade since Arnould and Thompson published their article that christened a prominent stream of consumer research with the moniker consumer culture theory (CCT; Arnould and Thompson 2005). In this article, they focused on the twenty years prior to the publication of the article. In three decades, including the period since the CCT-christening publication, CCT has become an influential and highly present movement in the consumer research field. The highly visible scholars leading the CCT movement draw a significant number of doctoral students who wish to work in this genre. A successful conference series assembles some of the brightest minds in the field every year. Multiple international doctoral seminars are organized on this topic. Key journals in the fields of consumer research and marketing have representatives of CCT in their editorial teams and boards. These are all indications that in a very short time the CCT movement has gathered much momentum and has become very successful.

At the 2015 CCT Conference in Fayetteville, Arkansas, Sidney J. Levy, a leading and foundational scholar in marketing and consumer research and a key influence in the development of ideas that merged into the CCT movement gave a keynote speech that explored the "roots and development of CCT" (Levy 2015). This is an invaluable contribution to our understanding of disciplinary evolution. In this chapter, we wish to take a similar approach, but with a critical lens. We will contextualize the evolution of CCT within a longer history not only of the consumer research and marketing fields but also of human evolution and philosophical ideas in general. Our goal is to understand both the past and envision a future—that is, the reasons and the necessities that gave birth to CCT, as well as the needed critical evaluation and renewal to foster further development of thought. We hope this critique and renewal could propel CCT to spaces beyond the once-spectacular—but now somewhat theoretically moribund—intellectual orbit and to become an emancipatory force for humanity: after all consumer culture is now the globally pervasive ethos and zeitgeist (Featherstone 1983, 2007), and critical and liberatory CCT work should help make people's lives more meaningful.

In what follows, we have a simple three-part structure: review, critique, and renewal. We critically review, very briefly, the history of CCT, then present the key points of the critique of the movement including our own critique, and finally suggest some avenues for a meaningful renewal of CCT to engage the passion and commitment of researchers and students for advancing the understanding of and ameliorating the human condition. There have, of course, been other critiques of and calls for renewal of the CCT corpus of knowledge—content, philosophies, and methods—and these are examined briefly in the chapter. What we add to these critical views is a broader global and deeper historical perspective, and suggest renewal directions that have hitherto received little attention.

Review

Historical Backdrop

Although CCT-like scholarship had been going on since the 1980s (and even earlier by scholars like Sidney Levy), the CCT brand began its life with the publication of the inaugural article, "Consumer Culture Theory (CCT): Twenty Years of Research," by Arnould and Thompson in 2005 in the *Journal of Consumer Research* (*JCR*). This article was at once exciting in its promise and disappointing in its coverage of work and theories that enabled the CCT brand to emerge. Hegel, Marx, Weber—not to mention many other stalwarts in the Western intellectual traditions with relevant works on consumers and culture, let alone the ancient Eastern alternatives and the newer postcolonial reverberating discourses—did not exist in the history of theories of consumer culture depicted in this *JCR* article. The authors chose to limit their review largely to twenty years of publications in one journal, *JCR*, indicating that many other publications could not be included due to space limitations. All the left-out publications that were mentioned were journals (with the order of "Culture" and "Consumption" in the name of the journal *CMC* reversed); seminal books on consumer culture did not figure even as "left out" items. All these "limits" reinforced the strong bias in the discipline in favor of one journal that is lionized and against books, which—when we look at key contributions to consumer culture literatures across disciplines and historical epochs—have had much greater impact and staying power than journal articles, including those published in *JCR*, most of which are forgotten soon after they appear in print and indeed fail to generate excitement in general public intellectual forums.

In the first Heretical Consumer Research (HCR) meeting in 1996 in Tucson, Arizona, two distinct approaches surfaced to getting groundbreaking research and theoretical advancements in consumer research heard. One emphasized the significance and necessity of publishing these new perspectives in *JCR*, then considered to be the top journal in the field. The other approach emphasized the importance of keeping the integrity of the work produced and expressed the concern that trying to publish in *JCR* might require softening of ideas and findings that might be difficult to digest by membership of the editorial board of a journal that harbored established and largely conventional business-school-based scholars in the field. Clearly, colleagues in the first camp were later very successful in publishing in *JCR* and proved that it could be done without too much compromise. It is largely this group of consumer researchers who were active participants in early HCR meetings that established and now constitute the core scholars of the CCT school. It needs to be said, however, that they do not owe this success to their participation in HCR, and that HCR had very different aims and content from CCT, in order to dispel the rumors that CCT is a child of HCR, even if HCR helped a group of CCT scholars with similar aims to find and support each other.

In the second meeting of HCR in Estes Park, Colorado, another difference in approaches surfaced. One approach argued that the term *heretical* ought to be dropped for fear that the "center" of the discipline would never accept the perspectives proposed by this movement. The second approach argued that the movement ought to claim the "center" as heretical. This difference further defined the approach that CCT scholars later took in, indeed, constituting part of the center. Their success in becoming highly present as associate editors, editors, and editorial board members of *JCR* cannot be denied. The ideological fallout of this has been as expected: because heresy cannot be central and because the center cannot be heretical, the growing centrality of CCT has purged the movement of any desire to be sharply radical and critical of contemporary consumer culture, while maintaining some chic and nugatory jibes at overtly psychoeconomic (i.e., the previous and continuing non-CCT) approaches to consumer behavior.

Evolutionary Trajectory of CCT

Within a very short time, the CCT brand became very successful in attracting many scholars and, especially important, many doctoral students to the universities of the key CCT scholars. Multiple seminars, modeled after the intensive doctoral seminars that were organized by Dominique Bouchet in Denmark beginning in 1995—the Bouchet-led seminars that many later-to-be-central CCT scholars had attended as faculty or as doctoral students—were started to acculturate new doctoral students to the major tenets of CCT. Publications in highly regarded journals in the tradition of CCT became numerous. Eventually, a CCT conference series was initiated, and it continues successfully every year.

What have the CCT articles in *JCR* achieved, in intellectual and knowledge-systemic terms? In succinct terms, the following have certainly been successful achievements of the CCT movement:

- Opening the disciplinary space of consumer research to philosophical knowledge traditions other than positivist logical empiricism (e.g., Holbrook and O'Shaughnessy 1988; Hudson and Ozanne 1988; Thompson, Locander, and Pollio 1989);

- Bringing in research literatures outside the traditional psychoeconomic ones, such as anthropology (e.g., Joy 2001; Sherry 1983), ethnography (Peñaloza 1994), literary theory (e.g., Brown 1999, Stern 1989), semiology (Holbrook and Grayson 1986; Mick 1986; Sherry and Camargo 1987), and more; and
- Creating room for discursive, introspective, narrative styles of writing (e.g., Holbrook 1987) and for naturalistic field reportage (e.g., Belk, Wallendorf, and Sherry 1989).

In the disciplines of marketing and consumer behavior—fields that suppressed almost all perspectives except the North American idea of positivist science and scientific advancement—Arnould and Thompson's (2005) intervention with the idea of CCT was welcome and courageous. They gave voice to a growing desire among interpretive consumer research academics (e.g., Sherry 1991) to be recognized and understood as a valid and needed school of knowledge generation for a deeper understanding of the human condition. They also managed to create "turf" for scholars who wanted to pursue this line of scholarship—not as lush a turf as the mainstream one but a comfortable turf nonetheless (Dholakia 2012, 224)—and some professional recognition of the alternative turf so that positions in academic departments would be available for CCT-oriented scholars.

The risk of such aims, however, has historically always been that such efforts can easily turn into a path of careerism and self-promotion rather than a concern for intellectual advancement for humanity and the universe. To resist this tendency, members and leaders of a movement have to reject tirelessly the impulses toward templates of all kinds and allow refreshment of all ideas. Has a state of simmering intellectual renewal continued in CCT, or has the "movement" ceased to be a movement and become, of course, not a mainstream but a significant sidestream for those choosing to navigate the waters in interpretive canoes and kayaks rather than in statistically powered motorboats?

Critique

As we begin our critique, we acknowledge that the CCT movement's attempt to bring greater attention to theories and methods that can bring a deeper understanding of cultural and individual processes that motivate consumer behaviors and experiences is admirable, as is the movement's goal to bring recognition to and academic positions for scholars who are expanding consumer research horizons. There are, however, limitations of the movement—some recognized, and others not addressed as fully as we think is necessary. In the rest of this section, we first review some existing CCT critiques and then offer a critique of our own.

Seeds of Discontent and Urgings for Renewal

As its success grew, some criticism of the CCT school began to be heard. Becoming aware of these criticisms, Askegaard and Linnet (2011) published an article in *Marketing Theory* that called for an expansion of the contextualization of CCT studies beyond the "sociocultural context" that they argued was brought to consumer research by CCT. This article also presented a quite thorough review of the literature since the Arnould and Thompson (2005) piece in *JCR*. Their review saves us from having to present an overview of this literature. The expansion Askegaard and Linnet (2011) called for was to contextualize consumer research studies in "systemic and structuring influences of market and social systems." Although a welcome opening to broader perspectives, their proposed contextualization can be argued to be insufficient. As some of the following critiques we discuss also express, the ideological and historical factors beyond the market-hegemonic and "social" influences are in great need of being brought into the picture. Although CCT has "culture" in its name, it can be argued that the cultural is often limited to the economic and the social—and that, too, at individual and group levels, and not the systemic level—in CCT studies.

In a chapter commenting on the state of CCT, Moisander, Peñaloza, and Valtonen (2009) express several significant concerns regarding the current status of CCT that we share. Indeed, a field that was opening many new and exciting avenues has been closed off by some of the declarations on behalf of CCT by some leaders of CCT. A new dogma—regarding correct ways, and by implication incorrect ways, of doing consumer culture research and producing new theory—has begun to emerge. Worthy papers presenting new theoretical developments and insights have been rejected by editors and reviewers who belong to the CCT school because the authors resisted following the CCT template for performing and reporting research. The template follows greatly the preferred North American methods and styles. Moisander, Peñaloza, and Valtonen (2009) have done an excellent job in situating and analyzing the CCT shortcomings and potentials in this respect. In this chapter, we shall try not to repeat what they have accomplished but to address and expand on additional concerns and critique that the CCT field needs for its reinvigoration.

Fitchett, Patsiaouras, and Davies (2014) have also addressed the ideological limits of CCT. They identify a "neoliberal sentiment" in CCT, what we consider to be the result of a lack of attention to the political dimension of culture. Fitchett, Patsiaouras, and Davies focus on the CCT school's emphasis on consumer subjectivities and also a worldview that universalizes the market and consumption. Another commentary on CCT—by Cova, Maclaran, and Bradshaw (2013)—also stresses CCT's ideological limitations. In this elegant commentary, they situate CCT in the time frame of postmodern and post-postmodern movements and, interestingly, contrast it to communism, as they also see its potentials of accommodating communism, possibly by continually rejecting it or, as they propose, as an "ideological counterpoint" (Cova, Maclaran, and Bradshaw 2013, 221).

In the United States, and by extension in much of the Western world, from the 1940s, social science scholarship has been—relatively invisibly—constrained by a "plastic cage" (Brown 1995), crafted assiduously in Cold War-addled America by the Rand Corporation and its far-reaching and research-shaping tentacles in all major universities (Amadae 2003). The result has been an intellectual space that pervades almost all of Western social sciences, especially on the North American side of the Atlantic, and is unquestioning of capitalism and implacably hostile to communism and even to socialism. With the abject irrelevance of the Cold War from 1990 onward, some segments of the humanities and a few sections of social sciences (e.g., Hardt and Negri 2001; Passavant and Dean 2004) have managed to explicitly and daringly step out of the plastic cage. As the critique by Cova, Maclaran, and Bradshaw (2013) shows, however, CCT leaders have chosen not only *not* to challenge the methodological aspects of rational choice (neo)liberalism but also to remain within the ideological boundaries of the plastic cage (see also Askegaard 2014). This is partly perhaps due to the subtle surveillance exercised by the business school systems (i.e., the dean's office)—systems often supported by generous donors who owe their success and wealth to capitalist enterprises. The well-endowed B-schools provide the CCT leaders their professional daily bread (or should we say "cake," à la the likely misattributed phrase of Marie Antoinette?) and lavish oft-lucrative research-support rewards on top scholars but also monitor carefully any intellectual research and pedagogic transgressions that may question the fundamental tenets of the capitalist system.

Our Critique

We critique CCT along the following dimensions: overly strict adherence to certain methods, near-exclusive reliance on midrange theory, political orientations, and styles of presentation of research. We also critique on three broader dimensions as well: what we call a temporal trap; in a similar vein, a spatial trap; and a trap arising from ways of filtering theory. Together, these limitations and myopic orientations have brought the *innovative* scholarly practices—that were opening the field to new perspectives and insights in the decades preceding the "branded success" of CCT—to a near-screeching halt. Let us review these problematic dimensions.

Methodological Rigidities

CCT scholars have continued the North American scientific ideology that has equated scientificity with certain methods of data collection. Clearly, CCT scholars are not fond of numeric or quantitative data collection as the only form of generating empirical data, yet we do not see a thorough understanding of the implications of the distinction between measuring data points and generating rich text in the discussions of methods in the CCT literature. Therefore, to respond to criticisms from the quantitative research proponents that qualitative data generated and its analysis do not meet validity and reliability standards, which are products of and required in quantitative measurements, CCT scholars take a defensive position and try to argue for equivalents in generated texts and their analyses.

There are of course historical *JCR* pieces that are not based on generated rich texts but on archival texts and materials (Karababa and Ger 2011). These are, however, typical descriptive studies that do not critically explain why what they describe is happening at the time and the context that they study. Consequently, we are left with "this is what happened" without an understanding of why it happened at that time and place. The theories that are used in these papers are used to verify the descriptions rather than question them. This is part of the ideological bias we talk about, and—despite some evidence of opening the methodological space—these historical studies do not provide a strong alternative to the preferred rich-text methods of CCT.

Two dimensions of this shortsightedness can be mentioned. First, until the North American emergence and then dominance of a certain flavor of science, with its globally imposed positivist and realist philosophies of empiricism, social scientists across the Eurasian continent and elsewhere readily recognized a much wider array of empirical study. A great many major contributors to social sciences—whose works still resonate and inform much of our social knowledge today—did empirical observations that, under the domineering and prevalent North American influence, would be deemed unscientific today. Marx and Weber are just two examples. When Marx wrote *Capital* and Weber wrote *The Protestant Ethic and the Spirit of Capitalism*, they were clearly basing their analyses on empirical observations of historical trends—of social, economic, and political conditions and events—observations that may be called *grand observation*. Although today the term "observation" is used mostly for observations of individual or group behaviors—and "grand observation" would not be included among "scientific" methods—the soundness of the analyses of Marx and Weber is evidenced in the contemporary human condition and by the continuing influence of these two figures in contemporary social science theories advanced by current scholars (see, e.g., Fuchs and Dyer-Witheford 2013).

Second, the central purposes of generating data points and generating rich text are different, regardless of whether they may be considered complementary or incompatible. Data points are conducive to verifying what facts and relationships exist—that is, *what is*. They are utilized to find *measures of central tendency* and *norm(al)s*. Rich text is needed to identify *what can be*, the potentials and possibilities, and is conducive to recognizing *exceptions to norms* and complex *underlying patterns* that produce the measurable data points. Trying to force the purposes and principles of one onto the other can only inhibit humanity's capability to understand and express itself.

In both respects, the approach of the CCT school—with the passage of time—has been veering closer to conventional and North American interpretations of scientific methods, analyses, and purposes. This, indeed, results in an ideological bias as has been addressed by Moisander, Peñaloza, and Valtonen (2009); by Cova, Maclaran, and Bradshaw (2013); and by Fitchett, Patsiaouras, and Davies (2014). Much of the work coming out in the CCT literature tends to reinforce workings of the market and consumption, as well as the consumer subjectivity, a continuation of "what is" the current human experience in the realm of consumption, and CCT publications in *JCR* continue to evidence this (e.g., Bardhi and Eckhardt 2012; Dolbec and Fischer 2015; Martin and Schouten 2014). An excerpt from a recent *JCR* article (Giesler and Thompson 2016) on "a tutorial in consumer research" is a further example:

> Consumer researchers have become increasingly sensitized to the dynamic nature of market and consumption systems, as evidenced by recent scholarship on market emergence, the legitimation of consumption practices, consumer subject formation, value co-creation, brand audience dissipation and risk acculturation.
>
> (Giesler and Thompson, 2016)

Theoretical Range

Like the overall field of consumer research—of which CCT is a subfield—the early possibilities of building big-scale or grand theories have evaporated. CCT work, like other consumer research work, is mainly about exploring midrange theoretical avenues. A kind of inferiority complex that existed in conventional consumer research toward psychology and social psychology has continued among CCT scholars, this time toward disciplines such as sociology and anthropology. Such an inferiority complex leads to the notion that grand theories are not the domain of consumer research. In effect, this is a surprising continuation of a sense that CCT is still connected to the mundane daily aspects of business or organizations, and not a repudiation of the beholdenness of consumer research to business—a repudiation often claimed by Association of Consumer Research (ACR), *Journal of Consumer Research* (*JCR*), and CCT leaders. Yet, the limit put on scholars of the field against grand theory seems to be a remnant of the past and must be transcended if renewal is the goal.

This is an unfortunate stance because the market is the most hegemonic institution of this current period of history and consumer subjectivity is the current dominant form of subjecthood (Firat and Dholakia 2016). As such, one would think that as closet students of marketing—the founding discipline of the consumer research field that is devoted to investigating the institutionalized practices of the market—scholars of consumer research might be the ones in the best position to decipher, in a grand fashion, the implications and possible future(s) of the contemporary human condition. Such potential is stifled when there is a lack of attention to—and often avoidance of—grand theories of consumption and consumerism (cf. Firat 1987).

There are of course no specific edicts against grand theory in CCT works. The lack of grand theory work is the result of the invisible college of CCT standard setters who send out the inclusionary signals that favor midrange works and exclusionary signals that urge those wishing to do grand projects to explore other, "broader" disciplinary pastures like sociology and anthropology and not to pollute CCT field with sweeping ideas that may not meet empirical-verifiability claims patterned loosely after positivist falsification norms.

Political Orientations

The spaces where people desire, dream, acquire, consume, and commune—the consumptionscapes of life, to use a term inspired from Appadurai (1990)—represent the prime terrain where most of CCT research occurs. Such spaces are also complex arenas of ideological play, but this is usually not evident in most of CCT work (for exceptions, see Varman and Belk 2009; Varman and Vikas 2007).

The treatment of the ideological character of marketspaces and con-sumptionscapes, the arenas of consumption, can take many forms (for examples, see Dholakia 2015). The range includes treating these as ideology-free spaces, purely hedonic arenas for engaging in acts of consumption. Matters of ideology are for realms other than consumption, such as religion and politics. In another mode of treatment, the ideological character of consumptionscapes is acknowledged but from a celebra-tory or at least a mixed-valenced position. In traditional pre-CCT-era consumer research, consumptionscapes were the desired, aspired ideo-logical spaces (Levy 1959)—dominions where triumphal forces of free markets and unfettered capitalism opened up an abundance of fulfilling consumption choice opportunities. A lot of CCT work has introduced a mixed-valenced treatment of consumptionscapes, treating such spaces as contested, conflicted, and muddled. Missing to a great extent are treatments that take a critical view of ideology and consumptionscapes. The few CCT works in this mode attract rather limited attention (e.g., Varman and Belk 2009; Varman and Vikas 2007). Pushing the critical envelope even further, there are consumptionscapes—mostly away from the limelight of the "advanced West"—where there is crass marketplace-linked violence, with tacit support of megabrands. The corporate brand-owning actors sometimes acquire the Janus face of monsters while turned toward the largely invisible subaltern end – the end that is away from the Western media gaze (Banerjee 2008, 2011; Varman and Al-Amoudi 2016); while retaining the demeanor of endearing charmers in the media-exposed settings of the West. CCT research, vastly underpowered in critical dimensions in general, ignores such necro-leaning or other duplicitous aspects of consumptionscapes and marketscapes.

Even more pronounced is the attention given to the economic dimension of even social relationships. Although the term "culture" is prominent in the CCT school's name, it is present only in meaning and representations of consumer discourses regarding commodities, which in a culture of consumption also include identities, lifestyles, and community memberships that become commodified as market-supplied and market-enabled "things" to be consumed. Consequently—the market being the modern institution of the economic—these "things," even when purely iconic, always represent economic relations. In this form, culture is reduced to or regresses to its economic content, and the necessity to break out of the hegemony of the economic and expand and explode into the cultural for a complete presentation of the human condition is hindered. The complexity of the cultural textuality of human existence is unidimensionalized in its representation. We see this, for example, in the attention to creation of value, which continues the tradition of focus on exchange or economic value central to conventional ideology (Schau, Muñiz, and Arnould 2009)

Styles of Presentation

There is also some rigidity in CCT writing styles. How quotations from interviews are presented, or how these texts are discussed are expected to follow a strict format that, again, follows very much a North American style. A Continental European style that prefers longer and more complex sentence structures, less direct expression, and less attention to detail with greater attention to core arguments and ideas is often shunned. CCT reviewers require referencing extant literature and representing findings in terms of existing theories—and largely using *JCR* as the source—rather than presenting new theoretical formulations, which is a result of the focus on midrange theory rather than attempts at new grand theory. Whereas European scholars often expect the readers to have knowledge of existing literature and, therefore, do not stress referencing of every possible source, the North American style is to exhibit knowledge through references rather than through content and weight of argument. Unfortunately, styles different from the North American norms—when attempted by some CCT authors—often result in rejections by key CCT journals. We expand on the "northern bias" of consumer culture work—including the work outside the CCT mold—in the later section on the "spatial trap."

The Temporality Trap

Despite its pervasive contemporary presence, consumer culture is a historically temporary culture. Its origins are in the modern construction of life, especially economic life that eventually gained a dominant position in late modernity in relation to other domains of culture, such as the political and social domains. As the economic domain of culture gained the upper hand, the *Homo economicus* identity of the human individual also became more prominent in defining the human condition and eventually led to the citizen subjectivity of individuals in modern life to transform into the consumer subjectivity (Lury 1996; Schama 1990), and modern culture transformed into consumer culture.

Despite some claims—viewpoints that emerged at the end of the Cold War—that we have reached "the end of history" with the henceforth forever-dominant capitalist market system (Fukuyama 2006), a review of human history indicates that all systems, orders, and organizations of life have been and are likely to continue to be temporary. Consumer culture, which is arguably the dominant form of culture in late modernity, is unlikely to be an exception to this historical experience. Consequently, basing a whole discipline of inquiry into the human condition on a temporary condition is risky for providing lasting contributions to human knowledge. Yet, despite the institution of the market and consumer subjectivity being temporary to contemporary human condition, CCT scholars still often focus on studying market creation and dynamics and consumer actions (cf. Dolbec and Fischer 2015; Martin and Schouten 2014).

The key ideological and philosophical weakness of the CCT movement is evident in the choice of its name. Consumer culture is, after all, a particular and temporal period in human history. It is based in the history of modernity, the growing hegemony of the market, and the consumerization of the human being (Dholakia 2013), but for a block of time, and neither universal nor forever. By focusing on a temporal and contextual subjectivity thrust upon the human being, a subjectivity that makes the human being subservient to the logic of the market and the economic her or his master, CCT can only help perpetuate conditions that have many harmful consequences, from disenchantment of lives, to destruction of the environments within which humans exist. The CCT brand chooses to work with and remain loyal to constructs that are temporally and contextually bound and that carry historical baggage that intern humans to conditions that they can often do better without. These are conditions that humans could escape from, if scholars had the will to articulate potentials with new constructs that would present insights into "what can be" when, instead, sticking to past constructs that derive from the modern order, an approach that is bound to perpetuate "what is."

The Spatial Trap

Along with the temporality trap, CCT school's North American bias exhibits itself in more than methods; it is present in subjects and sites chosen for study. Many CCT studies so far have been done in North America. In cases where sites that are European at the margin—such as Iceland, Greenland, and Turkey—are researched, the subjects of study extend the interests originated in the consumer culture of North America. Brand communities, identity projects, fashion, meanings, commodities, and structures of consumption constitute much of this interest. Problems and new theory and frameworks arising from experiences of people in regions of the world other than North America find resistance and rejection in prominent journals (Eckhardt and Dholakia 2013). The ethnocentric orientation—dominant in conventional perspectives—that anything new can only come out of the West, specifically North America is, unfortunately, continued in CCT.

It needs to be noted that influential consumer culture research that is outside the B-school settings also suffers from what Don Slater (2010)—one of the most influential non-B-school consumer culture theorists—calls the "north" bias, leading to the following state of affairs:

> The only questions that can be asked, the only findings that make sense, are those that would occur to a northern academic who is concerned (probably rightly) about US shopping malls and credit card debt, and who presumes to speak in the name of those she or he regards as victims [for B-school CCT work, participants rather than victims] of these processes. The issue is about articulation of voices within an epistemological field—of opening the study of consumption to many agendas, many politics; it is about democracy and ethics—ensuring that the northern academic . . . is one voice within the field rather than the one defining it. (p. 282)

This is a sentiment coming from a researcher who *is* a genuinely critical theorist. Even he, with his strong, system-challenging critical voice, is concerned about the "north" bias in consumer culture work and is advocating openness and multivocality. In the uncritical B-school CCT work, the barriers to first recognizing and then overcoming the north bias are much higher, but—in our view—must be scaled, if CCT work is to have significant global impact.

The Theory-Filtering Trap

Although not unique to CCT—the *problematique* we raise here is endemic to consumer research and marketing scholarship overall—the surprising thing is how quickly CCT work has fallen in a theory-filtering trap. Essentially, the observed tendency in the consumer research and marketing fields is that a diligent—and also usually prominent—scholar explores a new social theoretical field in depth and then brings insights and ideas from this field into the discipline via one or more "seminal" (for the discipline of course, not globally) article(s) that achieve(s) iconic status and is (are) cited very widely. Most subsequent scholars that are influenced by these pioneering pieces then cite the original concept-rich article(s), and then begin to cite each other. There is almost no desire to go back to the original social theoretical field(s). As a result, (a) the perspective filtered by the pioneering scholar prevails, (b) alternate perspectives and intellectual influences (in the base social theoretical field) that may have been deliberately sidestepped or inadvertently underplayed by the pioneering scholar hardly ever find their way into the discipline, and (c) the evolving intellectual trajectory of the base social theoretical field is neglected—in effect, the base social theoretical field gets frozen in the time when the "pioneering" article(s) was (were) authored. These problematic patterns have very much taken root in CCT work.

To its credit, the CCT movement has tried to counter these tendencies with its Canon of Classics seminars directed at young doctoral and postdoctoral scholars. The young scholars attending these seminars are encouraged to read and discuss some prominent key social theorists—in philosophy, social sciences, and humanities—something that the seminars in mainstream consumer research subfields fail to do. There are, however, fundamental problems in the CCT approach, including but not limited to these: (1) canonization is, of course, an act of freezing knowledge, and also a disciplining act (Foucault 1972/2010); (2) in the CCT way, the young scholars are strongly advised to follow the interpretation of the "canon" offered by the CCT leaders and admonished and warned when they try to stray on to other pathways. In effect, there is a recanonization of the canon, in the CCT mold—and the straying and errant young scholars, if any, are stopped (metaphorically, of course) by attack dogs and machine-gun-equipped watchtowers (see Dholakia 2012, 224).

Renewal

We are hopeful that the aforementioned shortcomings and blind spots in CCT work are surmountable and will be overcome. For this, the leaders of the CCT school have to, once again, be open to a multiplicity of viewpoints, methods, and philosophical perspectives. The passion for opening up the field to articulation of potentials and possibilities of change—possibilities that have been sapped and halted over several years—needs to be restored and reinvigorated. In what follows, we suggest some pathways for renewal—and of course these can be debated, enlarged, modified, refuted, and supplemented.

Now that the CCT school is successfully established, there is a need to return to a passion for opening the field to new ideas and theoretical insights. Clearly, for a renewal, first the limitations and shortcomings we discussed need to be transcended. Initially, this requires these to be recognized as shortcomings. Then, the trends that led to these must be reversed. We feel, however, that the most important step is to recognize that all concepts and constructs we are currently utilizing to explore the human condition owe much to modern thought and have been and still are instrumental not only in understanding the discourses that govern contemporary conditions but also in constructing them. The constructs "the market," "consumer," "consumption," and "consumer culture" are, without doubt, significant among these. Consequently, we need to discover the concepts and constructs that will help us recognize alternative discourses that will allow the construction of alternative organizations of life (cf. Fırat and Dholakia 2016). Only then are we likely to be able to propose insights that can help humanity overcome the entrapments of modernity and envision alternatives.

Neither in an ordinal nor in an exhaustive fashion, we offer the following range of avenues and possibilities for renewal, reinvigoration and reinvention in the CCT field. We have deliberately worded these in the "From . . . to" format—even though such a format could be criticized as being a bit formulaic—to provoke discourse, discussion, and debate:

- From supravocality to multivocality: For reasons that we have outlined in this chapter, the CCT body of work is largely characterized by a my-way-or-highway type supravocality, an ersatz quasi canonization of positions, stances, methods, and styles that have become entrenched and unquestioned. A multivocal opening of CCT conceptual spaces is a strong first imperative.
- From feigned neutrality to explicated positions: Although not original to CCT—the institutions of ACR and *JCR* have long feigned both a neutrality across multiple disciplines and ideological positions and a freedom from beholdenness to business school interests—CCT has "upped the ante" of this game by its seemingly defiant-oppositional

position vis-à-vis mainstream consumer-business research, yet—in reality—very much serving the interests it appears to oppose. In terms of analogy to U.S. politics, it is a bit like the seemingly probusiness stance of Republicans and the seemingly prolabor stance of Democrats, yet with the lived reality showing that big businesses actually flourish more when Democrats are in power (Miller and Schofield 2008). To be credible to the very large world of social sciences and humanities, and not just to some business school subgroups, CCT researchers need to explicate their stances and positions in open ways.

- From consumer to postconsumer: Even as they bring into question the viability and sustainability of the first C in CCT, various types of postconsumer subjectivities—construer (Fırat and Dholakia 2016), designer (Trabucco 2012), prosumer (Ritzer 2015), produser (Bruns 2013), craft maker (Campbell 2005) and more—are gaining ground, intersecting, and often converging. CCT does often look at consumer cocreation, but the pressing imperative—from the critical renewal angle—is to locate and analyze these subjectivities in the overall systemic production-consumption nexus and the associated economic and cultural politics.

- From theory application to theory creation: Indeed, when scholars from almost all other social science fields—including sociology, anthropology, history, and philosophy—are developing theories about marketing and consumption phenomena, it is discouraging that CCT colleagues are more fond of applying these theories than creating theories, especially because the phenomena in focus are the ones CCT researchers should have closer understanding of than broader social science and humanities disciplines. A confidence in the possibility that grand theories can be developed by consumer research scholars would help in this respect.

- From confirming the status quo to exploring the potentials: The methods most often used by CCT members are indeed more conducive to exploring the exceptions, possibilities, and potentials of "what can be" as opposed to generalizations that confirm "what is." We suggest that CCT scholars take advantage of this opportunity to present humanity with insightful and feasible alternative ways of living, being, and organizing life that have the potential of relieving humanity from the many ills it faces today.

Of course, each of these themes of transition requires an article-length, even a book-length, treatment, and this cannot be done within the confines of a chapter such as this. But even if a subset of these transitions is undertaken seriously, CCT can regain its innovative and path-breaking potential that it once had (see, e.g., some of the exciting pre-CCT ideas in select chapters of Fırat, Dholakia, and Bagozzi (1987).

Concluding Comments

This chapter reviewed the origins and trajectory of CCT, discussed some of its limitations, and proposed what we think is needed for renewal that could move CCT to new horizons and assure its place in the history of human knowledge. We applaud the CCT movement for what it has started but believe that radical renewal is needed if it is to leave a cherished legacy. The ingredients, tools, and activist champions for renewal of CCT and related conceptual terrains are readily available. What is missing, and needs to be created, is the openness to these forces of renewal and change.

We—as authors of this critical review—regard ourselves not as central CCT scholars but as general and critical applied social science scholars interested in consumer culture, globalization, and markets, as well as in other research topics. Thus, we cannot offer a voice laden with CCT authority (though we do have claim to perhaps the strongest, established critical voice in the field). Therefore, in conclusion, we do want to offer a consumer culture research voice that is imbued with strong authority, because of the impact of his work:

> The problem is that in equating the study of consumption with the study of consumer culture as a social problem [social phenomenon, for CCT work] we constitute our very object of study within a narrow, singular analytical framework in which the scholar's own social and political location becomes unreflexive, unchallenged, and, yes, moralistic. (p. 282)

These comments from Slater are part of a panel discussion on "Critical and Moral Stances in Consumer Studies" published in the *Journal of Consumer Culture* (*JoCC*) in 2010. Slater, after his reflections on the state of (non-B-school) scholarship on consumer culture—which, of course, is largely critical—seeks an escape from the problems he lists by emphasizing his (current) Latourian poststructural approaches to studying consumer culture by "engaging with the myriad and contradictory ways in which the machines of social life are assembled and can be disassembled" (284). Although, for theoretical advance and renewal, we do encourage such poststructural—and reflexive—work in CCT, we also feel the need for solid and foundational critical structurally based CCT scholarship; after all, poststructuralism makes a lot more sense when the limits of structuralism have been reached, and these limiting horizons have not even been approached in CCT work. Again in conclusion, therefore, we also endorse a position favored by Sharon Zukin (2010) in the same panel discussion piece in *JoCC*. She wants consumer culture work to focus on

> the economic institutions that speak to us as one-dimensional consumers, ignoring that consumption, like production, breeds inequality, environmental harm, and false hopes for success . . . as we know

well today, overconsumption in rich countries is closely connected to production in poor regions of the world. The point of our research should be to focus people's minds on the political-economic structures that make this connection possible. (286–7)

Bibliography

Amadae, Sonja Michelle. *Rationalizing Capitalist Democracy: The Cold War Origins of Rational Choice Liberalism.* Chicago: University of Chicago Press, 2003.

Appadurai, Arjun. "Disjuncture and Difference in the Global Cultural Economy." *Theory, Culture and Society* 7, no. 2 (1990): 295–310.

Arnould, Eric J. and Craig J. Thompson. "Consumer Culture Theory (CCT): Twenty Years of Research." *Journal of Consumer Research* 31, no. 4 (2005): 868–82.

Askegaard, Søren. "Consumer Culture Theory: Neo-Liberalism's 'Useful Idiots'?" *Marketing Theory* 14, no. 4 (2014): 507–11.

———— and Jeppe Trolle Linnet. "Towards an Epistemology of Consumer Culture Theory: Phenomenology and the Context of Context." *Marketing Theory* 11, no. 4 (2011): 381–404.

Banerjee, Bobby S. "Necrocapitalism." *Organization Studies* 29, no. 12 (2008): 1541–63.

————. "Voices of the Governed: Towards a Theory of the Translocal." *Organization* 18, no. 3 (2011): 323–44.

Bardhi, Fleura and Giana M. Eckhardt. "Access-Based Consumption: The Case of Car Sharing." *Journal of Consumer Research* 39, no. 4 (2012): 881–98.

Belk, Russell W., Melanie Wallendorf, and John F. Sherry, Jr. "The Sacred and the Profane in Consumer Behavior: Theodicy on the Odyssey." *Journal of Consumer Research* 16, no. 1 (1989): 1–38.

Brown, Stephen. "Marketing and Literature: The Anxiety of Academic Influence." *Journal of Marketing* 63, no. 1 (1999): 1–15.

Brown, Wendy. *States of Injury: Power and Freedom in Late Modernity.* Princeton, NJ: Princeton University Press, 1995.

Bruns, Axel. "From Prosumption to Produsage." In *Handbook on the Digital Creative Economy*, edited by Ruth Towse and Christian Handke, Cheltenham, UK: Edward Elgar, 2013: 67–78.

Campbell, Colin. "The Craft Consumer Culture, Craft and Consumption in a Postmodern Society." *Journal of Consumer Culture* 5, no. 1 (2005): 23–42.

Cova, Bernard, Pauline Maclaran, and Alan Bradshaw. "Rethinking Consumer Culture Theory from the Postmodern to the Communist Horizon." *Marketing Theory* 13, no. 2 (2013): 213–25.

Dholakia, Nikhilesh. "Being Critical in Marketing Studies: The Imperative of Macro Perspectives." *Journal of Macromarketing* 32, no. 2 (2012): 220–5.

————. "Fusing Back the Human, Radically." In *Humanistic Marketing*, 137–49. Edited by Richard J. Varey and Michael Pirson. London: Palgrave Macmillan, 2013.

————. "Marketing as Mystification." *Marketing Theory* 16, no. 3 (2015): 401–26.

Dolbec, Pierre-Yann and Eileen Fischer. "Refashioning a Field? Connected Consumers and Institutional Dynamics in Markets." *Journal of Consumer Research* 41, no. 6 (2015): 1447–68.

Eckhardt, Giana M. and Nikhilesh Dholakia. "Addressing the Mega Imbalance: Interpretive Exploration of Asia." *Qualitative Market Research: An International Journal* 16, no. 1 (2013): 4–11.

————, and Rohit Varman. "Ideology for the 10 Billion: Introduction to Globalization of Marketing Ideology." *Journal of Macromarketing* 33, no. 1 (2013): 7–12.

Ertimur, Burçak and Gokcen Coskuner Balli. "Navigating the Institutional Logics of Markets: Implications for Strategic Brand Management," *Journal of Marketing* 79, no. 2 (2015): 40–61.
Featherstone, Mike. "Consumer Culture: An Introduction." *Theory, Culture & Society* 1, no. 3 (1983): 4–9.
———. *Consumer Culture and Postmodernism*. London: Sage, 2007.
Figueiredo, Bernardo and Daiane Scaraboto. "Systemic Value Creation: A Value-in-Action Perspective on Collaborative Consumer Networks," *Journal of Consumer Research* 43, no. 4 (2016): 509–33.
Fırat, A. Fuat. "The Social Construction of Consumption Patterns: Understanding Macro Consumption Phenomena." In *Philosophical and Radical Thought in Marketing*, 251–67. Edited by A. F. Fırat, N. Dholakia, and R. P. Bagozzi. Lexington, MA: Lexington Books, 1987.
——— and Nikhilesh Dholakia. *Consuming People: From Political Economy to Theaters of Consumption*. London: Routledge, 1998.
———. "From Consumer to Construer: Travels in Human Subjectivity." *Journal of Consumer Culture* (2016).
——— and Richard P. Bagozzi, eds. *Philosophical and Radical Thought in Marketing*. Lexington, MA: Lexington Books, 1987.
Fitchett, James A., Georgios Patsiaouras, and Andrea Davies. "Myth and Ideology in Consumer Culture Theory." *Marketing Theory* 14, no. 4 (2014): 495–506.
Foucault, Michel. *The Archaeology of Knowledge*. New York: Vintage Books, 1972/2010.
Fuchs, Christian and Nick Dyer-Witheford. "Karl Marx@ Internet Studies." *New Media & Society* 15, no. 5 (2013): 782–96.
Fukuyama, Francis. *The End of History and the Last Man*. New York: Simon and Schuster, 2006.
Giesler, Marcus. "How Doppelgänger Brand Images Influence the Market Creation Process: Longitudinal Insights from the Rise of Botox Cosmetic," *Journal of Marketing* 76, no. 6 (2012): 55–68.
——— and Eileen Fischer. "Editorial: Market System Dynamics," *Marketing Theory* (Forthcoming).
——— and Craig J. Thompson. "Process Theorization in Cultural Consumer Research." *Journal of Consumer Research* 43, no. 4 (2016): 497–508.
——— and Ela Veresiu. "Creating the Responsible Consumer: Moralistic Governance Regimes and Consumer Subjectivity," *Journal of Consumer Research* 41, no. 3 (2014): 840–57.
Hardt, Michael and Antonio Negri. *Empire*. Cambridge, MA: Harvard University Press, 2001.
Holbrook, Morris B. "An Audiovisual Inventory of Some Fanatic Consumer Behavior: The 25-Cent Tour of a Jazz Collector's Home." *Advances in Consumer Research* 14, no. 1 (1987): 144–9
——— and Mark W. Grayson. "The Semiology of Cinematic Consumption: Symbolic Consumer Behavior in Out of Africa." *Journal of Consumer Research* 13, no. 3 (1986): 374–81.
——— and John O'Shaughnessy. "On the Scientific Status of Consumer Research and the Need for an Interpretive Approach to Studying Consumption Behavior." *Journal of Consumer Research* 15, no. 3 (1988): 398–402.
Hudson, Laurel Anderson and Julie L. Ozanne. "Alternative Ways of Seeking Knowledge in Consumer Research." *Journal of Consumer Research* 14, no. 4 (1988): 508–21.
Humphreys, Ashlee. "Semiotic Structure and the Legitimation of Consumption Practices: The Case of Casino Gambling," *Journal of Consumer Research* 37, no. 3 (2010): 490–510.

Joy, Annamma. "Gift Giving in Hong Kong and the Continuum of Social Ties." *Journal of Consumer Research* 28, no. 2 (2001): 239–56.

Karababa, Eminegül and Güliz Ger. "Early Ottoman Coffeehouse Culture and the Formation of the Consumer Subject." *Journal of Consumer Research* 37, no. 5 (2011): 737–60.

Levy, Sidney J. "Symbols for Sale." *Harvard Business Review* 37, no. 4 (1959): 117–24.

———. "Roots and Development of Consumer Culture Theory." Presented at the *Consumer Culture Theory Conference*, Fayetteville, AR, 2015.

Lury, Celia. *Consumer Culture*. New Brunswick, NJ: Rutgers University Press, 1996.

Martin, Diane M. and John W. Schouten. "Consumption-Driven Market Emergence." *Journal of Consumer Research* 40, no. 5 (2014): 855–70.

Mick, David Glen. "Consumer Research and Semiotics: Exploring the Morphology of Signs, Symbols, and Significance." *Journal of Consumer Research* 13, no. 3 (1986): 196–213.

Miller, Gary and Norman Schofield. "The Transformation of the Republican and Democratic Party Coalitions in the US." *Perspectives on Politics* 6, no. 3 (2008): 433–50.

Moisander, Johanna, Lisa Peñaloza, and Anu Valtonen. "From CCT to CCC: Building Consumer Culture Community." In *Explorations in Consumer Culture Theory*, 7–33. Edited by J. F. Sherry, Jr. and E. Fischer. London: Routledge, 2009.

Parmentier, Marie-Agnés and Eileen Fischer. "Things Fall Apart: The Dynamics of Brand Audience Dissipation," *Journal of Consumer Research* 28, no. 5 (2015): 1228–51.

Passavant, Paul Andrew and Jodi Dean. *Empire's New Clothes: Reading Hardt and Negri*. Hove, UK: Psychology Press, 2004.

Peñaloza, Lisa. "Atravesando Fronteras/Border Crossings: A Critical Ethnographic Exploration of the Consumer Acculturation of Mexican Immigrants." *Journal of Consumer Research* 21, no. 1 (1994): 32–54.

Ritzer, George. "Prosumer Capitalism." *The Sociological Quarterly* 56, no. 3 (2015): 413–45.

Schama, Simon. *Citizens: A Chronicle of the French Revolution*. New York: Vintage Books, 1990.

Schau, Hope J., Albert M. Muñiz, and Eric J. Arnould. "How Brand Community Practices Create Value." *Journal of Marketing* 73, no. 5 (2009): 30–51.

Sherry, John F., Jr. "Gift Giving in Anthropological Perspective." *Journal of Consumer Research* 10, no. 2 (1983): 157–68.

———. "Postmodern Alternatives: The Interpretive Turn in Consumer Research." In *Handbook of Consumer Behavior*, 548–91. Edited by Thomas S. Robertson and Harold H. Kassarjian. Englewood Cliffs, NJ: Prentice-Hall, 1991.

——— and Eduardo G. Camargo. "May Your Life Be Marvelous: English Language Labelling and the Semiotics of Japanese Promotion." *Journal of Consumer Research* 14, no. 2 (1987): 174–88.

Slater, Don. "The Moral Seriousness of Consumption." *Journal of Consumer Culture* 10, no. 2 (2010): 280–4.

Stern, Barbara B. "Literary Criticism and Consumer Research: Overview and Illustrative Analysis." *Journal of Consumer Research* 16, no. 3 (1989): 322–34.

Thompson, Craig J., William B. Locander, and Howard R. Pollio. "Putting Consumer Experience Back into Consumer Research: The Philosophy and Method of Existential-Phenomenology." *Journal of Consumer Research* 16, no. 2 (1989): 133–46.

Trabucco, Francesco. "How Design Relates to Scientific Research." In *Design Research: Between Scientific Research and Project Praxis*, 35–44. Edited by L. Rampino. Milano. Italy: Francoangeli, 2012.

Varman, Rohit and Ismael Al-Amoudi. "Accumulation through Derealization: How Corporate Violence Remains Unchecked." *Human Relations* (2016).
—— and Russell W. Belk. "Nationalism and Ideology in an Anticonsumption Movement." *Journal of Consumer Research* 36, no. 4 (2009): 686–700.
—— and Ram Manohar Vikas. "Freedom and Consumption: Toward Conceptualizing Systemic Constraints for Subaltern Consumers in a Capitalist Society." *Consumption Markets and Culture* 10, no. 2 (2007): 117–31.
Zukin, Sharon. "Do We Want to Change the World?" *Journal of Consumer Culture* 10, no. 2 (2010): 285–7.

12 Consumer Culture Strategy

Douglas B. Holt

I propose consumer culture strategy (CCS) as the "theory-in-practice" complement to the high-theoretical academic ambitions of consumer culture theory (CCT). The goal of CCS is to unlock what I believe to be the great potential of consumer culture scholarship to impact important social and environmental problems.

Many scholars gravitate to CCT because they are committed to the pursuit of academic research that has real impact on societal issues that are important to them, and CCT is potentially a superb springboard to achieve these ambitions. CCT is an improvised discipline that was patched together in an open-ended manner as the loyal opposition to the conventions of the very dominant quantitative traditions of consumer research in marketing departments (dominated in large part by statistical models adapted from engineering and by experimental studies of decision making). Once the gates were opened, the flood began: researchers were inspired by an amazingly diverse set of intellectual traditions and methods and introduced the tools they were most excited about, and next-generation scholars proceeded to work with these puzzle pieces and cobble them together. I believe that we've ended up with a very distinctive discipline that has become, in an unintended-consequences sort of way, much more than merely a sect of antipositivist consumer researchers. We have unknowingly assembled a research model, skillset and wide portfolio of intellectual tools that, in combination, has unique power to help solve particularly challenging social and environmental issues.

The leaders of CCT have worked tenaciously to legitimatize CCT (in the eyes of the dominant disciplines in marketing primarily) as a rigorous social scientific endeavor. Yet, ironically, an unintentional consequence of this ambition is that it has disabled the potential societal impact of CCT research. Very little CCT research has had a significant societal impact to date—developing theories that inform new approaches to tackling important issues or generating unique and valuable insights into key policy debates. This relevance problem is due, I will argue, to the particular way in which CCT's gatekeepers have defined the "right" way to do CCT and the knowledge contributions that we should aim for.

I eagerly helped to erect these gates back in the 1990s. I have been a vocal proponent of the theory-building approach eventually branded by Arnould and Thompson (2005) as CCT (see, e.g., Holt 1995). Early on, I was something of a firebrand supporting this approach and have written many of my academic papers with exactly the CCT mode of contribution in mind. So, this essay is also a reflexive exercise in which I draw from my own evolution as a scholar to challenge the discipline to step back and reflect on the successful institutionalization of CCT.

Here, I unpack this fundamental contradiction and propose that we consecrate a new type of knowledge goal, which I call consumer culture strategy. As I develop this argument, please note that CCS is an alternative mode of theory development, distinctive from and complementary to CCT. It not an "applied" version of CCT. My goal is to encourage fellow scholars of consumer culture and marketing to formalize CCS as alternative pathway to make important scholarly contributions and build academic careers alongside CCT.

CCT Paradigm

Let's begin with the key axioms of the CCT paradigm and then draw out the contrasts with CCS. CCT has come to be organized around an idiosyncratic academic paradigm—"What are the desired knowledge goals that we should all strive for, and how should one do the research that achieves these goals?"—that is unique in the academy to my knowledge:

1. CCT consecrates a diverse interdisciplinary range of what I will call "high social theory": very abstract theory that is decoupled from contexts and intended to explain how the social world works in its entirety. For example, favorites have included actor-network theory, practice theory, Foucault's theory of power, and Butler's theory of performativity. To be successful in CCT, one has to master a wide variety of very challenging theories embedded in rich intellectual traditions (hence the arrival of theory "finishing schools" at Southern Denmark University and Bilkent University).
2. CCT strives for a natural science–styled ideal of academic contribution that focuses upon extending highly abstract "generalizable" theories, which exist largely within other academic disciplines (anthropology, sociology, cultural studies, media studies, etc.).
3. CCT requires modest engagement with a wide range of substantive literatures outside of marketing. Many CCT papers engage specific topics that have generated intensive research from scholars in many disciplines beyond marketing. The norm in CCT is to ritually acknowledge the nonmarketing literature but not treat it as the focus of the research. So, CCT requires the ability to locate and quickly get a handle on a substantive literature, often a literature that one had little exposure to previously. To be productive in CCT, one has to be a substantive nomad,

able to read new literatures sufficiently to be able to represent them in a credible manner in article-length research in short order, because there will be another such literature to master tomorrow.

4. CCT takes a holistic and "discovery-oriented" approach to research, drawing from grounded theory, the extended case method, and the like, which is highly sensitized to cultural interpretation.

This patchwork academic model is quite unique. One can find scholars with even broader and more erudite knowledge of social theory in the humanities, but they aren't much concerned with substantive literatures and explicit theory building and few do primary empirical research. Likewise, one can find many more impressive works of empirical research in the social sciences, but these works are almost always produced by subdisciplinary specialists who master a much narrower range of theory, with their disciplines encouraging them to ignore the remaining ninety-nine percent.

The Flaw: Narrow Specification of Theory Contribution

The potential to apply this distinctive expertise to help solve challenging social and environmental problems is mostly dormant because these CCT axioms disallow research designed to effectively pursue these goals. CCT's myopic specification of theory contribution that consecrates only high social theory is the culprit. If you follow the aforementioned CCT axioms, as most CCT scholars now believe they must, then it's virtually impossible to come up with ideas that have real-world impact, despite one's passionate intentions.

Formalizing the theory model as CCT has been terrific for developing CCT as an academic brand, as it provides a credible claim to the rest of the marketing discipline that we're doing "real science," fighting against the powers that be who often dismissed our work as just interpreting stuff and spinning out idiosyncratic description. But in making this type of theory advance the sole definition of academic contribution, we end up working on ever-more-nuanced tweaks of ever more esoteric and abstract concepts, a pursuit that is necessarily far removed from a focused investigation of worldly problems. So, although many scholars add implications sections in their introductions and conclusions that seek to connect the dots to key societal issues, these connections are necessarily weak, underspecifying the issue and largely ignoring the insights developed by other scholars who actually focus on the issue.

New Focus: Contribute to Theory-in-Practice

This essay reflects my intellectual evolution over the past fifteen years, which began—of all places—at the Harvard Business School. HBS has a very pragmatic orientation, seeking to be the locus of all important ideas that managers rely upon. So, while on the faculty, I was strongly

encouraged to pursue theory building that would actually make a difference in business. This emphasis required that I invert my favored CCT
approach to research. Instead of starting with the academic literature
and asking, "Where are the theoretical gaps?" I started with the world
of management and asked, "Where are the weaknesses in practice that
better theory could improve upon?"

I focused my efforts on branding because my background in social
and cultural theory provided me with tools that had obvious application
to the phenomenon but had not yet been applied well in either practice or the academic literature. I first synthesized the dominant theory
of branding, as practiced for decades by the leading consumer marketing companies, consultancies, and ad agencies and formalized later on
by psychologists in marketing departments. Both in practice and in the
academy, brand theory was dominated by what I called the *mindshare
model* (Holt 2004). Critiquing this model from the lens of a variety of
social-cultural theoretic traditions, I was able to show that it had a number of glaring shortcomings—in particular that it was a present-tense
model abstracted from society and history and so could not possibly
explain how brands emerged or faded. This critique provided the template for the research to follow: I conducted several dozen brand gene-
alogies (historical sociocultural analyses) from which, by comparing the
many cases in search of a common explanation, I developed a new branding model (what I call *cultural branding*) that explains how powerful
(iconic) brands emerge and then wax and wane over time. I continued
this work for nearly a decade, revising and extending the original theory
(e.g., Holt and Cameron 2010). This research proved to be the most
intellectually challenging and empirically rigorous of any work that I've
done in my career.

This model became widely influential in business around the world
and was also embraced by CCT academics. I attribute this success to the
fact that I focused so intensively on building what I will call *theory-in-
practice*: beginning with existing theory that is dominant in the world of
practice (not just in academic articles), drawing selectively and syntheti-
cally on sociocultural intellectual traditions that allowed me to find ways
to dramatically improve this model, and then demonstrating to practitioners that my model explained the brands they most wanted to emulate
much better than the mindshare model.

If, instead, I had sought to publish my branding research in the *Journal
of Consumer Research* (*JCR*), I would never have been allowed to
develop theory in this "unorthodox" manner and, so, would never have
been able to impact practice in this way. The work would also have been
empirically compromised: the key insights driving the cultural branding
model came from the case comparisons across many brand cases. And
demonstrating that the model held up across a wide variety of cases also
made it much more convincing. Yet it's impossible to do such detailed,

multiple-case analysis in CCT due to the word constraints of journal articles. Books still are not given much credit.

In 2004, I moved to Oxford and organized the marketing department (which I called Marketing, Culture & Society) with this same focus on theory-in-practice, but with an emphasis on social and environmental issues rather than commercial marketing. My research focused first on public health in Africa (McKnight and Holt 2014) and then on sustainable consumption (Holt 2012), sustainable economy (Holt 2014) and creating political will for climate policy (Holt 2015). I approached each of these projects using the same research logic as I did with branding, which I formalize here as CCS. Let me briefly reference these projects to highlight four key differences between CCS and CCT.

CCS Axioms

Designing research projects to contribute to solving an important societal issue changes everything about the research. Here I detail the key contrasts between CCS and CCT.

Contribute to Issue Theory

Many social and environmental issues are so widespread and important that they have generated a body of theory specifically devoted to the issue. Many thousands of scholars have devoted their careers to advancing understanding of a particular issue, which accumulates into a particular kind of theory-in-practice that we might call "issue theory"—interdisciplinary constellations of theory that are particular to an issue. For example, there are tens of thousands of academic articles that have been published on climate change. These issue theories usually draw selectively from more general theories, specifying how the theory works with respect to the issue in a much more detailed and nuanced manner than one would find in the general literature on the theory and often extending or modifying the theory to get better traction on the issue. The intellectual conversation driving efforts to solve such issues centers on issue theory because it is necessarily more precise, customized to the particulars of the issue.

For example, behavioral scientists and political scientists have analyzed why climate change is such a challenging issue to organize citizens to participate in collective action. Their issue-specific theorizing provides an important baseline specification of the problem that scholars from other disciplines (such as myself) can then engage. The issue itself is of such importance that there is a large body of theory that is organized around understanding its particular characteristics. Articles and books rarely abstract away from the issue—improving understanding of the issue is the ultimate objective. There are many such issues that would benefit from the varieties of theory that CCT scholars draw from, but only if the orientation of the research is focused squarely at the issue itself rather than trying to extract "implications" from high theory research.

Become an Issue Expert (It's Not Just a Case)

The conventional logic of CCT is to select a case (or multiple cases) that provides a good venue to explore the theory that you want to extend. It doesn't matter at all how seemingly trivial or marginal is the case (in fact, studying the margins is often helpful theoretically) because the focus is on the abstract theoretical conversation, not the case itself. In CCS, this logic is inverted: the focus of the research is an issue that you want to help solve. Issues such as climate change, global poverty, and gun violence aren't just cases. They're hugely important and deserving of theoretical work that is focused squarely on the problem, that never abstracts away, whose contribution is judged against other theories of the problem.

Treating issues as the focal phenomenon rather than as a "case of" an abstract interest demands that the researcher becoming truly expert on the issue, a standard of expertise that is far higher than CCT norms for substantive topics. To publish in CCT requires becoming competent enough to be credible among peers who mostly have marginal knowledge of the subject—typically a very low bar. To have impact in CCS requires that one benchmark expertise against those who have devoted their careers to the issue, reading across literatures that are at a far remove from typical CCT haunts. So, CCS often requires devoting years to a particular issue and developing programmatic research that unfolds over a number of papers or even a book. This is a radical departure from CCT norms—a career killer given the norms of the field.

Develop the Research Question to Address the Gaps in Practice

In CCT, scholars develop research questions to address conceptual gaps in a body of high theory. In CCS, the analytic goal is reversed: one starts with a major gap or bottleneck in practice—a potential solution that isn't working, a solution pathway that's been ignored, and so forth. The goal is to leverage theory to address the gap.

In our work on vaccination delivery systems in Africa (McKnight and Holt 2014), we began with the Expanded Program on Immunisation (EPI), a massive effort to dramatically improve childhood vaccination rates in the very poorest countries, spearheaded by the Bill & Melinda Gates Foundation. The program has been very successful in general but failed in certain countries and certain regions within countries—a contextual failure that conventional models couldn't explain and so couldn't fix. Because the EPI model was based upon providing free vaccines, we hypothesized that the bottlenecks were occurring due to problems in the public health systems that we could pinpoint, drawing upon marketing and consumer culture theories and techniques. We structured an ethnographic research project to explain why vaccination rates were very low in the Oromia region of Ethiopia.

In another example, sustainable consumption has been on the global environmental agenda since the Rio Earth Summit of 1991. Although many CCT scholars have worked on sustainable consumption, the research—constructed within the CCT paradigm—engages other academic scholarship on the topic and so, necessarily, has remained at the periphery of practice. Research is focused on theory rather than allowed to address the most fundamental practical question as the focus of the research: why have three decades of efforts to promote sustainable consumption—in which the theory-in-practice aligned quite closely with the assumptions of many academics working on the topic—failed time and again? Applying the CCS approach, I examined a major multiyear American campaign to drive sustainable consumption—the campaign against bottled water—which failed badly (Holt 2012). My goal was to build an explanation for why the campaign failed and, in so doing, develop a more accurate and useful theory explaining how it is that certain consumption patterns become unsustainable or sustainable.

Likewise, the starting point for my work on building strategy to drive the political will to pass a major carbon tax in the United States (the policy most people believe is the only possible solution to stop runaway climate change) was the failure of many massive campaigns run by all major environmental organizations in the United States to build such a movement in 2007–2009. I hypothesized that I could extend my work on branding to both explain the failures and also build a new strategy that would work much better (Holt 2015).

Contribute to Theory-in-Practice

Focusing on issue theory requires roving outside the comfortable domain of academic journals. The community of intellectual stakeholders who advance ideas on major social and environmental issues is usually quite diverse and extends far beyond the usual circle of academics. In fact, academics often make up a small percentage of the community. For one to have impact, then, it is necessary to treat all ideas that have gained traction among stakeholders as legitimate, as "theory" that one should engage in one's research. For example, in my work on climate change, I needed not only to read up on all of the scientific research on the topic but also to engage all of the work that's sought to influence climate movement strategy: from popular figures like Al Gore, Bill McKibben, and Naomi Klein and the major environmental organizations like the Sierra Club, Greenpeace, Friends of the Earth, and 350.org; to far-flung academic literatures in science communication, political science, sociology, history, psychology, and even philosophy.

Draw upon CCT Theories as a Selective Tool Kit

Theory is just as important in CCS as CCT. (It has little to do with conventional "applied" research in which theory fades away, with only a nod in the distance.) But instead of a deep investigation into a single theory as CCT requires, in CCS one picks selectively from the wide range of sociocultural theories the constructs and frameworks that are most helpful to solve the problem. Often this requires synthesizing theories or repurposing them, using them in novel ways. The holistic interdisciplinary worldview of CCT becomes particularly useful in advancing solutions that single "silver bullet" approaches to theory application simply miss. Most big, thorny social issues require a holistic lens that moves across markets, consumption, economy, technology, society, and culture, requiring historic, semiotic, and ethnographic lenses. So CCT, treated as a tool kit, becomes a powerful approach to generate new insights.

Become a Strategic Theorist: Build Problem-Solving Models

The resulting theoretical advance from a CCS study should provide direct insights into filling the gap identified at the beginning of the research. In other words, the theory should be *strategic*. Many of us work in marketing departments and teach marketing, which requires that we become adept at a problem-solving strategic approach that is largely alien to the social sciences. Putting the CCT's eclectic approach to theory and research into a problem-solving strategy model yields powerful insights that other disciplines simply can't produce.

In our work on EPI vaccination, we developed a new model that led directly to several major changes in how public health systems administer vaccines that, we argued, would significantly increase vaccination rates. In my work on sustainable consumption, I developed an alternative social constructionist model of unsustainable markets that led directly to alternative strategies for driving sustainable consumption. In my work on sustainable economy, my analysis led to the development of an entirely different alternative economy strategy from that which is commonly pursued. In my work on climate change, I used the theory I developed to motivate a new movement strategy that would address the weaknesses of past efforts.

The analytic challenge of CCS research, then, is strategy development—an iterative tacking back and forth between analysis of the issue on the ground, the particular theories that seem to be most helpful in interpreting this data, with a continual focus to build a strategy model that opens up new and better solutions to the issue. To help solve complex social problems in this way is particularly challenging and intellectually exciting. This kind of theoretic sleuthing work couldn't be more different from the usual approach taken in applied research. The idea of application suggests a simple connecting of the dots: the big theory has all of the answers and one only needs to figure out how it applies particularly to a specific case. Applied social science usually doesn't work, for reasons I developed previously, which is why we need CCS.

Concluding Thoughts

What Is "Scholarship" in CCT?

Until we consecrate the CCS paradigm, which uses our oddly power-ful discipline in an entirely new way, we are not tapping into its true potential. To build a CCS tradition in academic marketing departments requires broadening paradigmatic norms. If CCT scholars are going to be allowed to do impactful research, then we must open the field up to "theorizing issues" in addition to reworking high social theory. For many CCTers, the pursuit of better high social theory is a very satisfying enterprise, an end in itself. So be it. And, for the many who want their theoretical work to have real impact on the world, CCT remains a crucial foundation for CCS. Becoming expert in working with a wide range of theory across disciplines is the real strength of CCT. What differs is how one organizes the conversation that one wants to engage: in CCT the ideal is to converse with the theory masters and their acolytes, whereas in CCS the ideal is to converse with the very best and most impactful ideas that are used today to understand major social issues and guide their solutions. This choice of conversation changes everything about the research: the research design, what a literature review looks like, how the analysis is conducted, the theory that the project engages, and the ultimate theoretical contribution. As a result, CCS research is not easily published in CCT outlets. I haven't even tried, as I know it would be a frustrating experience.

And it's not clear that such research should be published in CCT-favored journals. If one is aiming for journals, then the usual circuit of *Journal of Consumer Research, Consumption, Markets and Culture,Marketing Theory*, and the *Journal of Consumer Culture* is not ideal. CCS research is best suited for publication in journals that are organized around issues, rather than disciplines, because this is where the scholarly conversation is the richest, most sophisticated, and most influential. And the most impactful issue theory research is to be found in books, not journal arti-cles. Our field has never credited books appropriately, so this is a major institutional challenge for advancing CCS.

Will CCS Give Up Our Hard-Won Institutional Legitimacy?

Clawing our way to scientific legitimacy by making sciency claims about the merits of our theory and methods is the hard and slow "red ocean" path for CCT to earn status and institutional credibility. Today, the market for ideas is no longer centered in the university but rather in the global, digitized "idea discourse" that circulates among the intelligentsia and chattering classes worldwide. Winning in this idea discourse today drives legitimacy and institutional rewards within the academy. Bringing ideas to the table that provide powerful and novel pathways to solving social problems gain particular traction in this discourse today. Take, for instance, Paul Collier, a respected developmental economics academic who became one of the most influential scholars in his field when he published an issue-theory focused, strategically oriented book, *The Bottom Billion*, which presented a new analysis and solution for poverty in sub-Saharan Africa. The same can be said of Abhijit Banerjee and Esther Duflo's *Poor Economics*. Both are applied "nonacademic" books in that the research is one-hundred-percent oriented to solving crucial social problems rather than building disciplinary theory. Yet both do so in a conceptually sophisticated manner that belies the "application" label. One could argue that these three academics are now the most influential in their field globally as the result of such work. I have no doubt that CCT researchers can follow the same path if it they were to embrace CCS.

Bibliography

Arnould, Eric and Craig J. Thompson. "Consumer Culture Theory (CCT): Twenty Years of Research." *Journal of Consumer Research* 31, no. 4 (2005): 868–82.

Holt, Douglas B. "How Consumers Consume: A Typology of Consumption Practices." *Journal of Consumer Research* 22 (June 1995): 1–16.

———. *How Brands Become Icons: The Principles of Cultural Branding.* Cambridge, MA: Harvard Business School Press, 2004.

———. "Constructing Sustainable Consumption: From Ethical Values to the Cultural Transformation of Unsustainable Markets." *The Annals of the American Academy of Political and Social Science* 644, no. 1 (2012): 236–55.

———. "Why the Sustainable Economy Movement Hasn't Scaled: Toward a Strategy That Empowers Main Street." In *Sustainable Lifestyles and the Quest for Plenitude.* Edited by Juliet Schor and Craig Thompson. New Haven, CT: Yale University Press, 2014.

———. *Branding Climate.* Cultural Strategy Group Inc, brandclimate.org (Working paper 2015).

——— and Douglas Cameron. *Cultural Strategy: Using Innovative Ideologies to Build Breakthrough Brands.* Oxford: Oxford University Press, 2010.

McKnight, Jacob and Douglas B. Holt. "Designing the Expanded Programme on Immunisation (EPI) as a Service: Prioritising Patients over Administrative Logic." *Global Public Health* 9, no. 10 (2014): 1152–66.

13 Redressing an Alleged Lacuna

Scholarly Models for an Engaged Ethnology of Consumer Culture

Eric J. Arnould

Introduction

Consumer culture theory (CCT) has recently been taken to task by a number of authors, including some in this volume, for its inattention to culture and cultural context (ironically enough), its overemphasis on issues of individual identity and agentic selfhood, and its lack of a critical perspective (Askegaard and Linnet 2011; Fırat and Dholakia, this volume; Fitchett, Patsiaouras, and Davies 2014; Graeber 2011; Moisander, Peñaloza, and Valtonen 2009). Although the facticity of the critique is debatable, the merits of the positions propounded by the critics are well taken. It is my contention that whatever fault there may be lies not with conceptualization of CCT per se (Arnould and Thompson 2005; Thompson, Arnould, and Giesler 2013) the problem lies instead with institutional factors. These include the shallow social science training of many students of management and marketing today, with presentism in theorization, and with ethnocentric and anachronistic biases in these disciplines that naturalize individual agency and marginalize if not ignore cultural and historical variation, and the contingency of social theory. In short, shortcomings in CCT are indeed due to the influence of neoliberal, utilitarian ideology or "practical reason" on the practice of marketing and consumption scholarship. My suggestion in what follows is that familiarization with two important critics of these cultural biases in twentieth-century social science, and emulation of their mode of working, would contribute to correcting the alleged shortcomings in this disciplinary tendency.

The chapter begins with a discussion of Marcel Mauss and continues with one of his intellectual heirs, Marshall Sahlins, recognizing both as worthy descendants of that "wicked company" who populated the European Enlightenment (Blom 2010). In each case I highlight some major works, some contributions to method, and action research or what some in critical theory might call positive critique (Murray, Ozanne, and Shapiro 1994).

Marcel Mauss

As Emile Durkheim's nephew and heir, Marcel Mauss's significant contributions to modern social science now receive the attention they deserve. Durkheim's influence loomed large in Mauss's education and professional life as Mauss curated decades of scholarship through the journal *l'Année Sociologique* that Durkheim founded. Born in 1872, Mauss lived until 1952. It is fair to say that he was an eminently modern figure, part of the formative era of social science. Mauss was one of those polymaths that hardly exist today, mastering both ancient and modern languages, philosophy, religion, history, political science, and of course sociology through his wide reading of the social sciences in the service of the *l'Année Sociologique*. Mauss eventually became an armchair ethnologist, his theorization based on ethnographic case material. Indeed, he modernized and systematized the science of cultural comparison, rejecting the descriptive and evolutionist treatments of earlier scholars. Mauss's ethnology espoused a positivist social science based on observable, knowable "facts."

Unlike Durkheim, Mauss always sought out the materiality of social forms in time and space, as well as the sociology of material forms. His work always examines the interconnection of language (that is to say, symbolic representation), action, and personal experience. Mauss espoused grounding analyses of contemporary phenomena in historical context. And he saw social science as produced by social scientists' translations of varied local meanings (*concret figuré*) into abstract conceptual terms (*concret pensé*, Dubar 1969; James 1998).

Mauss is known for several important texts all infused with that characteristic depth of historical and ethnological scholarship that has made them classics. These include: a) *An Essay on the Nature and Function of Sacrifice* (1899), which inspired, among others, Daniel Miller's (1998) *A Theory of Shopping*; b) *An Essay on the General Theory of Magic* (1904) with Henri Hubert, often critiqued but which subsequent scholarship on magic generally comments and extends; and c) *Primitive Classification* written with Durkheim (Durkheim and Mauss 1963/1903). It is little used in consumer research and marketing but is foundational to Lévi-Strauss' structuralism and aligned with the well-known work in consumer research of Greimas. Mauss' most famous work is the *Essay on the Gift* that appeared in the *l'Année Sociologique* in 1924. Two other important texts are "Techniques of the Body" (1935) and "A Category of the Human Mind: The Notion of Person; the Notion of Self" (1985/1938).

The Gift

Mauss (1990/1924) is most famous in anthropology and consumer research for the essay on the gift. The Maussian model shows that people, objects, and social relations form a cogenerative whole, a significant accomplishment that is still not widely digested. When people transact with each other in gift and commodity relations, they create and re-create this system in systematically variable ways. Basing himself on the best scholarship available at the turn of the twentieth century, Mauss sought to show that, right across the globe and as far back as he could go in human history, cycles of obligatory returns of gifts effected major transfer of goods and, in so doing, organized social life.

The book begins with a synthesis of the ethnographic work on the northwest coast Native American institution of the potlatch. The potlach is a kind of agonistic exchange, elaborate gift-giving celebrations given to legitimate the transfer of titles or to obtain recognition of ones right to a title. Mauss argues that the potlatch is an example of a total system of giving. Spelled out, this means that each gift is part of a system of reciprocity that engages the honor of giver and recipient and the groups they represent. It is a total system in that every item of status or of spiritual or material possession is implicated for everyone in the whole community. In significant measure, this is because all these things are the product of the labor of groups in the society, organized by group leaders (McCall 1982). The rule that every gift has to be returned in some specified way sets up a perpetual cycle of exchanges both within and between generations and across the society. And where does the system get its energy? In each instance, from individuals who gain renown by mobilizing the labor of their kin in acts of largesse or lose honor through default, as the kin group shames defaulters, and the whole business sanctioned by beliefs that transcendent forces punish those who do not reciprocate.

Historically, potlatches were exercises in power in which massive acts of generosity produced indebtedness among the receiving clans and their representatives and honor among the givers. Only a greater counter gift could cancel prior potlatch debts, which thus set up an escalating cycle of gifts and counter gifts. At one time, the catalog of transfers that mapped all the obligations between the clans within various tribal groups, and individuals within those clans, could describe the potlatching cultures that extended from today's Oregon all the way to the hinterlands of contemporary British Columbia. It is not too much to say that the cycling gift system between persons, things, and the environment was the society. In CCT, Mauss's theoretical genius in defining the potlatch is brilliantly demonstrated by Weinberger and Wallendorf's (2012) recent study of the role of Mardi Gras gifting in the reproduction of social structure in south Louisiana.

The Gift then goes to Melanesians and an extended discussion of the Kula system of circulation, and on to Polynesia, and then eventually to ancient Roman, German, and ultimately Indian Vedic texts. It appears to veer off into arcane debates on ancient law, but in fact the second part of the text is about contemporary politics and economics. And, although it is concerned with rethinking social policy before the advent of the European welfare state, it simultaneously offers a critique of British utilitarian philosophy. Mauss essentially argues that the gift provides an alternative empirically based model of the social contract to the Hobbesian one. I will return to this point.

After the northwest coast, Mauss turns his attention to Melanesia, the home of the now justly famous Kula. These are systems of totalized competitive giving that incorporate in their cycles all things and services and all persons on the huge arc of islands that make up the system. Early observers never really appreciated the scale or social significance of the Kula, hence limiting Mauss's own analysis. But this has been rectified by subsequent scholarship, notably by Weiner (1976, 1992) and contributors to an amazing edited collection (Leach and Leach 1983).

In the discussion of the circulation of gifts, Mauss's contribution is threefold. First, it offers an ethnological model of human sociality that is an alternative to that imagined by Hobbes and his descendants.

Second, it synthesizes the three normative obligations that compose the gift system, namely those of giving, receiving, and reciprocating. One is obligated to give because giving creates obligations among others; it is foundational to relationships. Failing to give puts one beyond the pale of social life. One is obligated to receive because refusal creates a conflict and forecloses the possibility of relationship. When it came to the obligation to reciprocate, Mauss's theory takes a Durkheimian detour as he invokes a religious idea, that of the Maori hau, which he associates with the sacred. Subsequent scholarship has found sociological explanations for reciprocation; theories related to the fundamental inalienability of gifted objects (Godelier 2004; Sahlins 1976; Weiner 1976, 1992); or the ideas of restitution and completion (McCall 1982; Sahlins 1976), respectively.

In Mauss's theory the three obligations are of equal importance. Here a key point is the convenient inconvenience that in gift exchanges that do not involve money, gifts and counter gifts cannot easily "cancel" one another because they always involve exchanges of things that are in some sense incommensurate. No two potlatch "coppers," Kula necklaces or armbands, or even dinner parties are exactly alike.

According to Mauss, these obligations form the core of social relations in societies without centralized authority but continue to animate social relations even within more complex polities (Hyde 1979), even if in our own, the obligation to receive sometimes seems to trump the other two. Thus, Cancian (1966) believes Americans attempt to maximize the equality of exchange when giving gifts. Exchange partners attempt to modulate their relationship by using gifts to maintain the desired degree of intimacy. And Caplow (1982) found that American Christmas gifts are frequently scaled to the kinship relationships between donor and recipient.

One of Mauss's key points, as Mary Douglas (1990) insisted, is that the idea of a pure "disinterested" gift is a contradiction. A gift without the possibility of return is an act of symbolic violence that disempowers the recipient. Moreover, if we ignore the universal fact of obligation in the circulation of gifts, we make our own experiences of interpersonal debt, moral responsibility, and obligation incomprehensible, something CCT scholarship has recognized (Bradford 2009; Bradford and Sherry 2015). To avoid feeling inferior and to safeguard reputation, the recipient must reciprocate. Failure to reciprocate appropriately can result in an asymmetrical relationship (Sahlins 1976). On the other hand, within culturally prescribed bounds, the reciprocity involved in gift exchange cannot be more balanced than are the respective social positions of donor and recipient. Otherwise, participants risk imputations of either of ostentation or meanness (van Baal 1975). "Giving too much, too little, or [too early or] too late can strain a relationship to the point of dissolution" (Sherry 1983, 158).

A third key contribution in *The Gift* is to pose the question "What force is there in the thing which one gives which forces the receiver to return it?" (Mauss 1925, 33). Behind this question lies a fundamental Durkheimian question: "Since people create things with their hands and construe the world . . . with their minds, why then do their products . . . compel them rather than vice versa?" (Jenkins 1998, 85). Now this led Mauss, heir to Durkheim after all, to investigate religious causes in ideas like Polynesian mana and the Maori hau.

But Mauss also proposed a more sociological idea about the sociological force in things. In total prestations—that is, gifts between social groups—Mauss said things are related in some degree as persons and persons in some degree as things. Or, as Strathern (1990, 189) says, in a gift economy, persons and things are "personified": a process that makes people's relations visible. And as Weiner says, "where exchange is the basic framework around which formal patterns of social interaction are organized, objects become highly significant because in their manner of presentation-quality, quantity, and the like- they can be read as objectification of desire and intent" (1976, 212). Thus, the famous Kula valuables in Melanesian circulation systems are valued because of the genealogy of their successive trustees. In contemporary times, this is a bit like the idea of provenance, where works of art acquire worth from the succession of owners. The general point is that every exchange, as it embodies some degree of sociability, cannot be understood in its material terms apart from its social terms, and vice versa. Objects become containers for the being of the donor, who gives a portion of that being to the recipient; there is an inevitable symbolic encoding of the gift with connotative meaning (Sherry 1983, 159). The basic idea Mauss explored in *The Gift* is that things have motivational force. And this idea is very much alive today in posthumanist scholarship for example.

As mentioned, *The Gift* constitutes an intentional critique of utilitarian philosophy. The first element of critique is that utilitarian thought is based on an impoverished concept of the person seen as an independent individual instead of as a social being, which links to Mauss's subsequent essay on the nature of the self, discussed next. What Mauss shows in the analysis of gift giving and ancient comparative law is that, in short, a proper analysis of social life cannot begin with the individual. The second point of critique is that of cultural relativism: rather than fixed by nature (or "evolution"), social relations change with changes in the modes of economic production and circulation. The third point of critique is its simplistic view of methodological individualism and its lack of appreciation of the essentially normative construction of political action (Blommaert 2016). This is the Hobbesian view that absent the state, self-interested actors are inclined to a state of war. The general point, as both Douglas (1990) and Sahlins (1972) have pointed out, is that there are alternative normative foundations for circulation, for social security, and for the pursuit of personal recognition to the so-called free market. Mauss discovered a mechanism, the gift economy, by which individual desires, but not interests (because the latter is a construct specific to market economies) combine to make a social system, without engaging primarily in market exchange. Phrased another way, Mauss shows against methodological individualism on the one hand and Durkheimian social determinism on the other, that there is a third model of action in which liberty and obligation are commingled.

"A Category of the Human Mind: The Notion of Person; the Notion of Self"

In this paper originally from 1938, Mauss sets out the proposition that the category of the self-directed, "privately conscious, autonomous person, congruent with the public endorsement and sanctioning of individual identity and agency" (James 1998, 15) is not a human universal but a product of Western, and perhaps now, global history. This is an idea that entails a foundational critique of both Western economics and psychology. It is an idea Campbell (1987) developed further in his study of the emergence of the Western consuming self from the Reformation forward.

Mauss's interest in the self has to do with his post-Durkheimian idea of the total social fact. This is his claim that the social is only real when integrated into a system of meanings. That social

> system must also be embodied in individual experience, and that, from two different viewpoints: first, in an individual history . . . and after that, in . . . a system of interpretation accounting for the aspects of all modes of behavior simultaneously, physical, physiological, psychical and sociological . . . Only to study that fragment of our life which is our life in society is not enough. (Lévi-Strauss 1987/1950, 26)

Mauss (1985/1938, 3) makes it "plain, particularly to us, that there has never existed a human being who has not been aware, not only of his body, but also at the same time of his individuality, both spiritual and physical." But the aim of the essay is elsewhere; that is, to explore how "over the centuries, in numerous societies, how has it slowly evolved—not the sense of 'self' (*me*)—but the notion or concept that men in different ages have formed of it"

So, following the ethnological method he employed in the work on sacrifice, magic, and the gift, he sets out exploring how and where various conceptions associated with the modern, Western self develop. He starts as always with the concrete. Thus, he first shows how ideas of role and role performance are deeply rooted in clan-based societies in which individuals inherit spirits, names, or titles and represent groups on important public and ritual occasions. Later he explores the principle of the moral person as developed in Roman law from ideas around the persona or public mask, worn literally by theatrical performers and figuratively by public figures. He further situates the idea of the volitional, conscious person in practices associated with Stoic philosophy.

He then goes on to discuss the contribution of Christianity, arguing that "it is Christians who have made a metaphysical entity of the 'moral person' (*personne morale*), after they became aware of its religious power. Our own notion of the human person is still basically the Christian one" (p.19). He points out how centuries of debate about the nature of the soul versus the body explored questions of determinism versus free will.

Eventually he identifies the origin of the idea of "the me." He says it is to "thought that is discursive, clear and deductive, that the Renaissance and Descartes address themselves in order to understand their nature. It is thought that contains the revolutionary '*Cogito ergo sum*'" (p.21). And finally, as expressed in characteristically comparative form, the

> ideas of the Moravian Brothers, the Puritans, the Wesleyans and the Pietists are those which form the basis on which is established the notion: the "person" (*personne*) equals the "self" (*moi*); the "self" (*moi*) equals consciousness, and is its primordial category (p.21).

That is, detailed analysis of concrete, empirical evidence leads to the formulation of a theoretical idea. This is territory revisited by Campbell (1987) in his discussion of the emergence of the Romantic, self-improving consumer self that is pervasive today (Askegaard and Eckhardt 2012; Moisio and Beruchashvili 2010).

Mauss extends his thinking into the origins of the social science focus on the individual by arguing that

> the one who founded all science and all action on the "self" (*moi*), was Fichte. Kant had already made of the individual consciousness . . . the

condition for Practical Reason. It was Fichte who made of it as well the category of the "self" (*moi*), the condition of consciousness and of science.

Johann Fichte (1762–1814), a student of Kant, originated the then-controversial idea that the phenomenal world arises from self-consciousness, the activity of the ego, and moral awareness. The latter point is important to Mauss's position as a sociologist because Fichte argued that the existence of other rational subjects somehow summons the subject or self into self-awareness as an individual.

Mauss's account is historical, anthropological, and genealogical in a Foucauldian sense, though that association is anachronistic. He succeeds in making the ancient past contemporary and pertinent, while rendering our own preconceptions about the self contingent and indeed problematic. What Mauss's essay also suggests is the same sort of groundwork that he develops with regard to the European self be pursued in other cultural contexts. For Mauss is clear that what we call individuals among non-Western peoples must be foundationally different. More recent anthropological work, although adopting contemporary terminologies, seems to confirm Mauss's relativistic view of selfhood (Hallowell 1955; Ho 1995; White and Kirkpatrick 1985). This work is an invitation for consumer culture theorists to develop more culturally relative conceptions of the relationship between consumption and identity, a topic relatively untouched in anthropological work and consumer psychology.

"Techniques of the Body"

In this paper from 1934, Mauss returned to this theme of understanding human phenomena holistically. He was staking out the crucial value for the human sciences of a study of the manner in which each society imposes a rigorously determined use of the body upon the individual through biosocial means (Lévi-Strauss 1987/1950; Maynard, Greenfield, and Childs 1999). Although taken up by some students of the anthropology of ritual, craft, sport, music, and dance and as foundational to a theory of material culture (Gélard 2013; Warnier 1999), it seems to me that insofar as the body is the site of consumption, and overwhelmingly consumer objects are the instruments of bodily technique, that this paper is of considerable significance to CCT as well.

The text has four parts: first, an introduction to the idea of body technique or "habitus" and some examples; second, a simple taxonomy; third, an enumeration of techniques over the life course; and fourth, a conclusion that emphasizes that the "habitus" constitutes a total social fact, being biopsychosocial. Mauss tried to insist on the body as the primordial human tool, but he never excises the role of instruments in forming and being formed by bodies. In this essay, we find a more sociologically grounded precursor of Belk's (1988) ideas, but at the same time he lacked a more elaborate theory of materiality (Miller 1987).

In this essay, Mauss is the originator of the concept of habitus, a construct made famous by another Durkheimian, Bourdieu (1977). Mauss says,

> I have had this notion of the social nature of the "habitus" for many years . . . The word translates infinitely better than "habitude" (habit or custom), the "exis", the "acquired ability" and "faculty" of Aristotle (who was a psychologist) . . . These "habits" do not just vary with individuals and their imitations, they vary especially between societies, educations, proprieties and fashions, prestiges. In them we should see the techniques and work of collective and individual practical reason (p.73)

Further, he argues that it is purposeful activities that both suppose and generate knowledge, what he himself called practical rather than discursive knowledge, but always social, culturally specific knowledge.

Consistent with his key concept of the total social fact, Mauss understood that asserting the causal priority of bio-psychical or sociocultural is ill-starred. The two are mutual translations, but in which sociological structures have priority (Sahlins 1996). Phrased another way, Mauss sought to socialize the organic endowment of the living human body. Our most natural daily activities, he argued—walking, eating, sleeping, even swimming—are collectively instigated, as are also procreation, emotional expressions, and illness. As these activities are available to others' recognition and evaluation, they form part of the social makeup of individuals.

He argued explicitly that culture and social structure leave their imprint on individuals through the training of the child's bodily needs and activities; through socialization, the body becomes a cultural artifact. At the same time, bodily techniques exhibit great individual accessibility and variability, as the quadrennial Olympic Games dramatically remind us.

To illustrate his contemporary relevance, Mauss offers a wonderfully prescient example of the effect of consumption on body techniques. Reflecting on his time in the hospital after World War I, he remarks,

> I wondered where previously I had seen girls walking as my nurses walked. I had the time to think about it. At last I realized that it was at the cinema. Returning to France, I noticed how common this gait was, especially in Paris; the girls were French and they too were walking in this way. In fact, American walking fashions had begun to arrive over here, thanks to the cinema (p.72).

The spread of Southern Californian "Valley speak" and urban hip-hop lingo, attire, postures, and gaits are contemporary examples of diffusion of bodily consumer practice Mauss identified from the earliest days

234 Eric J. Arnould

of the cinema but about which rather little has been written. Perhaps Thompson and Üstüner (2015) point a way forward in understanding consumer bodily technique as Maussian total social facts.

Another point worth extracting from this essay is captured in Mauss's remark that "the body is man's first and most natural instrument. Or more accurately, not to speak of instruments, man's first and most natural technical object, and at the same time technical means, is his body" (p.75). But at the same time, almost all of his examples evoke the materiality of bodily practices. That is, when Mauss wrote of specific techniques, he also made reference to a world of materiality, or what he referred to as "instruments" or "supplementary means" (Thompson and Üstüner, 2015, 83). Thus practical knowledge, habitus, and materials together form a total system of materiality. And this point, in turn, leads Mauss to call into question the ontological utility of ad hoc typologies of action. As he says, all such bodily techniques share the qualities of being effective in the eyes of practitioners and traditional—in other words, cultural. "It is thanks to society that there is the certainty of pre-prepared movements, domination of the conscious over emotion and unconsciousness" (p.86). And finally, again foreshadowing Clifford Geertz of the Balinese cock-fight or Bourdieuan taste regimes more generally, he adds that techniques of the self of necessity refer to "the notion we have of the activity of the consciousness as being above all a system of symbolic assemblages" (p.76)

One final point comes from his last paragraph where he points out that traditional Indian and Chinese scholarship has far advanced study of the relationship between bodily techniques and altered states of consciousness and, for that reason, should be the object of further study. It seems this opening toward non-Western science of the body and its techniques remains relatively virgin territory (cf. Askegaard and Eckhardt 2012).

Evolutionary psychology and neuromarketing and neuro-consumer research would seem to have it that humans are a product of their bodies, but Mauss took pains to demonstrate that it is the other way around. Human societies have at all times and in all places turned the body into a product both of techniques, what today we call practices, and its representations (Sahlins 1996). In this way, Mauss is a precursor to contemporary Butlerian gender studies, on the one hand, and actor network and practice theory, on the other, but the enemy now as then of simplistic evolutionary thinking. Still the recent Nordic walking and Mars Coat King studies respectively, are among the few real Maussian studies of a market-mediated technique as material practice and consumer assemblage (Bettany 2007; Shove and Pantzar 2005). Surely there is room for more.

Ethnological Method

I do not discuss Mauss's book-length text on ethnological method but point to some aspects of his practice that I think respond to the critical call for more attention to context—that is, to the meso level of analysis.

As seen in his major works and more anecdotally in the shorter texts I reviewed, Mauss typically begins by trying to sort out an ontological conundrum. What compels reciprocity? What is this thing called "me"? In order to answer this, he typically turns to an exemplary concrete case of the phenomena in question (*concret figuré*). He then identifies native terms and categories and explicates them in terms of social institutions of the cultural context in question. Indeed, it is through this procedure that some native concepts like mana or potlatch, for instance, have become scientific constructs. He is scrupulous about sources and historical context. On this basis, he then builds up comparisons, drawing upon similar phenomena among neighboring cultural contexts and then moving farther afield, while attempting to control the dimensions of contrast of his examples. Finally, he brings in possible parallels from contexts further afield and historical periods different from those with which he begins. It is through this kind of controlled cultural comparison that he builds up syncretic theoretical models like those of the gift, sacrifice, magic, the self, and so on (*concret pensé*). He scrupulously builds up theory from specific empirical materials rather than personal intuitions or taken-for-granted assumptions. He demonstrates rather than claims and, in so doing, often uses examples to upend, reverse, or transform principles or theories that in the light of the empirical evidence appear faulty. Sometimes all this takes the form of an extended "black swan" sort of argument.

Mauss's descendants, anthropologists Claude Lévi-Strauss and Philippe Descola have deployed effectively this same ethnological technique. And we can see echoes of this method in some studies in CCT that have pushed the envelope in terms of understanding categories like the fetish, the gift, and inalienable wealth (Curasi, Price, and Arnould 2004; Fernandez and Lastovicka 2011; Giesler 2006; Joy 2001; Weinberger and Wallendorf 2012).

Action Research

Finally, one other important aspect of Mauss's career that I think responds to criticism of the CCT approach in consumption studies is that Mauss was no ivory tower purist. Instead he was a committed lifelong socialist. For example, he wrote a column in the radical newspaper *l'Humanité*. He was a close friend to Jean Jaurès, the martyred French socialist leader, and he was deeply engaged in the cooperative movement. He was highly critical of the totalitarian tendencies evident in the socialist movements in Russia after the 1917 revolution, seeing no solution to the problem of societal anomie there. In the aftermath of the World War I in *l'Humanité*, he wrote polemically and at length in defense of the construct of the nation not as a purified conservative expression of an ethnic identity as in German National Socialism but as a progressive hybrid expression of the collectivity. In 1921 he drew up a plan calling for the state to provide material assistance and social protection—hat is, what we call today "*l'état providence*" or a social safety net. His political experience seems to have nourished the critical and nonpartisan but impassioned perspective about the constitution of civil society one can find in works like the essay *The Gift*. To my mind, it is the combination of Mauss's impeccable, comparative, and historical scholarship combined with his commitment to resolving wicked social problems that makes Mauss an admirable role model of the engaged public intellectual still today (Fournier 2006; Godelier 2004; Schlanger 1998).

Marshall Sahlins

Sahlins earned his Ph.D. in anthropology at Columbia University in 1954. His main intellectual influences included Leslie White, Karl Polanyi, and Julian Steward, mentors who influenced his perennial interest in the cultural economy and in culture and historical change. In the late 1960s, he spent two years in Paris, where he was deeply influenced by structuralist and Marxist anthropology. Sahlins's work has focused on demonstrating the power that culture has to shape people's perceptions and actions. He has been particularly interested in demonstrating that culture has a unique power to motivate people, which is not derived from the economy. His early career work was engaged with anthropological debates of the day, but his midcareer work focused on debunking the idea of "economically rational" man, the progressive notion of economic history, and demonstrating that economic systems adapted to particular circumstances in culturally specific ways. Two books punctuated this period, *Stone Age Economics* and *Culture and Practical Reason*. After the latter book, his focus shifted to the relationship between history and anthropology and the way different cultures understand and make history. His many students of relevant interest to CCT include Grant McCracken, author of *Culture and Consumption* I and II; Rita Denny, co-author of *Doing Anthropology in Consumer Research* and the *Handbook of Anthropology in Business*; and David Graeber, author of *Toward an Anthropological Theory of Value* and *Debt: The First 5,000 Years*.

Stone Age Economics

The book title is a typical Sahlinsian joke; it refers not to the economic systems of Stone Age societies, although it does focus on non- or pre-market societies, but instead refers to the rudimentary state of historically and culturally informed economic theory. It contains a number of important essays. "The Original Affluent Society" shows that aboriginal hunting and gathering bands were not materially poor if judged by their own cultural standards. Economically, they sought sufficiency and acquired their material needs without exhaustive labor because of their minute knowledge of their physical environment and their adaptive ingenuity. This essay is an important empirical critique of the assumption that scarcity is the foundational driver of human economic activity. "The Domestic Mode of Production," which is composed of two essays, uses the findings of the Russian agronomist Chayanov (who wrote in the 1920s) to explain what governs the intensity of the work life of household groups in different tribal and peasant economies. He shows that labor intensity is generally inversely proportional to the ratio of productive to nonproductive labor. Absent external constraint, peasant households do not maximize their economic productivity. Further, he shows that the Neolithic revolution was not so much a revolution in productivity, as social evolutionists have argued, but one in social organization that led to an increase in human industriousness and fueled the emergence of city-states. This perspective is perhaps helpful in thinking through how industrial capitalism become consumer capitalism or how consumer capitalism might become a postconsumer economy—again, Sahlins's attempts to complexify our understanding of the relationships between environment, culture, and economy.

"The Spirit of the Gift" offers a reinterpretation of Mauss's rationale for the obligatory repayment of gifts found in primitive societies. He suggests that the hau, far from being primarily a sacred principle, as Mauss argued, is instead a productive principle. The gift is the embodiment of creative activity; it embodies the activity of some definite agents. Thus, circulation is motivated by persons' and groups' desire to reduce or at least moderate their dependence upon the creative power of another as materialized in the gift. Further, we are dealing with a type of society that does not envision individual gain via reduction of others' outcomes. Instead, one gains in honor and prestige as much through others' failure of generous expenditure as through one's own largesse. Advantage or increase must be acknowledged by a return.

Further, and this is crucial, not two, but three parties are involved in the circulation of the gift. The benefit that a second party derives from passing on a gift to a third belongs to the first, original giver, which in much tribal usage is a collective entity that holds resources in trust: ancestors, the "forest," the clan. The idea that gift exchange entails three parties is something consumer culture theorists have found in intergenerational giving where cherished possessions are transformed into inalienable wealth—that is, things that should be given by not sold (Bradford 2009; Curasi, Price and Arnould 2004; Epp and Price 2010; Weiner 1992). Curiously, in situations where a third party is clearly engaged in contemporary contexts (i.e., the contemporary gift store, where people buy gifts to give to others), the implications of the tripartite structure were not developed (Sherry, McGrath, and Levy 1993). Nor have they in the context of the massive practice of in-store gift returns that follow major holidays. Consumer researchers initially adopted a bilateral exchange logic that obscures meso-level systemic dimensions (Sherry 1983). Recent CCT research has demonstrated that the circulation of gifted objects brings forth Mauss's idea of total prestation and noted the importance of the circulation of physical objects in the establishment of intracommunity relationships among multiple actors (Bradford 2009; Bradford and Sherry 2015; Giesler 2006; Weinberger and Wallendorf 2012).

In addition, Sahlins repeats and extends Mauss's argument about how reciprocal gift giving maintains peaceful relationships among stateless bands and tribes who have no institutionalized sphere of political life. "On the Sociology of Primitive Exchange" is a long essay that adopts very much Mauss's ethnological method. With supporting evidence focused on reciprocity and kinship distance, kinship rank, and wealth, drawn from a global ethnographic sample, Sahlins shows how different forms of exchange express social distance: to each social relationship is attached a permissible mode of circulation and exchange. Although the ethnographic detail is perhaps exotic and outdated, it alerts us to the actual complexity of the circulation of things, relationships, and meanings in our own societies.

This essay contains the famous formulation of generalized, balanced, and negative reciprocity, with Sahlins showing that cross-culturally there is an inverse relationship between our sense of mutual implication with others and the dominant logic of exchange between us. There is much of interest in this formulation. First, generalized reciprocity not only is evident as a mechanism that creates, maintains, and symbolizes close ties but also is often extended to relative strangers as found in acts of charity or even in random acts of courtesy, as in crowd-funded projects when the latter fail. "Gifts make friends" as Sahlins (1972, 186) says; the gesture of giving always contains the potential for further sociality.

Balanced reciprocity is also paradoxical because, as Caplow (1982) and others (Cheal 1988) studying contemporary gift giving in Euro-American contexts have noted, partners are inclined to seek for what they can count as a rough equivalency—this, of course, being culturally determined rather than subject to standard accounting principles. On the other hand, theoretically balanced reciprocity resembles market exchange in that it could be self-liquidating if people did in fact resort to auditing these exchanges in search of true equivalency. Consequently, in consumer culture as Cheal (1988) points out, the cycle of gift transactions provides a recurring opportunities to celebrate mutual affection and the continuity of interpersonal attachments through invented rites that affirm the maintenance of social bonds. This affirmation helps account for the otherwise curious persistence of quasi-religious holidays in secular contexts, the acceptance of so-called Hallmark holidays, and the diffusion of Christmas gift giving to non-Christian cultural contexts.

And finally, there is negative reciprocity, which Sahlins himself glosses as "chicanery" and some equate with self-interested market maximizing. But there are unresolved problems here. First it has been shown in "pure" market contexts as diverse as fine art auctions and financial trading floors that these are infused with the other two exchange principles. Second, it seems to some that a better example of negative reciprocity is, in fact, the gift that admits no return as seen in some potlatch examples and in some contemporary "charitable" giving, which in fact is much the same thing. As stated earlier, the gift that admits no return is a truly antisocial action, an act of power that places the recipient in a permanently dependent position vis-à-vis the giver.

Of course, Sahlins's early work has its weaknesses. First, it rather loses the perspective, as Mauss did not, that non-Western societies are not the sediment of transacting individuals but the product of social relations among groups in which individuals may not have appeared except as representatives of groups. Second, Sahlins pays almost no attention to the variable relationship between money and gift giving. Third, things have neither biography nor agency in Sahlins's treatment as we now recognize they do; here, they are mere counters in circulatory movements. Finally, of course, he ignores not only production but also consumption in favor of distribution or circulation. A later book corrects some of these weaknesses.

Culture and Practical Reason

The second early book that CCT scholars should know is a continuation of the themes initiated in the earlier text in pursuing the critique of the utilitarian presuppositions in North American social theory. The first part of the book is a reflection on two ideas of the nature of culture, a culturological idea of culture that is Maussian, Boasian, Douglasian, and Geertzian in character and a practical idea of culture, a kind of reactive, utilitarian functionalism that explains cultural phenomena in terms of some other teleology (e.g., functional utility or adaptive superiority).

As Sahlins positions himself within a culturalist camp, his main opponent is utility theory and specifically the presumption that culture is the product of individuals pursuing their self-interest through rational actions (Sahlins 1976, vii). Instead, as against both utilitarianism generally and a tendency in American anthropology (L. Pospisil, H.K. Schneider, J. Stewart, M. Harris), Sahlins argues that although there is a materialist "base" for cultural difference, the quality of culture is such that it always adapts to environmental opportunities and constraints through specific cultural schemes. Given cultural schemes are never the only ones possible and never determined exclusively by material forces (Sahlins 1976, viii). This is an important point in the critique of globalization of consumption seen as McDonaldization (Ritzer 2009), for example.

Instead, Sahlins argues that the material causes must be the product of a symbolic system of meaningful values because the general determinations of purposeful material action are always subject to the specific formulations of culture (Sahlins 1976, 57). Moreover, because culture is a symbolic system, it maintains a fundamental autonomy of material factors. And therefore, the reason the dominant discourse in (Western) society proclaims the teleological finality of material rationality is because our cultural apparatus is hidden behind the experience of bourgeois subjectivity, the individually differentiated organization of consumption (Hau, accessed 30/09/2016.). For Sahlins, utility values are differential cultural values, not determinants of the cultural order.

Of special interest to students of consumption is "La Pensée Bourgeoise," which contains some rather messy materials about consumer preferences in the United States. He shows preferences exemplify a structural logic and cultural continuity that operates independently of functional necessity. By focusing on the semiotic dimensions of the objects people value, Sahlins makes the telling point that production is a system of cultural intentions, as he illustrates by reference to food and fashion.

One of the pithy arguments he makes is that we can think of the economy as the "organizing instance" of market society, as is kinship in stateless societies or sacred kingship in ancient empires. And like all organizing instances, it imposes an order of meanings. Utility, he says, is a candidate for its core symbol, something we see expressed in a host of marketing tactics, perhaps most concisely in the single word, "sale." Scarcity, one of the supposed natural motors of economic activity, too, he argues, is socially constructed (e.g., beef cheek is scarce but cheap; comparatively, sirloin is relatively less scarce but pricey). Commodities he points out, as will be no news today in CCT, are organized as orders of symbolic difference. And perhaps more boldly, he argues that people, in turn, are organized by these orders of things—again, no news today to those familiar with the concept of consumer tribes (Shankar, Cova, and Kozinets 2011). The market economy constantly charts new territories of differences (as he says, fashion is custom in the guise of a departure from custom).

Expanding on the nature of things, Sahlins offers the following argument. Fashioning products always renders material a symbolic conception. And systematic variation in objective features of such products serves as the medium of a vast and dynamic conceptual scheme, in part, he says, because each difference is developed with a view toward the master symbol, "utility" (made in y; new and improved; now with/without [ingredient] x; 20% off, organic, fairly traded, etc.). By the systematic arrangement of meaningful differences assigned to concrete commercial things, the cultural order is realized as an order of goods. Production (consumption) is thus the reproduction of the cultural in a system of objects. The reader will immediately detect a resonance with early Baudrillard (Graeber 2011).

Sahlins offers a claim in this text that both assimilates Western societies into the purview of anthropology and identifies it in terms of a compelling distinction from the kinds of societies anthropologists originally set out to understand. And this distinction is simultaneously an invitation to take up consumption as an appropriate topic for anthropological inquiry. His claim is that it is the symbolic constitution of the economy, in contrast to the symbolic constitution of kinship, kingship, or religion in other sociocultural contexts, that determines the organization of Western society and that sets "la pensée bourgeoise" apart from "la pensée sauvage" that preoccupied social scientists like Durkheim (1963), Levy-Bruhl (1923) or Lévi-Strauss (1966).

Recent Work

Perhaps the most interesting recent work both for scholars and critics of consumer culture appeared in *Current Anthropology* (1996) and later in book form (Sahlins 2008). It is a culmination of Sahlins's analysis of Euro-American "native anthropology"—that is, those axiomatic elements that infuse popular and social scientific discourse. It is a genealogical analysis of the idea of need. His argument is almost theological; he says, for example, "Originally, need had distinguished mankind from God's self-sufficient perfection."

Echoing Mauss (1938) in style and substance, and via a long genealogical argument, Sahlins shows how the idea of endless needs is based on the development of theological themes. The need for things, as well as for society itself as nothing more than a vehicle of individual need fulfillment, was the outcome of the expulsion from paradise, where we may note neither were there things (Adam and Eve were naked after all) nor society (they were alone with God and his works): "Originally understood by the Church Fathers as a form of bondage, each man's endless and hopeless attention to his own desires became, in the liberal-bourgeois ideology, the condition of freedom itself" (Sahlins 1996, 397). Sahlins expands,

> The original evil and source of vast sadness in [St.] Augustine, the needs of the body became simply "natural" in Hobbes or at least a "necessary evil" in Baron d'Holbach, to end in Adam Smith or Milton Friedman as the supreme source of social virtue. (Sahlins 1996, 398)

Thus, as he says, Western philosophy and social thought turn necessity into virtue; need becomes the alpha and omega of human motivation. In his argument, Sahlins provides ammunition to those critics of CCT's celebratory examination of the uses of consumption in identity work or community building as a longstanding element of liberal ideology. But at the same time, he shows that the critique of consumption excess descends from an older strand of the same Judeo-Christian ideology that can be found in St. Augustine and the medieval church fathers.

Sahlins takes up another matter in this paper, namely the perceived biological determinism underlying the way things appear to be in consumer culture. For it appears "in people's existential awareness, cultural forms of every description are produced and reproduced as the objects or projects of their corporeal feelings" (1996, 401). In other words, "in our subjective experience, culture is an epiphenomenon of an economy of the relief of bodily aches," (1996, 401)—that is, our desires conceived of as based in our physiology, a position rearticulated both in CCT (Belk, Ger, and Askegaard 2003) and evolutionary consumer psychology. And again, Sahlins is quick to point out that this conception is linked to the long-standing Judeo-Christian belief in the divided and opposed aspects of selfhood, the animalist body, and the soulful, spiritual intellect. Not only that, but it appears in some of this work as if God, the original invisible hand and its operationalization competition, has been supplanted by nature, and its operationalization, natural selection.

One of Sahlins's concluding points in this deconstruction of the ideas of biological determinism of culture and the supposed innateness of consumer needs is that "the critical discovery of anthropology has been that human needs and drives are indeterminate as regards their object because bodily satisfactions are specified in and through symbolic values-and variously so in different cultural-symbolic schemes" (1996, 404). It is this ethnological assertion that should inspire consumer culture theorists in making sense of our many cultures of consumption. Indeed it should impel consumer culture theories toward "a methodological cosmopolitanism" (Sahlins 1996, 425), the constitution of [CCT] in and as a series of cultural-ontological variations, which would allow the construction of more adequate ethnographic and interpretive schemata.

Historical Method

The historical turn in CCT may take inspiration from Sahlins's work of the past thirty years. It has focused on a twin project of rewriting history culturally and culture historically, while insisting on the priority of cultural templates for action and interpretation in making sense of history and culture. As he says,

> What guides my response is a concern to show that commonsense bourgeois realism, when taken as a historiographic conceit, is a kind of symbolic violence done to other times and other customs. I want to suggest that one cannot do good history, not even contemporary history, without regard for ideas, actions, and ontologies that are not and never were our own. (Sahlins 1995, 14)

Perhaps more generally Sahlins has tried to work out a method to deal with the point that "cultural change, externally induced yet indigenously orchestrated, has been going on for millennia" (1986, viii). This is a broadside against the practical reason evident in work as apparently different from Rostow's *The Stage of Economic Growth* and Ritzer's *The McDonaldization of Society* that implies that cultures assimilated into the current consumer culture globalization possess "no autonomous cultural logic" (viii). In contrast, Sahlins asserts that each culture produces its own historicity and may in fact assert its own temporalities. Moreover, he intends to do this by adducing written and oral historical sources to show how history is culturally patterned and how cultural schemas are historically constituted, reproduced, and thereby transformed. However, Sahlins is quick to insist that there is no "true" historical account anywhere, only preexistant schemas that interpret events in their own terms and then determine creative action as their own intersubjective unfolding as historical praxis (Abrahamson 1986). These points are important for consumer culture researchers who have taken up a process turn in analysis (Humphreys 2010; Karababa and Ger 2011; Thompson and Giesler 2016) but who in their accounts have perhaps somewhat neglected what Williams (1977) would refer to as residual and emergent cultural schema and counterhistories with subversive agendas.

One of the key entries in this historicizing project is Sahlins's reconstructions of the initial apotheosis, and subsequent murder of Captain Cook in Hawaii (Sahlins1985, 1995). He insists that Cook's murder makes logical sense on the basis of complex ethnographic evidence involving beliefs about deities as applied to Captain Cook, humans' relationship to the divine, the ritual calendar, kinship, kingship, political divisions, and so on. It thereby contains a critique of the supposed universality of "practical reason," the presumption of the universality of which would rob cultures of cultural specificity, and in which Cook's death would be reduced to a fight over material goods. The theoretical point Sahlins makes is that mythopraxes are generative systems of foundational meaning, a point developed in some recent CCT scholarship (Dong and Tian 2009; Thompson and Tian 2008; Thompson and Üstüner 2015).

Methodologically, then, Sahlins wants to show first how practices implement received cultural templates for action and interpretation in empirical contexts. Still, "every reproduction of culture is an alteration, insofar as in action, the categories by which a present world is orchestrated pick up some novel empirical content" (Sahlins 1986, 144). Of course, especially contemporary contexts may contain actors, things, and processes that are neither deducible from the received cultural templates nor intrinsic to them and that may channel both practice and the results of practice in novel directions. These may even contradict the templates. This point seems particularly relevant to scholars trying to make sense of commercially motivated and mediated innovations in global consumer culture.

Next, he introduces the idea of prescription, routine enactment via tacit or explicit rules, or performances embedded in actors' strategic moves that enact cultural templates. These arguments are similar to those offered in practice theory. Sociocultural dynamism stems from the latter even as those able to act strategically are already culturally scripted. Individuals assume a heteroglossic relationship to culture's intersubjective concepts. Thus, social life amounts to "a continuous rearrangement of [cultural] categories in the projects of personal being" (Sahlins 2005, 285). Individuals' improvisations can have structural effects—albeit within limits set by cultural logic, institutional freedom, and social position. Hence, he concludes, "people change their culture"; indeed, "that's all they ever do" (Sahlins 2005, 287).

A final point is to expose the mythical structuring of cultural performances or alternatively their enactment as habitus, as techniques of the body in Maussian terms. Discussions of myth in consumer culture seem not too distant from this logic, even if the techniques of the body have been somewhat neglected relative to the mythopraxic dimensions of consumption. That is, I think CCT treats myth as more than mere interpretive frameworks within which practice becomes meaningful. Of course, this idealism is what some have criticized (Cova, et al. 2013; Fitchett et al. 2014). In CCT, it seems to me that studies have tended to look at the performative nature of myth or at habitus in structuring consumption but not both together. Perhaps I am mistaken. In any case, we can see that Sahlins is working toward a poststructuralist epistemology from his structural Marxism.

Sahlins has also been at pains to develop extended historical examples to reject apocalyptic post-isms that equate the current historical epoch with the death knell of cultural difference, as well as the kind of hand-wringing, postcolonialist identity politics that rejects the possibility of scientific understanding of others' cultures. In this regard, he likes to point to the fact that despite colonialism, genocide, globalization, and global warming, foraging peoples, who we might consider among the most threatened by these phenomena, persist. Thus, culture matters (1993, 1999a, 1999b). CCT is well placed to contribute to theoretically grounded rejections of simplistic globalization theory via demonstrations of glocalization (Watson 1995; Askegaard, Kjeldgaard, and Arnould forthcoming).

Action Research

Like Mauss before him, Sahlins has been an activist cultural critic. He is, for example, the inventor of the "teach-in" at the University of Michigan in 1965 that aimed to appropriate universities to teach opposition to the

Vietnam War, rather than boycott them. He wrote in opposition to the war in the popular media and visited and wrote about Vietnam at the time. He continues to write against the military use of anthropologists, sometimes rationalized as instilling cultural relativism in the military. He says, for example, "Of course it is the opposite of cultural relativism—cultural cynicism one might call it—since the object is to appropriate the cultural practices of others to one's own purposes, notably the purpose of dominating them" (http://aaanewsinfo.blogspot.com/2007/11/aaaboard-statement-on-hts.html). He has also written scathingly (and humorously) about the infusion and consequences of neoliberal ideology in higher education (Sahlins 2009).

Sahlins has taken on the Confucius Institute. The Confucius Institute is an ambitious worldwide project devoted to teaching Chinese language and culture sponsored by the Chinese government. Based on a global investigation, Sahlins shows that this is a propaganda instrument of the Chinese Communist Party, one that actively undermines academic integrity and free inquiry into Chinese society and government policies. He has played a significant role in reining in the institute's activities (http://apjjf.org/2014/12/46/Marshall-Sahlins/4220.html).

Discussion

In my assessment, Mauss and Sahlins are exemplars of traditions of public scholarship that conjure their radical Enlightenment forebears (Blom 2010) and provide role models for CCT today. First, both have contributed foundational theoretical ideas that continue to resonate in contemporary consumption scholarship, among which are the gift, nonmarket principles of exchange, magic, sacrifice, the performative body, and the symbolic and ideological constitution of consumption as a cultural system. Second, both adopt a critically relativist perspective toward axioms and constructs that orient scholarly practice. Third, both are resolutely committed to the virtue of emic realities, both historical and contemporary, in developing inductive theory. They investigate deeply in specific contexts but draw on complementary situations to bring light to their analyses. Further, both insist on the necessity of grounding interpretations of events and individual action in cultural, linguistic, and historical contexts—that is, methodological holism. Fourth, both engage a virtuous circle of practice between theory, critique, and constructive social action. The results are intellectual immortality.

These comments lead to several modest proposals for future work in CCT. First, in the spirit of both authors, we might produce more work critical of the taken-for-granted categories adopted in conventional consumer research insofar as they reflect an ethnocentric "pensée bourgeoise," constructs such as need—a critique begun by Sahlins—but also motivation, decision, utility, biological determinism, and the like.

Second, in the spirit of Mauss, more work on alternative modes of circulation is needed, a project already begun (Eckhardt and Bardhi 2016; Figueiredo and Scaraboto forthcoming; Lamberton and Rose 2012; Scaraboto 2015). Third, as we have virtually no comparative cultural analyses of consumption phenomena in CCT, following Mauss, we might develop such ethnological reflections. These could take the form of a kind of cross-cultural meta-analysis. Fourth, the trend toward more processual, cultural-historical work is worthy of more attention (Thompson and Giesler, 2016). Finally, these authors provide cover for those inclined toward more critical CCT, but one that recognizes that there is space between unreflective paeans to "consumer sovereignty" and equally unreflective resurrections of vulgar Marxism (Earley 2014; Graeber 2011; Jafari and Goulding 2008).

Bibliography

Abramson, Allen. Review of *Islands of History*, by M. Sahlins (Chicago: University of Chicago Press, 1985). *Man* 21 (Spring 1986): 581.

Arnould, Eric J. and Craig J. Thompson. "Consumer Culture Theory (CCT): Twenty Years of Research." *Journal of Consumer Research* 31 (March 2005): 868–83.

Askegaard, Søren and Jeppe Trolle Linnet. "Towards an Epistemology of Consumer Culture Theory: Phenomenology and the Context of Context." *Marketing Theory* 11, no. 4 (2011): 381–404.

Askegaard, Søren and Giana M. Eckhardt. "Glocal Yoga: Re-Appropriation in the Indian Consumptionscape." *Marketing Theory* 12 (March 2012): 45–60.

Askegaard, Søren, Dannie Kjeldgaard, Eric Arnould. "Programmatic Authenticity: Culinary Place Branding in Greenland," In *Handbook of Place Branding*. Edited by Andrea Campelo, Gloucestershire, UK: Edward Elgar Publishing (forthcoming).

Belk, Russell W. "Possessions and the Extended Self." *Journal of Consumer Research* 15 (September 1988): 139–68.

———, Guliz Ger, and Søren Askegaard. "The Fire of Desire: A Multisited Inquiry into Consumer Passion." *Journal of Consumer Research* 30 (December 2003): 326–51.

Bettany, Shona. "The Material Semiotics of Consumption or Where (and What) Are the Objects in Consumer Culture Theory?" In *Consumer Culture Theory*, 41–56. Edited by Russell W. Belk and John F. Sherry. Research in Consumer Behavior, Vol. 11. Bingley: Emerald Group Publishing, 2007.

Blom, Philipp. *A Wicked Company: The Forgotten Radicalism of the European Enlightenment*. New York: Basic Books, 2010.

Blommaert, Jan. "Mathematics and Its Ideologies: An Anthropologist's Observations,2016." https://jmeblommaert.wordpress.com/2016/07/23/mathematics-and-its-ideologies-an-anthropologists-observations/.

Bourdieu, Pierrre. *Outline of a Theory of Practice*, Translated by Richard Nice. Cambridge: Cambridge University Press, 1977.

Bradford, Tonya Williams. "Intergenerationally Gifted Asset Dispositions." *Journal of Consumer Research* 36 (June 2009): 93–111.

——— and John F. Sherry, Jr. "Domesticating Public Space through Ritual: Tailgating as Vestaval." *Journal of Consumer Research* 42 (June 2015): 130–51.

Campbell, Colin. *The Romantic Ethic and the Spirit of Modern Consumerism*. Cambridge: Blackwell, 1987.

Cancian, Frank. "Maximization as Norm, Strategy, and Theory: A Comment on Programmatic Statements in Economic Anthropology." *American Anthropologist* 68 (April 1966): 465–70.

Caplow, Theodore. "Christmas Gifts and Kin Networks." *American Sociological Review* 47 (June 1982): 383–92.

Cheal, David. *The Gift Economy*. New York: Routledge, Chapman & Hall, 1988.

Cova, Bernard, Pauline; Maclaran and Alan Bradshaw. "Rethinking consumer culture theory from the postmodern to the communist horizon." *Marketing Theory* 13 (June 2013): 213–25.

Curasi, Carolyn Folkman, Linda L. Price, and Eric J. Arnould. "How Individuals' Cherished Possessions Become Families' Inalienable Wealth." *Journal of Consumer Research* 31 (December 2004): 609–22.

Dong, Lily and Kelly Tian. "The Use of Western Brands in Asserting Chinese National Identity." *Journal of Consumer Research* 36 (October 2009): 504–23.

Douglas, Mary. "Forward: No Free Gifts." In *The Gift*, ix–xxiii. Edited by Marcel Mauss. London: Routledge, 1990.

Dubar, Claude. "La Méthode de Marcel Mauss." *Revue Française de Sociologie* 10 (October–December 1969): 515–21.

Durkheim, Emile and Marcel Mauss. *Primitive Classification*. Chicago: University of Chicago Press, 1963/1903.

Earley, Amanda. "Connecting Contexts: A Badiouian Epistemology for Consumer Culture Theory." *Marketing Theory* 14 (March 2014): 73–96.

Eckhardt, Giana M. and Fleura Bardhi. "The Relationship between Access Practices and Economic Systems." *Journal of the Association of Consumer Research* 1 (April 2016): 210–25.

Epp, Amber M. and Linda L. Price. "The Storied Life of Singularized Objects: Forces of Agency and Network Transformation." *Journal of Consumer Research* 36 (February 2010): 820–37.

Fernandez, Karen V. and John L. Lastovicka. "Making Magic: Fetishes in Contemporary Consumption." *Journal of Consumer Research* 38 (August 2011): 278–99.

Figueiredo, Bernardo and Daiane Scaraboto. "The Systemic Creation of Value through Circulation in Collaborative Consumer Networks." *Journal of Consumer Research* (December 2016): 509–33.

Fırat, Fuat and Nikhilesh Dholakia. "The Consumer Culture Theory Movement: Critique and Renewal" (this volume).

Fitchett, James A., Georgios Patsiaouras, and Andrea Davies. "Myth and Ideology in Consumer Culture Theory." *Marketing Theory* 14, no. 4 (2014): 495–506.

Fournier, Marcel. *Marcel Mauss: A Biography*. Princeton: Princeton University Press, 2006.

Gélard, Marie-Luce. "Les Techniques du Corps" de Marcel Mauss; Renouveau Ou Retour Sur Une Question Annexe?" In *Marcel Mauss, L'Anthropologie de L'un et du Multiple*, 81–100. Edited by E. Dianteill. Paris: Presses Universitaires de France, 2013.

Giesler, Markus. "Consumer Gift Systems." *Journal of Consumer Research* 33 (September 2006): 283–90.

Godelier, Maurice. "What Mauss Did Not Say." In *Values and Valuables*, 3–21. Edited by C. Werner and D. Bell. Walnut Creek, CA: Altamira Press, 2004.

Graeber, David. "Consumption." *Current Anthropology* 52 (August 2011): 489–511.

Hallowell, A. I. *Culture and Experience*. Philadelphia: University of Pennsylvania Press, 1955.

Hau, Mark "Producing Culture: A Reading of Marshall Sahlins' Culture and Practical Reason." http://socanth101.blogspot.dk/2012/02/producing-culture-reading-of-marshall.html, accessed 30/09/2016.

Ho, D. Y. F. "Selfhood and Identity in Confucianism, Taoism, Buddhism, and Hinduism: Contrasts with the West." *Journal for the Theory of Social Behaviour* 25, no. 2 (1995): 115–39.

Humphreys, Ashlee. "Semiotic Structure and the Legitimation of Consumption Practices: The Case of Casino Gambling." *Journal of Consumer Research* 37 (October 2010): 490–510.

Hyde, Lewis. *The Gift, Imagination and the Erotic Life of Property*. New York: Vintage Books, 1979.

Jafari, Aliakbar and Christina Goulding. "'We Are Not Terrorists!' UK-Based Iranians, Consumption Practices and the 'Torn Self'." *Consumption, Markets & Culture* 11 (June 2008): 73–91.

James, Wendy. "'One of Us': Marcel Mauss and English Anthropology." In *Marcel Mauss: A Centenary Tribute*, 3–28. Edited by Wendy James and N. J. Allen. New York: Bergahnn Books, 1998.

Jenkins, Tim. "Derrida's Reading of Mauss." In *Marcel Mauss: A Centenary Tribute*, 83–96. Edited by Wendy James and N. J. Allen. New York: Bergahnn Books, 1998.

Joy, Annamma. "Gift Giving in Hong Kong and the Continuum of Social Ties." *Journal of Consumer Research* 28 (September 2001): 239–56.

Karababa, Eminegül and Güliz Ger. "Early Modern Ottoman Coffeehouse Culture and the Formation of the Consumer Subject." *Journal of Consumer Research* 37 (February 2011): 737–60.

Lamberton, Cait Poynor and Randall L. Rose. "When Is Ours Better than Mine? A Framework for Understanding and Altering Participation in Commercial Sharing Systems." *Journal of Marketing* 76 (July 2012): 109–25.

Leach, Jerry W. and Edmund Leach, eds. *The Kula: New Perspectives on Massim Exchange*. London: Cambridge University Press, 1983.

Lévi-Strauss, Claude. *The Savage Mind*. Chicago: Chicago University Press, 1966.

———. *Introduction to the Work of Marcel Mauss*, trans. Felicity Baker. London: Routledge & Kegan Paul, 1987/1950.

Levy-Bruhl, Lucien. *Primitive Mentality*. London: George Allen & Unwin, 1923.

Mauss, Marcel. "Les Techniques Du Corps." *Journal de Psychologie* 32, nos. 3–4 (1934), 3–23.

———. "A Category of the Human Mind: The Notion of Person; the Notion of Self" (trans. W. D. Halls). In *The Category of the Person: Anthropology, Philosophy, History*, 1–25. Edited by Michael Carrithers, Steven Collins, and Steven Lukes. Cambridge: Cambridge University Press, 1985/1938.

———. *The Gift: Essay on the Form and Function of Exchange*. London: Routledge, 1990/1924.

Maynard, Ashley E., Patricia M. Greenfield, and Carla P. Childs. "Culture, History, Biology, and Body: Native and Non-Native Acquisition of Technological Skill." *Ethos* 27 (September 1999): 379–402.

McCall, Grant. "Association and Power in Reciprocity and Requital: More on Mauss and the Maori." *Oceania* 52 (June 1982): 303–19.

Miller, Daniel. *Material Culture and Mass Consumption*. New York: Basil Blackwell, 1987.

———. *A Theory of Shopping*. Ithaca: Cornell University Press, 1998.

Moisander, Johanna, Lisa Peñaloza, and Anu Valtonen. "From CCT to CCC: Building Consumer Culture Community." In *Explorations in Consumer Culture Theory*, 7–33. Edited by J. F. Sherry, Jr. and E. Fischer. London: Routledge, 2009.

Moisio, Risto and Mariam Beruchashvili. "Questing for Well-Being at Weight Watchers: The Role of the Spiritual-Therapeutic Model in a Support Group." *Journal of Consumer Research* 36 (February 2010): 857–75.

Murray, Jeff B., Julie L. Ozanne, and Jon M. Shapiro. "Revitalizing the Critical Imagination: Unleashing the Crouched Tiger." *Journal of Consumer Research* 21 (December 1994): 559–65.

Ritzer, George. *The McDonaldization of Society*. Los Angeles: Pine Forge Press, 2009.

Sahlins, Marshall. *Stone Age Economics*. New York: Aldine, 1972.

———. *Culture and Practical Reason*. Chicago: University of Chicago Press, 1976.

———. *Islands of History*. Chicago: University of Chicago Press, 1986.

———. "Goodbye to Tristes Tropes: Ethnography in the Context of Modern World History." *The Journal of Modern History* 65 (March 1993): 1–25.

———. *How "Natives" Think: About Captain Cook, for Example*. Chicago: University of Chicago Press, 1995.

———, Thomas Bargatzky, Nurit Bird-David, John Clammer, Jacques Hamel, Keiji Maegawa, and Jukka Siikala. "The Sadness of Sweetness: The Native Anthropology of Western Cosmology [and Comments and Reply]." *Current Anthropology* 37 (June 1996): 395–428.

———. "Two or Three Things That I Know about Culture." *The Journal of the Royal Anthropological Institute* 5 (September 1999): 399–421.

———. *The Western Illusion of Human Nature*. Ann Arbor: Prickly Paradigm Press, 2005.

———. *Culture in Practice: Selected Essays*. Cambridge: MIT Press and New York: Zero Books, 2008.

———. "The Conflicts of the Faculty." *Critical Inquiry* 35 (Summer 2009): 997–1017.

Scaraboto, Daiane. "Selling, Sharing, and Everything in between: The Hybrid Economies of Collaborative Networks." *Journal of Consumer Research* 42 (June 2015): 152–76.

Schlanger, Nathan. 1998. "The Study of Techniques as an Ideological Challenge: Technology, Nation and Humanity in the Work of Marcel Mauss." In *Marcel Mauss: A Centenary Tribute*, 192–212. Edited by Wendy James and N. J. Allen. New York: Bergahnn Books, 1998.

Shankar, Avi, Bernard Cova, and Robert Kozinets. *Consumer Tribes*. Oxon and New York: Routledge, 2011.

Sherry, John F., Jr. "Gift Giving in Anthropological Perspective." *Journal of Consumer Research* 10 (September 1983): 157–68.

———, Mary Ann McGrath, and Sidney J. Levy. "The Dark Side of the Gift." *Journal of Business Research* 28 (November 1993): 225–44.

Shove, Elizabeth and Mika Pantzar. "Consumers, Producers and Practices." *Journal of Consumer Culture* 5 (March 2005): 43–64.

Strathern, Marilyn. *The Gender of the Gift: Problems with Women and Problems with Society in Melanesia*. Berkeley and Los Angeles: University of California Press, 1990.Thompson, Craig T., Eric J. Arnould, and Markus Giesler. "Discursivity, Difference, and Dialogue: Genealogical Reflections on the CCT Heteroglossia." *Marketing Theory* 13 (June 2013): 149–74.

Thompson, Craig J. and Tuba Üstüner. "Women Skating on the Edge: Marketplace Performances as Ideological Edgework." *Journal of Consumer Research* 42 (August 2015): 235–65.

Thompson, Craig T. and Markus Giesler. "A Tutorial in Consumer Research: Process Theorization in Cultural Consumer Research." *Journal of Consumer Research* 43 (December 2016); 497–508. Thompson, Craig and Kelly Tian. "Reconstructing the South: How Commercial Myths Compete for Identity Value through the Ideological Shaping of Popular Memories and Countermemories." *Journal of Consumer Research* 34 (February 2008): 595–613.

Van Baal, Jan. *Reciprocity and the Position of Women*. Assen: Van Gorcum, 1975.

Warnier, Jean-Pierre. "Retour à Marcel Mauss." In *Construire la Culture Matérielle : L'homme qui pensait avec ses doigts*, 1–59. Paris: Presses Universitaires de France, 1999.

Watson, James, ed. *Golden Arches East*. Stanford: Stanford University Press; 1995.

Weinberger, Michelle F. and Melanie Wallendorf. "Gifting at the Intersection of Contemporary Moral and Market Economies." *Journal of Consumer Research* 39 (June 2012): 74–92.

Weiner, Annette B. *Women of Value, Men of Renown*. Austin: University of Texas, 1976.

———. *Inalienable Possessions: The Paradox of Keeping-While Giving*. Berkeley and Los Angeles: University of California, 1992.

White, Geoffrey M. and John Kirkpatrick, eds. *Person, Self and Experience: Exploring Pacific Ethnopsychologies*. Berkeley: University of California Press, 1985.

Williams, Raymond. *Marxism and Literature*. Oxford: Oxford University Press, 1977.

14 Brand Doings in a Performative Perspective

An Analysis of Conceptual Brand Discourses

Matthias Bode and Dannie Kjeldgaard

For eighty years, with almost admirable stoicism, the American Marketing Association (AMA) remains loyal to its brand definition. The definition in 2015 is in essence identical to the 1935 Definitions Report (Conejo and Wooliscroft 2015). A common critical reflection on that situation points out the lack of adjustment to fundamental changes in the social, economic, cultural, and historical environments in which brands are produced, negotiated, and consumed. And there is no shortage on working toward the "holy grail of defining 'brand' " (de Chernatony 2009). Scholars have discussed brands as symbolic repositories for living our lives (Fournier 1998); as cultural, ideological, and political objects (Schroeder and Salzer-Mörling 2006); as the basic prerequisite to a company's long-term market success (Kapferer 1997); as a self-help guide for improving one's life (Montoya 2002; Peters 1997); as the "core activity of capitalism" (Holt 2006); and the epitome of the decline of Western civilization (Klein 2000). However, the argument that "authors have failed to fully develop the brand construct and its boundaries" is still relevant (de Chernatony and Riley 1998, 417) and as a consequence hampers the development of branding theories (Gabbott and Jevons 2009, 119).

We contribute to the brand construct discussion from a consumer culture theory (CCT) perspective with a change of perspective. We are not presenting a final "correct, better, inclusive" definition. Our focus is rather on analyzing the development of brand definitions as discourses that construct the subjects and the worlds of which they speak, rather than just describing them differently.

We share the idea of branding as one of marketing's ideological foci (Banet-Weiser 2012; Levy and Luedicke 2013; Lury 2009). Furthermore, we also think that the construction of brand definitions has a certain persuasive power and rhetorical strength (Holt 2004). Our theoretical approach is therefore based upon metaphors (Lakoff and Johnson 1980) and current approaches on marketplace performativity (Mason, Kjellberg, and Hagberg 2015). The specific discursive framing of brands constitutes certain acts, skills, practices, and beliefs that have material effects on how brand managers, brand researchers, brand activists, media, government, nongovernmental organizations, and so forth enact brand-related practices.

In this chapter, we carry out a critical theoretical overview of paradigmatic brand and branding conceptions and advance a novel conceptual approach to brands and branding that draws on performance theory. We develop paradigmatic brand types (Goodyear 1996; Louro and Cunha 2001; Mazurek 2014) from the theoretical discussion of brands over the last fifty years, with an emphasis on rapprochements between socioculturally oriented conceptions of brands (Diamond et al. 2009; Holt 2004; Kozinets et al. 2002; McAlexander, Schouten, and Koenig 2002; Schau, Muñiz, and Arnould 2009) and more traditional brand-management frames.

The analysis will focus on three prototypical brand discourses that can be found in the (managerial and critical) academic brand management literature.

1. The brand-as-object: These definitional approaches focus on the product itself (the identification). As a reflection of brand theorization, the objective realities of the brand are basically the result of managerial efforts.
2. The brand-in-the-mind: This definitional frame focuses on the subjective reality of the consumer's brand perceptions (e.g., as associative networks). The consumer's mind becomes the locus to control, verify, and adjust intended brand realities.
3. The brand-in-culture: Here the focus shifts from the product and the consumer toward the wider sociocultural environment of the "brand habitat" (Sherry 2005) that resembles the idea of the "brandscape" (Sherry 1998), which is however more often used in a narrower spatial context. Typically, the brand is positioned in a cultural space as a configuration of meanings, which is contextually created by a wider range of stakeholders.

We argue that existing theory is mired in three fundamental assumptions: a dyadic comprehension of brand relations, an essentializing understanding of the brand, and a semantic notion of brand meaning. We propose a complementary branding model based on the idea of performativity, which connects to an emergent discussion of performative aspects in marketing (Araujo and Kjellberg 2010; Deighton 1992; Dion and Arnould. 2016; Holt and Thompson 2004; Lucarelli and Hallin 2015; Nakassis 2012) and the so-called performative turn in social science (Gond and Cabantous 2016; Madison and Hamera 2003).

The "brand-in-performances" frame goes beyond a symbolic perspective and focuses on brands coming alive in constellations of discourses, practices, meanings, and materialities. The brand has a relational existence, a relation between brand users, brand performances, and an observing audience, rather than "just" in the branded object, the mind of consumers, or cultural spaces. In this way our perspective links toward assemblage approaches (Canniford and Bajde 2015; Lury 2009; Parmentier and Fischer 2015). In their brand application, Onya and Ryan (2015) use the sociotechnical agencement concept to explain the wider contextuality of performativity, where the performative brand is a part and a consequence of an assemblage with different actors, agencies, materialities, and relations.

Our perspective also aligns with both the notion that marketing is intrinsically a performative discipline (Deighton 1992) and the approach to marketing practices from dramaturgical perspectives (Goulding and Saren 2016; Moisio and Arnould 2005; Shulman 2016). A performative perspective enables branding academics and practitioners to consider elements of the branding process that present theory does not consider. Calls in marketing—often emerging from B2B or nation brand cases—for branding conceptions that can encompass a multiactor perspective (Diamond et al. 2009; Merrilees and Herington 2012; Parmentier and Fischer 2015; Vallaster and von Wallpach 2013) and an emphasis on brand practices and participant networks (Mäläskä, Saraniemi, and Tähtinen 2011; Schau, Muñiz, and Arnould 2009) point to the fact that existing branding theory is found wanting. Clearly, significant advances in branding theory are still attainable, and the "loop of socio-cultural branding" (Diamond et al. 2009) should not be closed. In this chapter, we suggest that a branding conceptualization based on performance theory can meet the calls for new perspectives and mitigate limitations in existing theory.

Branding Metaphors We Live By

In the following argument, we provide a typological review and critique of predominant approaches in branding theory to identify the main assumptions about brands and branding in terms of *brand relations* (who are thought to be the main actors in the branding process?), *brand ontology* (what is the nature of "a brand"?) and finally *brand content* (the main assumption about the roles and function of brands in the market with a focus on the role of meaning).

In his introduction of a cultural branding model, Holt (2004, xii) mentions the rhetorical strength of existing traditional brand models. They frame how we think about brands and subsequently also act in a strategic perspective. It is the power of brand metaphors and sense-making mechanisms (Lakoff and Johnson 1980) that structures the way brands are treated in the academic literature and managed in practice (Davies and Chun 2003; Fillis and Rentschler 2008; Ng and Koller 2013; Stern 2006). In a similar way, Avis and Aitken (2015, 210) speak of a contingency between applying a certain brand lens and "finding" such brands in market practices. As branding metaphors are in themselves highly valued "idea brands" in the academic and consulting realm, there is a constant negotiation of the interpretive meaning of these sense-making mechanisms. In our attempt to describe conceptual differences in branding approaches, we do not assume a teleological evolution of brand paradigms, in the sense of a necessary evolution from naïve to current conceptions, as finalized, elaborated, and sophisticated "better" brand paradigms (Goodyear 1996).

Existing categorizations differ in their emphasis on academic or managerial brand discourses, the micro or macro level, and the use of historical time frames (see Wilson and Levy 2012; Broderick and de Chernatony 2009 and Low anf Fullerton 1994 for discussions of brand paradigms). We position our metaphor categorization of branding discourses by a primary focus on the theoretical discussion of brands, while acknowledging the multidirectional influence between brand academics and practitioners (as consultants or brand managers). We furthermore stress inherent assumptions, the explanatory potential, and performative effects of brand discourses, and less on the cause of the evolution of discourses. Our approach centers on stereotypical condensation rather than historical differentiation. The branding approaches do not replace each other but overlap; they can still all be present in the literature or in the way of thinking about brands, and they can appear in practice also in more hybrid versions.

The Brand-as-Object

Taking the example of the Coca-Cola brand, in this view the brand can be found in and on the product itself, in the Coca-Cola logo, the typical shape of the bottle, and the red color. This is how the brand can be identified and how this brand is differentiated from other soda drinks. In this way, the brand-as-object metaphor reflects theorization of brands as objective realities that emerge from the marketing managerial efforts. For Merz, He, and Vargo (2009, 330), such a perspective approaches the value of a brand as being embedded in the physical good. In the traditional marketing literature, the origin of this metaphor is rooted in the dominant transition from unbranded to branded goods in Western industrialized economies in the late nineteenth century, which coincides with the emergence of marketing as an academic discipline and business practice (Bartels 1988; Jones 1994; Maynard 1941; Merz, He, and Vargo 2009). Although the history of branding practices reaches further back (Eckhardt and Bengtsson 2010; Moore and Reid 2008; Roper and Parker 2006), a common approach is to separate such developments by the emergence of the "modern" brand (Avis and Aitken 2015).

The first conceptual discussions of brands (e.g., Findeisen 1924; Mataja 1910) were dominated by a focus on the functional benefits of branding: consumers could learn about products directly from the producer (through advertising), and they could demand these brands from their retailers. Before, when they were buying, for instance, coffee, they were dependent on whatever coffee the retailer sold them in a brown, unmarked bag. This focus is obvious in the definition of a brand proposed by the AMA in 1960, which is still in use (Aaker 1991; Keller 2008, 2; Kotler et al. 1996): "A name, term, sign, symbol, or design, or a combination of them, intended to identify the goods or services of one seller or group of sellers and to differentiate them from those of competitors." The identification and differentiation focus emphasizes the aspect of a visual and verbal marking of the product, which refers more to the legal definition of a trademark. This sense-making mechanism tends to frame branding in terms of its objective impact on a product: what a product looks like, how it is named, or how the logo is developed. As a consequence, the sensory-perceivable reality of a branded product becomes the focus of thinking about branding. There is a positivist logic of the brand-as-object paradigm that leads to a conception of the brand as a more static entity ("the branded product can only change when the company is changing the visual-verbal branding strategy"). The final brand is then the direct result of the activities that are subsumed under the name of brand management. The role of the consumer in this paradigm is reduced to be the final passive recipient of the finished brand as an object. The optional behavioral range for the consumer is limited to accepting or rejecting the brand, based on positive or negative brand attitudes.

This paradigm has been criticized in the literature already in the 1990s as being too product focused and too mechanical (Arnold 1992; Crainer 1995). Yet, this conceptualization still circulates in extant literature, as well as in marketing practice. It is this understanding of a brand-as-object that is often foregrounded in critical discussions about a managerial practice that focus only on brand management. When Rust and colleagues argue in favor of a managerial focus on customer equity instead of brand equity, they summarize the dangers of neglecting a more active customer, as

> most marketing managers speak about the value of a brand as though it were solid and monolithic . . . Managers begin to believe that the value of their brand is somehow intrinsic-that, like a diamond in a necklace, the brand has an objective, inherent value. (Rust, Zeithaml and Lemon 2004, 113)

In this way, managers appropriate their own ideological goal. Also in the brand-as-object frame, the finalized brand is a result of a relational process, in differentiating the brand from competing brands. However, the goal of brand management is to hide the artificial, constructive, and contextual process of developing a brand for the consumer. In the end, the consumer is supposed to perceive the brand "as if" it is a singular, autonomous entity, "as if" it is defined by inherent properties and not by external relations (Goldman 1992; Williamson 1978). In their response to the customer equity discussion, Leone and colleagues (2006) point out that there are understandings of a brand that also incorporate the more dynamic and idiosyncratic customer contribution to what a brand stands for. This brand metaphor can be called "brand-in-the-mind."

The Brand-in-the-Mind

With this metaphor, the brand cannot be found on a bottle. The brand Coca-Cola is rather made up of the associations that brand managers and consumers have with regard to "Coca-Cola." Mental construc- tions as "refreshment," "joy," and "fun" are what the brand is made of. Consumers might have a different idea of what a brand stands for from that of the responsible brand manager. In the brand-as-object paradigm, the interpretation would be that consumers misunderstood the brand promise and do not accept the brand as it is manifested in the market. The branding focus would then be directed toward a modified promo- tional strategy for better identification and differentiation of the brand for the target group of consumers.

Several developments challenged this sense-making mechanism for brands. First, advances were made in the development of a consumer behavior discipline, manifested in the first textbooks (Engel, Kollat, and Blackwell 1968; Howard and Sheth 1969; Nicosia 1966) and the foun- dation of the Association for Consumer Research (ACR) in 1969 and the *Journal of Consumer Research* in 1974. These processes intensified research on consumer decisions and information-stimuli processing. The former black box of the consumers' minds became an intensive research focus with implications for the marketing and branding literature. But the basic difference for new brand conceptions was coming into shape and to the attention of brand managers as seen, for example, in Ries and Trout's ideas, originally published in the early 1970s in a trade magazine that later became the best-selling publication *Positioning: The Battle for Your Mind* (1981). In this perspective, the "successful brand," usually via a fixed benefit-product category association, occupies a highly com- petitive position in the consumer's mind. The brand entity conceptually changes from the material object into a psychological entity, either in the consumer's or the brand manager's mind. These differences, between the consumer's and the company's idea of what the brand constitutes, is often discussed in the relationships between brand image (Levy 1959; Newman 1957) and brand identity (Aaker and Joachimsthaler 2000; Kapferer 1997). Brand image basically includes how actual, potential, or oppositional consumers perceive the brand. It finds expression in psycho- logical variables such as associative networks, brand knowledge, or feel- ings toward the brand: "a brand exists in the brain as a neural associative network" (Batey 2008, 114). Brand identity on the other hand focuses on the strategically defined idea of a brand, the brand essence, or brand vision (for a discussion of the relation and differences of image and identity, see Christensen and Askegaard 2001). As de Chernatony (2001, 19) phrases it, "Brands are complex offerings that are conceived in brand plans but ultimately they reside in consumers' minds."

The traditional brand management literature has produced a wide variety of brand identity models to guide strategic brand management process (Aaker and Joachimsthaler 2000). They all share the basic move away from the criticized focus on the brand "component parts: the brand name, its logo, design, or packaging, advertising or sponsorship" (Kapferer 1997, 11). Where these models differ is in the assumed relationship between brand image and identity and the chosen focus on the consumer's or the company's mind as the adequate managerial reference point. What they share is a basic assumption that what matters for a brand is not the object but "what resides in the minds of consumers" (Dahlen, Lange, and Smith 2010, 213) and hence a disentanglement of the brand from the material reality of the brand object toward mental constructions. The rise of neuropsychology has additionally enforced the idea that brands live and die in the mind of consumers (Gordon 2002; Plassmann, Ramsøy, and Milosavljevi 2012). As O'Shaughnessy (2006, 90) criticizes, these developments run the danger of treating concepts like brand images as real entities located in the mind.

A consequence of the changed role of subjective perceptions is the increased conceptual importance of the consumer who is not just the "receiver" of the brand anymore. The consumer has to conclude that a brand exists (conceptualized in constructs like "brand awareness" or "brand salience") and in a particular way (conceptualized in constructs like "brand associations" or "brand attitude"), based on the actions of strategic brand management. Without perceiving the brand, the brand would not enter the realm of material reality. In this sense, a working and successful brand is based on the application of a set of brand management tools, mediated through the consumer. The consumer's mind is then the locus to control, verify, and adjust the intended brand reality. When brands are predominantly relevant as psychological representations, brand management then logically becomes the management of these representations (Rosenbaum-Elliot, Percy, and Pervan 2015). Still, similar to the object paradigm, the brand is a static entity, which has to be adjusted from time to time.

The Brand-as-Culture

With this metaphor, the brand Coca-Cola is neither located on the product or in the mind of users. Rather, the brand Coca-Cola can be found in a cultural space as a configuration of meanings, which are contextually created—for example, a symbol for utopian internationalism, Americanness, capitalist globalization, world unity, or nostalgia (Kucuk 2015). With such a sense-making mechanism, brands are seen as the products of culture and reside in culture. In this way, the main empirical anchor point to locate brands moves away both from the product as object and the consumers' mind toward the broader construct of culture. The approach takes as a theoretical starting point the ideas of Sidney Levy (1959, 118) who suggested that "people buy things not only for what they can do, but also for what they mean." One factor was the realization that consumers are less passive than assumed in existing brand paradigms. In the brand-in-the-mind model, consumers are conceptualized as necessary participants in the branding process, as they have to develop a knowledge structure of brand-relevant information in their mind (Keller 2008). They can engage with a brand and develop knowledge structures, but they can also focus their mental energy on subjectively more important issues and avoid the brand or they can develop unintended brand information. In this model, brand management has either succeeded or failed in terms of activating the intended brand meaning in the minds of the consumers. The company can try to create a brand, but it is only the consumer who determines if a brand becomes alive and meaningful (Timacheff and Rand 2001).

In the brand-as-culture approach, the conceptualization of the consumer's contribution to the brand is fundamentally changed. Consumers are not the final arbiters anymore; they are now seen as active partners of marketers in creating a brand. Actual brand meanings are seen as co-authored by the consumer, not just adopted in the correct or wrong way (Bengtsson and Östberg 2006). Marketers and consumers are understood as engaging jointly in a cultural space producing the reality of the brand. As Sherry (2005) points out, this goes beyond a reception-theory recognition of active readers of a text toward agentic meaning processes by playfulness and actively searching for wider meanings ("questing"). This means the company has lost the exclusive control over brand meanings (Kelly 1998; Levine 2000; Veloutsou 2009, 128). The phenomenon is also realized by adherents of the brand-in-the-mind model: "Brand equity is increasingly built by activities outside the company's direct control" (Keller and Lehmann 2005, 27). However, the conclusions that brand scholars are drawing differ. In a cultural approach to branding, this is not seen as a problem to be solved but as a necessary and productive condition for the creation of meaningful brands. Examples are the strategic responses outlined by Fournier and Avery (2011) or Quinton (2013), which are based on degrees of conceding control to consumers or leveraging the situation by debate, dialogue, and interactions.

The theoretical constitution of the paradigm was informed and shaped by two different research streams that overlapped and influenced each other. First, in the 1990s the discussion about products turned into an increased focus on adding service aspects to create value. As "servitization" (Vandermerwe and Rada 1988), the discussion reflected the increasing significance of the service industry and hybridization of business models (e.g., cars + banking services, or restaurants + music CDs). In service marketing, the integrative, active element of the consumer in value creation was, by definition, already established. Furthermore, the rapid development in information and communication technologies like the Internet and Web 2.0 platforms increased the possibilities for consumers to actively participate in the branding process, through customizations, interactive communication, or personal communication with global network effects (McKenna 1995). A main discussion point was now how much the power base in the marketplace had shifted in favor of the consumer (Pires et al. 2006). For the brand manager, a typical recommendation was now that command-and-control branding does not work anymore online (Christodoulides et al. 2006). Mitchell (2001, 260) speaks of the outdated model of the traditional brand manager as an "inveterate control freak [who] . . . wants to control everything about his brand." Seminal publications that pooled these changes and tried to develop a coherent strategic response were by Prahalad and Ramaswamy on "value co-creation" (Prahalad and Ramaswamy (2002), and in the marketing field, the initial "Service-Dominant-Logic" paper by Stephen Vargo and Robert Lusch (2004). Lusch and Vargo (2006) framed consumers as cocreators of value, treating them as operant resources, endogenous to exchange and value creation instead of operand resources, where marketing is doing something with the passive consumers.

In a second research stream, the cocreation of value was approached as the cocreation of meaning. It was through the work of symbolic consumer behavior researchers like Elizabeth Hirschman and Morris Holbrook (1981) that the Levy position on the meanings in consumption was channeled into the CCT research program (Arnould and Thompson 2005). Although there are methodologically diverse conceptions of consumption meanings as more phenomenological, semiotic, postmodern, or psychological, a basic reference point is McCracken's (1986) model of meaning transfer. He describes first how culturally shared meanings can enter the life of consumers through brands, extends the authorship for brand meanings from companies to further cultural systems like fashion, and emphasizes the relevance of personalized meanings in relation to the managerial meaning intentions. Following this model, the meaning cocreation can then be defined as "the adaptation of culturally-shared meanings to the person's unique circumstance for purposes of individual communication and categorization" (Allen, Fournier, and Miller 2008, 786). This paradigmatic core is based on the dyad between the company and the consumer with brands forming part of a mediating cultural world (Schroeder and Salzer-Mörling 2006). In enriching psychological perspectives on branding, culture is elevated to play a decisive role in the potentiality and realization of brand meanings. First, culture becomes the inevitable background context for the company, the brand and the consumer. It is only within cultural systems that meanings can become possible: brands live in cultures (Holt 2004). This is a conceptual difference to the brand-in-the-mind theory, where the cultural context is an exogenous variable at best and information-distorting noise at worst. In this way, the brand becomes a dynamic entity, dependent on cultural codes, space, and time. Furthermore, cultural systems are analyzed in their role as a resource pool for creating meaning potentials (McCracken 1986) and as a meaning author outside of the company's sphere (Thompson and Tian 2008).

The research focus in the cultural brand paradigm is on the role of brands in consumer identity projects (Luedicke, Thompson, and Giesler 2010), consumer collectives as brand meaning authors (e.g., Kozinets 2007; McAlexander, Schouten, and Koenig 2002; Muñiz and O'Guinn 2001), and the emergence of oppositional brand meanings (Thompson and Arsel 2004) and their implications for brand strategy (Thompson, Rindfleisch, and Arsel 2006). The research has a strong consumer-driven tendency.

Efforts to also a more managerial point of view are less developed. An exception is the cultural branding model by Holt (2004, Holt and Cameron 2010), which concentrates on iconic brands that perform identity myths, and, to a lesser extent, McCracken's work (2005, 2009), and the role of formation of and competition in myth markets (Thompson and Tian 2008) and the implications for responding to and acting upon a multiplicity of actors with various personal and cultural goals around the brand (Borghini et al. 2009; Kozinets et al. 2002). A shared discussion between more managerially oriented marketing theory and the CCT field predominantly takes place around the idea of co-cocreation in service-dominant logic (e.g., Arnould, Price, and Malshe 2006; Jaworski and Kohli 2006). Further indications of building bridges are the broad acceptance of Fournier's (1998) work on subjective meanings and personal brand relationships as a seminal brand study, the prominent discussion of limitations in the psychological brand model (Keller and Lehmann 2005), and the publication of new hybrid textbooks, which try to combine a cultural brand model within a psychological brand frame (Dahlen, Lange, and Smith 2010).

Assumptions in Current Branding Theory

There is a set of shared assumptions about brands and branding that cuts across the three types of brand discourses. Although they appear in different versions in concrete examples of the discourses, in a stylized form they can be formulated as follows.

> Brand relations: The central constituent of the brand is the producer-consumer relationship. The brand-as-object approach considers the

producer to be the prime instigator and constructor of the brand and places less emphasis on the consumer. The brand-in-the-mind approach shifts emphasis to the consumer, and the more phenomenologically based parts of the brand-as-culture approach look at the role of brands in the lived experiences of consumers (e.g., Fournier 1998). The brand-as-culture approach looks at both producers and consumers as culturally embedded agents and advocates more and more a postdyadic perspective. However, rather than opening up the perspective qualitatively (e.g., in terms of assemblages or networks) the producer-consumer dyad still works as the primary relationship of branding, and the discussion is focused on the question of power relations between both entities (Schroeder 2009). The next logical step (and not the starting point) is then the quantitative extension via further influences.

Brand ontology: In the brand-as-object approach, the role of the brand is to be a material manifestation with the main functions of identification and differentiation, and in the brand-in-the-mind approach, the brand serves as a set of associations in consumers' minds. In the brand-as-culture approach, brands are manifestations of cultural meanings. The brand-as-culture approach characterizes the nature of the brand as either a produced, consumed, or interpreted object. Brands are related to wider cultural processes but are nevertheless thought of as quasi entities—for example, as "containers of myths" (Holt 2004) or a repository, storehouse, or powerhouse of meaning (Sherry 2005). For Lucarelli and Hallin (2015, 87) this understanding of brands runs into the danger of defining a brand by "the bundle of components that are said to constitute it and that have been included in it over time." It can be argued that newer approaches in the CCT field, like practice theories (Warde 2005), ANT applications (Bajde 2013), and philosophies of new materialities (Borgerson 2014), can both weaken and strengthen the objectified perspective in branding. Such approaches can, on the one hand, emphasize a more processual and network perspective with stronger performance and practice elements. On the other hand, the utilization of product affordances and object agencies can end up with fixed, stable categories rather than emphasizing consumption and brands as "continuous dynamic and relational accomplishments in intersectings of multiple practices in everyday life" (Halkier and Jensen 2011, 107),

Brand content: At first sight, the brand approaches differ in their conceptualization and terminology of brand content as associations and meanings. In the brand-as-object approach, the meaning of a brand is projected into the brand's object as an inherent value of the brand. "The brand is not the product, but it gives meaning and defines its identity in both time and space" (Kapferer 1997, 17). In the brand-in-the-mind approach, brand meanings are understood psychologically to be the result of consumers' perception and refer to the "semantic and symbolic features of a brand" (Batey 2008, 111). Within the brand-as-culture approach, a more semiotic and hermeneutical perspective emphasizes the continuous renegotiation of meanings. Instead of producing static meaning units, the diverse interpretations of consumers tend to foster more unstable, ambiguous, and dynamic meaning systems (Kucuk 2015; Mick and Buhl 1992; Scott 1994; Stern 2006).

Although the three approaches differ in assuming where meanings originate and in the degree of stability of meanings, they share a tendency to see meanings primarily in their relation to the object. For instance, what does the brand Starbucks stand for? What does it mean and for whom? Even if the brand meaning space is a contestable terrain, in the end, different actors construct a relationship between the brand Starbucks, for example, and its semantic meanings, which can range from "corporate interloper" to "a comfortable communal space in which consumers can relax and socialize" (Thompson, Rindfleisch, and Arsel 2006).

These main assumptions about brands and branding form the basis of a comparison of the explanatory value of these approaches with an approach based on the theories of performativity.

Performative Theory

The increased use of the noun "performance," the adjective "performative," or the verb "to perform" in current social science discussion has been discussed as an indication for a general "performative turn" (Alexander 2005, 415; Burke 2005, 35; Cherry 2008; Denzin 2001, 25; Kincheloe and McLaren 2005, 314; Roberts 2007, 52). The academic embodiment in the form of *performative social science* (PSS) can be defined as the open, inquiring, creative, dynamic, reflexive, and activist endeavor of research as a performance, by a performance, of a performance, and in a performance (Roberts 2008). PSS focuses on the doing, the active, the processual, and the lively instead of on fixed entities. As a boundary-crossing, interdisciplinary constellation, it is influenced by drama and theater studies, performance art, social science, ethnography, and linguistics. The concepts of social behavior as performance are strongly shaped by Goffman's concept of role-playing (1956) and Kenneth Burke's "situated modes of action" (1945) and further developed by the anthropologist Victor Turner (1982) and his works on rituals and social drama. The linguistic influence is especially strong through the concept of performativity as a qualitative transformation of the relationship between the symbolic and material sphere. This relates to a general tendency to integrate studying performances (as a more scientific endeavor) and doing performances (as a more aesthetic endeavor) (Schechner 2006, 2).

A performance in the PSS context can be understood as a framed behavioral event, which involves a performer and an audience (which can also be the performing self), and is characterized by an interplay between an actual performance and an existing blueprint for the performance. A performance is not an essential, inherent feature of an object but a relation between performers, actions, and audience. It is a marked or framed event, whereby the performative "frame" is often established by institutionalized settings or means of metacommunication, like a wink (Goffman 1974). In this sense, a performance can be characterized as restored (or twice-behaved) behavior (Schechner 2006, 34). There is no performance without an existing preperformance, without being based on preexisting models, scripts, or patterns. Every performance as an event is unique and different from each other in terms of the recombination and the context but is based on restored behavior by the constituent parts.

The term "performance" is not new in marketing discourse, but the specific conceptual use in a PSS sense is. A common understanding in marketing theory reduces a performance to entertainment and an artistic context (Bouissac 1987). An example is the research on concerts or musical performances (Minor et al. 2004). In a wider context, the use of performance related to the theater finds a solid application in the service delivery literature. The theater or drama frame is used metaphorically, so that consumers are treated like an audience in a play, and the servicescape becomes a stage setting for the performance (Bitner 1992; Booms and Bitner 1981; Grove and Fisk 1983; Grove, Fisk, and Dorsch 1998; Morgan, Watson, and Hemmington 2008). Closely related to this is the strategic use of the theater-performance metaphor in the work of Pine and Gilmore (1999) with their version of experience management. However, in PSS the "performance" term is not used exclusively for a performing art context. It rather focuses on performance aspects that combine aesthetic and social behavior. Performance is also used to denote a quantifiable, technical, evaluated performance, like a baseball-hitting performance (Holt 1995, 5), the successful or failing performance in games (Holbrook et al. 1984), or the performance of entities like brands or stocks (Deighton 1992, 362). This use of the "performance" term is usually not embedded in a separate theoretical context and plainly understood as behavior measured to a more or less explicit standard (Carlson 2006, 4).

The most advanced discussion of the performance term has been developed by Deighton (1992). He refers back to the conceptual work on performance in the social sciences and develops several categories and typologies of performances with an emphasis on the experienced quality of performances. His definition of a performance, incorporating the aspects of an audience, a reference standard, and a framing, comes close to the PSS conception. His insistence on an "obligation" between performer and audience also resonates with a critical PSS discussion about the relevance of an assumed responsibility of a performer to an audience (Hymes 1975). His main emphasis is on managerial options to shape the perception of market-initiated performances. Less developed is the notion of the consumer as an active subject involved in performances.

In a very broad sense the concept of performativity is used to indicate a performance-like quality in something. In a more specific sense, it implies the process of enactment through and in discursive formations. The use of the performativity concept is informed by the linguistic tradition of performance studies. It starts with the speech-act theory by Austin (1962) and further advanced by Searle (1969), with the famous example of "Yes, I take this woman to be my lawful wedded wife." These speech acts are performative in the sense that they are doing what they are referring to. The concept of "doing by saying" was later theoretically refined by Judith Butler with a focus on identity and gender. She understands gender as performative in the sense that "it is real only to the extent that it is performed" (Butler 1988, 528). Although the speech-act theory assumes a choosing subject, Butler extends the performative conception to the social realm in referring to the performance as a repetition of acts and a "reiterative and citational practice" (Butler 1993, 2). This conception relates to the aspect of restored behavior in a performance.

In marketing, the discussion of performativity enters in the form of the performative consequence of research methods and market actions. In making a difference, they have material consequences and "can help to bring into being what they also discover" (Law and Urry 2004, 392–3). Each segmentation or positioning research has always performative aspects of co-constructing the categories that are "discovered" (Hackley 2001; Heiskanen 2005; Venter, Wright, and Dibb 2015). In economics, Michel Callon (1998) has started an influential discussion in new approaches to the constitution (or formatting) of markets by the activities of social actors, like economists, lawyers, and marketers, which he calls "performativity of economics." Rather than taking markets as a given, the focus is on how markets are enacted by the relevant subjects. In his work, the economy is not something external that economists analyze. The tools of economics not only describe the economic world but also are used by market participants to make decisions about their own behavior, like trading strategies. In this way, economic models, concepts, and theories materially shape the behavior of economic actors. Economists then create market realities, when their models of how actors behave in a market influence market actors' behavior in such a way "that they better correspond to the model" (MacKenzie 2006, 19). This approach has also been applied in marketing theory (e.g., Araujo 2007; Dion and Arnould 2016; Kjellberg and Helgesson 2007, Lucarelli and Hallin 2015), although with a strong focus on the technical aspects of the necessary skills of market actors.

Studies of consumption and market rituals (see Otnes and Lowrey 2004 for an overview) are related to the performance and performativity approach. Typically, rituals are seen to be a reenactment of a script with the purpose of reflecting and maintaining a social order. However, rather than this relatively static and functional understanding of ritual, rituals have been suggested to have performative aspects (Bell 1997; Turner 1982). That is, rituals are "performative" both in a narrow sense, that rituals are performances involving actors and audience, but also in a wider sense, that ritual performances are not just the enactment of cultural structures but are creative and productive strategies and actions where actors create meaningful events out of situations characterized by indeterminacy (Brown 2003). Ritual hence is considered more open as a means through which participants construct a variety of meanings and purposes, and it stands in a dynamic relation to the social order in that it can fundamentally alter it. Rituals in such a perspective are characterized by both repeatability (a set frequency, a script) and emergence (dynamic meanings, alterations of the script, etc.). Furthermore, ritual is often characterized by a dynamic and ambiguous definition of actors and roles in terms of who is performing and who is observing, which connects with a performance perspective.

In the following sections, we suggest a further modification of the brand-as-culture approach. We argue that the currently discussed brand-as-culture frame can inhibit the analysis of significant brand processes. Existing theory underappreciates the multiplicity of brand authors in their shifting roles; a branding process that enacts the brand rather than modifies or shapes the brand as an entity in a cultural space; and the performative elements in the branding process.

Brand Relations as Brand Performances

As we have argued, one of the foundational assumptions of existing brand theory is the producer-consumer dyad. Advances in brand theory have concluded that branding is a matter of gestalts involving a multiplicity of actors pursuing and achieving various personal and cultural projects and goals (Diamond et al. 2009) and that brand value cocreation occurs in "collective enactment of practices, which favor investments in networks rather than firm-consumer dyads" (Schau, Muñiz, and Arnould 2009, 41). Although we concur with these conclusions, we argue that previous theories do not adequately conceptualize the network constitution of the brand beyond the producer-consumer dyad. These dyads are like a shadow myth that is only quantitatively expanded ("two plus *x* actors"), not qualitatively.

We argue for the value of applying a multiple-actor perspective on the branding process a priori rather than starting with the dyadic as the norm and then modifying it. With a performance perspective (Bell 1997; Schechner 2006), actors are not defined by institutional affiliation: "the subject works for Coca-Cola, therefore the subject belongs to the producer category." Rather than determining the actor as producer or consumer based on whether the actor is employed by the company, a performative perspective means looking at what roles are played in which performances: "In this performance, the subject acts as a consumer, a producer, and in a performer-audience-stage-citational references constellation."

Here the performance theory distinction between "make-belief" and "make-believe" helps to clarify further the processes of the individual role enactment of the performance participants (Schechner 2006, 42ff.). For a traditional theater perspective, the actor enters a theatrical stage to play a role. In a performance perspective, there is always an ambiguous mix of theatrical and everyday performances (see also the feedback-relations model of aesthetic performances and social dramas in Schechner 2006, 77). The more artistic, playful elements by brand actors to perform creative elements of brand engagements (e.g., citing advertising claims, using brand materials as accessories, incorporating the brand in stylized displays or sketches) are "make-believe" performances, pretending to be the actor he or she is playing with clear distinctions between the mimetic and the "real": "I am using the brand but I am not the manipulated dupe." On the other hand, "make-belief" performances blur the boundaries of "real" and pretend. Such performances (which would be a typical status display of a brand) become more theatrical so that the performance should have reality effects. A traditional actor perspective would try to frame these shifting role-identity relations with diverse links to the brand in reductive brand relationship, loyalty, or involvement concepts. This assumes role and identity as preexisting concepts rather than seeing their dynamics and tensions as coconstitutive. It also assumes that brand managers only focus on "make-belief" performances, for highly loyal, brand-loving consumers who perform the promised reality of the brand.

However, in a coconstitutive frame, taking up a role as a performer is at the same time redefining the performer's institutional role while changing roles permanently in a brand performance. Furthermore, the dynamic element implies also a quality of role fluidity. It is not so much about shifting from one role to another but about a quality of constant role renegotiations, of their definitions and qualities shifting across contexts. In the performative perspective, we can see a bartender playing with a branded drink, citing marketed properties of the brand like the Corona-lime drinking ritual, inviting customers to join in, and shifting from having a performative role to becoming an audience member observing the performances of others (customers). This kind of multiplicity of roles in connection with the practices and the shifting between roles cannot be adequately captured by the traditional dyadic perspective. Hence, it is not sufficient merely to add another type of actor in the branding process but rather to change the conceptual perspective.

We suggest that as an alternative to a dyadic perspective that brand researchers and practitioners frame the analysis of branding as a set of performances by multiple *enactors* as the basic condition of the branding process. This takes us beyond authoring or co-authoring of meanings and changes the focus to the activities and the practices—in short, the performative nature of branding.

The Brand Ontology as Processual

In existing brand theory, there is a tendency to essentialize the notion of the brand. "It" can be located in the mind of the consumer, in the authorial voice of the producer, and in culture (McCracken 2005). Furthermore, brands are often considered to have agentic qualities as, for example, being "performers of, and containers for, an identity myth" (Holt 2004, 14). The thinking in the cultural branding paradigm acknowledges a de-essentialized understanding of brand meaning but is nevertheless still caught in the notion of meaning as locatable essences, and brands and products as carriers of these essences, most notably espoused by the movement-of-meaning model (McCracken 1986; Holt (2004).

In a performative perspective, brand phenomena only exist in the performances of multiple brand enactors. This changes the main center for brand manager performances. First, it means a focus on the performance itself as brand engagement, rather than on the "final" brand result (Singh and Sonnenburg 2012). Second, rather than exploiting existing cultural resources (see, for example, the "resonance" concept of Fournier, Solomon, and Englis 2008), company branding activities are directed toward the development of the scripts and props, the setting of the stage, and the dramatizing of the whole value chain as a framing for multiple performances (Bell 1997). Examples are the iconic Coca-Cola Christmas commercials, where the arrival of a decorated delivery truck is linked to the Christmas season, or Oxfam Shelflife, which allows consumers to discover the stories, origins, and former uses of the donated products through a product QR code). In the cultural branding literature, one would assume that the brand contains mythical representation and norms of consumer performances.

In the performative view, performances by subjects acting as consumers or organizational members are made possible through the framing of the brand and the citationality of performances, also including the failing, reclassifying, inappropriate, insufficient, and mistaken potentialities (Nakassis 2012). In a related way, Parmentier and Fischer (2015) describe the activities of *America's Next Top Model* fans as reframing, remixing, and rejecting. We argue that this can make the brand meaningful as a social reality and not the other way around. This does not mean that there are no mythical elements but rather that these mythical elements allow for other meaningful practices and performance.

Performativity in a very broad sense is used to indicate a performance-like quality in something. In a more specific sense, used in a postmodern and poststructuralist context, it implies the process of enactment through and in discursive formations, informed by the linguistic tradition of Austin (1962) and Searle (1969) and later Judith Butler (1988). There is no "Coca-Cola Christmas nostalgia myth brand consumption" but only cited, reshaped, redone, varied doings of the brand in a continuous dynamic and relational way.

In this sense we refer to a performative branding frame that starts out but goes beyond "the social construction of the brand" (Muñiz and O'Guinn 2001) by arguing that "the brand" as a social reality emerges by way of a set of performative processes. There is hence an inseparability of the brand and performances.

Brand Content as Brand Doings in Becoming

When it comes to brand meanings, existing brand paradigms are unable not only to adequately capture the richness of the potentiality in emergent meanings but also, more importantly, to neglect the semiosis as the social and subjective meaning activities (Fiske 1990, 41). In psychological brand models, brand meanings become reified as either an essence hidden in the text or an independently existing cognitive representation. Rather, meaning is part of a relationship between the sign, other signs, and the sign user in a specific sociocultural context (Fiske 1990, 41). Although this general perspective is accepted in the cultural branding model (e.g., Diamond et al. 2009), the empirical reality in research is too often a separation of meanings from the meaning process in forms of meaning categories or meaning lists (e.g., Strizhakova, Coulter, Price 2008).

In a performative branding perspective, the implicit or explicit semantic meaning model would be in a first step replaced by a pragmatic meaning model with a focus on the meaning relationships and the uses of meanings (Jensen 1991; Mey 1993). In this way, the "cocreation of meaning" would be freed from a narrowly defined communication model like Hall's encoding-decoding model (1993/1980). In this model, the differences between the authorial potential meanings (in the sense of companies' brand meanings) and the realized meanings (in the sense of consumers' brand meanings) are based on socially distributed codes.

Although there have been wide criticisms of reductive elements in the encoding-decoding model (e.g., Wren-Lewis 1983), it still works as a backbone of the meaning models in the cultural branding model (Arnould and Thompson 2005, 874; Mick and Buhl 1992, 193). Meanings are conceptualized as hegemonic or oppositional meanings, in relation to contextually defined standards (Kozinets and Handelman 2004; Thompson and

Arsel 2004). But as Wren-Lewis (1983, 184) points out, "the fact that many decoders will come up with the same reading does not make that meaning an essential part of the text." Rather, there is a multiplicity of meanings that can become relevant and actualized in their specific uses. That is, meanings are performed.

Such performances among enactors of brand meanings may be multiple and ultimately point to the "unruliness" (Nakassis 2012) or "messiness" (Lucarelli and Hallin 2015) of the becoming of brands. In a performative perspective, a feature of the performance is the "consciousness of doubleness" for the performer and the audience, which can also be the performing self (Carlson 2006, 47). The reflexive performance is not just "doing" but also "showing the doing." In a theatrical performance, the actor plays the role of a magician while being aware of not "being" a magician. This goes beyond the act of "willing suspension of disbelief" where the audience believes temporarily in an illusion. For a performance perspective, it is the simultaneity of the "real" and the "illusory," the character of transition and "in- betweenness," that characterizes the consciousness (Schechner 1977).

Outlining a Performative Branding Model

On the basis of these performative perspectives on (1) brand relations, (2) brand ontology, and (3) brand content, we propose a performative branding model, which can enrich a cultural branding approach. From a performative perspective, the brand might be understood as a dynamic, relational potentiality that is materially and symbolically actualized in concrete spatio-temporal events involving brand enactors, performances, and audiences. We will now discuss this perspective in comparison to exiting brand as culture perspectives. As a caveat, it should be mentioned again that our categorizations are theoretical fictions in exaggerating typicality, whereas actual approaches are more diverse in the cultural and the performative branding category due to different, specific theoretical backgrounds inside the broad categories and individual applications.

Table 14.1 From brand culture to brand performances.

	Brand as culture	*Brand in performances*
Brand relations	dyadic subjects plus x	polyadic enactors
Brand ontology	the socially constructed brand entity	constellations of brand processes
Brand content	coconstructed meanings	doings in becoming
Methodological consequences	analysis of culture as text	analysis of culture as being performed

From Dyadic Subjects to Polyadic Enactors

In cultural branding approaches, there is a danger of starting the analysis with a producer-consumer dyad, which is then subsequently enlarged ("2 + *x*"). A performative analysis will always have a polyadic perspective on the key actors involved in the branding process as a starting process. This can be seen as a conceptual flattening of brand participants, who are understood as *en*actors. They are defined by the roles and scripts performed in the branding process rather than by institutional affiliations. An actor is usually seen as playing a role (acting out) and reproducing a prescribed role through acting close to the script, whereas an enactor is more often connected to play theory and improvisational theater, with greater freedom to perform a more loosely prescribed role (reacting to a script). The enactment also emphasizes the performative qualities of manifestations and (re)creations of the performed role (Cornelissen 2004). In this way enactors are considered active coconstituents of the brand rather than more passive actors.

From Socially Constructed Brands to Constellations of Brand Processes

We argue that the nature of "the brand" as an entity should be understood as the outcome of the range of practices and performances of a multitude of enactors. Hence, it is not "the brand" as such that performs but the range of enactors. The brand entity emerges through doings and the doing of other things than merely consuming or managing the brand. A narrow and static focus too often ends up in acknowledging the focal role of brands in culture and in the lives of consumers, either in a positive (accepting, loving, adoring) or negative (rejecting, hating, resisting) way. However, here we refer to the critical interjection of O'Guinn and Muñiz (2009, 178), who warned about forgetting the majority of brand cases, where consumers are not fanatics or anti-brand activists, where brands are not the center of life, and where brand relationships more often are "thin (but not negligible)." Such mundane performances, which are not necessarily centrally directed toward the brand and its meaning, are also constitutive of a brand and the role it is allowed to play in individual performance. An example is the widespread use of GIFs in social media interactions (Gensler, Völckner, Liu-Thompkins & Wiertz 2013). Although brands like Starbucks, Paramount, and Kraft are also actively producing brand-related GIFs, there is a flattened-out landscape of twenty-three million GIFs posted by users alone on Tumblr every day in 2015 (Isaac 2015). The brand typically plays an insignificant role in these performances, yet it is not a negligible role. It is not about brand lovers or haters. The brand becomes part of a frame for performing other central projects, like social communicative interactions, and hence also comes into being through this.

By having a multiplicity of performances, the brand—which does not have to be the focus of attention—"comes alive." We argue that the brand is a medium through which practices occur and also materializes from these practices and performances.

From Coconstructed Meanings to Doings in Becoming

Rather than understanding branding as a process of encoding and decoding by way of producers' and consumers' embeddedness in ideologies and mythologies of the market, we argue that meanings are performative outcomes. An example would be the binary discussion of authentic versus fake brands (Gundlach and Neville 2012). From a positivist discussion (where authenticity is located in the brand) to a psychological frame (where authentic brands are based on subjective associations) to a sociocultural frame (where the social constructiveness of authenticity as coconstructed meanings would be emphasized), the background assumption refers to authentic or inauthentic meanings. Recent empirical research by Liu and colleagues (2015) acknowledges a cultural pattern and adds a third logic of mixed authenticity perception to the binary system. A performative perspective emphasizes the performative acts of doubleness and in-betweenness, when brand enactors mix, remix, simulate, and play with "realness," "fakeness," and "factiousness" in diverse ways (see, e.g., Luvaas 2010; Nakassis 2012). This would also include brand enactors as brand managers. An example is Versace, who in 2013 launched the Versace Versus collection, which is based on Versace copies. Here the authentic brand is citing the fake brand that cites the authentic brand. Another example is the designer Sonique Saturday, who developed fake designer bags like the "You Fake Like This Birkin" handbag in 2015. As the handbags became successful, Gucci presented in 2016 the Gucci Ghost bag collection, imitating the fake bag design and being accused of copying the copy (Cuffe 2016). These performative acts are not just a multiplicity of meanings; they are brand doings in becoming with frames that go beyond the current focus on binary authenticity meanings.

From Culture as Text to an Analysis of Culture as Performed

In a performative perspective, the analytical focus would be the "world as performance" (Conquergood 1991). Methodologically, branding research would look into spatial and temporal constellations of performer, audience, stage, props, cited resources, embodied knowledge (e.g., as movements, gestures, habits, routines, and play), improvisations, and the actualized frames as ways of organizing information and perception.

An example would be the analysis of spatio-temporal brand stages enacted not only as a predefined stage ("with this brandfest consumers have a stage for their brand engagement") but also as quasi pop-ups by consumer enactors. As an illustration, consider the moments of engaging in the Coca-Cola "Share Happiness" campaign by playing with the shareable, split-can design. Or consider the change of the backstage and frontstage role, when backstage activities like logistics or production are framed as frontstage opportunities. An example is when the recording of music becomes a publicly shared art installation in the case of the artist PJ Harvey's ninth album in 2015, where delivery by drones and robots becomes a spectacle in itself. This is linked to the idea of transparent supply chains (New 2010). However, instead of focusing on the intended trust and reputation values to support the product brand, here the backstage activities are becoming additional values by themselves.

Although performative branding incidents often can be incorporated in cultural branding research projects, we should remind ourselves that every ontological positioning has subsequent epistemological ramifications. For a long time, the Geertzian "culture as a text" model was a guiding principle for the development of interpretive consumer research (ICR) and CCT. When ICR was coming into existence in the 1980s, the inspiration was the connected "blurred genres" position: applying perspectives, models, and ideas from the humanities in social science (O'Shaughnessy and Holbrook 1988). With a certain time delay, the crisis of representation (Clifford and Marcus 1986) entered the field of ICR with postmodern and postexperimental modes. This is what Denzin and Lincoln (2000, 2) called the sixth mode of qualitative inquiry. With explicit reference to this model, Sherry and Schouten (2002) demanded and defended the use of poetry, plays, short stories, and movies in consumer research.

Meanwhile, Denzin (2001, 2003) has introduced the seventh moment of qualitative research, which he calls "performance-based qualitative research." From that perspective, every research act itself is a coperformance, an interaction and participation in performances. Research becomes a dialogical performance, a continuous play with the oppositions of identity and difference: "the aim of the dialogical performance is to bring self and other together so that they can question, debate and challenge one another" (Conquergood 1985, 9). This means going beyond a cultural branding research logic of either being "neutral, objective, and detached" or being "subjectively immersed in the field."

For a performative research methodology, there is only the in-between of the "real" and the "illusory" position, where, for example, a consumer interview is neither the more or less distorted mirror of an external world or a representation of the consumer's inner world. Every interview will always be framed by confessional or biographical performances and commodified research results (for the media or the academic marketplace). For a performative perspective, the idea of an interview changes from an interpretation of a world into a reflexive relationship to the world it creates (Denzin 2001, 30).

And, last but not least, the presentation of branding research in a CCT frame is still, to a large extent, governed by the culture-as-text-scriptocentrism (Conquergood 2002; see also Parmentier and Fischer 2015). Knowledge is accepted and understood when it is secured in print. Performative branding would not replace texts with performances but modify the stance of textualism. There are aesthetic, ethical, and epistemic intertwinements when it comes to performative research that tries to re-create the tacit, masked, whispered, provisional, camouflaged, improvised, indirect, and hidden nature of brand performances. And the overarching goal would be to show how a performative branding approach can allow us to see, feel, hear, and think brands differently and beyond traditional branding approaches.

Bibliography

Aaker, David A. *Managing Brand Equity: Capitalizing on the Value of a Brand Name*. New York: Free Press, 1991.
———— and E. Joachimsthaler. *Brand Leadership*. London: Free Press, 2000.
Alexander, B. K. "Performance Ethnography: The Reenacting and Inciting of Culture." In *The Sage Handbook of Qualitative Research*, 411–41. Edited by D. K. Denzin and Y. S. Lincoln. Sage: Thousand Oaks, 2005.
Allen, Chris, Susan Fournier, and Felicia Miller. "Brands and Their Meaning Makers." In *Handbook of Consumer Psychology*, 781–821. Edited by Curtis Haugtvedt, Paul Herr, and Frank Kardes. New York: Lawrence Erlbaum, 2008.
Araujo, Luis. "Markets, Market-Making and Marketing." *Marketing Theory* 7, no. 3 (2007): 211–26.
———— and Hans Kjellberg. "Shaping Exchanges, Performing Markets: The Study of Marketing Practices." In *The SAGE Handbook of Marketing Theory*, 195–218. Edited by Pauline Maclaran, Michael Saren, Barbara Stern, and Mark Tadajewski. Los Angeles: SAGE, 2010.
Arnold, David. *The Handbook of Brand Management*. London: Economist Books, 1992.
Arnould, Eric J., Linda L. Price, and Avinash Malshe. "Toward a Cultural Resource-Based Theory of the Customer." In *The Service-Dominant Logic of Marketing: Dialog, Debate, and Directions*, 91–104. Edited by R. F. Lusch and S. L. Vargo. Armonk, NY: ME Sharpe, 2006.
———— and Craig J. Thompson. "Reflections: Consumer Culture Theory (CCT): Twenty Years of Research." *Journal of Consumer Research* 31, no. 3 (2005): 868–82.
Austin, John L. *How to Do Things With Words*. Cambridge: Harvard University Press, 1962.
Avis, Mark and Robert Aitken. "Intertwined: Brand Personification, Brand Personality and Brand Relationships in Historical Perspective." *Journal of Historical Research in Marketing* 7, no. 2 (2015): 208–31.
Bajde, Domen. "Consumer Culture Theory (Re)visits Actor–Network Theory Flattening Consumption Studies." *Marketing Theory* 13, no. 2 (2013): 227–42.
Banet-Weiser, Sarah. *Authentic™: The Politics of Ambivalence in a Brand Culture*. NYU Press, 2012.

Bartels, Robert. *The History of Marketing Thought*, 3rd ed. Columbus: Publishing Horizons, 1988.

Bastos, Wilson and Sidney J. Levy. "A History of the Concept of Branding: Practice and Theory." *Journal of Historical Research in Marketing* 4, no. 3 (2012): 347–68.

Batey, Mark. *Brand Meaning*. New York: Routledge, 2008.

Bell, C. *Ritual: Perspectives and Dimensions*. Oxford: Oxford University Press, 1997.

Bengtsson, A. and J. Östberg. "Researching the Cultures of Brands." In *Handbook of Qualitative Research Methods in Marketing*, 83–93. Edited by R. W. Belk. Cheltenham: Edward Elgar, 2006.

Bitner, Mary Jo. "Servicescapes: The Impact of Physical Surroundings on Customers and Employees." *Journal of Marketing* 56, no. 2 (1992): 57–71.

Booms, Bernard H. and Mary Jo Bitner. "Marketing Strategies and Organisational Structures." In *Marketing of Services*, 47–51. Edited by James H. Donnelly and William R. George. Chicago: American Marketing Association, 1981.

Borgerson, Janet L. "The Flickering Consumer: New Materialities and Consumer Research." In *Consumer Culture Theory (Research in Consumer Behavior*, Vol. 15, 125–44. Edited by Russell W. Belk, Linda Price, and Lisa Peñaloza. Emerald Group Publishing Limited, 2014.

Borghini et al. "Why Are Themed Brand Stores So Powerful? Retail Brand Ideology at American Girl Place." *Journal of Retailing* 85, no. 3 (2009): 363–75.

Bouissac, Paul. "The Marketing of Performance." In *Marketing and Semiotics: New Directions in the Study of Signs for Sale*, 391–406. Edited by Jean Umiker-Sebeok. Berlin: Mouton de Gruyter, 1987.

Brodie, Roderick J. and Leslie de Chernatony. "Towards New Conceptualizations of Branding: Theories of the Middle Range." *Marketing Theory* 9, no. 1 (2009): 95–100.

Brown, Gavin. "Theorizing Ritual as Performance: Explorations of Ritual Indeterminacy." *Journal of Ritual Studies* 17, no. 1 (2003): 3–18.

Brown, Stephen. "When Innovation Met Renovation: Back to the Future of Branding." *Marketing Intelligence & Planning* 33, no. 5 (2015): 634–55.

Burke, Kenneth. *A Grammar of Motives*. New York: Prentice-Hall Publishers, 1945.

Burke, Peter. "Performing History: The Importance of Occasions." *Rethinking History: The Journal of Theory and Practice* 9, no. 1 (2005): 35–52.

Butler, Judith. "Performative Acts and Gender Constitution: An Essay in Phenomenology and Feminist Theory." *Theatre Journal* 40, no. 4 (1988): 519–31.

———. *Bodies That Matter: On the Discursive Limits of Sex*. New York: Routledge, 1993.

Callon, Michel. "Introduction: The Embeddedness of Economic Markets in Economics." In *The Laws of the Market*, 1–57. Edited by Michel Callon. Oxford: Blackwell, 1998.

Canniford, Robin and Domen Bajde, eds. *Assembling Consumption: Researching Actors, Networks and Markets*. Abingdon, Oxon and New York, NY: Routledge, 2015.

Carlson, M. *Performance: A Critical Introduction*, 2nd ed. New York, NY: Routledge, 2006.

Cherry, S. "Parody as a Performative Analytic: Beyond Performativity as Metadiscourse." *Forum Qualitative Sozialforschung / Forum: Qualitative Social Research* 9, no. 2 (2008): Art. 25. http://nbnresolving.de/urn:nbn:de:0114-fqs0802258.

Christensen, Lars T. and Søren Askegaard. "Corporate Identity and Corporate Image Revisited: A Semiotic Perspective." *European Journal of Marketing* 35, nos. 3–4 (2001): 292–315.

Christodoulides, George, Leslie De Chernatony, Olivier Furrer, Eric Shiu, and Temi Abimbola. "Conceptualising and Measuring the Equity of Online Brands." *Journal of Marketing Management* 22, no. 7 (2006): 799–825.

Clifford, J. and G. E. Marcus, eds. *Writing Culture: The Poetics and Politics of Ethnography*. Berkeley, CA: University of California Press, 1986.

Conejo, Francisco and Ben Wooliscroft. "Brands Defined as Semiotic Marketing Systems." *Journal of Macromarketing* 35, no. 3 (2015): 287–301.

Conquergood, D. "Performing as a Moral Act: Ethical Dimensions of the Ethnography of Performance." *Literature in Performance* 5 (1985): 1–13.

———. "Rethinking Ethnography: Towards a Critical Cultural Politics." *Communication Monographs* 58 (1991):179–94.

———. "Performance Studies: Interventions and Radical Research." *Drama Review: A Journal of Performance Studies* 46, no. 2 (2012): 145–56.

Cornelissen, Joep P. "What Are We Playing At? Theatre, Organization, and the Use of Metaphor." *Organization Studies* 25, no. 5 (2004): 705–26.

Crainer, Stuart. *The Real Power of Brands: Making Brands Work for Competitive Advantage*. London: Pitman Publishing, 1995.

Cuffe, Alice. "Milan Fashion Week: Did Gucci Steal Their Latest Handbag Design?" *International Business Times*, February 25, 2016. www.ibtimes.co.uk/milan-fashion-week-did-gucci-steal-their-latest-handbag-design-1545992.

Dahlen, M., F. Lange, and T. Smith. *Marketing Communications: A Brand Narrative Approach*. Chichester: Wiley, 2010.

Davies, Gary and Rosa Chun. "The Use of Metaphor in the Exploration of the Brand Concept." *Journal of Marketing Management* 19, nos. 1–2 (2003): 45–71.

de Chernatony, Leslie. "Towards the Holy Grail of Defining 'Brand'." *Marketing Theory* 9, no. 1 (2009): 101–5.

——— and F. Dall'Olmo Riley. "Modelling the Components of the Brand." *European Journal of Marketing* 32, nos. 11–2 (1998): 1074–90.

Deighton, John. "The Consumption of Performance." *Journal of Consumer Research* 19, no. 3 (1992): 362–72.

Denzin, N. K. "The Seventh Moment: Qualitative Inquiry and the Practices of a More Radical Consumer Research." *Journal of Consumer Research* 28, no. 2 (2001): 324–30.

———. "The Call to Performance." *Symbolic Interaction* 26, no. 1 (2003): 187–207.

——— and Y. S. Lincoln. "The Discipline and Practice of Qualitative Research." In *Handbook of Qualitative Research*, 2nd ed., 1–29. Edited by N. K. Denzin and Y. S. Lincoln. Thousand Oaks, CA: Sage, 2000.

Diamond, Nina, John F. Sherry, Jr., Albert M. Muñiz, Jr., Mary Ann McGrath, Robert V. Kozinets, and Stefania Borghini. "American Girl and the Brand Gestalt: Closing the Loop on Sociocultural Branding Research." *Journal of Marketing* 73 (May 2009): 118–34.

Dion, Delphine and Eric Arnould. "Persona-Fied Brands: Managing Branded Persons through Persona." *Journal of Marketing Management* 32, nos. 1–2 (2016): 121–48.

Eckhardt, Giana M. and Anders Bengtsson. "A Brief History of Branding in China." *Journal of Macromarketing* 30, no. 3 (2010): 210–21.

Engel, James F., David T. Kollat, and Roger D. Blackwell. *Consumer Behavior*. New York: Holt, Rinehart and Winston, 1968.

Fillis, Ian and Ruth Rentschler. "Exploring Metaphor as an Alternative Marketing Language." *European Business Review* 20, no. 6 (2008): 492–514.

Findeisen, F. *Der Markenartikel im Rahmen der Absatzökonomik der Betriebe*. Berlin: Spaeth & Linde, 1924.

Fiske, John. *Introduction to Communication Studies*, 2nd ed. London: Routledge, 1990.

Fournier, Susan. "Consumers and Their Brands: Developing Relationship Theory in Consumer Research." *Journal of Consumer Research* 24 (March 1998): 343–52.

——— and Jill Avery. "The Uninvited Brand." *Business Horizons* 54, no. 3 (2011): 193–207.

———, Michael Solomon, and Basil Englis. "When Brands Resonate." In *Handbook of Brand and Experience Management*, 35–57. Edited by Bernd E. Schmitt and D. L. Rogers. Boston, MA, Cheltenham, UK and Northampton, MA, USA: Edward Elgar, 2008.

Gabbott, Mark and Colin Jevons. "Brand Community in Search of Theory: An Endless Spiral of Ambiguity." *Marketing Theory* 9, no. 1 (2009): 119–22.

Gardner, Burleigh B. and Sidney J. Levy. "The Product and the Brand." *Harvard Business Review* 33, no. 2 (1955): 33–9.

Gensler, S., F. Völckner, Y. Liu-Thompkins, and C. Wiertz. "Managing Brands in the Social Media Environment." *Journal of Interactive Marketing* 27, no. 4 (2013): 242–56.

Goffman, Erving. *The Presentation of Self in Everyday Life*. New York: Doubleday, 1956.

———. *Frame Analysis*. New York: Doubleday, 1974.

Goldman, R. *Reading Ads Socially*. London and New York, 1992.

Gond, J.-P. and L. Cabantous. "Chapter 47. Performativity: Towards a Performative Turn in Organizational Studies." In *The Routledge Companion to Philosophy in Organization Studies*, 508–16. Edited by R. Mir, H. Willmott, and M. Greenwood. Routledge, 2016.

Goodyear, Mary. "Divided by a Common Language." *Journal of the Market Research Society* 38, no. 2 (1996): 105–22.

Gordon, Wendy. "The Darkroom of the Mind: What Does Neuropsychology Now Tell Us About Brands?" *Journal of Consumer Behaviour* 1, no. 3 (2002): 280–92.

Goulding, Christina and Michael Saren. "Transformation, Transcendence, and Temporality in Theatrical Consumption." *Journal of Business Research* 69, no. 1 (2016): 216–23.

Grove, S. J. and R. P. Fisk. "The Dramaturgy of Service Exchange: An Analytical Framework for Services Marketing." In *Emerging Perspectives on Service Marketing*, 45–9. Chicago: American Marketing Association, 1983.

——— and Michael J. Dorsch. "Assessing the Theatrical Components of the Service Encounter: A Cluster Analysis Examination." *The Service Industries Journal* 18, no. 3 (1998): 116–34.

Gundlach, H. and B. Neville. "Authenticity: Further Theoretical and Practical Development." *Journal of Brand Management* 19, no. 6 (2012): 484–99.

Hackley, Christopher E. *Marketing and Social Construction: Exploring the Rhetorics of Managed Consumption*. London: Routledge, 2001.

Halkier, Bente and Iben Jensen. "Methodological Challenges in Using Practice Theory in Consumption Research: Examples from a Study on Handling Nutritional Contestations of Food Consumption." *Journal of Consumer Culture* 11, no. 1 (2011): 101–23.

Hall, Stuart. "Encoding/Decoding." In *Culture, Media, Language*, 128–38. Edited by Stuart Hall, Dorothy Hobson, Andrew Lowe, and Paul Willis. London: Hutchinson Education, 1980.

Heiskanen, Eva. "The Performative Nature of Consumer Research." *Journal of Consumer Policy* 28, no. 2 (2005): 179–201.

Hirschman, Elizabeth C. "Evolutionary Branding." *Psychology and Marketing* 27, no. 6 (2010): 568–83.

——— and Morris B. Holbrook, eds. *Symbolic Consumer Behavior*. Ann Arbor: Association of Consumer Research, 1981.

Holbrook, M. B., R. W. Chestnut, T. H. Oliva, and E. A. Greenleaf. "Play as Consumption Experience: The Roles of Emotions, Performance, and Personality in the Enjoyment of Games." *Journal of Consumer Research* 11, no. 2 (1984): 728–39.

Holt, Douglas B. "How Consumers Consume: A Typology of Consumption Practices." *Journal of Consumer Research* 22, no. 1 (1995): 1–16.

———. "Why Do Brands Cause Trouble? A Dialectical Theory of Consumer Culture and Branding." *Journal of Consumer Research* 29 (June 2002): 70–90.

———. *How Brands Become Icons: The Principles of Cultural Branding.* Boston, MA: Harvard Business School Press, 2004.

———. "Introduction: Toward a Sociology of Branding." *Journal of Consumer Culture* 6, no. 3 (2006): 299–302.

———. "Branding in the Age of Social Media." *Harvard Business Review* 94, no. 3 (2016): 40–8, 50.

——— and Craig J. Thompson. "Man-of-Action Heroes: The Pursuit of Heroic Masculinity in Everyday Consumption." *Journal of Consumer Research* 31 (September 2004): 425–40.

——— and Douglas Cameron. *Cultural Strategy: Using Innovative Ideologies to Build Breakthrough Brands.* Oxford: Oxford University Press, 2010.

Howard, J. A. and J. N. Sheth. *The Theory of Buyer Behavior.* New York: Wiley, 1969.

Hymes, D. "Breakthrough into Performance." In *Folklore: Performance and Communication*, 11–74. Edited by D. Ben-Amos and K. Goldstein. The Hague and Paris: Mouton, 1975.

Isaac, M. "For Mobile Messaging, GIFs Prove to Be Worth at Least a Thousand Words." *New York Times*, 2015. www.nytimes.com/2015/08/04/technology/gifs-go-beyond-emoji-to-express-thoughts-without-words.html.

Jaworski, Bernie and Ajay K. Kohli. "Co-Creating the Voice of the Customer." In *The Service-Dominant Logic of Marketing: Dialog, Debate, and Directions*, 109–17. Edited by Robert F. Lusch and Stephen L. Vargo. Armonk: ME Sharpe, 2005.

Jensen, K. B. "When Is Meaning? Communication Theory, Pragmatism and Mass Media Reception." *Communication Yearbook* 14 (1991): 3–32.

Jones, D. G. Brian. "Biography and the History of Marketing Thought: Henry Charles Taylor and Edward David Jones." In *Research in Marketing: Explorations in the History of Marketing (Supplement 6)*, 67–85. Edited by Jagdish N. Sheth and Ronald Fullerton. Westport: JAI Press, 1994.

Kapferer, Jean-Noël. *Strategic Brand Management: New Approaches to Creating and Evaluating Brand Equity*, 2nd ed. London: Kogan Page, 1997.

Keller, K. L. *Strategic Brand Management: Building, Measuring, and Managing Brand Equity*, 3rd ed. Upper Saddle River: Pearson Prentice Hall, 2008.

——— and D. R. Lehmann. *Brands and Branding: Research findings and Future Priorities.* MSI Special Report, No. 05–200. Cambridge, MA: Marketing Science Institute, 2005.

Kelly, K. *New Rules for the New Economy: 10 Radical Strategies for a Connected World.* New York: Viking, 1998.

Kincheloe, Joe L. and Peter McLaren. "Rethinking Critical Theory and Qualitative Research." In *The SAGE Handbook of Qualitative Research*, 303–42. Edited by Norman K. Denzin and Yvonna S. Lincoln. Thousand Oaks: Sage, 2005.

Kjellberg, H. and C.-F. Helgesson. "On the Nature of Markets and Their Practices." *Marketing Theory* 7, no. 2 (2007): 137–62.

Klein, Naomi. *No Logo: Taking Aim at the Brand Bullies.* New York: Picador, 2000.

Kotler, P., G. Armstrong, J. Saunders, and V. Wong. *Principles of Marketing.* Hemel Hempstead: Prentice Hall Europe, 1996.

Kozinets, R. V. "Inno-Tribes: Star-Trek as Wikimedia." In *Consumer Tribes*, 177–93. Edited by Bernard Cova, Robert V. Kozinets, and Avi Shankar. Oxford: Elsevier, 2007.

——— and J. M. Handelman. "Adversaries of Consumption: Consumer Movements, Activism, and Ideology." *Journal of Consumer Research* 31 (December 2004): 691–704.

Kozinets, Robert et al. "Themed Flagship Brand Stores in the New Millennium: Theory, Practice, Prospects." *Journal of Retailing* 78 (2002): 17–29.

Kucuk, S. Umit. "A Semiotic Analysis of Consumer-Generated Antibranding." *Marketing Theory* 15, no. 2 (2015): 243–64.

Lakoff, George and Mark Johnson. *Metaphors We Live by*. Chicago: University of Chicago Press, 1980.

Law, John and John Urry. "Enacting the Social." *Economy and Society* 33, no. 3 (2004): 390–410.

Leone, Robert P., Vithala R. Rao, Kevin Lane Keller, Anita Man Luo, Leigh McAlister, and Rajendra K. Srivastava. "Linking Brand Equity to Customer Equity." *Journal of Service Research* 9, no. 2 (2006): 125–38.

Levine, Rick. *The Cluetrain Manifesto: The End of Business as Usual.* Cambridge: Perseus Books, 2000.

Levitt, Theodore. "Exploit the Product Life Cycle." *Harvard Business Review* 43, no. 6 (1965): 81–94.

Levy, Sidney J. "Symbols for Sale." *Harvard Business Review* 37, no. 4 (1959): 117–24.

——— and Marius K. Luedicke. "From Marketing Ideology to Branding Ideology." *Journal of Macromarketing* 33, no. 1 (2013): 58–66.

Liu, Martin J., Natalia Yannopoulou, Xuemei Bian, and Richard Elliott. "Authenticity Perceptions in the Chinese Marketplace." *Journal of Business Research* 68, no. 1 (2015): 27–33.

Louro, Maria João and Paulo Vieira Cunha. "Brand Management Paradigms." *Journal of Marketing Management* 17, nos. 7–8 (2001): 849–75.

Low, George S. and Ronald A. Fullerton. "Brands, Brand Management, and the Brand Manager System: A Critical-Historical Evaluation." *Journal of Marketing Research* 31, no. 2 (1994): 173–90.

Lucarelli, Andrea and Anette Hallin. "Brand Transformation: A Performative Approach to Brand Regeneration." *Journal of Marketing Management* 31, nos. 1–2 (2015): 84–106.

Luedicke, Marius K., Craig J. Thompson, and Markus Giesler. "Consumer Identity Work as Moral Protagonism: How Myth and Ideology Animate a Brand-Mediated Moral Conflict." *Journal of Consumer Research* 36, no. 4 (2010): 1016–32.

Lury, Celia. "Brand as Assemblage." *Journal of Cultural Economy* 2, nos. 1–2 (2009): 67–82.

Lusch, R. F. and S. L. Vargo, eds. *The Service-Dominant Logic of Marketing: Dialog, Debate, and Directions*. Armonk, NY: ME Sharpe, 2006.

Luvaas, Brent. "Designer Vandalism: Indonesian Indie Fashion and the Cultural Practice of Cut 'n' Paste." *Visual Anthropology Review* 26, no. 1 (2010): 1–16.

MacKenzie, D. *An Engine, Not a Camera: How Financial Models Shape Markets*. Cambridge, MA: MIT Press, 2006.

Madison, D. Soyini and Judith Hamera, eds. *The SAGE Handbook of Performance Studies*. London: Sage, 2006.

Mäläskä, Minna, Saila Saraniemi, and Jaana Tähtinen. "Network Actors' Participation in B2B SME Branding." *Industrial Marketing Management* 40, no. 7 (2011): 1144–52.

Mason, Katy, Hans Kjellberg, and Johan Hagberg. "Exploring the Performativity of Marketing: Theories, Practices and Devices." *Journal of Marketing Management* 31, nos. 1–2 (2015): 1–15.

Mataja, Victor. *Die Reklame. Eine Untersuchung über Ankündigungswesen und Werbetätigkeit im Geschäftsleben.* Leipzig: Duncker & Humblot, 1910.

Maynard, Harold H. "Marketing Courses Prior to 1910." *Journal of Marketing* 6, no. 2 (1941): 382–4.

Mazurek, Marica. "Branding Paradigms and the Shift of Methodological Approaches to Branding." *Kybernetes* 43, nos. 3–4 (2014): 565–86.

McAlexander, James H., John W. Schouten, and Harold Koenig. "Building Brand Community." *Journal of Marketing* 66 (January 2002): 38–54.

McCracken, Grant. "Culture and Consumption: A Theoretical Account of the Structure and Movement of the Cultural Meaning of Consumer Goods." *Journal of Consumer Research* 13 (June 1986): 71–84.

———. *Culture and Consumption II: Markets, Meaning and Brand Management.* Bloomington: Indiana University Press, 2005.

———. *Chief Culture Officer: How to Create a Living, Breathing Corporation.* New York: Basic Books, 2009.

McKenna, Regis. "Real-Time Marketing." *Harvard Business Review* 73, no. 4 (1995): 87–95.

McNair, Malcolm P. "Trends in Large-Scale Retailing." *Harvard Business Review* 10, no. 1 (1931): 30–9.

Merrilees, B., D. Miller, and C. Herington. "Multiple Stakeholders and Multiple City Brand Meanings." *European Journal of Marketing* 46 (2012): 1032–47.

Merz, Michael A., Yi He, and Stephen L. Vargo. "The Evolving Brand Logic: A Service-Dominant Logic Perspective." *Journal of the Academy of Marketing Science* 37, no. 3 (2009): 328–44.

Mey, Jacob L. *Pragmatics: An Introduction.* Oxford: Blackwell, 1993.

Mick, David Glen and Claus Buhl. "A Meaning-Based Model of Advertising Experiences." *Journal of Consumer Research* 19 (December 1992): 317–38.

Minor, M. S., T. Wagner, F. J. Brewerton, and A. Hausman. "Rock On! An Elementary Model of Customer Satisfaction with Musical Performances." *Journal of Services Marketing* 18, no. 1 (2004): 7–18.

Mitchell, A. *Right Side Up: Building Brands in the Age of the Organized Consumer.* London: HarperCollinsBusiness, 2001.

Moisio, Risto and Eric J. Arnould. "Extending the Dramaturgical Framework in Marketing: Drama Structure, Drama Interaction and Drama Content in Shopping Experiences." *Journal of Consumer Behaviour* 4, no. 4 (2005): 246–56.

Montoya, P. *The Personal Branding Phenomenon: Realize Greater Influence, Explosive Income Growth and Rapid Career Advancement by Applying the Branding Techniques of Oprah, Martha and Michael.* Beaverton: Personal Branding Press, 2002.

Moore, Karl and Susan Reid. "The Birth of Brand: 4000 Years of Branding." *Business History* 50, no. 4 (2008): 419–32.

Morgan, M., P. Watson, and N. Hemmington. "Drama in the Dining Room: Theatrical Perspectives on the Foodservice Encounter." *Journal of Foodservice* 19, no. 2 (2008): 111–8.

Muñiz, A., Jr. and T. O'Guinn. "Brand Community." *Journal of Consumer Research* 27 (March 2001): 412–32.

Nakassis, C. V. "Brand, Citationality, Performativity." *American Anthropologist* 114, no. 4 (2012): 624–38.

New, Steve. "The Transparent Supply Chain." *Harvard Business Review* 88 (2010): 1–5.

Newman, Joseph William. *Motivation Research and Marketing Management.* Norwood: The Plimpton Press, 1957.

Ng, C. J. W. and V. Koller. "Deliberate Conventional Metaphor in Images: The Case of Corporate Branding Discourse." *Metaphor and Symbol* 28, no. 3 (2013): 131–47.

Nicosia, Francesco M. *Consumer Decision Process*. Englewood Cliffs: Prentice-Hall, 1966.

O'Guinn, Thomas C. and Albert Muñiz, Jr. "Collective Brand Relationships." In *Handbook of Brand Relations*, 173–94. Edited by Joseph Priester, Deborah MacInnis, and C. W. Park. New York, 2009.

Onyas, Winfred Ikiring and Annmarie Ryan. "Exploring the Brand's World-as-Assemblage: The Brand as a Market Shaping Device." *Journal of Marketing Management* 31, nos. 1–2 (2015): 141–66.

O'Shaughnessy, John. "Book Review: Philosophical Foundations of Cognitive Neuroscience." *Journal of Macromarketing* 26, no. 1 (2006): 88–97.

——— and M. B. Holbrook. "Understanding Consumer Behavior: The Linguistic Turn in Marketing Research." *Journal of the Market Research Society* 30, no. 2 (1988): 197–223.

Otnes, Cele C. and Tina M. Lowrey. *Contemporary Consumption Rituals. A Research Anthology*, Mahwah: Lawrence Erlbaum, 2004.

Ots, Mart and Benjamin Hartmann. "Media Brand Cultures: Researching and Theorizing How Consumers Engage in the Social Construction of Media Brands." In *Handbook of Media Branding*, 217–29. Edited by Siegert, Förster, Chan-Olmsted, and Ots. Heidelberg: Springer, 2015.

Parmentier, Marie-Agnès and Eileen Fischer. "Things Fall Apart: The Dynamics of Brand Audience Dissipation." *Journal of Consumer Research* 41, no. 5 (2015): 1228–51.

Peters, Tom. "The Brand Called You." *Fast Company* 10 (1997): 83.

Pine, B. Joseph and James H. Gilmore. *The Experience Economy: Work Is Theatre and Every Business Is a Stage*. Boston: Harvard Business School Press, 1999.

Pires, Guilherme D., John Stanton, and Paulo Rita. "The Internet, Consumer Empowerment and Marketing Strategies." *European Journal of Marketing* 40, nos. 9–10 (2006): 936–49.

Plassmann, H., T. Z. Ramsøy, and M. Milosavljevi. "Branding the Brain: A Critical Review and Outlook." *Journal of Consumer Psychology* 22, no. 1 (2012): 18–36.

Prahalad, C. K. and Venkatram Ramaswamy. "The Cocreation Connection." *Strategy and Business* 27, no. 2 (2002): 51–60.

Quinton, S. "The Community Brand Paradigm: A Response to Brand Management's Dilemma in the Digital Era." *Journal of Marketing Management* 29, nos. 7–8 (2013): 912–32.

Ries, Al and Jack Trout. *Positioning: The Battle for Your Mind*. New York: McGraw-Hill, 1981.

Roberts, Brian. "Performative Social Science: A Consideration of Skills, Purpose and Context." *Forum Qualitative Sozialforschung / Forum: Qualitative Social Research* 9, no. 2, Art. 58, 2008. www.qualitative-research.net/fqs-texte/2-08/08-2-58-e.htm.

Roper, S. and C. Parker. "Evolution of Branding Theory and Its Relevance to the Independent Retail Sector." *The Marketing Review* 6, no. 1 (2006): 55–71.

Rosenbaum-Elliot, *Richard,* Larry Percy, and Simon Pervan. *Strategic Brand Management*, 3rd ed. Oxford [et al.]: Oxford University Press, 2015.

Rust, Roland T., Valarie A. Zeithaml, and Katherine N. Lemon. "Customer-Centered Brand Management." *Harvard Business Review* 82, no. 9 (2004): 110–8.

Schau, Hope Jensen, Albert M. Muñiz, Jr., and Eric J. Arnould. "How Brand Community Practices Create Value." *Journal of Marketing* 73 (September 2009): 30–51.

Schechner, Richard. *Essays in Performance Theory*. New York, NY: Drama Book Specialists, 1977.

———. *Performance Studies: An Introduction*, 2nd ed. New York: Routledge, 2006.

Schroeder, Jonathan E. "The Cultural Codes of Branding." *Marketing Theory* 9, no. 1 (2009): 123–6.

——— and Miriam Salzer-Mörling. "The Cultural Codes of Branding." In *Brand Culture*, 3–16. Edited by Jonathan E. Schroeder and Miriam Salzer-Mörling. London: Routledge, 2005.

Scott, Linda M. "The Bridge from Text to Mind: Adapting Reader-Response Theory to Consumer Research." *Journal of Consumer Research* 21, no. 3 (1994): 461–79.

Searle, John R. *Speech Acts*. Cambridge: Harvard University Press, 1969.

Sherry, John F., Jr. "The Soul of the Company Store: Nike Town Chicago and the Emplaced Brandscape." In *ServiceScapes: The Concept of Place in Contemporary Markets*, 109–46. Edited by J. F. Sherry, Jr. Chicago, IL: NTC Business Books, 1998.

———. "Brand Meaning." In *Kellogg on Branding*, 40–69. Edited by Alice M. Tybout and Tim Calkins. Hoboken: Wiley, 2005.

——— and J. W. Schouten. "A Role for Poetry in Consumer Research." *Journal of Consumer Research* 29, no. 2 (2002): 218–34.

Shulman, David. *The Presentation of Self in Contemporary Social Life*. Los Angeles: SAGE, 2006.

Singh, Sangeeta and Stephan Sonnenburg. "Brand Performances in Social Media." *Journal of Interactive Marketing* 26, no. 4 (2012): 189–97.

Stern, Barbara B. "What Does Brand Mean? Historical-Analysis Method and Construct Definition." *Journal of the Academy of Marketing Science* 34, no. 2 (2006): 216–23.

Strizhakova, Yuliya, Robin Coulter, and Linda L. Price. "The Meanings of Branded Products: A Cross-National Scale Development and Meaning Assessment." *International Journal of Research in Marketing* 25, no. 2 (2008): 82–93.

Thompson, C. J. and Z. Arsel. "The Starbucks Brandscape and Consumers' (Anti-Corporate) Experiences of Glocalization." *Journal of Consumer Research* 31 (December 2004): 631–42.

———, A. Rindfleisch, and Z. Arsel. "Emotional Branding and the Strategic Value of the Doppelganger Brand Image." *Journal of Marketing* 70 (January 2006): 50–64.

——— and K. Tian. "Reconstructing the South: How Commercial Myths Compete for Identity Value through the Ideological Shaping of Popular Memories and Countermemories." *Journal of Consumer Research* 34 (February 2008): 595–613.

Timacheff, S. and D. E. Rand. *From Bricks to Clicks: Five Steps to Creating a Durable Online Brand*. New York: McGraw-Hill, 2001.

Turner, Victor Witter. *From Ritual to Theatre: The Human Seriousness of Play*. New York: PAJ Publications, 1982.

Vallaster, Christine and Sylvia von Wallpach. "An Online Discursive Inquiry into the Social Dynamics of Multi-Stakeholder Brand Meaning Co-Creation." *Journal of Business Research* 66, no. 9 (2013): 1505–15.

Vandermerwe, Sandra and Juan F. Rada. "Servitization of Business: Adding Value by Adding Services." *European Management Journal* 6 (Winter 1988): 315–24.

Vargo, Stephen L. and Robert F. Lusch. "Evolving to a New Dominant Logic for Marketing." *Journal of Marketing* 68, no. 1 (2004): 1–17.

Veloutsou, Cleopatra. "Brands as Relationship Facilitators in Consumer Markets." *Marketing Theory* 9 (March 2009): 127–30.

Venter, Peet, Alex Wright, and Sally Dibb. "Performing Market Segmentation: A Performative Perspective." *Journal of Marketing Management* 31, nos. 1–2 (2015): 62–83.

Warde, Alan. "Consumption and Theories of Practice." *Journal of Consumer Culture* 5, no. 2 (2005): 131–53.

Williamson, J. *Decoding Advertisements*. London, 1978.

Wren-Lewis, Justin. "The Encoding/Decoding Model: Criticisms and Redevelopments for Research on Decoding." *Media Culture & Society* 5, no. 2 (1983): 179–97.

Part IV
Poetry

15 Leakage

John W. Schouten

So I'm walking to work and the last gasp of winter
is piling up on the sidewalks
It's fine. I'm wearing my favorite Timberland boots
which I just spent 20 euros having re-heeled cuz I'd walked the old heels off
and I'm thinking I'm pretty smart
until about halfway to work when I start to feel this creeping coldness
in the balls of my feet. Yep, both of em
Turns out the boots have hairline cracks in the soles
right where they bend
And I'm thinking as I walk how all my life
my heroes have been dying
First there was JFK
and then the unthinkable, his brother Bobby
and when my father died I could barely contain
my anger. The grief came later, as it always does
And then I thought about my best friend
fighting against a shadowy beast that just grows
stronger and stronger with no place to grab
nowhere to grapple, no way to throw it to the ground
even for a minute and I'm thinking
Goddammit, these fucking soles looked fine
when I took em in, and these boots
I thought for sure I'd get another season out of em

16 Digital Self

Hilary Downey

A pursuit spent in waking
Hours, streaming secretly
Shadows, cast long; imperfect
Images loaded-lightly, lacking
Flawlessness; outward looking,
Inmost craving, for a gentle gaze
On tempered frames; sterile soft
Settings willing out blotches
To be barred; a filterscape
Of flaws censored by a constant
Cynicism; the digital self

Emotional effort edited re-visiting
The growing gallery, foraging for
Frailties in identity, imaginings,
Imagery; coarse colours cut through
With soft lenses, embrace fresh filters
Spanking software; to re-style a self
In whose image; in whose fashion

The Instagram aesthetic, commingling
Colours, light, filters, styling, to a
Crucial level. The art of crafting reactions
Without words; the look and feel of
People, places and things; the chasing of
Moments to shepherd the scene. Build
An art collection from fragments of life,
Inside the other side of Instagram; sleek
Visual journal, "#whywhiteworks", claimed
By hot Instagrammars. No simple posting,
Where sliding scales of beauty subsist; the
Desperate seeking personalization on point.

Where is real art anymore? Instead,
Imitating instants lacking originality

Observe this space. Sharing perfection
Versus authenticity; the delivered desire,
Chasing laudable moments the aesthetics
Of the bold. Trapped by the temptation of
An ideal self, hashtags and looks, recognition,
Reaction, representation, the flawless 'selfies'
Inspire shapes of satire, imitation; the
Paranoid, perfect on parade.

17 Guesswork

David Glen Mick

It does not matter
if the destiny of everything,
our sun, our theories,
is to collapse.
And it does not matter
if the invention of time
and the imagination of atoms
press down on our shoulders,
as we peer over the minima
that quarantine our species.

We predict anyway,
interpret anything,
what is obvious,
what is oddity,
as if our guesswork
and our thermometers
(both reliant on mercurial tongues)
were proxies for 50%
omnipotence.

Is there nothing else to do
but conjecture and argue
about the starless sky of noon
and the depthless pool of self,
the preference for fancy,
and the reverence for ease,
the blessed possessions,
and the skew-whiff decisions?

We bear more than Cassandra's agony
because our end is to know
what we will never know,
while we go on insisting otherwise.

18 Schooling

Pilar Rojas Gaviria

Petit assemblé,
You smile,
The music,
Fill your eyes!
Little creature of mine:
Are we without success?
The mafia team arrives . . .
Special needs don't be afraid,
Feel strong as you recover
From the soldiers: therapists and counsellors!
Flourishing,
Performing your glorious,
Grand plié!
An earthquake,
And we are drained.
I feel constrained,
The schooling market is taking over!
Stretch your muscles,
Dear, we are not yet done,
The army of normality seems
All around!
Flip and Flop,
And freeze,
And flow,
Arms fully engaged,
The undistinguished row ahead,
Speechless,
Though not afraid.

19 4play

John F. Sherry, Jr.

carelessly craning,
  casually covering his six,
he slathers base coat
  on the gritty dark side
of the sheltering wall,
  coaxing texture from gapped mortar
rimed with exhaust
  and mottled moss—
the pitted brick piss-bleached,
  studded with sheared bolts and wheat paste—
to set up for the main event,
  where soon he will inscribe
a love-spell to arouse
  his torpid town,
if only he's not caught.

20 Self-Service in the Fourth Circle of Hell

Sandra D. Smith

Shops glittering with baubles
The clouds are greying and the streets wet
A young couple sit in the café window
Nursing their coffees in the growing gloom
The busy noodle canteen, painted lucky red
Is full of workers and families buying dinner
A local drunk staggers towards the chip shop
His torn umbrella no match for the rain
A man in a coat clutches his side
Stumbling as he grimaces in pain
Then in the distance I see its outline
The self-service laundromat
Lit up, a beacon of purple neon

Inside, it's a mixture of souls
Taking refuge amidst the buzz and whirl
And smells of detergent and bleach
I load my soiled clothes into a spare machine
Beside the man wearing a cap, reading the local paper
He chews on a cheese sandwich, mouth open
Then looks up, finger waving towards a photograph
"Bloody miracle this was wasn't it?"
He sucks in the crumbs of his feast
"The woman got out alive when she should've drowned
Mind, the river sometimes spits back those it could've taken"
He has a mad intensity in his eyes
I nod and he looks back down

"What's this?" says the man in a suit, laughing
Naively holding a plastic bag of clothes
He loudly reads the signs placed around the room:
"NO BANGING ON THE MACHINES;
THIS CAMERA IS LOOKING AT YOU
READ THE INSTRUCTIONS CAREFULLY;
NO REFUNDS WILL BE GIVEN

That's customer service for you"
"You've dropped a sock," hisses the woman with a stick
He thanks her and she rasps back at him,
"When the Serpent bites, He leaves something behind
Something from which you can never be free"
Her face hollow with age, her tongue flickering
She moves slowly over to her corner
Back into the shadows

The student studying poetry croons to his audience,
"Remember the golden apple in Mammon's arbour
When it is bitten, it's all trickery and dust
How could he argue the infernal isn't so bad
When compared to the empyreal vaults of Heaven?"
The man in the suit is now thumping his machine
"The bastards have robbed me of my money"
The short, round woman presses the green button
"You need to read the instructions," she says
The old woman then slithers out into the darkness
And the student silently shuts his book
As the night closes in, we huddle in the warmth
Waiting for a miracle to occur.

21 Self(IE) Analysis

Terrance Gabel

I took it...
all I possibly could
then packed back up
about face
repelled away
by the human zoo
rest of L.A.

Look at me...
there exactly where
I so loved to flee

that last time
captured
about to escape
so little did I know
then
fifteen years ago

Snapped...
with a cheap Kodak
disposable
like that me
now showing
much more
than ever was
intended to be

Taken...
for a ride
to preserve
happiness, scant and intense
biked up and down
than long left beach coast
coasting, speeding along

helmedted head
theatrically staged
poorly focused
ignorant of cost
living a dream
thought lost

how many more
pieces of me
can I take?

There I am...
immortally the fore
young and strong
content
the sea the sun the sand
a distant background
an identity
never quite found

22 Waste Water Treatment

Roel Wijland

 # Love River

Big data settles like
rock snot
in the spotlight arcade.

Across the entire algae
value chain
latter day positivists
fish with a fork.

Fresh water miners
discharge neononsense in
the ultra-structured
porefields.[1]

Note

1 Dear Dr. Wijland
   I am writing to let you know that *International Aquatic Research* is now published by Springer and is accepting submissions via our open online submission system. I would like to encourage you to submit your next research article to the journal. By publishing you will benefit from rigorous peer review, high visibility and open access to all disciplines in Science, Technology and Medicine. We publish original research articles, short communications, and review articles in a broad range of areas relevant to all aspects of aquatic sciences, fresh water and marine waters.

Dear Dr. Wijland
   We would like to invite you to the *3rd Annual International Congress of Algae*. Session speakers and presentation proposals are under recruitment, and considering your background, we sincerely invite you to give a speech on '*Sea bass from Texas: Notes from the material poetics project at the San Francisco waste dump*' at the congress. Key topics include Waste Water Treatment, Harmful Algal Blooms and Algae in Carbon Capture. You will meet algae cultivation plant owners, technology providers for wastewater treatment, algae end market users & biotech investors from over 30 countries. We will once

again bring together experts and executives from academia and industry to focus on the research breakthroughs and solutions throughout the entire algae value chain.

Dear Dr. Wijland

The organizing committee of the *5th Annual World Congress of Food and Nutrition* would be honored to invite you to be a Chair/ Speaker of Theme 3: Nutraceuticals and Functional Foods while presenting about '*Anchors, mermaids, shower-curtain seaweeds and fish-shaped fish: The texture of poetic agency*'. If you would like to attend this event, the congress will become more perfect. It is co-organized with the Exhibition of Elder and Geriatrics Care. The scientific sessions will present the most recent advances in the fields of food science and engineering, detection and safety, the management of disease and so on. Do you have any suggestions about our program? Your precious comments will be highly appreciated. Famous attractions near the conference venue include Love River and the Urban Spotlight Arcade.

Part V
Conclusion

23 Distilling Insights to Mobilize Responses

Anticipating Trajectories of Research and Intervention

John F. Sherry, Jr. and Eileen Fischer

Having ricocheted from the premodern to the postmodern to the posthuman to the proto-Anthropocene, we invite our intrepid readers to pause their peripatetic journey and consider some of the waymarks that have nominally guided our progress. Chief among these are reflexivity, representation, and reformation. Other cairns include close observations, close readings, and close encounters. Socioeconomics, social engineering, and societal impact are striking blazes as well. Performances, practices, and precedents also point the way. Each of these indicators is considered in our interpretive summary.

Before we commence our wrapping up, let's take a moment to assess developments that have arisen since the publication of this volume's predecessor (Sherry and Fischer 2009). A professional society—the Consumer Culture Theory Consortium (CCTC)—has been established, and its Facebook page (www.facebook.com/groups/213134458706536/) boasts a following of several thousand. The CCTC board is international in its composition, reflecting the global character of the organization's membership. The annual CCT conference approaches its twelfth meeting, alternating sites every other year between North America and Europe. Many of the papers from these conferences are regularly published by Russ Belk and chairs in the Emerald series, *Research in Consumer Behavior*. CCTC confers the Sidney J. Levy Award annually to the best article based on a doctoral dissertation published in the *Journal of Consumer Research*. The chapters that appear in the present volume represent the diversity of orientation, topics, contexts, and controversies that animate our vibrant field. We address many of these aspects in this conclusion.

The Rethinking

In the spirit of "go big or go home," our volume opens with a swipe at ontology. Conjuring a literal ghost in the machine, a portending mech-animism of sentient things, Russ Belk ushers us eloquently into a brave new world. His sobering meditation on the potential redefinition of personhood seems the inevitable conclusion to his seminal inquiry into the extended self. The behavioral, legal, and ethical issues he considers to be a consequence of the impending singularity are profound and should become the foci of seminar discussions in classrooms, boardrooms, and legislative chambers.

Our poets might have heard Langston Hughes (1995) intone, "I, too, sing America," between the lines of Alladi Venkatesh's essay on the disentangling of economic capital from other forms, the better to understand them all in their influential mutuality. Venkatesh proposes a progressive activist research agenda, a program of institutional reform in the face of demographic change and in the service of liberal democracy. His call is all the more compelling for its being issued in a time of U.S. presidential transition, polarized politics, and resurgent global nationalism. The complex constellation of ethnicity as it bears upon consumption and identity politics will occupy CCT researchers worldwide for the foreseeable future.

Embarking upon a reformation that is ultimately resumed in the chapter by Bode and Kjeldgaard, Sidney Levy, arguably the godfather if not the grandfather of consumer culture theory, expounds upon his signature contribution to the field: the nature of the brand. Upon completing a (pre) historical overview of the evolution of the brand—a process of successive encompassment—that culminates in the inexorable emergence of the grand brand, Levy propounds a model of the ideal brand pyramid (IBP). The IBP is the metaphorical equivalent of the golden section, designed to help us understand the contemporary quintessence of the brand, which he finds skewing toward the aesthetic. We can imagine the labels of the vertices changing with the zeitgeist and the increasing sophistication of our theorizing, such that, for example, the "ecological" might rise to prominence on the agendas of future brandthropologists. So also will the "digital" and the "virtual."

Embeddedness is at the heart of the vignettes that Melanie Wallendorf uses to explore the moral dimension of pricing. Her buyers and sellers perform an embodied, communal process of exchange that confounds market and gift. Her recounting of a revelatory incident that theorists have labeled "lagniappe"—a small gift given by a merchant to a customer at time of purchase by way of good measure—is a compelling example of this interpenetration of spheres. The lagniappe is also implicit in a later chapter by Bradford and Sherry. Wallendorf suggests a social tinkering with conventional pricing strategies might produce outsized rewards for exchange partners, including a restoration of some of the organic social solidarity that nostalgic citizens seem to miss. Such quality of life issues shaped by consumption compose a worthy field of inquiry for CCT research.

The Revisiting

Using the secular ritual of the bridal shower—an arbitrarily efficient medium hedged about with ambivalence—to explore the complexity of postmodern gift giving, Tonya Bradford and John Sherry offer a synthetic interpretation that seeks to reconcile three conceptions of the gift. This complexity theme reverberates throughout the volume. Their exploration of the interplay of gift and market economies joins a growing list of investigations that probes the ritual underwriting of consumer culture. The analysis of ceremonial strolling by the Covas (Bernard and Véronique) and Hounaida El Jurdi is a case in point. These authors provide a different slant on the spatial turn in consumer research by focusing on the way that place is embodied by the traversal rather than the occupation of space. Further, their presentational strategy of autoethnographic reminiscence, playlet, and photography speaks to the challenge of representing research insights authentically that has captured the imagination of many of the volume's contributors. Continued ethnographic attention to consumption rituals should result in academic, managerial, and public policy contributions uniquely notched by CCT research.

At the time of this writing, actor Glenda Jackson has ended a twenty-five-year hiatus, returning to the stage to great critical acclaim in the title role of *King Lear*, whose leitmotif of disposition will not be lost on CCT researchers. Linda Scott's magisterial chronicle of the shifting oppression-empowerment dialectic in our theories of the entanglement of women and consumption vividly reminds us that consumption is a form of political power. In so doing, she calls attention to important neglected precedents, much as Arnould does in a later chapter. Her activist approach that implicates consumption in programs of social engineering is also echoed in later critical chapters by Fırat and Dholakia, as well as Holt. The nuanced and variable impact of gender-role fluidity on brand narratives that Maclaran and Otnes discover in their study suggests that both brands and social structure can be refreshed by consumers intrigued enough by managerial intervention that provokes and delights, rather than merely preserves inertial satisfaction. Such media reconfigurations are responsive to the criticism of the limiting cycle of self-fulfilling representations that Venkatesh levels in an earlier chapter. Gender fluidity and escalating social and mass mediation have become cultural cynosures, and their intersection should keep CCT researchers engaged for years to come.

The Reassessing

Once *les enfants terribles* of the field, chief now among *les éminences grises* of conscientious inquiry, Fuat Fırat and Nik Dholakia continue to hold what they see as our slow-moving feet of clay to the fire, to promote a disciplinary ethos of critical reflexivity. They remind us that CCT might rather be a movement than merely a moment, an emancipatory force that, if properly revitalized, would have wide-ranging scholarly consequences. Doug Holt, an early if not solitary proponent of applying a CCT approach to managerial challenges—that the subdiscipline has assumed a generally non- or antimanagerial stance is itself an interesting development—now advises that the field abstract its apparatus up to the level of strategy and focus on the solution of practical problems of genuinely societal import. He maintains that the social impact of developing theories-in-practice far outweighs the benefit of continuing to build elaborate crypto-positivist academic silos. Taken together, our trio of critics suggests that, because we have become a part of the problem, however unwittingly, we must now become part of the solution. We are urged to develop an engaged scholarship, and Eric Arnould's historically meticulous intellectual précis of two of CCT's underappreciated role models points the way toward a career that might handily combine a love of social scientific inquiry with a commitment to social activism. Weaponizing CCT to make it more suited to introspective evolution and culture change seems a reasonably radical expectation of future work.

Living up to his billing as the Antichrist of marketing, Stephen Brown shreds the conventions of academic writing in reminding us of the stylistic obligation that we owe our readers. Knowing that representation is intimately bound up with understanding, and believing that the urgency of our prose should be proportional to the urgency of our ideas, his typologizing of gambits and lampooning of conventional sectioning should serve as a primer for those who want their insights to be received authentically. [Note: One of the editors was pleased to expand the SNARS database by forwarding a copy of one of his own consumer research articles (Sherry 2009) that begins with the words "Urethral Awakening Dream."] His rhetorical challenge is accepted by the poets whose work we consider next.

As a capstone consideration of the influence that such new intellectual darlings as actor-network theory, assemblage theory, flat ontology theory and others are exerting on the field currently, Matthias Bode and Dannie Kjeldgaard use performance theory to explode our notion of how to understand phenomena that we have previously deemed known. Taking perhaps the most central unit of marketing—the brand—as their point of departure, they demonstrate how impoverished our previous conceptions have been, by dramatically illustrating the multiplicity of brand authors, by exploring entailing versus shaping processes of brand engagement, and by beginning a preliminary inventory of performative elements animating the brand. We can imagine the decentering effect that construing the fundamental concepts and notions of both marketing and consumer behavior as a form of improvisational theater might have upon the disciplines. Perhaps the most profound and intriguing immediate impact would be their opening up to a host of additional scholarly fields of inquiry. An ecumenical pursuit of enlightenment is a virtuous aspiration for CCT researchers to embrace.

The Poems

Poetry has been a part of the CCT tradition from the beginning. At the first annual conference at Notre Dame in 2006, poems were printed in large font on easel paper and posted on the walls outside of the meeting rooms, which sometimes resulted in clogged corridors as readers, clustered in the hallways, jostled shoulders with attendees rushing to the next session. Subsequently, many of those poems were published in *Consumer Culture Theory*, volume eleven of *Research in Consumer Behavior* (Belk and Sherry 2007). The following few years, poets read their work aloud in makeshift sessions and published their poems in outlets such as *Explorations in Consumer Culture Theory* (Sherry and Fischer 2009), *Culture Markets and Consumption*, and the *Journal of Business Research*. Beginning in 2010 with an inspiration by Roel Wijland, the poetry readings have been held in more intimate off-site venues, attracted a dedicated and growing audience, and become one of the highlights of the conference. Poems have been published in chapbook format as an unofficial "proceedings" of the event, under the following titles: *Canaries Coalmines Thunderstones*, *Coyotes Confessions Totems*, *Clarence Clobbers Tenderly*, *Cardinal Cuento Tianda*, *Caribou Coracle Terä*, *Chickasaw Craft Threnody*, and *Calabash Cadencé Taisgeadan*. At the time of this writing, an eighth chapbook is in production.

The poems in our present volume range widely across the consumption experience, sometimes amplifying and sometimes challenging the themes of the preceding chapters. We empathize with the artisanal self, fraught with anxiety. We bristle at the presumption of prediction. We sway with the subtle dance of accommodation and resistance. We peer voyeuristically at the earthy, erotic insurgency of street art. We rollick with the rogue's gallery of patronage that retail spectacle has encouraged. We marvel at the polyvocal perversity of poetry and are amused by the confusion of analects with analytics. As always, we continuously observe the interlacing of the material with the immaterial. And our emotions and interpretations deepen with each subsequent rereading. As the power of the spoken word is enormously moving, the reader is encouraged to voice the poems aloud to enhance appreciation.

The poets probe that lyrical moment of consumption that will evoke in readers a visceral and emotional comprehension of the researcher's insight. Their language thrums with intensity and precision. The lilt of Hilary Downey's phrase "sliding scales of beauty" insinuates the interplay of artifice and authenticity in the presentation of self and is mirrored by Terry Gabel's lamentation "disposable like that me," the frustration of trying to integrate a multiphrenic self. The close observation of John Sherry's playfully intoned "rimed with exhaust," which captures the subversive palimpsest of urban surfaces, is echoed in Sandy Smith's thunderous proclamation "NO REFUNDS WILL BE GIVEN," a voluptuous account of a sanctuary of eccentrics and everyday oracles whose performance more than compensates for servicescape shortfalls. The weary resignation in John W. Schouten's avowal "nowhere to grapple," which reflects the angry desperation of displacement in the face of loss, reverberates in Roel Wijland's assonant assertion of the "algae value chain," a sardonic commentary on disciplinary entrepreneurs engaged in a process of search engine suboptimization and authors' lifeworks being audited but unread. Finally, the unexpected imagery of Pilar Rojas Gaviria's cadenced "army of normality" will feel familiar to every CCT researcher bent upon resisting the tyranny of social institutions, as will David Mick's idiom "the skew-whiff decisions," deriding the arrogance and delusion of measurement. Somewhere between incantation and thick inscription, our poets attempt to transform, and not merely inform, the reader with their understandings. We hope this higher order goal will sustain our avant-garde as the field individuates.

Walking the Labyrinth

Taking our cue from the *passeggiata*, let's slow our pace in these concluding comments to savor what we've distilled from our contributors' insights. There seems to be a series of tensions or dialectics between the poles of which the field of CCT is unfolding. Will we reenact a dominant origin myth, and, like the larger consumer research discipline from which we calved, become either an ecumenical, big-tent enterprise or a Balkanized formation of circled wagons? The resolution of these tensions will likely tell the tale.

Academic and Interventionist Inclinations

On the one hand, it is clear that CCT is thriving either as a discipline unto itself or as the subdiscipline of multiple contiguous fields, complete with professional associations, conferences, and a handful of receptive journals. Short of possessing a flagship journal and an efficient networking system across its diverse camps, the domain seems well established. On the other hand, the application of CCT as a technology of influence in the managerial and public policy areas is in its infancy. Activists might look to organizations such as the Ethnographic Praxis in Industry Conference (EPIC) or causes such as the transformative consumer research (TCR) movement for guidance in creating a practical variation of CCT. Ideally, CCT inquirers will move beyond a "pure" and "applied" dichotomous view of the future and integrate their options.

Positivistic and Humanistic Inclinations

Although the preponderance of effort is devoted to crafting a CCT that is social scientific in character at its best and crypto-positivist at its worst, both the delayed arrival of the crisis of representation to consumer research and the discovery of consumption by humanities scholars and artists has helped fuel the rise of more humanistic treatments of consumption experience. As the field branches out in each of these directions, we currently see little more than an (un)easy coexistence of the trends, such as the curated galleries at the annual CCT conferences. We wonder what insightful hybrids will arise as these inclinations continue to bump up against one another.

Theoretical and Descriptive Inclinations

Ardent critics and brute empiricists alike have argued that, for better and for worse, the gatekeepers of CCT are consumed with theorizing as the touchstone of worthy contribution. The derogation of practices such as description ("Ah description, of all the arts least appreciated," keens poet Charles Wright (2008) in his "Homage to What's-His-Name") chafes those "slow professors" attuned to "reflective inquiry" (Berg and Seeber 2016, 53), interpretive inquiry (Geertz 1973), and arts-based research (Leavey 2015). More confounding still is the increasing interest in assemblage theory, which itself will require escalating levels of meticulous description to sustain its advance (as is implicit in the chapter by Bode and Kjeldgaard). A rebalancing of evaluative criteria and an expansion (and legitimization) of alt-outlets for scholarly work are possible ways of addressing this tension.

Quasi-Economic and Moral Inclinations

CCT research has traditionally focused on the economic sphere, even (perhaps especially) in the unpacking of the extraeconomic dimensions of consumer experience. Although predominantly positive in its orientation, CCT has taken normative positions, typically in respect to its nominal consideration of the managerial implications of its insights. There is a rising interest in the moral and ethical consequences of consumer behavior, with CCT researchers being challenged to take normative positions on insights impacting societal welfare (Sherry 2014). As in the TCR and critical marketing literatures, to whom many CCT researchers are active contributors, there should be ample opportunity in the CCT literature to explore the constructive and destructive consequences that consumption has upon the common good and to recommend appropriate interventions, complete with specific guidance.

Exclusive and Inclusive Inclinations

For all its accomplishments to date, as any insurrection might be, CCT has been fraught from the beginning with conflicting goals, mixed intentions, and blind ambitions that are constantly being confronted. We have a traditional North American, Western European, and Nordic core, a vital Eurasian, Asian, Australian, and Latin American periphery, and an African potentiality, with divisions and distinctions within and between the regions too numerous too chronicle. We have franchises in business schools and colleges of arts and sciences, commonly operating as silos, with differently sanctioned publication outlets. We have institutions like CCTC working to create bridges to all these constituencies, in the hope of creating a global system of like-minded scholars. With good work continuing to be produced in the regions and in the silos, and the creation of collaborative networks across boundaries of all kinds, the growth and individuation of the field can be encouraged.

Can we negotiate orthodoxies that do not ossify into dogmas and interrogate our beliefs in a way that encourages innovative inquiry? Can we account for the complexities of our cultures of consumption, including their antecedents and consequences, in a holistic fashion and harness their awesome energy in the service to the common good? Can we apply our research insights to the solution of important practical problems? Can we be a floor wax *and* a dessert topping? As Stephen Brown might conclude, "Don't touch that dial—stay tuned for the next thrilling episode of our octennial series on the ripening of consumer culture theory!"

Bibliography

Belk, Russell W. *Highways and Buyways: Naturalistic Research from the Consumer Behavior Odyssey.* Association for Consumer Research, 1991.
—— and John F. Sherry, Jr. *Consumer Culture Theory,* Vol. 11 of *Research in Consumer Behavior (with Russell Belk).* Oxford: Elsevier, 2007.
Berg, Maggie and Barbara Seeber. *The Slow Professor: Challenging the Culture of Speed in the Academy.* Toronto: University of Toronto Press, 2016.
Geertz, Clifford. *The Interpretation of Cultures.* New York: Basic Books, 1973.
Hughes, Langston. "I, Too, Sing America." In Arnold Rampersad (ed.) *The Collected Poems of Langston Hughes,* 46. New York: Vintage Books, 1995.
Leavey, Patricia. *Method Meets Art: Arts-Based Research Practice.* New York: Guilford Press, 2015.
Sherry, John F., Jr. "Leaving Black Rock City." *Studies in Symbolic Interaction* 33 (2009): 459–64.
——. "Slouching toward Utopia: When Marketing Is Society." In *Marketing and the Common Good: Essays on Societal Impact from Notre Dame,* 43–60. Edited by Patrick Murphy and John F. Sherry, Jr. New York: Routledge, 2014.
—— and Eileen Fischer. *Explorations in Consumer Culture Theory.* London: Routledge, 2009.
Wright, Charles. 2008. "Homage to What's-His-Name." *New York Review of Books.* April 3, 2008.

Index

in 186; authoritative statements
185; CARS (creating a research
space) 181; concluding chapters
190; could do better (CDB)
proviso 181; declarative statements
185; definitive statements 187;
enumerative statements 187;
GALS (gender affects literary
style) 182; informative statements
185; interrogative statements 186;
introductory paragraphs 176–7;
inventiveness in 186–7; narrative
statements 185–6; nonfiction
beginnings 178; novelists vs.
academics 177; opening sentences
175–6; postassimilationist
acculturation research and
183–4; retroactive statements 187;
SNARS selection process 179–80;
technoculture 184; titles 189–90
rich text 202
Ries, Al 256
Rifkin, Jeremy 7
rituals, as performative 265
robotics 24
robot motherhood 24
robots: Aibo 16–17; autonomy of
21–2; bigotry of 11; in call centers
21; as caregivers 16–17, 20;
controlling 12–13; criminal and
property laws for 10–11; emergency
guide 21; ethical 15; extended
self 18–19; fearful accounts of
17–18; harming humans 17;
intimate relationships with 11–12,
19–20; military 12–13; origins of
10; owning themselves 24; Paro
16–17, 20; as persons 8; projecting
human traits 18; punishment for
9–10; resource acquisition goals
15; rights as legal persons 22; as
security guards 21; self-preservation
drive of 15; sentient robots 14; for
sex 11–12, 19–20; as surrogate
selves 18–19; Three Laws of
Robotics 12; warfare 12–13, 22.
See also artificial intelligence (AI);
autonomous machines
role fluidity 266–7
role-playing concepts 262
Rorty, Amélie 7–8
Rose, Randall L. 191
Roux, Dominique 20–1

Rubin, Gayle 123–4
Rue Saint-Ferréol 140
"Russian doll" phenomenon 119
Rust, Roland T. 255
Ryan, Annmarie 253

Sahlins, Marshall: biography of 236;
Culture and Practical Reason
239–42; "Domestic Mode of
Production, The" 237; on free
market 230; "Original Affluent
Society, The" 236–7; "On the
Sociology of Primitive Exchange"
238; "Spirit of the Gift, The" 237;
Stone Age Economics 236–9
Sandikci, Özlem 186
Scaraboto, Daiane 119, 122
scarcity: as driver of human economic
activity 237; socially constructed
240
Schooling (Gaviria) 289
Schouten, John W. 156–7, 184, 186–7
Scott, Linda M. 190
Searle, John R. 264
secondary agency 6
Second Wave approach to
consumption 108, 109, 112, 124
security robots 21
self, the 230–2, 299–300
self-driving cars: children of 5;
criminal laws applied to 9–10;
examples of 6; human drivers vs.
5–6; licensed to themselves 5–6.
See also autonomous machines
self-gifts. *See* monadic gifts
Self(IE) Analysis (Gabel) 293
self-indulgence, rationalization for 91
self-ownership model 12, 13–14
self-service honesty 65–8
*Self-Service in the Fourth Circle of
Hell* (Smith) 291–2
sentience 14–16
"Service-Dominant-Logic" marketing
259
service marketing 259
service provider relationship
management (SPRM) 73
sex robots 11–12, 19–20
Sherlock (television show) 152, 160,
166
Sherry, John F., Jr. 87, 92, 130, 132,
186–7, 258, 300–1
Short, Sue 10

Printed in the United States
by Baker & Taylor Publisher Services